THE FLIGHTDECK SURVIVAL MANUAL

How to survive a career flying aeroplanes for a living

By James McBride

an imprint of
flightsofpassion.com

The Flightdeck Survival Manual.

Published by: flightsofpassion.com

www.flightsofpassion.com

🐦 @flightsopassion

First published 2014

PAPERBACK ISBN: 978-0-9931368-0-1

Cover Photo by Ray Farley

Some of these short stories first appeared in *Flight Training News*

The author has written a regular monthly column in this publication since 2006

This is the first time the stories have been published together

Survival of the fittest

Why call it 'The Flightdeck Survival Manual' and why start the book with the survival course story?

Well it basically gives the backstory to how hard military trainee aircrew have to work to ensure that they pass the courses which eventually lead up to them being fully qualified aviators. There are so many different courses which they have to succeed at and it feels like the threat of failure is around every corner, but when you pass each course, the exhilaration of each significant milestone is amazing. In a similar way, on the civilian route, it is a very long trail for an ab-initio pilot to achieve the status of qualified, employed, commercial aviator and nobody should underestimate the mountain you have to climb to get there.

Essentially this is why I have called the book the Survival Manual, because that's frankly what it is all about - surviving. You need to find a way to conquer all the challenges which come at you and keep on going. There will be many times when you feel like giving up, but the main thing to remember at all times is that pure ability is not the major factor. It is persistence that pays off in the end, just good old fashioned dogged determination. There are no natural born Aces, forget that, everybody is on the same mountain, aiming for the summit. The ones who fall, are either blown off the ridges by the strong winds of ill fortune or become dizzy and unfocused due to distraction from other parts of their life. Basically my advice is hang on tight and don't look down - focus on your current challenge.

In this book of short stories, I have tried to list many 'survival strategies' which I have found have worked for me and have ensured that I remained employed doing what I enjoy most. I have had over thirty years of practice at it, so clearly I must have done a few things right. Of course I have made many mistakes along the way and have learned much from so many of my fellow aviators and their mistakes also. It's okay to make mistakes, if we humans didn't make them, we wouldn't make anything. Just try not make them repetitively.

If you are reading this while starting your own career in aviation, I wish you good fortune. But remember, there is a school of thought which says you can make your own luck!

Fair winds and Blue Skies!

James McBride
November 2014

The Flightdeck Survival Manual.

LIST OF SHORT STORIES   PAGE

+   +   +

End of Course Official Photo 1984; Author at back with Bob Hubble false moustaches; we got into SO much trouble for this one!

February '84 RN Survival Course 'before' photo – we looked a lot older afterwards.

Survival course group photo.   *On the way home in Pusser's Limo.*

Author with QFI 'Three Bananas' – 1985

Stan Greenhow QFI, Plymouth 1983   *The 'Dunker' helicopter crash simulator - really not funny*

Harrier OCU Squadron 1986.   Lt Mark Boast, self & S/Lt John Broomfield

February 1984 – Outside Air Temperature, -4°C.

Somewhere in the New Forest, Southern England - Military Aircrew Survival Course.

I was thinking to myself, *HOW did it get this crazy?* As I slowly started to unzip the front of his flying suit and tried to recall the last time I had held another man's penis in my hands. It must have been a couple of years back I decided and even then I had worn rubber gloves. No such luxuries this time, I drew a slow deep breath, clenched my teeth and thought, *well let's get on with it then*. I looked up into his eyes and I knew then I had been right to keep his hands tied behind his back. Those blue eyes burned brightly right into mine – *oh yes... you hate me alright,* went through my mind as my fingers reached gently inside the zip...

+   +   +

An essential part of military aircrew training is teaching them how to survive in enemy territory and to avoid capture in the event that they find themselves on the wrong side of the lines. Back in the early 1980's the location for this training in one part of HM Armed Forces in the UK was an establishment called Stockfield Park, near Gosport in Hampshire. Our course of intrepid Naval Aviators arrived there in February and we were already aware of the reputation of the place. In addition to being a centre for medical facilities and having a decompression chamber, Stockfield Park was the launch point for the Navy's Escape and Evasion survival course. Each course was composed of Pilots, Observers and Aircrewmen. The first two roles were always filled with officer ranks whereas Aircrewmen were non-commissioned ranks – *this would be interesting then* I thought, with us all having to rough it together in the same Basha.

The first week of the course was spent mostly in lectures and theoretically our team was to have no contact with the previous team which was just returning from the operational area in the New Forest. Of course whenever we were told not to do something... Well we managed to get a good briefing from the senior guys who all looked pretty rough when they arrived back. The practical survival part of the course was about nine days long and in that time there was very little food. One of my friends had somehow managed to lose 20 pounds in weight – needless to say he looked gaunt when I first saw him.

Another one of our colleagues let us into the secret about the Beaulieu Road Hotel, quite close to Beaulieu Railway station. He said that the landlady there Mrs. McGrath was always amenable to giving food to 'survivors' who called in at the back kitchen door. Finally, perhaps the best piece of 'Intel' which we gleaned from our mates was the actual location where most of the surviving would take place - the King's Hat Enclosure in the woods of the New Forest. If there was ever a good place to bury some survival rations in advance... this was it! Well let's face it; the recruiters had done their job well. In one location they had put a group together of 20 or so bright minds, all physically fit, well disciplined and determined to succeed at their chosen profession – flying military aeroplanes for a living. No surprise then that we were all keen to ensure that we passed this particular course.

We learned a huge amount in those first five days about the theory of survival. What sort of food was possible to eat raw from the forest floor – fungi of all kinds, plants and animals etc. Even so, I remember thinking that some of them didn't really appear very tasty – I had never been very partial to slug omelette. Now it was Friday; the survival school was closed for the weekend and although some of our course went home, others stayed on and I got the Ordnance Survey map out of the New Forest. On the Saturday morning I drove to Kings Hat Enclosure after first visiting the supermarket to pick up "supplies" and some strong plastic sealable containers...

It only took around 30 minutes to locate where the makeshift campsite would be at Kings Hat, then I buried the containers in three places nearby. Plenty of blood sugar supplements would be waiting for us when we arrived. There were only a few other cars around, but I was very cautious because the instructors had let it be known that the area was being frequently observed by the National Park Rangers who were friends of theirs. At one point I thought I saw a National Park 4x4 vehicle, on the way into the carpark area, but I dismissed it, *probably just another Land-Rover.*

Although it made perfect sense to bury some vital ration supplements at the site, I still felt guilty because I was acting alone and of course in reality I was 'cheating'. If caught, I could expect to pay a high price for this, but at the same time I was absolutely determined that I was not going to faint with low blood sugar through lack of sustenance and neither were the other blokes in my team. We were already informed that the only rations given out by the instructors at the start was a small tin of Glucose tablets for each survivor – 24 to a tin and they were supposed to last us for nearly nine days! Once the deed was done and my containers buried, I drove quietly away in my little unnoticeable Ford Fiesta.

On the Monday morning I very nearly did faint though when the senior instructor Lieutenant Ben Arnold, greeted us with "Good morning Course, *does anybody here drive A FORD FIESTA...?"* There was silence in the room and I thought I was going to die, my heart nearly leapt through my chest wall and I swear all around could hear the palpitations. Then he continued.
"'Cos I was thinking of buying one that's all and wondered what they were like to drive?" Now THAT sounded false. I knew then that he couldn't pin anything on me, otherwise he would have said so straight away and he didn't seem to be looking in my direction either. There was a stirring behind me and Bill Roberts put his hand up and said,
"Yes Staff, I've got a Ford Fiesta and it's a nice drive..." to which the instructor replied, "Oh REALLY...?! What *COLOUR* is it?"

Now this was descending into farce – what on earth would the colour make to the driving qualities of the vehicle? Poor Bill said "It's a white one, Staff..." at which point the conversation ended as the Lieutenant pretended to lose interest. Perhaps if he had known mine was a blue one... things would have been different! I was so glad that I kept quiet, but poor Bill was now a marked man although bless him he never realised it. In fact they made him work so hard on the survival exercises in the Forest he even achieved a recommendation to do the SAS Combat Survival Instructors course at Hereford. Every time there was a need for a dummy to take a beating, or a fall-guy to play patsy over the next week or so, it was *"Sub-Lieutenant Bill Roberts... COME ON DOWN!"* And each time I confess I did feel a twinge of remorse for the fact that he was taking a pounding from the staff who were absolutely convinced that he had been cheating them. I think they thought he had lied about the colour of his car. One time, the staff needed a 'volunteer' to help them demonstrate Resistance to Interrogation ("R-to-I" as it is known in the trade). I didn't even have to guess who they were going to choose for the deliberate bullying, physical abuse and humiliation which they put him through in front of the whole course. Naturally they said it was good value because we were all learning, but the main thing that I was learning, was that sometimes it is good to keep one's mouth shut.

Before being dropped off in the forest as if we were 'downed aircrew', the staff had some special tasks for us. Firstly we were all made to pack our improvised rucksacks the night before and these were to be inspected prior to departure to ensure that there was no contraband (extra large bars of chocolate and the like) being brought along for the ride. Then on the morning of our departure there was more indignity for us to suffer as part of the conditioning process. In reality we were already 'in captivity' because we did not have a choice about where we were going or what we were doing. Now prior to setting off in the trucks to the forest, we were required to undergo a strip search. This included an inspection of all physical orifices and cavities, nose, mouth etc. They were thorough even to the point of telling each one of us while naked to "Bend over and spread your cheeks", to visually check that we were not concealing anything within the space separating our Gluteus Maximus muscles.

Due to our previous intelligence gathering we were already expecting this and the fact that the staff would spend a long time ripping apart all of our kit looking for contraband items such as money or food. The deal was that in addition to our 24 aircrew ration sweets, we were permitted to take one more item with us. The list was quite specific, either one of the following, half a packet of cigarettes (if we smoked) or a small bar of chocolate, small packet of sweets like wine gums. Although high-energy confectionery like Kendal Mint Cake for example was banned. One of our course, Lieutenant Archie Smith being a bit of an extrovert, decided that instead of half a pack of cigarettes, he would take a large cigar and put it in his rucksack. Poor Archie; the staff took a dim view of this when they found it and crushed it before giving him back his kit. In their words, "it did not survive the initial parachute landing..." *Bastards*. Once again the staff had the upper hand and if they wanted to move the goalposts, well they were moved and there was nothing we could do about it.

In my own case, I thought long and hard about preparing for the course and I was completely committed to getting through it with flying colours, but not too well as there was a risk of being recommended for the CSI course run by the SAS. That would not be good as far as I was concerned. My primary goal was to become a Naval Pilot and becoming Combat Survival Instructor, trained (beasted) by the SAS was not a necessary step in that process. To be sure of succeeding on this particular course, I decided that in addition to the pre-positioning of high-energy food in the forest, I would smuggle some money along also. Not only might the cash come in useful if we got chance to buy any food, but also it was a morale booster by virtue of the fact that 'they' (the Staff) didn't know about it. There really was only one location to hide the money and in my case when I bent over to 'spread my cheeks' for the visual inspection, I smiled as I had the satisfaction of thinking to myself – *Well Staff... you're close... but no cigar!*

They would have needed a rubber glove to find the tightly rolled and folded £20 note which was wrapped in a tied and shortened rubber condom. I managed to retrieve the currency a day later in the forest discreetly behind a tree, but that's enough detail I think on that matter.

Once all the kit inspection and strip searching was completed and we had got ourselves dressed again into flying suits, boots etc (remember this was February in the UK and we were outside) the final stage before loading into the trucks was the squad run. We had to get all of our kit on that we would be taking with us, including our backpacks made from parachute materials and sticks lashed together and form into one big squad. Then we were off for a 3 km run round the playing fields being herded and harried by the Staff. Several of our guys had problems as their packs disintegrated and they had to hold or carry what they could in their arms. Some of us helped them where we could if we had spare breath and arms to carry. If stuff was dropped we had to leave it – that was the rule. Now we were really 'on the run'.

+   +   +

A major part of the learning process appeared to be that all the survivors were required to undergo as much starvation as the staff could inflict within a nine day period. This, combined with lengthy route marches, blistered feet, sleep deprivation, aching muscles and various 'exercises' would ensure that by the end of day five we would develop what they laughingly referred to as "The Survivors' Shuffle". In fact they took great delight in demonstrating this to us in the lecture room. Head down, eyes half closed, shoulders drooping, hands loose at the sides, feet scuffing slowly along, the Chief Petty Officer had it down to a tee – sadistic bastard!

Of all the aspects of the survival course which we disliked, the pointless 'yomping' over miles and miles of countryside was the worst. It was deadly dull and sapped the energy more than anything else. The funny thing was of course that we had been schooled well in the art of survival in the field behind enemy lines. Rule Number One? Never move in day time, always lie low and only move at night. What did they make us do? Walk for miles and miles during daylight hours. This was intentional though and we knew it. They only had a few days to wear us down and to give us a proper taste of what it would be like for real. We were some of the fittest, most highly motivated personnel in the forces - which was why we were yomping everywhere or "mindless trogging" as we called it in our team.

The entire course was split into teams of three and my two colleagues were Robert, a full career officer Lieutenant who had already been in the Navy for several years and Jack an experienced Naval Rating who was going through for Aircrewman. To be honest the pilots and observers were a bit unfair to the Aircrewmen trainees as they seemed to consider them less able, so there was always a bit of friction there especially as they were 'other ranks', i.e. not Commissioned Officers. I suppose nicknames like 'Winchweight' or 'Dope-on-a-Rope' didn't really help to build a team spirit; doubtless they had names for us too.

The first day of lectures on the aircrew survival course set the tone for the rest when the Chief Instructor introduced himself and the rest of the 'Staff'. He was renowned for being expert in unarmed combat. Certainly with his crew cut hairstyle and obvious athletic physique, you would not wish to get on the wrong side of him – he also had a very loud voice.

"GENTLEMEN! Welcome to your Aircrew Survival course. I realise that most of you are Officers and some of you are senior in rank to some of the instructors on this course, however as far as we are concerned here for the next two and a half weeks while on course you are ALL junior to every STAFF member – IS THAT CLEAR!? You will refer to and address ALL members of the instructional team as STAFF". So that was how it was to be. We were put in our place right from the start and those of us with other ideas kept them to themselves. He continued.

"I want now to introduce to you a new concept Gentlemen...it is called DISLOCATION OF EXPECTATION. Otherwise known as 'surprise, surprise'. Get used to it. EXPECT the unexpected; THAT is what survival is all about..." Which kind of explained how our team ended up looking after 'The Prisoner' – that was certainly not what we expected.

+   +   +

It was about five days into the practical exercise, simulating being on the run, behind enemy lines in a foreign country and we had all spent the night sleeping rough under a disused railway arch in the middle of nowhere. One team had been given the job of taking an enemy prisoner with them and their brief was not only to prevent him escaping (because he would report the position of the team to enemy troops), but also to try to interrogate him for information. While we were making preparations for our uncomfortable night under the viaduct, I had chance to talk to my mate Tom on the team with the prisoner about how things were going. It seemed he was not best pleased with the situation.

"It's a f****** nightmare. He keeps trying to escape and running off then we have to find him and bring him back. The bloke's not said one word to us apart from name, rank and serial number and draggin' HIM everywhere with us... SUCH a pain in the arse". I sympathised with him especially as he continued to describe the events of the previous night. "You know we hardly got any sleep at all last night. We're all f***** from yomping all f****** day right? An' then this joker; GUNTER they call him on his East German dogtags; starts f****** running away while we're trying to get our heads down".

"Oh he's got a name then has he?" I remarked interested to hear about the dogtags. I noticed that the prisoner was wearing an East German flying suit and much of the time it seemed the team kept a hood over his head and now they were getting more organized about tying his hands behind his back. Tom smiled, "YEAH, he's got a name alright... we call him ****!" We both laughed at this, it was clear that Tom's team were fed up with this guy which coming on top of everything else was adding to the stress and exhausting the team even more than lack of food, too much yomping and sleep deprivation were doing alone. When we parted I looked back at Gunter sat on his own, hands behind his back away from the team now settling down for the night and wondered who he was. He was tall, lean and muscular with very short hair and piercing blue eyes – aged about 30, but very fit. He must have been 6'2" perhaps a bit taller. *Hmmm... probably SAS trainee,* I thought to myself. When they took his hood off it was clear that he was watching everything and everybody looking for yet another chance to become a nuisance. "Imbuggerance Factor' we used to call it and the Staff had provided a real corker this time. Poor Tom, I felt quite sorry for him.

Next morning it was our turn to get some bad news when the staff called over to our team, "MCBRIDE, JOHNSON! Get over here!" We walked over to where the briefing was being given individually to each team. It was apparent that Tom and his mates were being relieved of the prisoner scenario and they looked quite pleased with themselves until they were informed that they now had a stretcher case to carry along with the 3 members of another team. The route was over rough ground, moorland and through the forest for approximately 15 kilometres with the casualty (one of the course students) handcuffed to the stretcher and unable to get off it! Unbelievable. In addition to the stretcher, they had to carry all their makeshift packs between six of them. My blood ran cold when 'Staff' turned to us two now and I started to imagine all sorts of problems facing us...

It was the Chief Petty Officer, the sadistic one who did such a good imitation of the survivors' shuffle. He said, "Right. Your team has got the prisoner to take with you. There's the route on the map and the RV for all teams will be at the bend in the river".

"Okay thanks a lot Staff!" I said brightly with a grin, "we'd much rather have the prisoner than the stretcher", at which point Robert kicked me on the back of the leg as if to say, *For heaven's sake McBride don't wind them up?!* As we turned to go, the Chief said in a low voice, "O'course that prisoner is a right pain in the jacksie ya'know lads. I reckon yer should give him loadsa' water to drink but don't let him pee eh? Then he'll give you his information..." This was accompanied by a huge theatrical wink. We returned to where Jack was waiting with our kit and gave him the bad news – his face fell. He wasn't really enjoying this whole survival thing and you could tell. In some ways he had it harder than the rest of us, because we were highly motivated to pass knowing that if we did so, the Navy would train us to fly helicopters for free and then pay us money to do so – an amazing deal. Jack was in a different environment and his vision was much more limited. His was a world of pain and he was not a happy bunny.

I tried to reassure him that carrying the stretcher for 15 kilometres would be WAY worse than this, but he wasn't so sure. He had seen how frustrated the other team had been when they were custodians of 'the prisoner' and how much they had been messed about by him. Then I told him what the Chief had said to us about letting the prisoner drink as much as he wanted, but not to let him urinate until he had given us his information. This put a smile on his face and I could see then that we had another budding sadist in our midst – *ohh great!* In fact we said we would take it in turns to lead the prisoner and also make him carry some of our stuff for us. We went over to where Gunter had been sitting quietly in the background while the teams had all been loading up and shipping out. He was sat hands tied behind his back with his hood on, legs drawn up in front of him so his knees were bent. I checked the bonds behind his back and they were very loose... clearly he had been getting ready to make another bid for freedom! *Bloody Hell, just in time!*

I looked around the viaduct area, we were the last team there and even the staff were departing in their military 4x4s – we were on our own, good. I grabbed the prisoner by the arms and said quickly, "Pass me that fishing net we were given the other day will you?" to Robert and Jack. "Let's sort out the hands thing for good". Very carefully and diligently I tied his wrists together such that there was no way he was going to untie them at all. I ensured that he still had blood flow to the hands, but the wrists were secure and fingers well clear of the knot. Now I loosened the canvas hood from round his neck and took it off – he blinked and screwed his eyes up against the bright morning sunlight. It was time to have a little talk with Gunter.

"What's your name?" I barked at him, grabbing his dogtags to have a look, they looked foreign and the script was Germanic – *hmm very convincing. They really go to some lengths to get it right.* The text said:

> **Oberleutnant Gunter Kühler**
> **#66373451, A Rh+**

His voice was very flat and unemotional as he replied, "Gunter... Kühler... six six tree seven," I interrupted him, "Yeah mate we know all that, but what's your *real name?* Charles, George, Bill? Eh?" There was a long pause. I continued, "Look we're all just on a course here and we don't want to fail it so please let's try and get along and cooperate – it will be easier for you..." His blue piercing stare came right back at me, his eyes had adjusted to the light now and he moistened his lips with his tongue. I noted he had a very strong jaw line. *No fat on him and very fit indeed...the bastard MUST be SAS.*

He started to speak again, "Gunter... Kühler... six six tree seven tree fower fife wun". He had a slight Germanic accent which was heightened as he pronounced the three and the five. He did not look worried at all, just calm and in control of himself. He had some dirty streaks down his face and about five days stubble like the rest of us, but otherwise he was in top shape. I asked him, "Where are you from mate? Ever been to Hereford? Did you volunteer for this gig like us or were you chosen from a cast of thousands? Eh?" He looked at me and did not reply – silence. *Well he's going to play the straight game then – his choice.*

"Okay Gunter, well we've got a bit of hike to do, you're coming with us, so let's get on with it. On your feet mate..." He didn't move he just sat there with no reaction. Jack was getting restless and said so. He was about 3 metres away from us and was looking really aggressive – I thought he looked ready to punch Gunter in spite of any Geneva Convention, his patience was running out. I walked over to Jack and asked him to go with Robert a bit further away while I had a private chat with Gunter.

When I returned, I bent down and put my mouth close to Gunter's ear and explained what sort of psychopath Jack was and that if Gunter didn't want to come walkies, then Robert and I would put Gunter's hood back on, leave and let Jack deal with him, simple as that. I explained that maybe the prisoner was fit and strong, but with a hood over his head and hands tied securely behind his back he would be no match for one pissed off Matelot. He thought for a moment, and then he stood up. *Good we're back in business.*

That was a very long day as I recall. Most of the time we allowed Gunter to have his hood off because he moved quicker that way, otherwise he stumbled everywhere which although faintly amusing, was not contributing to our average speed over the ground. As this was day five or six without food, we were all a bit strung-out and short on temper to say the least. The last thing we needed was somebody to come along as a dead weight and start playing games with us. In our minds, Gunter had volunteered for this trip and we had offered to play nicely, but he was going to stick to the rules... tough call.

Being mindful of Tom's team and their bad experience, we made sure he was never allowed space to do a runner on us and we frequently rechecked the handcuffs – that fishing net was top quality and very strong. Whenever we stopped, we all had a drink and offered our 'canteens' to Gunter also. Of course it would not be proper to deny the prisoner liquid; that would be cruel. Privately we laughed about the fact that he was drinking, but not peeing and in fact in a strange way it kept our spirits up knowing that there was somebody who was much worse off than we were. Poor Gunter was oblivious to the CPO's suggestion and to our intentions.

Officers and Gentlemen? Well I suppose we had been at the start of this thing nearly a week before, but the veneer of civilisation had worn pretty thin by now and we were becoming animal-like. In fact later in the course this would be clearly demonstrated when the staff gave each team a live rabbit for dinner. By then we had all been 7 days without any rations and were half starved. They joked about the fact that on a previous course one team was so squeamish about eating the rabbit, they actually made a pet out of it and couldn't kill it. There were no such qualms with us three. We had it done and butchered within 10 minutes of getting our hands on bunny and the meat was in the pot on the fire – we actually made a glove puppet out of the remains... mind you we were a bit delirious by then!

We overtook the stretcher party halfway across boggy moorland after a couple of hours as they were negotiating getting the stretcher over a barbed wire fence. They all looked totally exhausted from the continuous effort – thank heavens the staff had chosen young Pete to be the casualty; at least he was light, even if he was a dead weight. Naturally he felt guilty about causing so much grief to his mates, but he was not having a nice time of it either. Being carried over rough ground, handcuffed to a stretcher is no picnic as I could see by the marks on his wrists.

We stopped again after another hour or so and had another drink. We offered it to Gunter, but he shook his head. "Ah! Not thirsty then...?" said Robert with a smirk, to which the prisoner grunted. It was clear he wanted to tell us something... but what could it be? Another couple of unintelligible grunts emanated from our unwelcome guest and this time they were accompanied by bodily movements which indicated that he was in some discomfort. "What's that Gunter old chap?" Robert teased, "Sorry old boy, you'll have to grunt more clearly! .....we're not getting your banter old man!"

This started me and Jack off and we began to giggle. Gunter looked at us all alarmed from one to the other and commenced his writhing motion again, trying to move his hands round to the front to show us what he meant, more grunting. Robert was enjoying himself as he said with mock petulance, "Ohh... DO Grunt-Up old chap. We can barely hear you! We'll have to start calling you GRUNTER!" There was loud guffawing now from Jack and me as we fell about laughing at the insanity of the situation. The only one not laughing had his hands securely tied behind his back. Then Robert feigned sudden realization, "Oh you want to URINATE... is that it?" Gunter nodded relieved that he had got the message over without saying any words, but his relief was only temporary and not the kind he had hoped for when Robert continued, "Well if you tell us ALL about your squadron in East Germany and which airbase you're stationed at, we can let you have a pee, wouldn't that be nice?" Gunter shook his head and I thought - *Oh dear this will only end in tears.* I should have gone into fortune telling.

+   +   +

We checked the map again, another couple of hours and we would arrive at the bend in the river RV. "Okay let's go. Gunter on your feet", he looked up at Robert and you could see he was angry, but he got up alright and started walking with us. The forest now gave way to another patch of open moor which was very boggy underfoot and the going was tough. In addition the clouds had gathered now and it began to drizzle, with occasional flurries of sleet as it was so cold. The next time we stopped was nearly in the middle of a bog and we consulted the map. At these times we were in the habit of putting Gunter's hood back on because it stopped him looking at us and in our minds gaining information that could be useful to him. We were a little way away from where he had been standing so we could talk without him hearing us when suddenly I looked up and saw him running away. It was a surprise to us because he was hooded with his hands tied behind his back and we were in the middle of a marsh.

Our surprise was not as much as the one he got as we all three rugby-tackled him and four of us ended in the freezing gooey mud together – it stank. Not only that, but of course we ended up on top of the prisoner and he had his hooded head well under the mud. When he came up he was gasping for air and appeared in a bad way.

"That was f****** stupid wasn't it?!" I shouted at him, stating the obvious as we dragged his hood off, "you could have really hurt yourself then you daft bugger!" To which he replied, "PISS!" – His first word other than name, rank and serial number for two days. *Ahh... now we're getting somewhere, this is progress.*

"We'll let you have a pee when you tell us the information we want to know, your Squadron number and airbase – WHAT ARE THEY?" Now - no answer again, but as we all got up out of the bog it seemed he was a little more compliant than before. We continued trogging towards the distant river and now in addition to being wet, cold, hungry and fatigued; we all stank of the fetid disgusting mud from the bog. The smell was enough to choke a goat.

An hour or so later caked with dried mud, we arrived at the river to be met by the Staff and the other teams. There was an exercise in river crossing to be undertaken. We put Gunter's hood back on and sat him down well away from the scene of the action while we tried to figure out the way to cross the river without getting any wetter. The Staff gave all teams the same equipment, a couple of poles and ropes etc and we got stuck in. Memorably one of the less competent teams ended up in the freezing water of the river much to the amusement of the Staff and the rest of us come to that. The water was not deep, but it really was very cold and fast flowing they were soaked and now faced yet another long route march into the evening with wet boots and clothing, not pleasant.

Finally with the challenge/exercise completed, all teams were given the map references for the nightstop location, just another 10 kilometres away. The stretcher teams were very glad to be relieved of their burden, but it seemed we still had ours with us. The senior instructor took us to one side before they left and informed us that the prisoner was now expecting to be released and to go in the vehicles with the Staff, but as Lieutenant Arnold explained with a false smile of sympathy, "Dislocation of Expectation, see?" With that and a cheery wave he hopped into the last departing Land-Rover and was gone. It was quiet now in the woodland around the river with the distant sound of the retreating teams ahead of us, we were the last to leave.

We went over to where Gunter had been sitting and got him on his feet – his head still hooded. It seemed that he had been sitting very still trying to listen for sounds while he was waiting and perhaps he was surprised to hear it was us, his jailors who came to him at the end, but he didn't say so. As usual he didn't say anything. Now we wanted him to move with us and told him we were going for another "little walk of ten kay" and suddenly, but slowly his legs bent underneath him, he sank to his knees. He grunted and shook his hood from side to side, clearly he planned to go nowhere. You had to say too that he still looked uncomfortable as well he might having not urinated for the best part of 12 hours, but having had plenty of water to drink.

I waved silently to Robert to walk away with me to discuss the latest situation out of earshot and left Jack standing over him. You could hear the birds now tweeting and warbling as well as the babbling river close by, we were about 20 metres away from them and we shared our ideas in low voices. I said, "Well we could threaten him with dragging him into the river for good 'ducking'. He's smart and knows how cold it is and the fact that he would quickly get hypothermia", Robert looked at me shocked and replied.
"Are you serious? Really?" to which I said, "No. Not really. But he doesn't know we wouldn't go through with it... Let's face it he thinks we're pretty close to the edge as it is, so he might believe it and start walking again". It was at this point that I became aware of a low repeated thudding sound, supplementing the pleasant melodies of the birds and the river. A sound that sounded just like... somebody punching a hooded, defenceless, tied up prisoner... We spun round to look and it was true!

"NO JACK! NO! FOR F**** SAKE! NOOOO!!!" we screamed, as both Robert and I sprinted the 20 metres like we were in a race for our lives - or that of Gunter anyway. Gunter was still kneeling up, but was unable to ride any of the punches some to his head and some to his body, his assailant was playing full-contact! We dived on top of Jack, knocking the hooded one over as we went past. Jack was screaming, swearing and crying at the same time, it was all too much for him. *S***! Now what??*

"JACK! OKAY MATE, calm down. Come on now; remember IT'S NOT FOR REAL!" It took us a good few minutes to get him relaxed again, most of it we were both on top of him holding him down and telling him repeatedly that it was just a survival course and nothing was real, Gunter was only play acting and very soon it would all be over and we could get on with our lives. I even remember saying to him, "Look in a hundred years time, we'll all be dead and it won't matter... Let's chill out boys..."

Robert took Jack away down the track a little in the direction we were going to leave. I was still out of breath, but was alone with the prisoner, I got him up on his knees again and took his hood off. He looked shocked and very pale. He wasn't angry anymore, just scared – that had been quite a fright for him. I said, "Look Gunter, or whatever your name is... we're sorry about that, but you can see what we're dealing with here. We're going to have to do this next march before nightfall and you're coming with us. It's not our fault the Staff decided to leave you in the exercise longer than you expected, but that's life mate. Now, come on, let's go..." I helped him to his feet and we kept his hood off now. The tracks were good and solid; we were making good time over the ground.

Two hours later and we entered a clearing in the forest, we were not planning to stop, we just happened to walk into it. At this time Gunter, who appeared to have been in pain ever since we left the river dropped to his knees again. In fact the pain seemed to have been abdominal rather than as a result of the minor beating which he had received, he only had a few bruises and cuts on his face anyway – and by that time we all looked a bit ropey. I went over to him and said kindly, "Hey it's not much further, only a few more klicks and we're done - then we can hand you over to the Staff".

Again the shake of the head, but now speech too. "No... NEED... A... PISS... PLEASE?" Of course the team had come this far and we were determined to win on this one. While he was holding his water, we held all the aces. I replied, "You can have a pee if you tell us what your squadron is and where you are based..." Then it all came as a rush, he was done in. "My base is Drewitz; Cottbus-Drewitz... erm, and I fly SU22's with JBG-37 Squadron. Now I NEED TO PISS!" I looked at Robert and Jack, then back at Gunter – Ouch! *Now we have a problem. After all he's been through, we can't untie his hands, he'll bloody kill us. Damn!*

Which is how it got THIS CRAZY. We three discussed it and we all decided that as I used to be a nurse, then I should go ahead and help the patient to get his relief by opening his zip and taking his penis out for him while he remained tied up. I explained this carefully to Gunter and he completely understood our position. In fact at that point I think he was in so much agony, he didn't care anymore.

So I leaned him forward with his shoulder against a tree while I unzipped the flying suit at the front. After all we had been through, I was keen to make sure he didn't end up wetting the front of his clothing too and as I reached inside to withdraw his penis he flinched in pain. When I withdrew my hand gently holding his member, the reason for the pain was clear to see. I looked down and blinked, his penis had a pink swollen ring behind the head where his foreskin had become massively inflated... *Oh F***! No wonder he couldn't pee. Now we really have got a problem.*

"Listen to me now mate and listen carefully. This exercise is over and we're not playing games anymore. You have got a SERIOUS medical condition and we have to solve it and quickly too, we don't have much time..." He looked at me and saw I was deadly serious. He also knew that something was really wrong with his genitals and although he didn't know why he was in so much pain, obviously I did. He nodded and winced, "Yes.... it's.... B.A.D..." he whispered – I wasn't sure if he meant the pain or the condition, but he was right on both counts.

"What you have got is called a Paraphimosis. Trust me on this one Gunter, I used to be a nurse. And what you have got to do now, RIGHT NOW, is to get your foreskin forward again over the head of your dick, 'cos if you don't it will act like a tourniquet and cut off the blood supply. Honestly, the head will go gangrenous, I don't need to explain anymore do I...?" His eyes were now screwed up tight against the pain, I wasted no time undoing the fishing net from round his wrists. I continued talking calmly and professionally to him explaining that he had to do it himself and the pain would be excruciating or else it would be emergency surgery. I backed away and left him to it. As I turned towards the other two, the scream which split the air in that wood was horrendous – they looked at me in horror. It seemed to go on for ages, a whole lungful of air anyway; it brought tears to my eyes as I shook my head to get rid of the sound and the mental image of his balloon like foreskin. *Ooooohh! No wonder the man was in pain – damn!* I mused. *But we were not to know, it wasn't really our fault. He should have said something earlier,* but he was very tough and was not going to give in easily.

When I rejoined my teammates his cries had reduced to low sobbing and finally just heavy breathing as he was able to empty his bladder and gain relief at last. I explained to them both what had occurred and they looked stunned. We were all so glad it was over. Jack said, "Yeah, but like he did give us his Squadron and everything din't he?" I smiled and replied, "I don't think that matters too much now mate, but yes he did do that didn't he".

Twenty minutes later we were all on our way again, Gunter walking without any bonds or other restrictions, although he did seem to be walking rather stiffly and just as it was getting dark we arrived at the rendezvous location – I was pleased to see the Forestry Commission sign as we arrived, 'Kings Hat Inclosure'.

It was time to build our Basha and get on with the last few days of the course. The Staff were pleased to see Gunter, although it seemed he was less than pleased to see them. Meanwhile I had been looking forward to some Mature English Cheddar (Marks and Spencer's finest) and maybe some Yorkie chocolate bar, followed by some dry roasted peanuts – assuming the squirrels had not beaten us to it. However we would have to wait until night came for the munching to begin. I looked up at the darkening sky through the trees – *Hmm, not long to go now...*

+   +   +

Basha Feb 1984, Navy aircrew survival course – roast squirrel on the menu

---

We all have Wings.

(Yes it really is true – but some of them are carelessly 'clipped' by Careers Advisers).

I glanced at the clock on the instrument panel and could see it was just over an hour to go to landing, and then I looked across the flightdeck of the Alitalia 767 at my colleague, "Are you okay for a few minutes? I'll just pop back and check the plumbing – you have control". He smiled and said,
"No probs Skip, I have control, the Minimum Safe Altitude is less than ten grand, so we'll go straight down to that if we lose the cabin".
"Roger that. I'll bring you a cup of tea on my way back". I checked my tie in the mirror on the back of the cockpit door and made my exit. Outside in the

forward galley there was a middle aged male passenger waiting for the lavatory, I nodded, smiled and said to him, "Hope you don't mind if I jump the queue, or you could take some flying lessons?" He replied affably with an American accent.

"No you go right ahead Sir, I wouldn't want to do your job" there was a pause so I enquired what line of work he was in, "W-a-y-ll, some call me a careers advisor".

I took a deep breath and exhaled slowly before I could trust myself to speak...

"Humph! Somebody gave me some career advice once and it was wrong, it took me ten years to work that out for myself. People should never say, 'No you can't', to an enthusiastic teenager when they talk about their ambition in life - never!"

+   +   +

When I was 15 years old, we had a 'Careers Master' at our school – or perhaps more correctly one of the teaching staff whose secondary duty it was to advise the pupils on their future careers. This was at the Grammar School I was attending; a type of educational establishment that was once quite popular, but these days... not so much. I clearly remember him asking me the question, "So McBride, what do you want to do when you leave school? Hmmm...?"

In those days all surnames were used when we were addressed by our tutors. I didn't even need to think about it, I was quite sure what I wanted to do, I replied "I'd like to fly Sir... with the Royal Air Force". There was a pause and then he snorted back at me.

"Don't be ridiculous McBride, think of something else which is possible, there's absolutely no chance of you getting into the RAF". To say I was crushed would be an understatement – I left his office feeling numb, dejected and downhearted. Strewth! Now what to do? Literally I couldn't get enthusiastic about anything else; ever since primary school I had wanted to fly. I remember saying to myself, *Well that's it then...*

My dad had been an Adjutant Flying Officer on a Hawker Typhoon squadron in the Second World War and although he became a dentist after de-mob, he often talked about flying. In fact his association with aviation preceded WW2, because in the late 1930's he was employed as a fitter on Halifax Bomber production at Rootes' factory at Speke airport in Liverpool. Before that he had done some flying on a Tiger Moth and even went solo, but he was debarred from acceptance as military aircrew by having to wear spectacles. Whatever; by the time I was 15 years of age, his enthusiasm had caught my imagination – well that and the books on the adventures of Major James Bigglesworth - just plain 'Biggles' to his fans.

Although my eyesight was not an issue, according to my "Careers Master" I was not being realistic in my ambition to become an RAF pilot, so I had to think of something else. Quite honestly, there was nothing else which interested me and therefore (to a disillusioned teenager) there was not much point in school... Needless to say my academic results suffered badly as my dream went unfulfilled. In my own mind, there really was no point. It took me ten years to learn the truth, that in this life you can do anything if you have enough perseverance and drive. Inside every one of us *"we all have wings"*, but some of us don't realise until it is too late - in my case, I was only just in time. It took me a whole decade to work out for myself that the Careers Master did not know what he was talking about.

When I was accepted for Military Flying Training, I was the happiest person alive; I knew I was one of the luckiest too. My energies were totally focused on success in that field for a very long time. In every training course, which usually had a pass/fail assessment, test or exam at the end of it, I watched some of my contemporaries fall by the wayside. In many cases, I observed that it wasn't necessarily their lack of ability which was to blame for their demise; it seemed that they just lost faith that they could do it too. I could see then, that although *"we all had wings... some of us didn't know why"*. Time passes and fast forward to a happy time in my flying career when I was not only flying nice shiny airliners for a living, but in my off-duty I was also flying Air Cadets for the Royal Air Force in the wonderful De Havilland Chipmunk. Each cadet got around 25 minutes airborne which included aerobatics if they wished and most of them were mad keen to experience the full package. We could get 5 consecutive flights on a full tank of gas.

Due to the operational requirements of the Chipmunk, we carried out 'running changes' – in other words, we kept the engine running while we swapped over the cadets in the backseat. Once strapped in and the canopy closed up again, it was possible to speak to them on the intercom and the first thing we established was their name – we never normally got to see or speak to them face to face as the tandem seating and intensive programme prevented this.

"Good morning, welcome to the Air Experience Flight, what's your name?" I said nice and clearly on the intercom – the throat mike sometimes distorted speech and it was worth making the effort to be well understood.

"Tiberius Sir!" came his reply much to my surprise, so I said,

"Err...say again chap, I didn't quite catch your name...". I was much more used to hearing Bill, George or Harry.

"Yes it is... **TIBERIUS** Sir, after the famous Roman General and thank you for taking me flying today Sir". Well, you learn something new every day.

"You are VERY welcome Tiberius and I hope you enjoy the flight, I guess your Mum and Dad are teachers then are they?" As we taxied out for the runway, I was simultaneously running through the pre-takeoff checks.

"My father is a Professor in history Sir and my mother is also a history teacher". Now that explained everything, after all who else would saddle their son with such a cross to bear in life. I shook my head, smiled and looked up - the weather was picture perfect with blue skies and a few fluffy clouds. I called on the intercom, "Are you all secure in the back Tiberius?" and with an affirmative response, I pushed the throttle to full power and we started to roll. Rudder to maintain straight as the revs increased and then more rudder as the tail came up and before you knew it we were airborne. Airspeed increasing rapidly now, Tiberius must be fairly lightweight, I thought to myself and we were down to just one hour's fuel in the tanks anyway. *"We all have wings..."*

The next 25 minutes of our lives passed far too quickly as we soared, dived, rolled, climbed and looped our way round the sky. Tiberius had done quite a bit of glider flying and it seemed like he was a natural on the stick. By the time we started our last dive towards the airfield close to maximum speed for the run-in and break to land he was laughing his head off and so was I. Our feeling of euphoria in the cockpit of that little 'plane was intense and if somebody had said; *"we could live, for a thousand years"* we would have believed them absolutely and totally. In all my time flying the Air Cadets in AEF flights, there were a few truly notable missions and this one was right up there.

Now we were taxiing back in again, high on adrenalin and both of us glowing from the magic of flight, REAL flight. I asked him about his ambition to fly and he told me that he had received 'some negative feedback from his Careers Adviser' – I could feel my blood pressure rising... *Grrrr!...never say "NO you can't" to an enthusiastic teenager...Never!* I spent the next two minutes explaining to him that if he really wanted to do something (anything) in life, it was possible if he wanted it badly enough. Nothing could stop him and he "should not listen to the poor advice of a Careers Master", he interrupted me,
"Actually Sir it's a computer. We put in all the data and the Careers advice comes out as a printout..." I was aghast. *A computer programme?* Was that all our young people are worth now, not even a human mentor to advise them?

"Listen to me Tiberius", we were coming to the parking position in dispersal and our time was very short, "...when the computer gives you its decision, next time, just enter the letters B-O-L-O-X many times over until it crashes, do you understand me? Good luck my friend, you can do it! *You can fly!"* The canopy was open now, propeller at idle and another cadet waiting. The sergeant was on the wing and pulled the intercom lead for the back-seater, another customer joined me and plugged in, I set 1100 rpm again before the plugs oiled up. I cleared my throat, for some reason there was a lump in it and then I took a deep breath.

"Ahem... Good morning! *Welcome to the Air Experience Flight, what's your name?"*

+   +   +

The lyrics of the song 'Never Tear Us Apart' by INXS have a special resonance for me. They go like this:

"We could live *for a **thousand** years, but if I **hurt** you, I'd make **wine** from your **tears**. I **told** you, that **we** could fly, 'cause **we all have wings,** but some of us **don't know why".***

The Coolest Job on the Planet.

It is sometimes easy to forget how lucky we are to be doing the job of our dreams. In 1999 I was taking part in the 'Airline' TV series about easyJet - I was one of the onscreen characters. During one programme, I made the comparison between flying airliners and being a bus driver – in fact I think I said in so many words that I thought of myself as just that, a "Bus driver" on an Orange "bus" (of course it was an orange Boeing 737, but let's not split hairs).

After the programme had been screened, one of the easyJet First Officers cornered me in the crewroom at Luton and complained that I had insulted our profession - especially as he had "spent so much money" on getting his pilot's licence. My response was simple, "Don't get me wrong mate, I think it's one of the coolest jobs on the planet, however don't build it up to be something that it's not. Even flying round the globe at 500 miles per hour, it's just another form of transportation and we're still only driving a bus!"

That's the reality, the truth of what we do. To many people these days, flying has become just another form of transportation - a quick way from A to B. The romance of aviation has been diluted by its easy availability to all and although we can mourn the passing of the glory days, when Croydon was London's main airport and all airliners had propellers, the positive side of the coin is that flying has never been so cheap for everybody – a new golden age is upon us. And one of the key factors involved in this revolution in air travel has been the explosive growth of Low Cost Carriers over the past few years.

Love 'em or hate 'em, they are here to stay, because in addition to taking market share from the legacy carriers, the LCCs have also developed a customer base of their own. As a direct consequence there are more jobs in the industry for all of us and that is really good news for those young aspiring Airline Pilots who want to 'live the dream'. But, as always in life, the principle of no pain, no gain applies. Paradoxically, even though the airline industry needs more pilots than ever before, the days of training, and in particular type ratings, being paid for by airlines are gone. There are some notable exceptions, however even those companies are becoming hard pressed to compete with those who let their new joining pilots fund their own flying training.

The origin of this new fashion is with the LCCs and the success they have had in changing the way pilots are employed in Europe. Take Ryanair, for example. Going back a number of years now, Ryanair announced that as part of their drive towards lower costs in all areas, they would charge candidate pilots for all of the job application process. I distinctly recall at the time there was a storm of protest and howls of derision from the pilot community in general, but here we are, some years later, and the airline has no shortage of applicants willing to pay to work for them or even be interviewed by them. So there has been a climate change in pilot recruitment in the recent past. It did not take Ryanair's competitors long to catch up, and now the majority of companies require some form of "self-investment" by new joining pilots.

But we should not delude ourselves. Even those of us who were lucky enough to be in the right place at the right time to get our type ratings paid for, still had to pay in some way for our training/qualifications. Whether it was to join the military, hours-build, self-improve, instruct flying or buy an off-the-shelf frozen ATPL course – we have all made sacrifices at some time or other. The obstacles that we have overcome to get into the front seats of powered aeroplanes have been substantial and could only have been achieved by obsessive fanatics. For all of us at some time or other, ANY sacrifice was worth it – the end result really did justify the means. And not just in a monetary sense, as the number of failed relationships and marriages will testify among those gaining their professional pilot licences.

On the positive side though, the career expectations of commercial aviators in UK (and Irish) airlines have never been so high. In the not-so-distant past, and speaking in very general terms, you could have said that most commercial pilots would take around five years to get into the right-hand seat of a jet airliner as a First Officer. It would then take another five years as a minimum to be promoted to Captain. With the rapid expansion of the airline industry in Europe and the corresponding need for airline pilots, expectations are heightened to such a level that if a newly-qualified frozen ATPL holder does not obtain their first "Jet Job" immediately, with the ink still wet on their licence, they are severely disappointed.

What's more, there is considerable pressure on Flight Training Managers and Chief Training Captains in the UK to promote from within and First Officers in the airlines also anticipate getting their command upgrade sooner than before, as many companies struggle to attract the experienced, type-rated, skippers they need to support their expansion. These are known in the trade as DECs (Direct Entry Captains) and are a highly prized commodity among recruitment departments. Innovative methods have been utilised recently by recruiters keen to get them in through the doors, examples include golden handshakes and 'finders fees' (bounty payments) – in some cases as much as

£20,000 as a lump sum. The employer who offered this amount to encourage B737 Training Captains to apply, forgot to mention that there were substantial strings attached and this sum was subject to income tax. Needless to say 60% of £20k is nowhere near as attractive as £20K in your pocket, but that's another story.

So what about my own career and where do I fit in with the whole scheme of things?

I have to say that I consider myself very fortunate to have been continuously employed flying aeroplanes of one sort or another since 1983. We all have "lucky breaks" at one time or another in our flying careers and mine came back in the halcyon days of late 1988 when I was working as an Air Taxi Pilot on light piston twins in Manchester and there was a "pilot shortage". I applied to the airlines and within a matter of weeks, separated by interviews and simulator assessments; I had three offers for positions as F/O on Jet Airliners by three major charter airlines in the UK.

These were (in the order which they happened), B727 based at MAN, B737 based at LTN and B757 based at MAN. My decision on which to accept was based simply upon getting the biggest and shiniest jet possible on my licence – which happened to be (in those days) the new glass cockpit 757. I was also dead lucky with the company which I joined. Air 2000 (as it was then known) was a brilliant, vibrant, shining star of a company in which to fly airliners – quite honestly I could not have chosen better. The operating standards were excellent and the *esprit de corps* on the line was incredible. At my interview the Chief Pilot (Bob Screen) asked me if I had any questions and I recall cheekily asking when I would be able to "get my command on the 757". Bearing in mind that I had around 1000 hours total time in my logbooks, this was pretty gamey, however the interview had gone well so I thought it would sound as if I were keen. The solemn reply was, "About five years from your type rating...*assuming* you are good enough" As it transpired, he was correct almost to the day – I guess that was one of the reasons why he was the CP.

A lot of water has passed under the bridge since then and now with 13,000 hours plus total time, mostly on airliners (B757, 767 and 737), I find myself spending much of my life instructing others in the gentle art of commercial operations in airliners. I am mindful of the sacrifices that many have made along the way and so I am particularly pleased when I witness the development and success of the next generation coming through. It's a good feeling to have played a part in that process and this was especially true at times while working for easyJet, when the advancement was so rapid that it hardly seemed five minutes after a new F/O had been line-trained on the new type before he or she was entering a Command Training Course.

Of course, being involved in commercial flight training is not all benevolence and happy times - on occasion there are tears too. Part of my role puts me in the examining seat of simulator sessions and commercial flights, where I am working on behalf of the regulatory authority to ensure that a certain standard of performance is met by the pilots who are being checked. Even so, I still think flying aeroplanes for a living *really* is one of the coolest jobs on the planet.

The Class of '83. Author standing on wing. With coursemates at RN Grading Flight. Bob Hubble, Gary Suffling, Tony Morris, Andy Gray, Louis Beardsworth, Nigel Crates, Tony Stevens

(When flying airliners is compared to a theatrical performance).

"All the World's a Stage...

...and all the men and women merely players". Now I know for a fact that Shakespeare didn't have Airline Pilots in mind when he wrote this, because he died nearly three hundred years before Orville and Wilbur got their act together. That being said however, it often fascinates me how life imitates art and vice versa. Really we are all actors in the play of our own lives, like Jim Carey in the film, 'The Truman Show'. Shakespeare's words still have resonance today and I suggest are particularly relevant to the world of commercial aviation.

Take for example the situation in the flightdeck of an airliner in flight. Here two or more players are performing their duties (roles) and all have scripts with which to play their part. The curtain rises as they report for duty in the briefing/crew room. The lead role is taken by 'the Commander' and this is true even in these days of enlightened CRM. Other members of the cast appear in supporting roles and the play gets under way. The scene changes throughout the performance and the various acts are played out with all the cast involved at some time or other.

The main story line from our perspective however is what is happening in that little room at the front of the aircraft where the pilots sit. Here we have the interaction between usually two main characters and they have to get their lines right. The script is provided for them by the Director, (that's *'Ops'* Director) and their familiarity with the speaking part is a key element to the success of the production.

If the players deviate from the prepared text, then they could potentially turn a drama into a tragedy and those fateful words will be recorded for posterity on the Cockpit Voice Recorder (CVR). An extreme example of this was the Captain of the B747 of Avianca airlines back in 1983, who decided to ad lib at a critical stage of his performance in the play, "Flight into Madrid". The accident report makes for grim reading and the end result (Controlled Flight Into Terrain or CFIT) is sadly predictable.

Cited in the accident report were, "procedural errors by the crew including the pilot not knowing his precise position before descending. Failure of the crew to react to GPWS warning and deficient teamwork on the flightdeck". My reference to deviating from the script however, refers to the response of the Captain to the Ground Proximity automated voice 'Pull-Up' warning. Recorded for posterity on the CVR was the sound in the cockpit of the GPWS, ***"Whoop! Whoop! Pull-Up!"*** to which the South American Captain replied with the immortal words, ***"Shut-Up Gringo!"*** Shortly afterwards, the aircraft with nearly 200 souls onboard ploughed into the side of a mountain on final approach for Madrid.

This accident has been used many times since then as an example of the 'Wrong Stuff' when teaching Crew Resource Management (CRM). Strangely enough, there was another accident in Spain just over a year later in early '85, where the aircraft Captain was heard on the CVR telling the GPWS to *"Shut-up!"* The Iberia B727 crashed into high ground near Bilbao in Northern Spain at 3400 feet above sea level while making an instrument approach to runway 30.

Of course this was in the days before CRM and without doubt many accidents have been prevented since the introduction of this particular subject to the airline crews' learning syllabus. Naturally there was resistance from pilots in the early 90s when CRM training became a mandatory requirement. As a group of people, airline pilots can be sceptical about the introduction of new techniques, although it helps them when the training is carried out by 'airframe drivers' who really know and understand the nature of the work we do. It is interesting to observe the reactions from fellow aviators on these CRM training courses and the interaction they have with their colleagues.

Certainly the more experienced pilots tend to be less enthusiastic than their junior peers. Naturally there is humour too. According to one senior pilot on a course I attended, the acronym CRM stands for "Captain's Right Mate!" This was accompanied by much guffawing on all sides of the room. It is strange though to observe, that the pilots who REALLY need CRM training are exactly the ones who won't listen.

We have all worked with pilots who are "a CRM nightmare" and usually they are oblivious to the effect they have on others at work. In the main they are aircraft Commanders and tend to be of the old school variety – invariably authoritarian in their approach to the task of managing their team, they will brook no dissent in the ranks. Now when these guys deviate from the script it is very difficult for the junior co-pilot to get them to conform to the SOP, (Standard Operating Procedures – includes SOP 'Calls')

When I first started flying airliners, I remember an anecdote told to me by one of the Captains while we were flying back across the Atlantic from the States on the B757. On a seven hour flight there is plenty of time to chat. He recalled when many years before he used to fly the Atlantic routes as a junior co-pilot on large propeller aircraft and in those days there were five crew members in the flightdeck. Captain and Co-pilot, Flight Eng, Radio Operator and Navigator.

He said that the old 'Atlantic Barons' of yore were really fearsome creatures and as a junior man you always had to watch your step. He told me about an old skipper who just would not give the correct response to the normal challenge/response checklist – perhaps he had been doing the job too long, but all the Co-pilots had to put with it or they would lose their job. Whatever the challenge was, he would reply in a laconic growl *"Onboard!"*

The scenario would go something like, *"Before start checklist lad!"*
"Right Sir... Erm...Trim?" the reply came back, *"Onboard!"*
"Fuel?", again *"Onboard!"*
"Parking brake?", *"Onboard!"* and so on to the end of the checklist. You can imagine sitting next to that man for most of the night, flying in a darkened noisy cockpit across the ocean was not the most desirable of flying experiences. If he was like that just in a normal situation, you can predict how difficult it would be to call "Go-Around!" if he had cocked up an approach to land. Thankfully in our enlightened post CRM invented age, creatures like this are rare animals indeed.

Of course not all of the senior men in our industry are difficult to get along with – far from it. Some of the most enjoyable flights I have undertaken have been in the company of Airline Captains who are in the autumn of their flying career. It was a few years ago now, that I had the pleasure of flying in a B737 flightdeck with a very senior chap who didn't have long to go. As it was, I was the 'Training Captain' and he was theoretically the 'trainee' – it was his annual line check. He chuckled as he told me that in a previous company for whom he had flown (based in the Middle East), they had used a grading system for performance which was A, B or C, with + or – on each grade. He said that all the Expat pilots out there only ever got awarded B minus, anything higher was reserved for the locals!

John was also a great fan of the theatre and therefore his flightdeck atmosphere always had a theatrical air to it. At one point, prior to our pushback as we were prepping the aircraft for flight, there was a loud "CRASH" from the forward galley just behind the flightdeck bulkhead, as our 'not so dainty' Senior Stewardess slammed one of the service carts (trolley) home into its' stowage. I looked across at John in mock alarm with raised eyebrows and he met my gaze. In a very theatrical voice and with a big grin he said, *"Ahah!... Noises OFF!"* This set the tone for the next few hours together and I enjoyed his company enormously. The flying went very well too and my written report reflected my confidence in his abilities as Aircraft Commander. After the narrative, I wrote at the end of the report, "Truly a Command Performance Skipper and definitely worthy of a B plus!" He thought that was funny.

These days while I am running the simulator from the instructor's position, I have a grandstand view of the performance given by the pilots up front – they are playing to an audience of one. I am keenly aware that it is a privilege to be there, in a similar way to a Priest in a confessional. More than that, I am also the director of the play in some ways too, as I have to judge whether more time in rehearsal is required to achieve a better standard of performance.

During training, there is much repetition of exercises in order to 'get it right' – just as in rehearsals for a major theatre production. Take the Engine Failure On Takeoff case for example. There is little margin for poor performance here and therefore the freeze and reposition buttons are used to facilitate the repeated exercise, often with a rebrief of what went wrong.

Of course towards the end of a four hour simulator slot, enthusiasm and concentration is difficult to maintain when you are in the position of the trainee, so I do my best to encourage them from the director's chair. *"Once more with feeling please chaps!"* or *"Let's take it from the top shall we?"* It's worth bearing in mind though, that because of the nature of the job we do, nothing is left to chance. Which is precisely why you won't hear the phrase, *"Oh well... it'll be alright on the night!*

The Lever of Shame

(Teaching airline pilots and how I learn so much from them...)

One of the problems with Line Training pilots on airliners is that you have difficulty assessing their spare mental capacity. Of course in the simulator it's simple, you just dial in the fault, or combination of faults and then make observations of the pilots' handling of the failure/s from the trainer's seat. By contrast, "failure management" cannot be assessed on the line. In times gone by, (and not so long ago either) there were stories about Training Captains on jet airliners, retarding a thrust lever to idle to see how the pilot would handle the aircraft on one engine for real! In the enlightened age in which we now work however, this sort of practice is not acceptable as the safety of the flight would be unnecessarily compromised. In addition the quality of simulation has improved to the point where it's just about as real as it gets.

It was not always like this in pilot training. I recall a story told to me by a civilian flying instructor close to retirement about the time when he was working in the RAF as a fitter. He was assigned to a squadron which used the Vickers Varsity for multi-engined pilot training and he smiled as he revealed that unofficially the aircraft was known as "The Flying Pig" due in part to its' handling qualities. He said that during one hot summer in the 1960s, morale was particularly low among the other ranks on the squadron, which was mainly a result of the high number of engine problems which they had to rectify. In those days, "single engine" work really was that and the instructor used to shut down one engine completely to ensure proper asymmetric conditions. One afternoon, a group of fitters was sitting on the grass outside the hangar goofing (watching aeroplanes) as Varsities were practising circuits and bumps.

The aeroplane on finals was making a single engined approach and this was evident by the stationary propeller on one side. What attracted the airmen's attention however were the puffs of black smoke which began to emanate from the live engine, along with accompanying slowing down of the prop on that side. Almost immediately the "dead engine" propeller started to rotate slowly along with more belches of black smoke. One can only imagine the frantic scene in the cockpit as the pilots tried to rush the restarting of the simulated failed motor – their hands must have been a blur on levers and switches as they tried to rescue the situation.

Unfortunately their efforts were in vain as the airspeed decayed, the nose was raised to stretch the power assisted glide and the aircraft crash-landed in the rough grass of the undershoot, wiping off the undercarriage along the way. The most remarkable part of the incident however, was the reaction of the groundcrew, who all gave a resounding cheer and applauded as it went in! My colleague assured me that the two pilots survived with only cuts and bruises and the morale on the squadron improved markedly for a week or two after the event.

It is interesting to watch the maturing of trainee pilots as they go through their line training these days. Their first stumbling attempts on the radio, the errors in performance calculations the lack of spare capacity to even complete the paperwork as the line flight progresses. The assistance of the safety pilot on the jumpseat is invaluable at this stage. Before long though, you can see them spread their wings and little by little grow in confidence until not only has the SP been released from the observer's seat, but they've passed their Final Line Check and are now fully online. Some of them make progress more rapidly than others and even appear full of confidence from the start.

During a descent into Nice in the 737 in autumn 1999, I remember one young chap who was very confident and he was acting as the handling pilot. Normally the approach controllers at Nice tend to leave you quite high for what seems like ages, then they suddenly clear you to descend to 6000 feet but with a "Maximum speed of 250 knots S'il vous plait!" Now this is easier said than done of course, as modern airliners can either go down or slow down – but it's a real problem to achieve both at the same time. Well young Gerry was quite switched on and had already slowed down when they levelled us off at Flight Level 200 or thereabouts. He immediately put the speedbrakes out at 250 knots when we were further cleared in our descent to 6000 feet and he ensured the thrust levers were at idle.

I had flown with him for a few days previously and had been impressed already by what I had seen - this was just a continuation of that good performance. My problem was that he seemed to take it all too much in his stride and even though our French colleague had tried to ruin his descent profile, he had been quick to react and therefore had the situation well under control. Now, as we descended towards minimum safe altitude out over the sea off the beautiful Cote d'Azur I thought I detected a trace of smugness in his manner as he called for the approach checklist.

Simultaneously the controller cut the corner on us as he turned us towards Cannes heading north, cleared us for further descent to 4000 feet on the QNH and we were going high and fast again. The weather was Cavok however so we could always convert to a visual approach if necessary. Gerry saw the steep profile and brought the speed back to 210 knots and called "Flap One!" At the same time, he called for the "Approach Checklist!" and I noted that his voice was slightly higher pitched than before. "Okay" I said, "I'll give you the approach checklist but you've got to answer in the style of Sean Connery". "What?" came the reply.

"Your responses have to be in the accent of Sean Connery". I said again.

"Yeah, in which film?" was his quick riposte.

"Well, BOND of course!" I paused as the altimeters unwound further and time started to telescope in towards us. "Right, here goes!" I said theatrically removing the checklist from its holder with a flourish.

"Altimeters?" I challenged, he called back "Checked and Set".

"Oh No, that was nowhere near good enough Gerry, let's try again shall we?" We both noted the coastline getting closer as he called for more flap and then "Gear down!"

"Listen, it's got to have more of a Scottish lilt to it and a bit of a lisp too, like this...*Chacked and Shett!*" The aircraft was level now and Gerry was anxious to deploy some more flap, I sensed the tension building nicely.
"Altimeters?" I called again, "Chacked and SHETT!" he responded as he turned the heading bug onto final approach for runway 04R.

"Approach Aids?", again he came back with "Chacked and SHETT!"

"Approach checklist complete", I confirmed as he called for landing flap to be deployed. His relief was palpable as we completed the landing checklist in the same manner without repetition. The landing was excellent and we taxied off the runway and were handed over to ground control for taxi instructions to the gate - another beautiful day in Nice. In his training file after the flight, I wrote that he was making excellent progress, but "Keep working on the Bond impressions..."

One of the most reassuring aspects of Gerry's flying was that he wasn't shy of using the speedbrake. Too many airline pilots consider their deployment of speedbrake, as a tacit admission of defeat in their attempts to produce the ideal descent. In fact the descent and initial part of the approach is a very dynamic time in any flight and there are many variables involved in the successful management of the vertical profile.

Recently during a night descent into Accra (Ghana) on the 757, I was the operating Captain and was continuously assessing the angle of glide by comparing our passing altitude with distance to touchdown. It was obvious that we were high on the profile and even though I had increased the speed with the engines at idle to correct back to the descent path, it just wasn't going to be enough. More drag was required. Now in all the best CRM (Crew Resource Management) textbooks there are lots of different interaction techniques aimed at keeping both pilots on an even keel. Transactional Analysis is often used to demonstrate the positive effects of wholesome behavioural trends. Much store is placed in being careful in what you say on the flightdeck, so that you don't inadvertently antagonise your working colleague/s.

Caution is advised when using humour – especially if it could be misconstrued as being implied criticism of the other pilot/s operational standards or competence. Well textbooks are all very well of course, but they cannot cover every possible scenario. Certainly they wouldn't have covered the very good working relationship between an experienced Senior First Officer and myself on that evening into Accra. It was obvious that I was unable to control the aircraft flightpath by speed alone and I would have to use the speedbrakes to slow us down and restore the energy levels.

I grimaced in the dark and with a shrug of my shoulders (all nonchalance itself), I simply announced, "Speedbrakes" and smoothly moved the lever all the way aft. I wasn't sure of what response I would get from my fellow aviator, but I couldn't have predicted his next words. In a very solemn, admonishing, voice he intoned, *"Ahh! The Lever of Shame!"*

I was still laughing as we taxied in about ten minutes later. As a choice one-liner, the thought of it still amuses me; however I would advise junior Co-Pilots to be careful where and with whom they use it!

Enemy at the Door

They used to say that everyone knew where they were on the day President Kennedy was shot. This was an indicator of the shocking nature of the breaking news. Those were innocent days of course and you could say it was the end of innocence for the United States. Certainly that tragic event and others like it had the effect of hardening the nation up for what was to come in future decades. All pilots will probably have perfect recollection of their whereabouts on September 11th, 2001. On that terrible day, the nature of our profession changed forever. Not just a case of 'no more flightdeck visitors', but throughout our industry the changes went far beyond this.

Airline security within the EU has always been pretty tight and this is especially true of the situation in the UK. Now of course, it's tighter than ever before. This includes, armoured cockpit doors, extra layers of passenger checks at every level, the employment of armed sky marshals travelling incognito on some services and much more besides. The Crews take a very different view of their role since 9/11 and gone is the innocent age of air travel where virtually everybody is nice and we could trust all of our customers.

It is sad to think that the terrorists, whose actions on the 11th September caused such carnage and destruction, were also fare paying customers of the airlines which they chose as their targets. The first to lose their lives during the attack were the flightdeck crews, as not only were they redundant to the terrorists' plans, but also they could have proved a serious impediment and prevented its' success. Not surprising then, that any attempt by anyone to enter the flightdeck while airborne these days is treated almost as if the 'enemy is at the door'.

It was not always like this and it is nice to recall the relaxing days of airline operations when we ran almost literally an 'open door' policy. The cabin crew came and went as they pleased and flightdeck visitors made a pleasant diversion on an otherwise potentially tedious flight with a long cruise segment. This was particularly true of the children who came into see us, many of whom would be quite in awe of what they observed while we cruised serenely at 35,000 feet at 500 mph. They asked funny questions at times of course; What does this switch do? How do you make it go up? It doesn't feel like we're moving does it? But the time passed more easily and it was always good PR for the company. Happy customers, meant potentially repeat business and therefore continued employment for all of us.

Some visitors were more memorable than others. Take Stelios for example, Chairman and founder of Easyjet. He often used to sit on the flightdeck jumpseat for takeoff and landing on the 737s we were operating and I vividly recall the first time for me which was on a flight from Nice to Luton when I was the Captain. The handling agent had already prewarned us that the 'great man' was checked in as a passenger and shortly before the rest of the passengers arrived, his larger than life personage filled the flightdeck doorway. He smiled broadly as we shook hands and said,

"Captain, may I have the pleasure of sitting with you both in the cockpit for takeoff and landing?" I replied,

"Well it's your aeroplane Stelios, I reckon you can sit where you like".

"But YOU are the aircraft Commander".

"True, but YOU pay my wages as the boss of the company".

"Well we could carry on like this all day, so I assume that's a yes then?" he said.

"Of course Stelios, make yourself at home". This was rather easier said than done in the confined space of the 737 cockpit. I had already confirmed that the F/O was happy to have the boss sitting with us and have never assumed their consent in the past. There were often stories from other co-pilots about how 'wicked Captain so and so' treated the flightdeck as their personal domain, which then lead to a less than harmonious working relationship. As far as I was concerned if the F/O said "No", then the answer was always "No".

On the flight to Luton it was nice to be able to have a chat with Stelios and I asked what he had been doing down in Nice? The date was in the spring of 1998 and at that time we had a not so huge fleet of just 6 tired old 737-300s.

"Well you know, I live in Monaco just around the corner from Nice and I have been working down there trying to find routes for the 12 new 737s which we have just ordered from Boeing and which start to deliver in August this year at the rate of one per month!"

"Oh?" I expressed surprise at this; I said naively, "I rather hoped you would have sorted that out by now?" Which just goes to prove that I am better off as a pilot and Stelios is much better at business. Within the next five years, the airline grew like topsy and before long our little orange bus company from Luton were carrying more passengers to European destinations than British Airways – something in the region of 25 million per annum by 2003. Now it's quite a big orange 'bus company (entirely Airbus with a fleet of 250+), but back then when we were so small, it was hard to visualise where the customers were going to come from. Glad I didn't give up the day job.

Funnily enough, a few years later, when I was a pilot manager for the company, I was given the unenviable task of interviewing Stelios (while he was still Chairman of easyJet) as part of an ASR (Air Safety Report) investigation. This occurred when one of the Captains had complained that Stelios's presence in the cockpit had been a flight safety hazard when he had flown on the jumpseat. Needless to say in all my dealings with Stelios he had always been the perfect gentleman and I had carried him onboard our flights in the flightdeck several times without incident.

The Captain on this flight however had been upset by Stelios asking a question about why the aircraft wasn't planning to make an autoland (low visibility) approach to the airport when the weather was bad. The skipper felt that his authority had been questioned/challenged and therefore had filed the report, citing reasons of 'Flight Safety'. The result of the investigation was that there had never been a safety issue and in fact it turned out that this particular Captain had always hated having visitors of any kind in his "office".

To complete the investigation I had to interview the Captain and I remember asking him the question, "So Bruce, how long is it that you've hated having non-operational personnel in the flightdeck?" To which he replied slowly, "Well... only the past 35 years or so". The case was closed very soon closed after this, but I think Stelios was rather less keen to sit in the cockpit on future flights. On another occasion in the distant past with a charter airline when I was operating as Captain to Las Palmas in the Canaries on the 757, I did actually call for one of the passengers to be sent up to see me after takeoff so I could give him a 'good old fashioned bollocking'. He was Judge James Pickles a famous member of the judiciary.

Prior to departing from Manchester, the Senior Steward (Jeremy) had asked him to move seats for takeoff as he had been given a seat in the emergency exit row, which must be occupied by fully Able Bodied People (ABPs). Justice Pickles actually had a disabled hand from an accident which he had suffered as a child, which Jeremy felt disbarred him from the category of ABP. ('Scuse the pun). Essentially the cabin crew must be satisfied that the passenger on an emergency exit row can open the emergency exit successfully – disability is not allowed.

Well there was a quite a scene in the cabin apparently and 'His Worship' was not of a mind for moving seats. With a Mexican standoff in progress and the ATC slot fast expiring, I asked Jeremy to pass the Captain's compliments to M'lud and to kindly inform him that, **"Either he moves in the next 30 seconds, or he is OFF the damn 'plane!"** That did the trick, but of course he was not a happy camper and insisted on, *"Seeing the Captain after takeoff!"*

Unfortunately he had temporarily forgotten where he was and that while onboard an aircraft, the **Captain's word** is law (UK's Air Navigation Order refers). Regrettably, he then tried to intimidate Jeremy by threatening *"To write about this incident in my newspaper column in the Daily Smudge".* Well, that did it for me and I was not going to miss the chance to give a judge a dressing down. When we had reached cruising altitude, I informed our Senior Steward that he could "Send that Judge in now".

Justice Pickles arrived full of bluster and bushy eyebrows and was exactly how I imagined he would be from his pictures in the press. I invited him to sit on the jumpseat in the flightdeck while we had our little chat. Specifically he wanted to see where the regulations were written which covered the legal situation which prevented him from sitting in an exit-row seat. I took some time to explain that all the relevant regulations regarding ABPs were in the operating manuals and legal documents carried onboard the aircraft, responding,

"No, you cannot look at them. Today you are a **passenger** Sir and will be accorded those courtesies and rights which THAT position warrants, but no more". I gave him my airline's business card and told him that if he had any questions regarding the application of the ANO in this circumstance, then he could kindly address those questions in writing to the Chief Pilot who would be happy to answer them. Now came the matter of attempting to intimidate our Senior Steward – he began to look particularly uncomfortable as I brought the subject up, although I smiled as I did so.

"SHAME on you Sir! You tried to abuse your position by threatening a crew member who was only doing his duty, *you should know better* – you will kindly make a formal apology to Jeremy as you pass through the galley on the way back to your seat!" And bless him, he did just that – Jeremy was delighted. In fact he was a lovely chap really and we were so impressed with his contrition that we extended the invitation to join us in the flightdeck for the descent and landing into Las Palmas. Ahh, those were the days when we could do such things. As he left the flight to go on his vacation, he was very complimentary about our crew and the airline, and assured that if he "mentioned the flight at all, it would be in glowing terms".

And what is my recollection of September 11th? Well I was actually flying as a passenger on an EasyJet flight to Belfast doing pilot recruiting duties as the attacks happened. We saw the second airliner hit the twin towers on the TV screen in the departure lounge at Luton and by the time we arrived in Belfast, the first tower had fallen – a tragic disaster of great magnitude and quite shocking for all of us in the hotel that night. It was a time when you just wanted to be home with the family and thanked God we didn't live in New York.

The next morning, I was still stunned by the appalling news and quite choked by the thoughts of what happened onboard those flights especially to the crews. I was on the 'phone to my wife and she said that my young son wanted to speak to me urgently – I thought, *Oh no, he's seen TV images of airliners crashing into buildings and although he's too young to understand, wants to tell me to take care while flying "my" aeroplane.* I waited, then his little voice came on the line – *I must tell him I'm on my way home.*

"Dad...?" He said, and something caught the back of my throat, *Dear God, he's only four.*
"Yes mate I'm here what is it?" Here it comes, phew this isn't going to be easy.
"Guess what Dad? .... I've got TRACY ISLAND!" He was ecstatic and wanted me to know how good he felt about his new toy.
"That's great news mate! Fantastic news, thank you for telling me about it. I can't wait to get home to play Thunderbirds with you".

Flying for easyJet from '97 to 2005   *(Ray Farley photo)*

Reality Check – keeping it real in the Simulator.

(Humour and Reality mixed together – a potent teaching combination for the brain).

Every six months, all commercial airline pilots spend up to two days in the simulator. This is usually in on two consecutive days of, four hour sessions when their skills and proficiency are tested in order to satisfy the requirements of the regulations. Once this is done, their licence is signed up by the examiner so that they can retain the privileges of their rating to operate Public Transport aircraft with passengers onboard. For many of us, it is a tense time in our lives. Complete failure of a Proficiency Check could ultimately result in unemployment and potentially loss of the licence which we have tried so hard to attain.

"Treat the Simulator like the real aircraft". I have lost count of the number of times I have said those words in pre simulator briefings. I often back it up by saying, *"What you are observed to do in the simulator, we have to assume that you would do in real life with the aircraft. If your approach to a runway is unstable and you subsequently decide to land from it, then I as the examiner have to assess that you would do the same on the line..."*

In the bad old days of simulator training and checking, candidates were given set-piece manoeuvres to fly in order that they could demonstrate their flying skills and proficiency. Often the pre-sim brief would be comprehensive and prescriptive such that little assessment of decision making processes was carried out. In its simplest form, it was 'Monkey see - Monkey do'. Now with the advent of NoTechs or None Technical Skills to give it the full title, simulator examiners are encouraged to assess thought processes, decision making qualities and interaction of pilots in the multi-crew environment. Of course this in itself is not possible unless the simulator experience is as real as it can be. Full motion Sims have come a long way in recent years and with the advances in computer technology, the exterior (visual) graphics are brilliant with wraparound (180°) vision helping pilots to believe they really are flying an airliner.

The way in which the 'check' of proficiency is conducted by the TRE (Type Rating Examiner) is just as important as the technology that is used to facilitate it. The CAA Training Standards department (Flight Operations Inspectorate) actively encourage the use of real time exercises, with minimal use of the 'freeze' and 'reposition' functions available in the Sim.

Naturally every time you freeze the motion in the middle of a flight, it has a really negative effect on the reality. During training however the freeze and reposition can be used to good effect when trainees require to practice and rehearse manoeuvres with which they are having trouble getting to grips with. The training of Engine Failure On Takeoff (EFOTO) technique is a good example of this, especially when this exercise needs to be trained to proficiency.

The introduction of LOFT (Line Oriented Flying Training) exercises, which began some years ago has been one of the cornerstones of the quiet revolution in Simulator training. During the LOFT part of the check, the candidates are given a Line Flight scenario which ideally should include Flightplans, weather/Notams, loading details, technical summary of the aircraft and even a CTOT (Calculated Take off Time – also known as an ATC Slot). As examiners we are recommended to interact as realistically as possible with the crew and to that end we have many 'hats' to wear.

The first and most obvious one is that of Air Traffic Controller and the TRE needs to be on the ball with respect to use of the R/T, especially with frequency changes. There is no point in briefing the crew to play it for real and then conducting the whole two Sim sessions on the same ATC frequency. Correct R/T procedures are the bread and butter of a Line Crew's workload and should come naturally to them. Moreover, incorrect R/T and the misuse of non-standard phraseology has been identified as key factors in many aviation accidents over the years.

There are many occasions when the crew have been 'handed over' to a new ATC unit, say from Tower to Approach and although they have correctly read back the digits of the new VHF frequency, this has been mis-selected on the VHF radio in use. In the dark at the back of the Sim, I am always pleased when I notice this and don't respond to their transmissions – just as it happens in real life. We have all done it and the first thing to do is cross-check that you have the correct frequency dialled up – I reckon 9 times out of 10 this will be the problem.

There are times when guys in the front probably feel cheesed off that the TRE is playing it this realistically, but that's our job. Sometimes it is necessary to hold back a little and be a bit passive, or even slightly incompetent as the controller – again this is real world here, as there are some destinations where ATC is renowned for being less than helpful. Not only will they (the controller) not spoonfeed the crew, they will even cock it up for them big style if you let them.

If the crew are going to learn the lesson of how this can happen, they may aswell do it in the Sim. Here we can rewind and replay as necessary to learn from the experience, rather than at some horrible Third World airport where a Go-Around or worse becomes essential for the safety of the flight. We're not talking about entrapment here, but the crew are responsible for keeping the flight safe. If we're talking about MSA (Minimum Safe Altitude) awareness, then that needs to be kept at a high level – even in the case of modern airliners fitted with advanced GPWS (Ground Proximity Warning Systems).

So a slightly duff controller may have descended an airliner to a Sector Safe Altitude (SSA) which subsequently becomes unsafe when further radar headings are given... It happens, not often, but the danger is there - so it has to happen in the synthetic world of the darkened electronic box on stilts. A controller can be distracted, get busy and for any one of a dozen reasons doesn't realise that the airliner is now heading towards high ground on an unsafe heading. Controlled Flight Into Terrain (CFIT) is one of the saddest type of accidents and accounts for a large percentage of hull losses still – always the root cause is human error/s, often coupled with deviation from accepted practice or Standard Operating Procedures (SOPs).

Part of the modern way of training means that crews are given the time to employ effective CRM and NoTechs in order to solve the problems which they are given in a safe and effective manner. This means bringing into the loop the assistance of and communication with the Cabin Crew. If an emergency landing is planned, then it is vital that the Cabin Crew are briefed in order to prepare the passengers for the event to ensure survivability is maximised. In the Sim the role of the SCCM (Senior Cabin Crew Member) is played by the TRE. I know that some examiners are in the habit of calling themselves "Doris" or "Cynthia" and perhaps putting on effeminate voices when they answer the intercom. Regardless of what you think of this from a gender bending viewpoint, I always answer the cabin interphone with my own name and try to refrain from any cross-dressing pretensions. I try to be James the Steward.

Although it's a serious business, there are occasions and appropriate moments for light relief. I remember several years ago conducting a proficiency check in the simulator on a B737 Captain who was nearing retirement. In actual fact the company had told him in no uncertain terms (and rather rudely) that they had no future use for him beyond the grand old age of 60 – he was at this time 59 years and 8 months old.

As his proficiency check was due to expire, he had been rostered for his last simulator session, I was his TRE and he was a very plain speaking Australian. He felt rather aggrieved that he was being discarded after they had used his last few months as Commander – he had spent a long time with the company. You can imagine that the atmosphere was not the most relaxed at first, especially when during the briefing he explained all of the circumstances.

I felt pity for the poor young inexperienced Co-Pilot who was going to have to put with two days of what might be quite difficult communication and CRM. Still, we all have our crosses to bear and while I conducted the check in a professional manner, I reasoned that the First Officer would probably learn something from the situation too. If nothing else he would learn a few new rude words to add to his vocabulary I mused, as the Aussie was keen to vent his spleen about what he thought of the way he had been treated.

On day one, they got airborne from East Midlands airport, bound for Manchester, only a 20 minute flight away, but as the TRE I decided it would be a little more expeditious if the Non-Precision Approach were carried out at the airport of departure. *Hmm...* I thought, how can I get them to return? It would have been easy to create a major system failure such that they wanted to put the aircraft on the ground as soon as possible, but there was a problem with that. Crews should not be put under undue stress with extra system failures when tasked with a Non-Precision Approach as this is not realistic. To be engaged in an NPA scenario will normally be the result of careful and time consuming preparations.

They were well into the SID (Standard Instrument Departure) now with the autopilot engaged and passing 4000 feet in the climb, albeit still a lot closer to EMA than MAN. I pressed the Cabin Call button and the chime sounded in the flightdeck overhead panel – bong! The Captain was flying and so he said to his right seater,

"Oi've got the ryedio Mate, you see what the steward wants". The F/O nodded and keyed the switch, *"Erm, yes, First Officer here, the Captain says what do you want?"*

"Hello, sorry to disturb you, it's James the Senior Steward at doors one", I said from my seat in the darkness of the back of the box, *"but there's a little old lady on row three who seems to be having a heart attack, with lots of chest pain and I think we should land as soon as possible..."* The Captain was listening to this too and I could see him nod in the semi-darkened cockpit. The F/O turned towards him not knowing what to say, with his eyebrows raised and eyes wide open. The Captain said to him.

"No worries Mate, tell 'em to make a PA for a doctor onboard, she might NOT be having a heart attack". Hmm, this was one Skipper who was not keen to return to East Mids. I thought. The F/O passed on the message and there was a pause, I replied.

"I've already done that and her son with whom she is travelling, says HE IS a Doctor and SHE IS HAVING A HEART ATTACK!"

"OW BAGGER! Tell ITC we're goin' back in and git the weather mate...I'll mike a PI announcement to explain to the Pax..." Said the Aussie ruefully, admitting defeat.
I was pleased that he had finally seen it my way and they then set up for the Non-Precision Approach when they learned that the ILS had just failed. The subsequent non-precision approach was soundly conducted as you would expect from an old campaigner and we moved on through the rest of the planned syllabus.

Midway through the second day of the Proficiency Check it was clear to me that they had both achieved a good standard and all the check items had been passed. They were carrying out the LOFT detail in real time and it was a complicated problem which was taking them some time to solve.

The aircraft Flaps had failed to retract properly and were jammed in the semi-deployed position; which meant they couldn't fly very far or very fast and had elected to take up a holding pattern to run through all of the QRH (Quick Reference Handbook) checklists. Anyone familiar with the B737 Flap checklists will tell you that they can be lengthy and sometimes a little confusing, but this Skipper was taking no chances and he tasked the F/O to carry them out methodically and slowly – I nodded approval in the darkness and smiled.

Bong! The cabin interphone chimed in the flightdeck overhead panel. The Captain looked over at the young Co-Pilot, *"Moy ryedio. Gow on mate, see what the old tart wants!"* he said and the F/O answered the intercom,

"The Captain says what do you want?" while he said this I could see that my Aussie friend was listening in on his audio panel.

"There's a little old lady in row three..." I began, smiling and you could see both of them tense up for the inevitable. I'll bet he's thinking Oh No – not again. I said "*... she says to tell the Captain... that she once had a problem with her Flaps!"* while trying hard to keep my face straight.

Without a pause the Skipper responded.

"WELL, TELL HER SHE'S GOT A FACKING GOOD MEMORY!!"

Living the Life of Reilly?

(Overrated occupation? Well you could say it has its ups and downs...)

There is a perhaps a popular misconception about the job which we airline pilots do. This misconceived idea centres on it being in some way a 'glamorous occupation'. It is easy to lay the blame for this at the door of the media industry, especially Hollywood and the films of the last 60 years or so since the end of the Second World War. Pilots and specifically 'Airline' pilots have always been depicted as having a fairly cushy existence. Apart from the few moments of high drama when they are called upon to save the day with a combination of macho decision making and superhuman flying skills; they are seen to be swanning around airport terminals, chatting up beautiful air 'hostesses' and generally having a great time.

Naturally our stereotype heroes are not unattractive to the eye, drive some very tasty motors and appear to be handsomely remunerated for what they do. In addition they seem to have boundless access to free air travel across the surface of the planet, with upgrades to Business or First Class being the norm and priority check-in at the airport. They only stay in the best hotels, their uniforms are all tailored to fit, they never seem to suffer routine illnesses and generally you get the impression that life could not be much better than this?!

It is surely the view of some airline senior managers. I remember exactly the words of a CEO of a previous company for whom I worked that in his opinion we were all "Overpaid Prima Donnas!" Interestingly enough this man had been in aircraft engineering for many years in his early life and one got the impression that he harboured a deep seated grudge/jealousy which stemmed from those times. In our company at that time, we were seen as a necessary evil and he didn't feel that we pilots should be paid any more than the girls in the typing pool... Of course if the secretarial staff could actually fly aeroplanes then you could have had sympathy with his viewpoint, but as it was they couldn't fly and we couldn't type, so tough!

Leonardo DiCaprio and his role in the recent film 'Catch Me if You Can' is a prime example of how we are viewed by the media and therefore the public at large. In fact his character was a real freeloader who contributed literally nothing to society at all. He played a conman who spent several years of his life wearing airline pilots' wings, staying at swanky hotels (all expenses paid) and chasing beautiful women without having to touch the controls of an aircraft – the phrase "Nice work if you can get it" comes to mind. There is a wonderful moment in the film when he is trotting through the airport terminal in his Captain's uniform on his way somewhere, with six or seven gorgeous women dressed as stewardesses in his entourage – it's a lovely image, pure tinsel town!

So it is no surprise then that the public have a certain image of our occupation, but what's it really like? Are we actually, "living the life of Reilly?" Well there are some very good things about being an airline pilot; such as the lack of traffic congestion on our way to report for work. This is not the result of a police escort every time or special routing for our journey. No, the real reason that we are not impeded in our progress to the airport is that normally the roads are empty in the middle of the night! In the early hours of the morning, not surprisingly the vast majority of the population is asleep. The myth about the cars we drive is also debunked by the fact that most pilots seem to have what they endearingly call 'an airport car'.

There is little point in driving an expensive, high performance, limited edition sports car only to leave it in some poorly lit, hardly patrolled, crime ridden airport staff car park while you are away from home for a week. So the airline pilot is often to be seen vacating some diminutive, scruffy vehicle which has been twice round the clock and is not likely to be stolen or damaged by anyone. Even if it were; the machine would be so unloved that the aviating owner would not give the matter a second thought as they filled in the insurance claim form.

Mind you, some of my brother pilots take this to extremes. Like my good friend Simon, an airline Captain who worked with me at Luton for many years and who owned THE most disgusting example from the Skoda Company which I had ever had the misfortune to be given a lift in. I well recall him confiding in me that this was his 'airport car' and trying to justify the ownership of the repulsive vehicle. While giving me a lift to the pub one night, his fiancée Ana was coming also and sensitive to my feelings on the subject, he said he hoped that I didn't mind, being seen getting out of the back of the Skoda. To which I replied, "I'd rather be seen getting out of the back of a Sheep!"

These days of course, the position of 'Pilot' doesn't seem to be as prestigious as once it was. Because of heightened security levels at all the airports, the pilots and cabin crew are subject to the same checks as the passengers. While it is acknowledged that all the extra screening, results in stress and frustration for the travelling public, imagine what it is like to go through the same process five or six times in a week when you are just trying to go to work? Not only that, but philosophically you must also know this heavy handed screening, is there to protect you (the aircrew) first and foremost from the possibility of a repeat of 9/11 (hijack) or some form of homemade bomb onboard your aircraft. The question has never been answered as to why the pilots are so carefully checked when they are the ones most at risk and have most to lose (their lives) by the unlawful interference of a terrorist.

What on earth would a pilot be putting a penknife in their bag for when they have access to the aircraft crash-axe on the flightdeck? Or even to give them the controls of the aeroplane itself? If a pilot wanted to terminate the flight all he/she needs to do is roll inverted and pull, it's as simple as that – naturally this would be into Canary Wharf or similar Al Qaeda target. So there really is no point in making the aircrew take off their shoes and belts; x-ray their mobiles; confiscate their perfumes/toiletries (in excess of 100mls) or even to give them ID cards at all?!

If the Department for Transport had a really good joined up think about it, they would put everybody through the same security checkpoints and all crew and passengers would have boarding cards, simple as that. The airports could make huge savings on ID processing units and separate staff access channels. They could all be done away with and the savings that are made from not having to employ as many staff could be spent on improving facilities for the passengers. In fact the boarding of the aircraft would be less likely to be delayed by crews waiting to go through the single access point for staff which is the operational Achilles Heel of most airports now. Heathrow is a good example of this where the crew buses wait in a line to go through the screening to get airside. The wait can be as long as an hour and has been responsible for many delayed departures in recent months.

When it comes to pilots' terms and conditions, these have been eroded by a huge amount over the past couple of decades, compared with other professions. Whereas the occupation used to attract quite good remuneration and substantial time off the roster to enjoy with family and friends, the last twenty or thirty years has seen a shift of emphasis by the financial directors in airlines. The laws of supply and demand mean that would be airline pilots are now forced to pay for more and more of their training and when they finally make it to the front seat of an airliner they are subject to harsher Ts & Cs than at any other time in the history of commercial aviation.

Add all this to the recurrent checks of their technical competence which they are obliged to undergo twice annually, stiff medical examinations, random drug and alcohol testing, the aforementioned security stresses, antisocial working hours combined with tough time zone changes and fewer perks of the job – it is surprising that there are enough applicants to fill the vacancies. Then there are certain modern airline companies who publicly threaten to sack any of their pilots who make mistakes... Fortunately most airlines still have an endemic 'blame free' culture which is conducive to crew reporting their own errors such that they and others may learn from them and this is how it should be of course.

It is not just the new generation of pilots who feel the pressures of the industry. In the case of some of the more senior pilots, they are tasked with unenviable rostered duties. Like a Training Captain whose roster had him positioning from his home base by air to Gatwick in the afternoon of day one, then working in the simulator for two nights running. The roster read; report for briefing at 2300 for a midnight start to finish at 0400, then a debrief for the crew after that, get back to the hotel, try to sleep during the day while the cleaning staff worked all around servicing rooms, then report to the Sim again at 2300. The best part of it was that after the second night in the Sim, the Trainer was required to position by taxi to Heathrow at 0500 with a day's rest (Sic) in another noisy hotel and report for duty later that evening to fly an overnight flight (doing Line Training) halfway across the earth's surface to another continent.

After this flight was over, he was planned to wait in the airport departure lounge for four hours to catch another flight, this time as a passenger to position to his final destination! Needless to say I was pretty knackered after that one, but I consoled myself with an old saying which I often heard while working in the military; "If you can't take a joke... you shouldn't have joined!" Oh and by the way, 'positioning' is also known as '*deadheading*' which is a beautifully descriptive term for the way you feel as a positioning crewmember.

Even the most senior managers have it tough at times too. I recall a brief meeting with the Chief Pilot of an airline I used to work for many years ago when we were in danger of being taken over by a rival firm. It was a hostile takeover and the most senior executives were working extreme hours in order to fend it off. The Chief Pilot looked pretty haggard when we saw him and during the brief chat it was obvious that he feared the worst. As we broke up to go our separate ways and having spread the reality of the situation among us, he gave us a sardonic shrug of his shoulders accompanied by the words which only recently had been sent down from the board to inspire the troops, "Ah well, *Share the Dream!*" This was a perfect example of the fact that even at the highest levels of the profession there are good times and bad. If you are going to be a manager, get ready to roll with the punches, get knocked down and come back for more.

Airline Flight Engineers are a dying breed in commercial aviation, however they are also going to be sadly missed by the majority of pilots whom have had the good fortune to have worked with them. They are a source of much wisdom as many of them have been flying longer than they would care to admit to – in essence, they have seen it all. One such gentleman was a certain Jon Manson (East African Airways) who was asked what he planned to do with his upcoming retirement.

Basically the question was posed such that the young First Officer wanted to know if he would miss the flying. Jon said he had given it some thought and he reckoned that there would be times when he might miss it all so he had made plans to ensure that he would have fewer regrets. He said, "I'm going to fit a Flight Engineers panel in the cupboard under the stairs at home and at about 9 o'clock on some evenings, I'll say goodnight to my wife and pop in there for the rest of the night with the door closed. She'll come and get me out in the morning then drive me round the estate for an hour or so before bringing me back home, whereupon I'll have a couple of whiskies and go to bed for the rest of the day... which is what I seem to have been doing for the past thirty years!"

At my home on the wall of the downstairs loo, I have a framed cartoon which someone once gave me as a present; it is entitled 'The Life of a Pilot'. It is an amusing series of little hand-drawn sketches of events which are the downside of being an airline pilot.

The last scene shows a harrowed mum with two young kids at the kitchen table, there is an empty chair at the other end. One child says, "What does Dad look like?" and the other one replies, "I saw him once!"

Yes it is still the best job on the planet, but you've got to say it does have its negative aspects too. People entering our profession should be absolutely certain of what they are letting themselves in for before they start.

"Captain, you *must* listen to me!"

(An important concept for all new Co-Pilots to grasp – the Monitoring Pilot Role).

The use of modern Crew Resource Management (CRM) in airline operations is a real problem for some pilots – it shouldn't be, but it is. You see in days of old and we're talking more than 20 years or ago, the Captain had the absolute authority over the crew and the crew were all obliged to accept his decision making without question. The advent of the Flight Data Recorder (FDR) and Cockpit Voice Recorder (CVR) on commercial aircraft paved the way for in-depth analysis of accident causes. This started to happen firstly in the US, sponsored by NASA in the 1970s – the rest of the world soon followed suit.

Poor decision making by flightcrew was identified as a key causal factor in some hull loss accidents and the inability of crews to respond appropriately to situations they found themselves in was often the origin. This could be caused by a loss of situational awareness which lead to the wrong decision/s being made. Much research was undertaken in the 1980s and the result of this was that the CAA in the UK introduced a mandatory requirement in 1992 for all commercial operators to conduct CRM training as part of the conditions to continue to maintain their Air Operators Certificate (AOC). Behavioural marker systems were developed in order that the training and guidance on the development of positive aspects of CRM could be standardised and all commercial operators were required to appoint CRM Instructors.

During the study of accidents which involved the inappropriate response by flightcrew, it became apparent that some situations carried more risk than others. One of the predisposing factors was the much talked about 'steep gradient' across the cockpit in terms of seniority and experience. This would occur when a very experienced Captain was paired to operate with a junior First Officer with relatively little flying experience. A classic example of the potentially disastrous consequences of this crew pairing is the report of the near accident with the Dornier 328 at Sumburgh airport a few years ago. Take one very experienced Captain (18,000 flying hours) and sit him next to a Co-Pilot with very few hours in his logbook, (his first commercial job) and there are two ingredients for the disaster recipe already. One of the problems with 'steep gradient' in the flightdeck is communication, or lack of it, which was certainly a factor in this incident.

The junior pilot is keenly aware of the seniority issue and that often inhibits their input when timely intervention is actually a necessity to ensure the safety of the flight. There have been many examples of this sort of accident over the years and it is a relief to see that finally we are now seeing reports of incidents which happened that did not result in an accident. In the case of the flight at Sumburgh, the result of the aircraft flying into the high ground at Fitful Head would most certainly have lead to a loss of not only the 'hull' but also the lives of all those onboard. The First Officer in his Air Safety Report stated that when it got to the point of him considering "taking control of the aircraft", to have done so while manoeuvring at low level might have placed the aircraft in a more hazardous situation. Logically, this statement indicates that he had already left it too late and that he should have intervened earlier in the flight.

In fact he must have felt huge pressure at this stage, because although he was not the handling pilot of the aircraft, he was the Monitoring Pilot who had already called ATC to tell them that they (the crew) were "...happy to continue and visual". This apparently was on the "Commander's instruction" according to the report. Of course the question "Visual with what?" comes to mind, because it obviously wasn't the runway and presumably not the high ground covered by low cloud either. From the official report, when the aircraft was "0.6nm from the coastline as shown on the radar display and at a Mode C altitude of 700ft" the approach controller transmitted, *"...just to confirm you are visual with Fitful Head?"* To which the response from the F/O was *"Affirm"*.

The situation in which he found himself is surprisingly common in my experience, whereby the junior monitoring pilot is coerced into making a statement on the R/T to Air Traffic which is not entirely true. *"Yeah, tell 'em WE are visual!"* is an oft repeated instruction from the left-hand seat which will be familiar to many First Officers and it is right there and then that they have the problem. Notice the use of the plural "We" implying that if the transmission is made as instructed, then the F/O is in agreement with the course of action. If he/she makes the radio call exactly as asked, then they are an accessory after the fact and thus share the responsibility for the Commander's decision.

I know why the Captain may make this request of his otherwise reluctant accomplice – in fact I have done so on occasions myself in the past. It is often more expeditious to obtain clearance for a visual approach to the runway, rather than having to stick with ATC radar headings on to some form of radio navigation approach aid. The Captain will probably be using his local knowledge to judge the positioning of the aircraft such that he shortens the distance and time to touchdown. The real problem occurs of course when the skipper gets it wrong - as in this case. Even when the Captain does cock it up, there is still support from the junior pilot who will still hope he can salvage the arrival and thus avoid the embarrassment of an unnecessary Go-around. (From CRM this is an example I think of 'Risky Shift' – where the team's decision is likely to be riskier than one made by a lone member).

I remember training a new Captain on a B737 coming into land at Liverpool several years ago and we were given clearance to self-position on to finals for runway 09 over the River Mersey. There was some patchy cloud around, but I was confident we would be able to crack a visual approach. He was the handling pilot and I was sat in the right-hand seat as we went downwind decelerating and descending with speedbrakes deployed. As we were south of the runway heading west, I had the better view from the F/O's seat and the new skipper was relying on my judgement for when to turn right onto baseleg, heading north.

I was conscious of the prohibited zone out to the west at the Capenhurst Nuclear facility and was keen to ensure we turned inside it on to finals (notice the unconscious use of the term "We" here and I wasn't even flying it). Well of course runway 09 is not the usual runway for landing at Liverpool and it is also rare to be given vectors on to what was effectively a downwind leg for the visual approach − the visual picture which I was seeing was from an unfamiliar perspective. (Notice all the excuses I am making for myself here...) Thinking about it later, I reckon that ATC probably did it deliberately so that we would be more likely to declare "Visual" and the radar man could release us to the Tower frequency.

Anyway, I could see the runway and also knew that if we kept it tight we could avoid the cloud which appeared to be out on long finals − i.e. over 4 miles out. "Yes, turn now!" I said with confidence at the same time as operating flaps, gear and reaching for the checklist, "WE are visual, turning right base" I confirmed for the tower. While running through the landing checklist for the trainee Captain I was also trying to monitor our positioning outside the flightdeck windows and now realised that the cloud on finals was a lot closer than I had anticipated.

In addition we were monstrously high for a straight-in visual approach; we needed more air distance that just was not available to us. This was really disappointing as we could see the threshold of the runway (albeit a little more 'plan-form' than usual) but we couldn't extend the base turn anymore due to the cloud − we would have to Go-around. With a big sigh of resignation, I said, "I'm sorry mate, I've cocked it up, we'll have to Go-around − we're too high to make it" and I noted the altimeter which was reading nearly 1000 feet. His reply took me by surprise.
"It's okay, I think I can get it in from here, we'll continue..."
"No. No. It's my fault, don't worry, we WILL have to Go-around, I'll tell ATC".

Now, he was the junior pilot and although he was sitting in the Captain's seat, he was obviously aware of 'the gradient'. Not only that, but he wanted **US** to succeed so much that he was prepared to continue the approach to prevent my embarrassment, even though **_he_** had not made the decision to start the baseleg turn so early − that error of judgement had clearly been mine.

On another occasion I was flying a 737 as Captain and handling pilot on final approach into Liverpool and we had a flap problem. This was the final sector of a four sector day, we were flying back into our home base in good weather and the flight was ahead of schedule − I had estimated that we would be on stand about five minutes early. I had called for "Gear down, Flap Fifteen" and then called for the landing flap, "Flap Thirty". A warning light and Flap

Disagree message indicated that the flaps had jammed at 15 degrees and would not deploy further, we were now about 5 miles out on final approach. "Oh!?" was my initial response and I looked over at the young Dutch First Officer next to me, he was just as puzzled. I thought about the scheduled time of arrival and considered the effect of the flaps on the landing distance. The runway was dry with about ten knots headwind component – easy job.

"No problem, we can easily land in the 'Flap Fifteen' config – just press the GPWS Flap Override switch and give me Autobrake Three please". The F/O was keen to oblige and we continued the approach. I thought about it for a few seconds, we were now at about 1000 feet on finals. "No Erik, we've got to Go Around" I said, explaining to him "we haven't done the QRH drill for the flap condition". (QRH = Quick Reference Handbook, list of non-normal checklists from Boeing).
"Are you sure?" He replied, the disappointment in his voice was audible. We had been cleared for landing and the runway looked so inviting. I smiled and was grateful for his supporting attitude to my original decision, even though I had made the wrong one momentarily.

"Yes my friend, I really am sure, I will explain later, but we have to do the QRH drill before we land and we don't have time on this approach, tell ATC we're Going Around please". From 1000 feet on finals and with as gentle a touch as I could manage we flew a Go-Around manoeuvre into a wide visual circuit. I spoke to the passengers to explain and apologised for our late arrival into Liverpool and we carried out the full QRH drill for Flap Disagree (with the lever position). The subsequent landing was uneventful and we left the flaps down for the engineers to inspect when we came onto stand.

What I didn't have time to explain to the F/O at the time, was that I had just completed an investigation into a very serious incident which had recently occurred with one of our company's aircraft. On that occasion the flightcrew had made an approach and landing with one engine shutdown after it had been severely damaged by a birdstrike on takeoff. The actual flight had landed safely, however in the time that the aircraft was airborne, the pilots had not carried out any QRH drills and therefore were found to be negligent. This was in spite of the fact that the flight had safely been diverted to another airfield.

In our situation with the jammed flaps; although I knew that to land with Flap 15 was not a problem to us from the performance point of view, we had not completed the checklists which Standard Operating Procedures demanded, therefore we were at fault. After we had completed all the paperwork in the crewroom, I explained this to the young Co-Pilot and emphasised to him that just because I was 'The Boss' on the flightdeck, he must speak up when, or if, he had reservations about a proposed course of action. It didn't help matters that I was also his Line Manager on the ground of course.

Thinking about it all some years later is interesting. These days in my role as a 'Trainer' and not a Manager, I find myself being consulted by younger pilots who need advice or guidance from time to time. In our industry, Trainers are often easier to approach than Managers and 'off the record' conversations are commonplace. Like the bright young F/O who sought my opinion last year after he had operated a flight with a Captain the day before and they had made a successful landing after an unstable approach.

During the approach, the F/O had made his concerns known to the Captain, but the Commander had assured him that all was well and the aircraft was under control. Sometimes, in the heat of the moment it is a difficult call to decide if an approach has become 'unstable', especially when it is a visual approach to a runway being flown by the other pilot.

The criteria which he described to me were marginal, however they clearly fitted the final approach just into the unstable category – a report should be filed - but here was his problem. Not only did the Captain try to persuade him that the approach and landing were stable, but he actively encouraged him not to file the Air Safety Report (ASR) which the situation justified. I expressed my sympathy with the F/O but stated that the Flight Data Monitoring system would pick it up and it would be better to 'fess up earlier rather than later. As it had only happened the day before, there was still time to get the ASR in the system without any apparent delay. I also advised him that he must talk again to the Captain immediately to let him know what he was doing, in order that the Captain did not feel upstaged.

I reflected that in days of old there would not have been an issue here. A good First Officer would be expected to follow the Captain's instructions and wishes to the letter and would not have to make the difficult decision which now faced my young colleague. When we discussed the event more closely, it transpired that the Captain had not appeared to have taken any notice of the F/O's wish to commence a Go-Around.

When we talked about the form of words used by the F/O as monitoring pilot, clearly their impact was insufficient to evince the correct response. We talked about the necessity for a form of words that would alert an unresponsive Commander that he must come up with an appropriate reaction or face the consequences. I reminded him of the phrase which was taught to me many years ago and which had been formulated after many such events were analysed by the airline which became ThomsonFly. "Captain you MUST listen to me!"

The formality of the structure of the sentence and the emphasis on the word **MUST** are not accidental. In addition, the delivery and gravitas of this announcement has the power to cut across the Flightdeck Gradient in times of extreme need. Used sparingly, at the right moment in time, these are five words which could prevent disaster.

Although I never had to use them myself, they were always there in my toolkit as a Co-Pilot and I had even rehearsed saying them. We do not know exactly what was said in the cockpit on the flight to Sumburgh, (no CVR) but if these words had been used, then the outcome may well have been very different.

"Running out of airlines..."

(Leaving the company? Never slam the door on your way out, you may want to get back in!)

A colleague of mine faced a curious situation a while back. It was over a weekend and the company for whom he was working, had rostered him to work in the Simulator for four days continuously as the Instructor/Examiner for recurrent training. The Thursday and Friday details went well, but then came Saturday and Sunday. In the hotel on the Saturday morning, he received a call from the Crewing department.

"We can't find a Captain for this afternoon's Sim session, stay at the hotel and we'll get back to you". Well, considering that he was in a nice room in a four star hotel with plenty to keep himself occupied, he didn't need telling twice. An hour or two went by as he amused himself with surfing the internet, doing some reading and writing and generally having a relaxing time. He called crewing again as the report time for the Sim session approached.

"No, we still can't find a Captain, so we're going to lose the Sim for the four hour session, sorry 'bout that. We hope to try and find one for tomorrow's Simulator booking, we'll keep you posted".

He had made some more enquiries elsewhere and got the background to explain the missing aviator and the story turned out like this. A Captain (let's call him X) who had previously worked for the airline, until recently and who had decided on the spur of the moment to go elsewhere, had informed the company that he wished to return.

As a consequence, the company had taken off the original rostered Skipper for the weekend Sim (LPC/OPC) and sent him abroad so that Captain X could take his place. In a way this was quite smart thinking on behalf of the crewing department, as they would then have another Captain on line very quickly which would help from the resources point of view.

What they had not bargained for was that Captain X would become a no-show at the last minute and they would then be faced with trying to cover a Sim slot in London at short notice over the weekend. It was a problem which they could not solve and they lost two days of simulator time, a total of 8 hours and also the use of their TRE and an experienced Line First Officer. The weird thing was that Captain X had already been swapping between a couple of other airlines in the previous 18 months or so and this was his third airline which he had re-entered, albeit unsuccessfully.

The comment was made by one of the frustrated crewing staff on the telephone, *"he's **running out of airlines** to work for, this guy..."* The obvious implication here was that he would be unlikely to be re-employed now that he had let them down so badly at a critical time. When this story was relayed to me, it got me thinking about other pilots I have known in the past and the sometimes odd career choices they had made.

Everything happens for a reason however and I know from personal experience that it is not easy to see things clearly at times. This is especially true when emotions come into play. There have been times in my own career for example when I have been ready to make a decision which has been more affected by my emotional state, rather than a logical/analytical viewpoint. In the early days at Easyjet, (late 1990's) there were many times when I felt I could have resigned and walked away without a backward glance.

I know that in the first 18 months when I worked for the company, there was a huge turnover of pilots. I think we lost something like 35% or so from memory. Mostly I think it was probably due to the fact that the company was changing SO rapidly and that most people have a problem with a shifting working environment over which they have little or no control. How many times do we hear our colleagues complaining about the fact that the company has 'moved the goalposts'? It has got to be said too, that at some times, the changes were not always for the better and many of my colleagues at that time got tired of waiting for our lot to improve.

Although it was a frustrating time for many of us, the funny thing was that for every low point or trough, there was inevitably an upturn just around the corner. It was an emotional rollercoaster ride in many ways; the 'lows' were bad but the 'highs' were terrific. In my case I hung on in there for 7 years plus and at the end I had no regrets.

We used to laugh and say that being in the company for one year was a bit like being employed for 7 years in a 'normal' airline. Dog years we used to call it, and after what felt like 49 years of continuous employment, it was certainly time for me to leave. I don't mean to knock it though, because many of my friends still work there and they still enjoy it despite all that has happened over the years – for some of them the grass on the other side of the fence was never greener and they know the deal they have is fine for their lifestyle, but there were others who left and then came back...

Inevitably their timing was poor. Some of them left the company just before the Share Option allocation was made in the spring of the year 2000 which was given to incentivise the long-term employees, including all the pilots who had been there since the beginning. (These Share Options would eventually be worth tens of thousands of pounds to us over the next few years after the company floated on the stock exchange).

When Easyjet bought the competitor Low-Cost Airline 'GO' back in April 2003, all the current GO pilots received substantial sums of money as part of the deal because they were all effectively shareholders in the company. I often overheard Easyjet pilots complaining that this was "not fair" because they didn't receive any money.

My answer to this was always, that you had to be in the right place at the right time. As an example I referred to our own windfall as Easyjet crews when the company went PLC three years earlier and although none of us had predicted this, it was well received nonetheless. If someone offers you a huge chunk of money to carry on working for a company which you enjoy working for anyway, you would welcome that too. So much for the fortunes of those who jump ship at the wrong time, how is it possible to predict what the best time is going to be?

Many years ago I had the privilege of flying with a very experienced airline Captain called Peter who taught me many things. One of which was to be careful not to assume that your position is always secure. He ruefully told me the story of how, many years earlier; he had been on a trip to the west coast of the USA and was enjoying a relaxing evening in the bar in Los Angeles in the company of his crew.

One of them asked him if he had heard the rumours about the possible redundancies at the airline, to which he replied that no he hadn't, but went on to say, "with my position being so far up the seniority list, they will have to lay-off a whole load of pilots before I get the chop..." Overnight Sir Freddie lost the battle to save the company and Laker Airways ceased operations the following morning. Peter was then looking for work along with all the other ex-Laker pilots.

Another example of not assuming anything was in the final week of Air Europe's activities when the airline was clearly in severe financial distress. Word spread round the terminal among the staff at Gatwick that the Finance Director had been seen and heard "whistling cheerfully in the corridor - so everything must be okay now". This was only days before the end and is a sad reminder of how much we all hope for the best where our employer is concerned.

One person who clearly was not convinced by the whistling was the Air Europe B757 Captain who made a point of replenishing his £1000 Captain's Float one day before the company ceased trading and parked their fleet on Gatwick's West Apron. When asked by the cashier, (as she handed over the money, which he put into his flightbag), if he had heard anything about the company's future, he replied that he had not... which may or may not have been true.

I have some thoughts to offer pilots on what to consider when thinking about changing from one airline to another. The grass really is always greener on the other side of the fence – do not make your decision to move in haste. Watch your exits – never slam the door on the way out, you will regret it eventually. Think about how this particular move you are considering is going to look on your CV – too many airlines is not a good sign.

On the other hand, don't stay with your current employer just because it's the easy option – movement in the industry is good for all of us. This is especially true if you sincerely believe that some sort of 'Glass Ceiling' has been placed on your career – pilots moving companies often leave their past behind and have a fresh start. Always resign politely and in writing – there is nothing to be gained by deliberately upsetting people before you leave. Remember that all the senior managers in the industry talk to each other – verbal references are easy to obtain and can just as easily stop you getting the next job.

It's always who you know, that is important at the end of the day – focus on building a network of colleagues and friends with whom you have good relations. When you reach more senior levels in the industry, this will avoid you even requiring an interview for a new position at times. Believe me, it is such a wonderful feeling when that happens.

In the past few years I have had to make some important career choices myself. While doing so, I have been conscious that really sound advice about where to go in your career, is hard to come by, even though I have spent the better part of 25 years doing this sort of thing for a living. I asked all of my mates what they thought about the various options with which I was faced and some of the replies were thought provoking, while others were contradictory and some were just plain way off target.

What I felt I really needed to do was to sit down and hold up my career and CV against the current market situation in the airline industry. I then spent some time researching all the factors which were effective or could be so, before deciding what to do. The careful analysis of this research was invaluable to me as I was then able to see all the alternatives with a clarity that I had not achieved before.

Although clairvoyance is not one of the qualifications which I possess, I am fortunate to know plenty of people who can give me the rounded perspective on where the airline industry is going and what is happening currently. There are plenty of differing opinions out there, but taking all of them into consideration is important if you want to make the best quality decision about your own career – this is similar to the way in which we ask our pilots to utilise a decision making tool (GRADE* or DODAR* for example) when faced with technical or emergency situations in the aircraft.

As a professional pilot if you are considering further career progression, you should spend time talking with your peers and also try to obtain high quality career advice which should ensure that you don't face the ignominy of "Running out of airlines..."

*Note: The acronym 'GRADE' stands for, Gather, (information) Review, Analyse, Decide (& Do), Evaluate. The other tool 'DODAR' stands for Diagnose, Options, Decision, Action, Review.

A Day at the Movies.

(Get a large bag of popcorn and a soft drink – the big picture is just about to start).

I always said I wouldn't do it again. I always said I would stick to my guns. I said to myself things like, "I don't need the money, I don't need the kudos and *humph*, I certainly don't need the *stress*!" No, I really did not intend to get involved with any 'Start-Up' airline ever again...

My experiences in the past had taught me enough to know that getting involved in a start-up is an emotional roller-coaster of the first order. Since my departure from the Big Orange Company, (May 2005) life had been substantially less demanding. I had been home more often and for longer periods; not much in the way of difficult decision making to be done; no more office politics; the flying had been relaxed and pretty leisurely for the most part and yet... something was missing. I grudgingly had to admit that being right in there at the heart of it all had been such a buzz. To see and be part of an airline growing from four tired old aeroplanes through to over 100 units in just 7 frantic years was **exhilarating** – there's no other word for it.

But exhilaration comes at a price. With the excitement comes pain – growing pains. I knew all too well what that felt like. The pain comes from the fact that start-up companies commonly grow so fast at first that everything changes all the time, but some important things don't change fast enough to keep pace. To sum up, there are not enough people employed to do all the jobs as the fleet and destination network expands. There is "overstretch" on people and resources to an amazing degree.

Only the strong survive and in this supercharged corporate environment while high-performers prosper, less committed employees fall by the wayside. Oh yes, there is enough stress for all of us in this phase of an airline's development. Often it comes down to the crews to perform above and beyond the call of duty to maintain the growth surge which is lead by the commercial department – and all of this I know.

So when I got the 'phonecall, I should have said "Thanks for the offer, but I'm really not interested in being part of your start-up airline". But I didn't, because I WAS curious and, well... life had been a little bit TOO quiet at times over the past couple of years, which brings me to my 'Day at the Movies'. You know sometimes when you experience an event in your life which is really intense and even a little bit emotional?

In flying, this could be the day of your First Solo, or maybe first time VMC on top on your own in a flying machine, thinking "Now - all I have to do is get down..." Or maybe when unforecast bad weather interferes while you're flying and ramps up the workload for you? Well, whatever the event, all of a sudden you get a flashback moment and the life event which you're caught up in seems "just like a scene from that film!" It can be an emotional high, a depressing low or a thrilling adrenaline rush, but you can just picture it all happening in your mind's eye.

So now we're all milling in and around our new crewroom. Pilots and cabin crew, some of us are in uniform and some in plain clothes. A feeling of expectation fills the air. Today we're going to fly - well, maybe. Our Boeing 767 is 'Tech' at the moment; the engineers are working flat-out to get her serviceable. They have fitted a replacement Fuel Control Unit (FCU) to the right engine and as the name implies, this is a fairly important piece of kit when it comes to power delivery.

The job has not been an easy one and they have been working double shifts to get it done, late finishes and early starts. As there is only one airliner in the fleet at the moment (the second one currently in Brunei with its engines in Singapore being refurbished) we have only the one airframe option for flight. The sky is blue and from where we are, we can see the tail of the machine jutting out from behind the hangar reflecting purple in the sunshine.

Joining this airline has been an act of faith so far for most of us. Kevin Costner's film 'Field of Dreams' comes to mind, along with its famous strap line "If you build it they will come!" Just now however our hopes and dreams seem to be a little on the optimistic side as real world 'Defect Rectification' is taking place only a hundred metres from where we are. The engineers have been working hard to produce a serviceable ship for us and we are conscious of their efforts, but we REALLY need this...

The company has been a long time in the process of formation and most of the Cabin Crew have been employed since April with little to do except training – they have been very patiently waiting for this day. Part of the plan today is to fly the Cabin Crew as a Familiarisation Flight – the majority of them have never flown before so it's important we give them as much exposure to the environment as possible. The training value will be excellent, but right now (late morning) we are going nowhere and are firmly adhering to Terra Firma.

In our industry, although most of us are upbeat most of the time, there are always the Nay-Sayers not far away. They are those who rejoice in others' failure and who are quick to say "I told you so". They say things like, "It'll never work!", "They've not yet been granted an AOC, they've only got one old aeroplane and even that's gone Tech!" Poisonous, negative vibes on the internet are one manifestation of this. It's not just the Cabin Crew who are keen to fly.

Those of us who have been in the game for a long time, also know that credibility is at stake here - damaging rumours have been circulating that the airline will never get off the ground. In the case of a 'Start-Up', these can mean the death knell if they gain enough momentum – we need to fly! Goose and Maverick on the ramp at Miramar come to mind in the film Top Gun, "I feel the need... *the need for SPEED!*" 'High fives' then as they boarded their F14 Tomcat – 'low fives' for us today as we sit in the crewroom with hands clasped below the table in hope.

Lunchtime comes and goes. It is important to stay focused. Two of the pilots now have to leave. They are trainees who we were going to do Base Training circuits with, but they have commitments elsewhere. If the aircraft had been serviceable first thing in the morning, it could have been done, but now we're out of time, so this training detail will have to be postponed. We still want to fly the two sectors with the Cabin Crew onboard as they will also be used for Line Training one of the new Captains, with me in the right-hand seat acting as First Officer.

With the way things are at present though, it's quite depressing, just like that time in the film 'The Full Monty' when the redundant steelworkers were queuing at the dole office for benefit payments. Mental note to myself, I must keep busy.

While catching up on some admin work, I liken our aeroplane to the 'Millennium Falcon' in Star Wars. The Falcon (grounded with Tech problems) had also seen better days and so much was riding on it being serviceable in time. I wonder to myself, *are we wasting our time here today?* Our own Millennium Falcon seems to have a great affinity with the surface of our planet and the maintenance hangar. We delay the flightplan with ATC yet again – this time indefinitely. It's just not our day today.

Mixed messages are now coming from engineering and I try not to get involved – it's much better to let our Chief Engineer deal with it all, I know this from experience. They will call us when they are ready for us and not before, the maintenance team already know the pressure's on. Sometimes I think they pay us (flightcrew) for the time we spend on the ground. I know for a fact that many of my contemporaries feel the same; flying is much easier in the air. As soon as you get the wheels up, your problems are solved.

Certainly most of our troubles are left behind at this point, or to be more correct it happens earlier than this, at V1. V1 is the speed when we have to fly of course. It is the point in the takeoff at which the decision to stop must already have been made, in other words if "Stop!" has not been called by the time the call of "Vee One!" is made, then we go. I recall many years ago seeing an amusing sticker on an airline pilot's flightbag which said *"Happiness is V1 at Lagos!"* which made quite a statement about the way in which many of my colleagues view that particular airport.

Recently I mentioned this to some Virgin Nigeria pilots whom I was training in the 737 Simulator and when they heard it they roared laughing thinking it was very funny indeed. They even wanted to find out where to buy the sticker for themselves, so it's nice to know this joke transcends the barriers of race and culture – I guess they don't think much of their hometown either...

The Chief Engineer approaches to break my reverie. "They're ready to complete the engine ground runs and would like the pilots to help them". I reply,

"Excellent news, let's go". It feels just like the scene when the actor Michael Keaton makes the famous announcement "It's *Showtime!*" as Beetlejuice in the film of the same name and we all start to get our gear together to go flying. I start to think this could really work today. As only engine ground testing is planned, we leave the Cabin Crew behind at the offices and make our way round to the security gate to the maintenance area. The ride is pleasant in the sunshine and we are given a lift in the quality manager's car, removing kiddie seat and child's bike before we can all get in. The crew at this point consists of the Chief Engineer and three pilots including me, with our quality manager driving – a bit of a squash in a Vauxhall Astra, but then we are reaching for the stars today. *Ahhhh, don't you just love start-up airlines?*

We board the 767 and liaise with the maintenance team. It is clear they have all been working very hard during the previous days and nights, but are now in sight of the finish, with just the engine ground runs to do. We talk about what needs to be done and start to prep the flightdeck. Ideally we will carry out the engine testing, and then if all goes well, the engineers will get off at the terminal and we will fly the two training sectors.

The idle power ground runs have been done, but now they need partial power and takeoff power runs to try and match the fuel delivery of the new FCU to the one already installed on the other engine – it's not going to be a five minute job. In our discussions we realise that because most of the Cabin Crew do not have their own airside ID cards, it will not be possible now to get them through airport security to fly with us... "Dear Lord give me strength, they've only been employed since April!" I say to no-one in particular as I conduct a careful walkround of the exterior – it has now been decided that we should board them all through the maintenance area and keep them onboard during the engine runs prior to flight.

Back in the flightdeck, I have a perfect view of the security gate and we are now waiting for the rest of the crew to join us. It will take some time as they have to walk round from the offices in a gaggle and of course they will have had to get their high-vis jackets on etc. etc. *If you build it they will come.* Costner's refrain goes through my brain. Everything is done; we just need to wait for them. All of a sudden here they are.

It is barely 30 minutes later and they are waiting the other side of the security barrier, but as it's after 5pm now and there is no security officer manning it. More delay as we request the attendance of the security staff, who when they arrive insist upon body searching everyone, including those of us pilots who came through the gate an hour before and have been onboard the aircraft since then. No I cannot explain it either, but have to caution a couple of my colleagues who are about to have a fit of the giggles in front of security, which would be counterproductive to say the least. I thank the security officers politely for their kind assistance; see them to the door and then go to brief the Cabin Crew.

They have two senior crew trainers with them and I explain what we are going to do – for the most part the cabin will be theirs, however they will need to sit down when we do the high power engine runs just in case something goes awry. Like the brakes failing perhaps, that would make for an interesting situation on the cargo apron where we are scheduled to run the engines up to full power. Finally we are on our way and both engines light-up easily with normal parameters, this is looking good. We taxy round to the cargo apron and put the brakes on in the correct position abeam one of the freighter stands.

By this time the flightdeck is pretty well a full house, what with our Chief Engineer, both pilots' seats filled and two other engineers sitting on the cockpit floor behind our seats. One of them has a laptop and is reading from the diagnostic programme the guidelines for assessing the engine instrument values – Fuel Flow versus N2 RPM etc. these are also compared with EPR (Engine Pressure Ratio) readings to confirm the actual power output from the engine. It's the right engine that's had the FCU change so we are concentrating on those gauges, but we are also 'clocking' the indications on the left side too to ensure they are comparable, as that is our 'normal' engine.

I am aware that in the cabin the trainers are making good use of the PA system and getting the Cabin Crew to practice safety demonstrations and other duties which are best learned on a live aircraft. After some time revving the right engine up to partial power settings, the engineers want to test the higher output indications. So far it has been going swimmingly, but we are not home and dry yet. I make a PA to the Cabin Crew and ask them all to sit down while we do this.

We also obtain permission from ATC – this one is going to be noisy. Under the engineers' instructions, we move the right thrust lever forward to nearly full power, while maintaining the left at high power also, the brakes are holding and the noise is phenomenal, even in here. Then an Apollo 13 moment... "Erm Houston we have a problem..." The right gauges are nowhere near balanced to the left engine, with EPR matched, the N2 is way off and so is the rate at which it is burning fuel. We bring the power back to idle again and all is fairly quiet. It's certainly gone quiet in the cabin, as according to our quality man; there are quite a number of worried faces back there and then I recall that the majority of them have never flown before as crew. *Some white faces in there and some red ones in here.*

We shutdown on the cargo ramp and the engineers go out onto the apron to make adjustments to the FCU on the right engine. *This is turning out to be rather a long day,* I think to myself as the shadows lengthen and the sun goes down in our faces, *and it's not over yet.* Adjustments complete, we start again and go through similar procedures.

Fortunately they have hit the sweet spot and this motor is now performing in a very similar manner to the one on the opposite side, although we still have the throttle slam tests to do. This is done just as it sounds and for those of us with mechanical empathy; it's really hard to do without wincing. Large bypass fan engines do not take kindly to this kind of abuse by the operator, but it is vital to make sure they don't stall or surge under rapid accelerations – this is the only way to do that. The engine passes the test with flying colours and we make our way to the main apron and shutdown again.

While the engineers go through their paperwork and complete all the relevant sections of the Techlog, which takes them over half an hour, we prepare the aircraft for flight. The flightplan has been delayed yet again and soon we have the Millennium Falcon moving under her own steam towards the runway. It IS a good feeling. On the flightdeck, our Chief Engineer sits anxiously on the spare crewseat while I guide the Capt Under Training along the taxiway from the right-hand seat. The Cabin Secure check comes through on the intercom, all of our checks in the flightdeck are complete and we call "Ready for departure".

"Roger, Golf Charlie Uniform, surface wind two niner zero at ten knots; landing traffic at four miles, cleared immediate takeoff!" This from ATC, with a Bmi Baby 737 on short finals. I acknowledge with more nonchalance than I am feeling right now "Golf Charlie Uniform, **Rolling**". I know that if we have to abort the takeoff the one on finals will have to go-around, but the engineers have signed off the aircraft, the ground-runs have all been passed and... so what if the aeroplane has sat on the ground for months, you've just got to believe in the system.

"Thrust set!" I call monitoring the power settings like a hawk, "Eighty knots", and the response comes back, "Check" from the handling pilot. It's looking really good now as the speed really starts to build up rapidly. The engines are not perfectly matched, but pretty damn close and I know I've seen a lot worse on the line in the past**.** **"Vee One, Rotate!"** and the other pilot's hand comes off the thrust levers – we are committed to fly.

As the pitch attitude stabilises at 17 degrees nose-up there are two indications of "Positive Climb" and the handling pilot calls "Gear-Up". I reach forward and raise the landing gear for the first time on this airframe in a long time. There is the usual rumbling, grinding sounds as the gear stows, but then the lights go out and we are on our way.

In Houston Mission Control, I can imagine them all cheering, hooting and giving a standing ovation – life is pretty good here too as we start to accelerate and retract the flaps. *Yes, we are truly paid for the time we spend on the ground,* I muse as I read aloud the after takeoff checklist.

Ninety minutes later and our mission is complete. We have flown two line training sectors, carried out some valuable Cabin Crew training, got the aircraft serviceable again and feel like we've recovered some street cred for the airline. East Midlands is in darkness as we make our final approach to land in the Millennium Falcon and at the end of a very long day at the movies I really only have one concern.

If the new Captain Under Training was playing the part of Han Solo and the young, handsome First Officer was Luke Skywalker, that only left one flightcrew member who could have been me...

Strewth, surely I wasn't playing the part of Chewbacca?!?

With Mum & Dad -'Wings' Award Day – 1985.   *Dad (centre) with 193 Sqdn 1944*

Teaching Monkeys to Fly

It is a long time ago since I heard the words but, I clearly remember him saying them, "Don't worry lad, we can even teach Monkeys to fly aeroplanes!" The flying instructor was Stan Greenhow and the place was the military establishment at Plymouth Roborough back in late '83. At the time I was being taught to fly the De Havilland Chipmunk, with the rest of my Navy Fleet Air Arm classmates. Of course Stan wasn't being literal, but what he was saying to us, was that we should feel confident that somehow they would be able to teach us to the required standard to pass the course. After all, if a Monkey could be taught to do it, then we humans shouldn't have a problem!?

But there was another message here too. Stan was saying to us – "Look, I have a novel way of getting through to you. I am going to present information to you in a different, yet interesting way. I am going to challenge you and yet reassure you. I am going to make you work hard, but you will thank me for it later". Oh yes, Stan was very special. He was an ex military pilot from WW2, very much retired and was literally a legend in his own lifetime to those who met him. A wonderful character, quite scary at times, but boy did we learn at a terrific rate under his tutelage. Since then I think of him from time to time – one of the greatest flying instructors we ever met. If anyone really could teach a monkey to fly, it would have been Stan the man!

In the intervening period, I have also heard references to Monkeys flying aeroplanes. How often do QFIs use the term, "Monkey see, Monkey do" for example? This implies that *if* a demonstration of skills is good enough, then the trainee will pick it up straight away and be able to replicate the manoeuvre precisely. On a similar theme, I recall that one of my RAF QFIs on the old Jet Provost was known as 'Three Bananas'. Flight Lieutenant McKenzie was an Australian pilot who had recently left the RAAF to join the UK Royal Air Force when the Aussies retired their Grumman Trackers.

He was also a great teacher and one of the reasons for this was that he always had a different way of passing on the information and demystifying the art of aviating. How he got his peculiar name was from teaching spinning in the JP. Considering that we all had less than 100 hours flying experience, to be taught spinning in a jet aircraft, (even one as docile as the JP) was quite a challenge. This was especially true for the Middle Eastern pilots who came through the RAF Fast Jet training system, some of whom had a very limited understanding of the English language.

Flt Lt McKenzie used to make the subject of spinning less terrifying by saying that he would count the turns in the spin while the student was flying and when the stude heard the words "Recover NOW!" they should apply the full spin recovery technique in an expeditious manner.
"The way I will do it is to count like this on the intercom, *One Banana, Two Bananas... Recover NOW!"* He would chant in the briefing room preflight and everyone thought this was funny, so through humour the bad spell was broken and the challenge was met. The funniest thing was that he was known as 'Three Bananas' because he never said it – he always shouted for recovery after Two! Secretly, I think he was actually not very keen on spinning and it was his own way of confronting that situation...

Of course Monkeys are keen on bananas and in some ways Flt Lt McKenzie was teaching us Monkeys to fly. His demonstrations were always faultless; he was a wonderful teacher and a great pilot. Those of us who were lucky enough to fly with him appreciated his talents a great deal.

These days I find myself in similar territory while teaching the TRTO conversion course students how to fly airliners like the B757. When you look at them closely, these are incredibly complicated machines, worth millions of dollars and the prospect of actually getting airborne in one is at first overwhelming. Bear in mind that the trainees coming through now frequently have less than 200 hours total flying time, the ink on their frozen ATPL is still wet and the biggest flying machine they have ever taken control of had a total of four seats...

The first time I meet them is often in the briefing room prior to their simulator session. They have just spent the best part of the previous six weeks in the classroom, going through the CBT (Computer Based Training) course to gain the knowledge of the technical side of the aircraft. Consider that there are miles and miles of wiring and almost as many miles of hydraulic pipes in these aeroplanes. They cost a fortune to design, build and maintain with every major system having one back-up system, sometimes two. While on the flightdeck there are several computers linked to Inertial Reference Systems for navigation, first designed by NASA containing Laser Ring Gyros, with just two frail human beings sat on the top of the rocket! When you have only 165 flying hours ever in your logbook, passing a TRTO Type conversion course is the toughest job on Earth – it is a mountain to climb and they know it. Not only this, but there is another complication, for many of the students, English is not their first language – for some of them are from Kazakhstan.

Occasionally when I enter the briefing room, I think I can almost smell their fear, I can certainly see it in their eyes. They are literally terrified that they will not be able to achieve the required standard and fail the course. If that occurs then they will have lost more than their life savings, because by and large, most of the trainees are in debt up to their necks to pay for all the training so far. *'**Please** get me through this...?!'*

Yes I am telepathic aswell, as their thought waves hit me through the ether from the other side of the briefing table. My response is, *'Phew! That's a big Ask!'* These TRTO courses were designed for pilots with 1000 hours plus, mostly upgrading their equipment from turboprops, so their experience level is far beyond the ken of the present trainees. However we live in the modern world and must move with the times – it's called progress I guess that we should run our trainee pilots through courses that stretch their skills and resources to the limits. To get through the course comfortably, means a learning rate which follows an upward curve that is sometimes exponential.

Ultra-friendly and mega-reassuring is my Modus Operandi from Day One. I'm going to take them on a journey and MUST have their complete confidence and trust. When things get complicated I ensure that I dumb it down immediately – "look how easy it is", I will say, explaining the method of calculating the descent from Cruise altitude in the 757. Just use simple maths, think of Three times your altitude and add a few miles for slowing down. From 30,000 feet altitude, you're going to need ninety miles, plus maybe ten or so to slow down to minimum speed to start putting the flaps out. From 25,000 feet you will need 75 miles and so on. I make sure that I use lots of sketches on the whiteboard and this helps to get the message across in any language.

One example where a combination of sketch and humour tend to break through is while teaching the Engine Failure On Takeoff (EFOTO). Low-houred students tend to find the EFOTO Sim detail which occurs at around Full Flight Sim Four (FF4) in the course, a real challenge. By this time they have only just gained proficiency at flying the 'aircraft' with two engines and with everything else working (especially the autopilot), when all of a sudden it's time to attempt single engined flying. Remember that the last time these pilots flew a twin on one engine; it was a light piston aeroplane with dinky little levers and pedals with correspondingly small control forces. Now they are faced with huge control pressures/movements and flying controls that seem massive by comparison – you must bear in mind that ergonomically, the Boeing engineers designed their 1980s flightdecks to fit the average Texan pilot and he's a big guy!

Again, it's necessary to cut straight through the ephemera and get right into the important bits that they need to know. I have a favourite sketch which I produce on the whiteboard which tends to cover EFOTO in only a few minutes. There is little time for niceties, really simple words are used and again a little humour is injected to keep their attention.

"Look, imagine a *rabbit* sitting next to the runway watching a 757 taking-off, but it's actually on the grass in the undershoot looking *down* the runway, this is what he sees" and so on, building the picture so that the trainees feel they are actually there. I then make sure they feel fully prepared for the session and also pretend that I am giving them a big secret that many EFOTO control problems come from putting in "Not enough Rudder!" Now this really is true and it's the most common fault, but introducing it at the end of the brief helps them to commit it to memory. Additionally they feel they have now been given a piece of magic information which will improve their flying skills. This is only partly true of course, what will improve their performance in the Sim is the *psychological confidence* which they get from having been given this 'Top Tip'.

The delivery of the information is vitally important too, especially checking for understanding at every stage. Don't go too fast, keep the words simple and vary the intonation a lot. It takes practice and sometimes lots of patience to keep saying the same thing in different ways until the penny drops. You can see it in their eyes, which is why eye contact is so vital to the process – these Monkeys are actually quite intelligent, but when they 'Max-out' (information overload), then as an instructor you have a problem and have to reduce your delivery rate. It's actually a lot more tiring doing a proper instructional session as a TRI (Type Rating Instructor) than it is when carrying out a TRE detail as an examiner. When you are examining, there is sometimes little to say and certainly no training input while the test items are being observed – so all you can do is sit behind the crew and make notes of your observations.

These TRTO Airliner Conversion courses must be among the most pressurised learning experiences in the world of aviation. There is a limited amount of time to gain proficiency and if a trainee is under-performing halfway through the course there is very little slack to allow them to regain the standard required by the LST. If I am involved in several of the TRI sessions of the course, then even I am feeling the pressure as it is a race against time to get them to assimilate enough information. Whenever there is the opportunity and if my Monkeys are performing well, I force the pace a little to get ahead of the programme. This ensures that they have some spare capacity to cope when the tougher details arrive – like the dreaded FF4. If there is one place on the course where they will hit quicksand this is the one. However with the right preparation and ensuring they are focused confidently on the high value aspects, we triumph over adversity with no missed items to carry forward to Sim FF5.

Sometimes my Monkeys come out literally exhausted (me too of course) and we all feel the relief when I hit the 'Off Motion' button for the last time. Their experience of the previous four hours has been intense concentration, with me hanging on at the back of the centre console as we practice and repeat the most complicated flying manoeuvres they have ever attempted. There is often a moment just as we cross the electric drawbridge with our flightbags, armfuls of books and aeronautical charts when I look back at them and smile. In their faces they look drained, but there is something else – they carry with them the warm glow of achievement from having mastered skills they never thought possible. I giggle when I say to them, "Hey, it's funny you know, some people think flying airliners is **boring?!**' and they always shake their heads.

There is a serious side to all this though, because in our industry we now have pilots coming through to fly our airliners with less flying experience than ever before. With the advent of the new Multi-Pilot Licence, (MPL) this situation will only worsen in the short term. I can imagine the more senior members of our profession shaking their heads in dismay when they find out the level of *inexperience* sitting next to them in the flightdeck. Sadly there will inevitably be times in the future when this lack of experience on the flightdeck will be a causal factor in aviation incidents and accidents – some would say this is the price we have to pay for progress. Of course the underlying cause is cost. Our accountant friends who count the beans in the airline industry (the financial directors) are obsessed with 'bottom line'. They know that less experienced crew will accept lesser terms and conditions and some companies shamelessly exploit this to the extent that their junior co-pilots are actually paying to work for the company. In spite of what the future holds, the accountants should be happy though because they will get what they wanted. After all, *if you pay peanuts, you will get Monkeys!*

----

*Just in case some of what I have written is taken the wrong way by my fellow aviators, I would like to say that I do **not** think of pilots as being apelike. Far from it, I believe that flying aeroplanes is an exacting, professional, challenging task which takes great skill, dexterity and intelligence to do well. There are only small percentages of any population who can do what we do on a daily basis and I have the greatest respect for my peers. Now pass me another banana, I'm going to fly a Raw Data ILS ☺*
P.S. The Kazakh for Rabbit is "Koy-Yon".

The 'F' Word. (With apologies to Gordon Ramsay).

(Pain is only temporary – Failure lasts a lifetime!)

Is there an Elephant in the room? Yes it's here and the word begins with an 'F'. I am talking about *Failures* in flying training and that is the 'F' word which no-one in our world likes to talk about.

You see much of flying aeroplanes is all about confidence and positive attitudes. In modern parlance, "It's a head-trip". When it comes down to it, pilots are responsible for the defeat of gravity and through the use of technology and the employment aerodynamic principles, we regularly achieve what was not possible before the Wright brothers came along. In some ways this makes pilots a bit different because to go so far away from the earth's surface without visible means of support is not a natural thing to do. Learning how to do the unnatural, implies that certain skills are mastered which permit otherwise ordinary human beings to do extraordinary things.

Although some of the basic skills are not that difficult to acquire – 'pull the stick back and the houses get smaller' – combining all of the essential elements together to form one very effective aeroplane operator is the key to the whole thing. Knowledge needs to be mixed with skills and experience through the medium of training to get the end product. That product is a pilot who is honed to perfection and fitted to the task (in theory), but even they are not infallible. The truism here is that if human beings did not make mistakes, they wouldn't make anything. Even highly qualified, experienced aviators with impeccable training backgrounds fail to achieve the required standard at certain times in their professional lives.

I recall one very senior KLM DC10 Captain who had worked for the company virtually since the end of the Second World War, telling me how he cocked up his very last Simulator Check prior to his retirement. In those days it was called "The Base Check" and was two days in the Sim – replaced now by the Licence Proficiency Check (LPC), same thing really. When he told me about the event it was with both candour and sheepishness and I got the distinct impression he was not a little ashamed of what he had done. His training department were even more surprised of course and immediately rescheduled another check which he passed with ease. In his case it wasn't that he couldn't perform to the required standard, after all he had done so continuously for many years, but he just let his guard drop towards the end of his career – he took his eye off the ball.

For me the fascinating thing was that he was one of the most careful guys around – he was really sharp and did not take risks when he flew. In fact when he told me about his last flight and the subsequent retirement party, the thing which stuck in my mind was that he actually carried out an autoland for his final landing into Schiphol – incredible. You would have thought that a pilot with 20,000 plus flying hours on everything from Lancaster bombers through DC3s, right up to widebody jet transports would want to have the satisfaction of putting his last aircraft down on the runway with his own hand, but no, not Captain Gerry Gardner. God bless you Gerry, you were an inspiration to many who flew with you I am sure.

Normally though, pilots fail courses and checks a lot earlier than six months before they are due to retire. Usually the failures come during the early days of flying when the trainee does not appreciate the way the system works. For example in the military flying training system, everybody lives under the fear of the axe, of getting "the chop". There is a whole different language associated with this phenomenon. A final review flight with a very senior flying instructor (perhaps the Chief Instructor or his deputy), is known as a "Thinly Disguised Chop Ride" and sometimes it is blindingly obvious to all around except the poor trainee who is being set up to fail.

By that time of course, the evidence is clear that they have not achieved the required standard of piloting and therefore it is necessary for someone to go and do the deed. This instructor/examiner will make every effort to put the student at their ease, such that their own conscience is clear once the axe has fallen – not for nothing are they often known as "the smiling assassin!"

It is important to realise though that the trainee themselves shoulders most of the responsibility for their own situation. That may sound odd, but when I see some students struggling with their airliner conversion courses, the words "It wasn't compulsory" come to mind. Each aviator who decides they are going to go 'professional' whether it's military or civil decides his or her own destiny. If it was easy, everybody would do it. One of the major problems which we see in training is people deluding themselves that they are actually better than they are at what they do – in other words there is sometimes a severe mismatch between confidence and ability.

This is often noticeable later on when Senior First Officers in the airlines approach the time when they upgrade to Captain. The vast majority of SFOs sincerely believe they are ready to make the transition quite a long time before they really are. Some who push for their Command Course (or are pushed forward by the company) then struggle to make the grade and fail the course. Failing a Command Course is just about the worst thing you can do to your career as a commercial airline pilot. It is a very public situation (everyone at your base knows you went on the course) and to come back to the crewroom still in the right-hand seat is ignominious to say the least.

My advice to SFOs who feel they are ready, is to listen to their peers and trainers – if there is doubt among them, don't go for the course. The other Line Skippers with whom you operate will give a good feel for it and if you ask them they will be honest about how they see your prospects.

Failure to meet the standard required can of course occur a lot earlier in the career of a commercial pilot. Prior to the airliner conversion course taking place, there is usually an assessment of an applicant's abilities in the simulator and the report from that session is always a sound indicator of the trainee's potential. I know of one trainee who gave just about the worst performance I have seen during his assessment and I wrote the report to reflect this, advising him not to waste his money on a self-funded airliner type rating course.

Unfortunately he didn't seem to want to listen and went ahead with the course anyway, resulting in a catastrophic situation where he had spent a huge amount of money and failed to get the rating. Not only that but all the way through his training, the instructors reported that he wasn't able to hack it and by the end of it, the company had to say there was nothing else they could do. This particular pilot had bitten off more than he could chew, but if he had taken notice of his initial reports, then he could have made the decision to stop earlier than he did.

Stress plays an influential part in the way pilots perform during training and the most common stressors are, Bereavement (close relative or friend), Divorce/Separation, Moving House, Long Separation from Family, Illness, Financial problems. If you are experiencing one or more of these top stressors in your life, then you should not be attempting to pass a flying training course where you have to give 100% to get through.

The adverse effects of stress are well known and if you just look at the cognitive symptoms you will note immediately that they are incompatible with mastering the necessary skills to defeat gravity. Forgetfulness, preoccupation and difficulty in concentrating, combined with indecisiveness, work mistakes and excessive worry are the primary symptoms, but these are then joined by decrease in creativity and loss of sense of humour, which lead to increased stress related performance errors.

The cure is in your own hands. Have a good look at your life and be honest about where you are and what you are doing. Are you stressed, or are you in a situation which could become stressful? If so, then you must either do something to reduce the effects of stress prior to starting an important course, or delay the course until you can sort your life out. Coping strategies include, removing the stressor or changing the way in which you think about it. Perhaps you could seek training in common stress reduction techniques – meditation, yoga, relaxation therapies etc. Most of all, it will help to talk to somebody and that could even be a trained counsellor.

Whatever you do, *please do something,* the problem will not just go away on its own and if you start an intensive flying training course without de-stressing your life, then you have only got one person to blame when you fail.

Capt Gary Hudson (LPC) taxying in at Baghdad - VVIP flight.   Note the nice crease in the shirt sleeve.

Command Performance.

("The best game in town" – being in the lefthand seat of an airliner).

Sometimes things are not always what they seem. A good example of this is the old story about the two pilots flying an airliner together into Gatwick, when the First Officer was the "handling" pilot and made a particularly firm landing. After taking control from him as the aircraft decelerated to taxi speed, the Captain said that he would say goodbye to the passengers.

From his seat on the right-hand side of the flightdeck, the F/O saw him pick up the microphone for the PA and apologise to the passengers in the cabin "for the rather rough landing which was done by the Co-Pilot!" Needless to say there was a frosty atmosphere after this and the F/O felt very embarrassed by what had happened.

It's a small world, of course and a week later saw the pair operating together again – this time the Captain was the flying pilot, when he really crunched it into Manchester. As they taxied off the runway in silence, the F/O volunteered to say goodbye to the passengers on the PA system and then to the Captain's horror, proceeded to tell all in the cabin that it was

"...the Captain who made that terrible landing and it was to be hoped he would get better at it in the future..."

"What the Hell did you say that for!?" Shouted the Captain as the F/O went white as a sheet. He replied,

"Well you did it to me last week in Gatwick...." To which the Captain retorted,

"Yes but I didn't press the bloody button!"

The importance of pilots having really good situational awareness (or S.A. as it is known) cannot be overemphasised. For example in the above situation, if the First Officer had been really sharp, he would have known that the Captain had not actually transmitted the words on the PA. There are far more important examples of lapses of SA which have lead crews and particularly aircraft Captains to make poor quality decisions.

Consider the case of a B757 getting airborne from a UK airfield some years back, when all of a sudden a message and a warning light illuminated in the flightdeck indicating that one of the emergency doors was open. The Captain elected to return to the airport of departure and land rather than continue the flight. Although the decision to return was not unsafe, neither was it particularly smart. The reason is that all Boeing airliners have what are called "plug-type" doors, such that when closed they cannot possibly be opened from the inside once the cabin is pressurised.

If this Captain had been a little more experienced or had better technical systems S.A. then he would have known this and continued the flight. The cause of the warning is/was a microswitch misalignment and provided that the cabin pressure shows no faults, then the warning of a door being "open" is spurious. To be fair to the airline though, they were very kind to the skipper - who had been recently promoted. After an interview with the Fleet Manager, during which he admitted his lack of technical awareness of the 757 door system, he returned to the line with the matter closed... just like the door had been from the beginning.

Another example of sub-prime Command Decision Making was when a B757 was held down at Flight Level 290 after departing a Scottish airfield en-route to Cyprus. Now a night flight to Cyprus from Scotland is not the most desirable of duties, but the flight was made even less so, when the Captain observed the warning message *"Insufficient Fuel"* on the screen of the Flight Management Computer (FMC).

At the time he had been off the radio and the First Officer had been in control while the skipper had been making a PA announcement to the cabin. Unknown to the Captain, the F/O had activated and executed FL290 as the cruise altitude all the way to Cyprus, which was substantially lower than the FL350 they were expecting. The rules of garbage in, garbage out then applied and the FMC quite rightly indicated that the aircraft did not have enough fuel onboard to fly at the lower level all the way to the other end of the Med.

If the Captain had taken a little more time over the decision making process and perhaps discussed it more deeply with the F/O, the flight might well have continued to Larnaca without a hitch. Instead, they both convinced themselves that there was a major fuel leak from the centre tank and declared an emergency, diverting into Luton for maintenance. The engineers could find no evidence of any fuel leak and after refuelling, the aircraft departed again for Cyprus, hours behind schedule and with the crew well into discretion.

Things went from bad to worse however, because the engineers filed a damning report at Luton, the airline's Flight Operations Director was alerted to the events and by the morning when the aircraft returned to the UK both pilots' careers had taken a nosedive. The moral of the story is stick to the Standard Operating Procedures (SOPs), which means that if one pilot makes a change to the active route in the FMC they MUST ensure the other pilot is in the loop.

In a former life (as we say in the trade), I was heavily involved with the upgrading of First Officers to Captains – the Command Upgrade Process. Being part of the system which selected, rejected or deferred hundreds of pilots who were being considered for promotion was quite illuminating. I was fortunate to gain a terrific insight into what goes to make a good Captain and what constitutes "the wrong stuff". It was not uncommon to be asked to investigate the reasons why an aircraft was diverted for what appeared to be insufficient cause.

An occasion I recall was when a 737 routing from Scotland to a London airport diverted into Birmingham after a fuel tank gauge had failed. Because the fuel gauge on one wing had all of a sudden begun to indicate zero, the recently upgraded Skipper decided that this could mean they had "lost" all of the fuel from that side. It was an embarrassing incident for the pilots, but one which caused much mirth among the crewroom pundits.

Even worse was to come for the poor Captain when only a week later they elected to divert into Birmingham again! This time because the airframe they were flying was not fit to carry out an autoland in poor visibility. The parallels were coincidental, the route was from Scotland to London and the destination airport was shrouded in fog – but then it had been all morning, so why get airborne from Glasgow? Now the crewroom gossip merchants had a field day. They put the rumour round that the Captain was trying to start a new base in Birmingham – all on their own!

I lost count of the number of times airliners diverted from Liverpool having flown from Belfast, just 25 minutes away due to bad weather which they knew about before they launched... Really not a clever thing to do. One of these flights diverted twice. The first time they ended up in East Midlands (EMA) after circling over the Liverpool airport for the best part of an hour, then after refuelling in EMA they set off again (20 minute flight) to find themselves in the same position – this time the passengers ended up in Leeds Bradford!

A much more serious incident occurred some years later when an aircraft with the same company ended up in a similar situation – i.e. diverting due to weather over a relatively short distance in the UK. In essence the diversion could have been avoided if the pilots had made the decision to sit tight and wait for the destination weather to improve rather than pressing-on.

Well they left their decision making too late, ran below their reserves and ended up declaring a "Fuel Emergency" during their arrival into their diversion airport. The saddest thing was that during the callout of the emergency services, one of the Fire Engines in the local town accidentally ran down and killed a pensioner while rushing to the airport. The quality of Command Decision Making on the flightdeck can have far reaching consequences.

The most important part of all this however is that we learn from our mistakes and the errors of others to further improve our own performance, which is why feedback loops in Flight Safety systems are so vital. Knowledge is power as they say and in this case the knowledge gained from the close shaves of others gives us the power to change for the better the ways in which we operate. A perfect example of this was the Kegworth accident where the British Midlands 737 crew failed to identify the correct engine which was failing. They were so unlucky in many ways and judged to be less than competent in others, but our profession learned huge lessons from the accident. The real tragedy of course was that 47 people died in that process.

As we taxied out in our Air India coloured B767 at London Heathrow the night after the BA 777 accident to commence our takeoff roll from runway 27L, we had a chance to observe the wreckage of Speedbird 038. A dramatic scene indeed, lit as it was by the emergency floodlights and still surrounded by what seemed like a hundred vehicles. There was little time for reflection though as we were very soon cleared for line up and our focus was on the job in hand. Later there would be time to think about it all and the overriding thought was how lucky they had been.

Regardless of what had lead up to the crash-landing, the fact remains that Boeing build a very strong airframe and for 100+ passengers and crew to survive a complete hull-loss was a brilliant result. Of course the AAIB investigation was only just beginning, but there were more lessons for us to learn about fuel icing as a result. More than once I have heard my more senior colleagues say, *"The day you stop learning, is the day you should stop flying!"* Never a truer word was said.

The term, "The Right Stuff" came from Tom Wolfe's 1970's book based around the NASA Mercury Space programme, in fact he actually brought this expression into common usage in the English language, although perhaps he was not the first to use it. In those early days of manned spaceflight, having the "Right Stuff" was more to do with astronauts demonstrating courage, fortitude, resilience and the ability to function effectively under extremely stressful conditions.

Since then the term has been more casually applied to all sorts of other situations, not least by inverting it as *"The Wrong Stuff"* to title a TV programme on the mistakes which airline pilots make. Last month's *From the Flightdeck* focussed on some of the negative situations which can arise as a result of poor Command Decision making, but these are exceptional cases.

The vast majority of Command Decisions in the airline industry which occur on a daily basis are perfectly safe and completely sound, which lead to entirely uneventful outcomes – this is the essential nature of our business. As I am fond of replying to people when they say that they have seen contestants on the Krypton Factor TV programme landing aeroplanes in the simulator, "they only have to get it right once!" Airline pilots have to get it right every time, day in day out as part of their working lives in all weathers and in every corner of the globe.

It is always easy to be wise after the event and as the saying goes, 'Hindsight is 20/20 vision'. While working as a Pilot Manager for a former employer, it would often fall to me to carry out an investigation into the decision making of some of our Airline Captains. Normally this would be sent to me by way of an emailed report from the Operations Centre who had been responsible for running the flying programme at the time of the incident.

It was not uncommon to find that these reports were already biased and critical of the outcome, implying that the crew had been in error even *before* all the facts were known. I soon learned that it was necessary to establish exactly what the facts were before even approaching an assessment regarding the quality of the decision. A good example of this was when I received an email on a Monday morning from our Ops people asking me to investigate the circumstances surrounding a medical diversion into Bristol airport over the weekend.

According to the Ops. Report, it would have been preferable for the aircraft, a B737 from Northern UK Enroute to Malaga to have diverted into Gatwick. Their question was why had this not occurred? It turned out that the Bristol diversion was operationally less desirable for the company. In cases like this when a diversion seems likely, it is normal for the flightcrew to call the company on company VHF frequency and find out which is the preferred alternate from the commercial aspect. All things being equal then, that is where the aircraft will make an approach to land.

I contacted the Captain and the First Officer to ask them for their version of the events and to ask why they appeared not to have spoken to the company before electing to 'dive' into Bristol. The answer which returned surprised me in some ways yet not in others. They said the passenger appeared to be very unwell with a suspected heart attack and they needed to make a decision on the diversion airfield fairly quickly. One of the other passengers had responded to the PA "Is there a doctor onboard?" and was tending to the sick traveller, but the news coming from the cabin was not encouraging and time was now precious.

The aircraft was routing southbound along the A25 airway down the England/Wales border and they (the pilots) were favouring Bristol. It was the nearest sizable airport with good medical facilities, perfect weather and was one of our company's crewbases. They had already waited a few minutes for Operations to give them their preferred commercial alternate and when the call came back, the pilots were asked *could they divert into Nice!?*

Needless to say they decided that a trip to the French Riviera would not be in the passenger's best interests, so they continued with their own plan – less than twenty five minutes later the aircraft was on the ground in Bristol and the passenger was on his way to hospital (he survived). Now good CRM works both ways and one of the best weapons in an airline Commander's armoury is high quality support from the ground. Without doubt on this occasion, that was lacking primarily due to one Operations employee's incomplete knowledge of geography. The case was rapidly closed with some feedback from myself on the crew's behalf regarding better operational support/communications required.

Bristol airport was also the location of another sick passenger event which had a happy ending. The aircraft was just boarding passengers when one of them, a senior gentleman suffered a massive heart attack, collapsing in the aisle. Immediately the cabin crew's excellent training kicked into action and they began to administer cardiac massage and resuscitation. The aircraft Captain came out from the flightdeck and made a perfectly correct assessment of the nature of the medical emergency, returned to the cockpit and made the Mayday call for urgent medical assistance.

Due to the swift response from Captain and crew in administering first aid and ensuring the prompt arrival of expert medical personnel, Sir Ranulph Fiennes survived the experience; made a full recovery and the rest as they say is history. The Captain then played a pivotal role in debriefing/counselling his shocked crew members and managing the handling of the passengers to ensure minimum disruption to their schedule. This was truly a "Command Performance" par excellence for which the Commander and crew were rewarded with the company's top honour of a Gold award in recognition of their efforts.

Big airlines and jet airliners are not the only place where you can find examples of above average performance by commercial pilots. I remember many years ago when I was a pilot with a Manchester based Air Taxi operator flying PA31 Piper Chieftains, that we had a major incident with one of our aircraft flying the night mail to Belfast across the Irish Sea. He was flying single crew and had taken off from East Midlands airport when he found problems with retracting the landing gear. After carrying out all the recommended checklist items, the Captain established that he could only get one of the main gear legs to lock down.

The prospect which faced him now was a partial gear up landing with a full load of mail onboard, during the winter at night. Fortunately Manchester were very obliging to him and offered the use of their (at the time) only runway for the exercise. There was then a long wait as the Captain went into the hold for an hour over Manchester at 6000 feet to burn off fuel before commencing the approach. Avgas is a highly inflammable substance of course and as only the right (starboard) main leg was locked down, the left (port) leg locked up with the nosegear partially extended, there was always the possibility of fuel tank rupture and subsequent fire after touchdown. Also a lighter weight for landing would be good from the aeroplane handling point of view, giving a slower stalling speed and less stress on the wing left (port) wing as it scraped along the runway.

The landing was textbook however and there was no fire, in fact there was barely enough fuel onboard for a go-around. Not only that, but the pilot stop-cocked both engines on landing, such that the propellers were stationary when the port prop touched the surface of Manchester's runway 24, thereby preventing the engine from being shock-loaded – brilliant! After the event, the Captain (who was locally feted as a hero and deservedly so) was asked if there was anything he would have done differently next time?

He stated that his one regret was to have opened the little crew hatch so early (6000 feet) before commencing his approach – it was then a very cold descent with 100+ mph winds whistling through the gap in the door into the cockpit. This Captain was one *cool operator* in more ways than one! The reason that I know so much about the incident is that I got a call at around 11pm that night while I was at home on standby to say, "We need you to fly a tonne of mail to Belfast that was inadvertently delivered to Manchester..." Half an hour later I arrived at the airport to find the mail being transferred to one of the spare aircraft which was being fuelled up for me to take across the Irish Sea. Of the hero pilot there was neither sight nor sound, he had obviously taken the rest of the night off!

It is true to say that there are so many good examples of above average Captaincy in the commercial airline world; it is difficult to pick which ones to talk about, although it makes it easy for me to fill a column like this. In the UK certainly, I believe we are blessed with the finest standard of commercial operations in the world. In my opinion a significant part of this well deserved reputation is played by the airline Captains across the board – quite simply they *ARE* the best in the business!

Footnote: The writer has made his own fair share of mistakes down the years while flying aeroplanes and does not believe himself to be infallible. It should be noted however that while, not making mistakes is important, learning not to make them again is really essential. This is why "no-blame" cultures within aviation companies (especially airlines) are vital for the benefit of all.

Another empty kitchen?

(Seriously? Yes I am afraid there are some in our profession who think this way).

Back in the late eighties when I joined my first airline, the actual mechanics of pilot selection were not quite so sophisticated as they are these days. In the words of the Chief Pilot then, "The modern airliner is so easy to fly, that's it's more important to find out if you can sit next to the bloke for four hours on a night Tenerife". Of course this was back in the days when very few women did the job and then it was assumed that you really would be sitting next to a 'bloke', in whichever rank.

So rare was it for us to fly airliners with women pilots that I distinctly remember my first time. Now bearing in mind that when I left school I was employed as a Nurse for several years and have an open mind where working women are concerned, even I felt a little bit weird when we reported for duty. I need not have worried however; my First Officer was very competent and great fun to fly with. She had a lovely sense of humour and a charismatic personality.

It's got to be said she was a great pilot and a good work colleague. At the end of the day, I turned to her and said, "Do you know that was my first time - doing that with a woman... and it wasn't as bad as I thought it was going to be!" Fortunately she took it as the joke I had intended and we both laughed out loud. In fact she was with me on the day of my last flight with the company and it was a bit of an emotional one really, but that as they say is another story.

Roll the clock forward to 1998 some ten years later and it was not uncommon at easyJet for two women pilots to fly together. As a committed equal opportunities employer with an abhorrence of tradition, the big orange airline made sure they employed plenty of the fairer sex in the flightdeck. I remember being vaguely disturbed on one flight however, when I worked with one of the female F/Os (Lisa) from Luton and while we were in the cruise I asked her where she had been to the previous day.

She said she had flown "to Athens and back with Captain Suzanne" and I made a face at her, wrinkling my nose, pretending to dislike the idea of two women operating the 737 together. I should have left it at that, but I was curious.

"What on earth did you two talk about in here?" I asked not knowing the reply.

"Well we talked about curtain materials and interior design mostly!"

I was too shocked to speak. I am sure Lisa said it to wind me up and it worked, as soon as I could get my words together I said,

"In here...? In this *hallowed* place, the FLIGHTDECK? You talked about GIRLIE things?! *Arrrgh!* LISA, I think I'm going to be sick!"

She laughed her head off at this and kept reminding me of it for the rest of the day.

There is one characteristic which most of the female pilots I have flown with share and that is they have above average flying ability and I suppose you can understand why this is. We still have a mainly male dominated industry and to get to fly a jet airliner, they have to be better than average (or very lucky) to succeed. There have been phases however when companies have positively encouraged applicants from both women and ethnic minority groups so that the demographic make-up of their employees is more representative of general society. In fact not so many years ago there was a popular belief among prospective trainee airline pilots that to be either female or from an ethnic minority (or both) would be a real asset for the interview with British Airways. Times change though and this is certainly no longer the case if it ever existed.

No. The real person they are looking for is... wait for it... YOU! Just be yourself. How many times have you heard it, but it IS so true. You don't have to be of a particular sex, or colour or religion. Think about how many aircraft takeoff and land around the world each day. Or even just in the UK alone - how many pilots are working to fly the line to keep the airline companies running to schedule, to keep Heathrow as nearly the busiest airport in the world?

All those male and female pilots out there doing the job and every day a certain percentage of them retire, or lose their medicals or leave the profession for other reasons. While all the time the industry continues to expand at a certain rate each year, each month, each week. It used to be 15% per annum, year on year expansion that was talked about, however in the current climate I am sure this is down to single figures, but it is still growing and will do so for as long as economists can predict. There is a job for you, of that you can be sure.

In a former company I spent plenty of time assessing and recruiting pilots as part of my role and many of the applicants we saw were for Ab-Initio training schemes. We used to have a bank of questions which we knew would produce either the right, right answers or the right *wrong* answers if you know what I mean. Questions such as, "If your friends were asked to use three words to describe you, what would they say?"

Of course we were looking for words here like, dedicated, professional, outgoing, stable, conscientious, honest, diligent, sharp, etc. etc. All very well if you have heard the question before or even thought about it, but if you had not prepared for the interview, then it would come as something as a shock. The worst interviewees I think were the ones who just did not have much to say. Those were hard work because as assessors we were always being positive and hoping that this particular candidate is going to tick all the boxes for us so that we can recommend him/her for the position/course.

We were not alone in our hopes for the applicants who were entering the profession right at the start, as was proven from my conversation recently with one of the senior Heads of Training of a large training establishment at Gatwick. He said that he had been involved in preparing applicants for their interviews with the airlines, along with his deputy (another very experienced airline Training Captain). One day a couple of years ago they sent twelve of their pilots out to be assessed by two major airlines in the UK, six went to airline X and six went to airline Y. They waited nervously in the office in Gatwick for the feedback from the recruitment manager from each airline to see how their protégés had fared. The call finally came in late afternoon from each airline – five of the pilots had passed in each case, to which the Head of Training replied, "okay we'll send you one more tomorrow if you can interview him then?" Of course, his plan was to send the failed applicant in each group to the opposite airline and... success! All twelve were employed!

In his own words, "Sometimes no matter how much you prepare them, they can still get it wrong on the day, or they may flunk a few of the important questions". So it is important to keep in mind that not all employers will think the same about each person. So often, it is personalities that come into play, even when the assessments are supposed to be completely objective.

As a candidate all you can do is to prepare in every way possible to make sure you prove how much you want the job and are willing and able to do whatever it takes to get it and be good at it. I used to say, "If they give me an interview, I'll talk my way in!" Which summarised my attitude to the assessment process at that time. Mind you I also used to be so enamoured with being paid to fly aeroplanes, I used to say "I'd do this job for twenty pounds a week", but I haven't said that for quite some years now.

Of course, it's not all about how you answer the questions, interact with others, play as part of the team, complete your psychometric test paper – it's also about how you look. Make sure you have a good think about that too before you enter the interview room, because airlines just do not employ scruffy pilots. You may be the 'Ace of the base', but you are not going to even get close enough to the Simulator to prove it if the assessors do not like the way you are presented. If you have not polished your shoes since the first day of 'big school' then now is the time to do so.

My senior colleague from Gatwick again drew on his experience to make the point about the fact that 'dress' is vitally important. When applying for a job as an airline pilot (or even trainee airline pilot) then you cannot look too conformist. One of the pilots he interviewed was hanging in the balance, but both of the assessors were distracted by the suit he was wearing which was clearly much too big for him and of quite a bright colour.

At the end of the interview they decided to give him some feedback as to why he had been unsuccessful and in addition to talking the applicant through the points where he had let himself down with the answers to the questions, they mentioned the ill fitting suit. Following which there was a long pause and the pilot replied,

"Yes, but my girlfriend bought it specially for me to wear at this interview".

The moral of the story has got to be, buy your own interview suit!

Remember: Be positive, be cheerful, don't be dull. Do all your preparation beforehand and make sure you know what to expect. Take care (and pride) in your appearance. Try not say negative things, turn them into positive ones.

Whose Fuel is it Anyway?

(We do use a lot of it to get around – but who owns it?)

Oil has reached a record $120 per barrel in the past year or two and smaller (50 seat) jet airliners have been axed as they became uneconomical. As corporate brinksmanship is being played out with North Sea pipelines and international supplies, it is perhaps a good time to reflect on the subject of fuel.

I remember sometime ago, flying along at cruising altitude and having a long discussion about fuel. My trainee pilot was asking about the policy of fuel loading as part of flight planning and this then went on to the wider subject of how we burn the fuel in flight.

For example, he had noted that we were "running late" – flying a few minutes behind the schedule and asked why we didn't "fly faster to make up the time?". I countered this question with another question, "Whose fuel is that in there?" pointing to the fuel gauges. Well he was a little bit stumped for an answer, so he tried with "Well the company bought it, so maybe it's Stelios's?" (You can guess whom we worked for) I laughed and said,

"Nope, it's certainly not his fuel... and it's not theirs either", pointing back at the flightdeck door indicating the passengers, "even though they have paid for their seats, it is not their fuel". He frowned and said,

"Well whose is it then?" I decided to tell him.

"It's ours. It's yours and mine! You see once we have pushed back and started engines, all of the gas in the tanks is owned by us and what we do with it is really our concern and nobody else's. That fuel means everything to us, it's what keeps us airborne and in so doing it gives us time. Yes, fuel equals time, thinking time, decision making time, call it what you will, but when we are flying fuel is *time*, end of story".

At this point we were flying in a Boeing 737-700, one of the New Generation Boeing 737s with all singing all dancing modern EFIS displays – just like a mini 747-400. We continued our conversation as currently there was not a lot to do. I asked him what speed is our normal cruising speed in the -700,

"Well it depends on a few things, but essentially we cruise at the ECON cruise speed as determined by the Flight Management Computer", he correctly replied.

"Yes but what is that, roughly, disregarding massive headwinds or tailwinds?" Once again he was correct when he said, "erm, it's about Mach 0.78... ish".

"Good", I was pleased that he remembered, "but what is the maximum we can go flat-out? What is our limiting Mach number?" He thought about it for a few seconds and the answer came to him.

"It's Mach 0.82" he looked relieved when I said, "Absolutely right, so in essence when we say that we are cruising at ECON cruise speed, we are actually flying at about 96% of the maximum speed for the aircraft anyway. You see it's got a Mach .78 wing, so it's doing exactly what the designers said it would do", I went on to explain, "we could cruise a bit faster, but not much, however what we would do is burn a whole load more fuel – today on this route, we would lose several hundred kilogrammes to shave just a couple of minutes off the arrival time".

More importantly of course you have to keep a broad view of the situation. Why was the aircraft running late? It was most unlikely to have been a result of the crew not turning up for work on time and was more probably down to somebody else's incompetence on the ground prior to departure.

To get an airliner ready for service, a substantial number of people need to work together in a coordinated way for an ontime despatch from the gate. It only takes one or two of those people to be deficient at their jobs, for the aircraft departure to be delayed and this can happen in a huge variety of ways. No matter how long how you fly the line, there will always be something which surprises you.

An example is the incident which occurred a few years ago while on the ramp in India. The Air India 767 was being made ready for flight and because the aircraft's Auxiliary Power Unit (APU) was unserviceable, we were reliant upon the supply of electrical power from the ground.

Now Ground Power Units (or GPUs as they are known) are occasionally unreliable and it is not uncommon for the diesel driven generator to drop off line, or to pack up altogether. Halfway through passenger boarding, there was a loud electrical "clunk" in the flightdeck and all the lights went out – additionally from our point of view, the computers dumped all their information which then required reprogramming which was singularly disappointing.

I enquired from the Air India engineer what the problem was, assuming that it was yet another GPU failure to be surprised by his answer. "The GPU ran out of diesel!" Well there you go - my flightdeck colleagues and I laughed at the fact that the GPU had not actually failed as normal, but there had been a human factors error in the chain which broke, leading to the AC power loss onboard the aircraft. It was the first time we had ever heard of this reason for GPU failure, but then as we know, we have not seen everything yet.

Which brings us back to the question of possibly cruising faster to reduce the arrival delay, when we, are not responsible for it and it is likely to have been an act of negligence or incompetence on the part of one of 'another part of the team'. At this point in the flightdeck discussion, I always ask the question,

"Why should we use up OUR precious fuel, in order to cover up the cause of a departure delay which is clearly the responsibility of somebody else?"

Well logic dictates that there is no point of course. No point at all, in spending a large amount of money (and planet's resources) in order to save maybe only a few minutes and to hide the fact that somebody forgot to check that a GPU had enough diesel in it.

What I do advise my colleagues however, is to assure the passengers on the PA system that we are doing all in our power to get them to their destination as soon as possible. Well, when we are flying (economically) at 96% of the maximum speed of the airframe this is true enough isn't it? The PR effect costs nothing and works wonders on the morale of the passengers, assuming they can understand English.

When I passed my B757 command course back in the early 90's and went for an interview with the Director of Flight Operations (DFO) of the airline, I distinctly recall his words to me on the subject of fuel. "In your first 12 months in the left-hand seat, do not feel pressured to minimise the fuel which you load for the flight – take as much as you want to carry".

Wise words indeed and I have repeated them many times when I have had the pleasure of overseeing others move from the right to the left seat. Any excess fuel is valuable thinking time as you arrive at your destination and in the early days of a jet airliner command, such time is important for young Captains. There are numerous examples throughout commercial aviation of pilots running out of ideas (and fuel) and sometimes both simultaneously. If only more of them had been fortunate enough to have bosses like our old DFO from those days in Air2000, perhaps the world of airline flying would be a little less stressful.

Of course the reason it is not, is because of the price of the stuff and the fact that it costs fuel to carry fuel. In round numbers it costs about 4% per tonne per hour on the Boeings – I guess Airbus must be similar. Now this may not seem much, but if you are running a fleet of 100+ aircraft and they are being utilised for 11 or 12 hours per day airborne every day of the year – it all adds up. Quite simply the fuel bills are colossal and they are the largest single cost factor in commercial airline flying. Training pilots not to use so much of the resource while flying is reasonably simple and there are various ways in which crews can be encouraged to fly economically, yet safely.

It *is* an emotive issue though and you cannot order your highly paid airline commanders to take less gas. Part of the reason they are so highly paid, is that they make critical decisions on things like fuel loads as part of their working lives. The route, the time of arrival at destination, the weather forecast, the technical state of the aircraft; there are many factors to be taken into consideration when deciding on the fuel load, however in this digital, computer literate age you will not hear Captains carrying "half a tonne extra for the wife and kids".

They may however rely on that sixth sense which tells them, 'today does not have a good feeling to it – maybe we'll round up the fuel on the flightplan'.

In fact even in our modern age, it's somehow comforting to know that we are still very much human and experience counts for an awful lot.

Nostalgia ain't what it used to be...

(They say that "If you can remember the '60s – you weren't really there...")

It is true to say that the job of "Airline Pilot" has changed a lot over the decades and none more so than in the last years since 9/11. Overnight our profession changed from being safe and efficient operators/managers of commercial flights to being right on the frontline in the prevention of terrorism. Worse still, airline crews (along with other airside workers) are now subject to excessive security searches and overzealous interpretation of rules by petty minded individuals at staff search points all over the UK, with local rules applied.

Finally, if we (the flight crews) find this a little hard to bear or voice our safety concerns with respect to increased stress levels from fighting to get through security, just to get to work; we are told that *we* are deficient in *our* CRM skills! Fancy that? The illogical and inconsistent application of security search regulations for staff search units all across the country is somehow our fault?!

It wasn't always like this. Maybe there were happier times in our past, times when we were not sealed into that little room in the pointy bit where the pilots sit. In those days too when I was in the right-hand seat, my more senior colleagues used to reminisce about the earlier times when it seems life was better, the job was more fun and the people less stressed. In fact pilots were also paid more in relative terms to the rest of the professions. I lost count of the number of times I heard Captains say something like, "I have never earned as much since the time when I was flying the 'Seven Oh Seven', running guns for Colonel Ghadaffi!" Of course THAT was a job without too much of a company pension plan, but what the heck? If the salary is large enough in the short to medium term, then you are not going to worry too much about the long term future.

I was enlightened to learn that it was not just the quality of employment which had changed over the years, but the build quality of the aircraft too it seemed. Often a Captain would say to me, "look at this, they don't make 'em like they used to", indicating the ripples in the skin of the Boeing 757 fuselage behind the trailing edge of the wing. The contrast here was with the early models and the popularly held view that Boeing were now using thinner sheet metal for the more recently built machines – apparently the early examples had no ripples in the fuselage. There would often be the accompanying comment which went something along the lines of "and we won't be seeing these airframes working in Africa in twenty years time", (like the 707s and 727s of the previous generation).

There were also many stories about the extraordinary activities which the crews used to get up to downroute and the senior guys used to tell of riotous parties and multifarious crazy antics which often embroiled them in controversial situations with the local law enforcement agencies.

Like the time when at an after flight crew party in an hotel in India, the First Officer and the Senior Stewardess decided to do a little shopping. Unfortunately they were still in their uniforms and 'three sheets to the wind', when they hopped into the back of a taxi outside the hotel. For some reason the taxi driver left them alone there for a few minutes while he went inside the hotel lobby to talk to the concierge and when he came out – the taxi was gone, weaving its way up the road into the busy Bombay traffic. The two crew members had decided that this was going to be a 'self-drive hire arrangement', but they had not bargained on the tenacity of a breadline taxi driver who could see his livelihood slipping away.

Giving chase with a fellow taxi driver in another cab, the locals soon rounded up quite a posse of Indians chasing the cowboys. Imagine the visual image as the two drunken crewmembers crunched the gears in the little black cab all the way to the Gate of India, struggling through the madness of traffic while all around them, everyone stared...

After all, you never see a white man driving a cab in Bombay, least of all one with three gold bars on his epaulettes and with a pretty white woman shouting and singing out of the window dressed as an air stewardess. By the time they reached the quayside at the Gate of India, the angry mob had nearly caught them up and as the traffic was at a standstill, they abandoned the transport and ran across the road, straight through the front doors of the prestigious, five star Taj Mahal Hotel and... kept running, straight out of the back of the building and up the street, leaving chaos in the lobby as fifty Indian taxi drivers arrived with a hullabaloo, to be delayed by the obstructive doormen.

Our two intrepid heroes then rushed straight into the nearest Police Station to explain they had been the victims of mistaken identity and could they please have Police protection from some outraged citizens! In the end they were shunted out of the back door of the Police Station and given a ride back to their hotel in a Police car.

All's well that ends well and the two miscreants rejoined the rest of their crew in the hotel to regale them with tales of their exploits in the bar later that evening. When the now Senior Captain told me this story I was sceptical at first, until I heard it verified by another pilot who worked for the same outfit at the time.

If I had any doubts about the fact that I had missed some really good parties in the past, these were dispelled when I first started flying the Boeing 757 back in '89. My company had just obtained their ETOPS clearance and the routes to Florida had recently been announced.

On this particular day I was flying with a senior and distinguished Captain who had served his time with Laker Airways on the DC10 – he was well acquainted with the charms of the New World, especially Bangor Maine in northeast United States where our crew slip/techstop was being planned for. Although the winters in that part of the world can be quite extreme, the runway at Bangor (KBGR) was always kept clear for the KC135 Tankers of the Air National Guard which needed to be able to provide Air to Air refuelling capability 365 days per year for the USAF. On the day when I reported for duty at Manchester to operate a Mediterranean out and back flight with this Captain, he had just been up to the management office to tell them their choice of airport was wrong.

He was keen to tell me about his encounter and to educate me as to the reasons why Bangor Maine was such an unsuitable place to slip the crews. His main reasoning seemed to be that there had been quite a lot of debauched behaviour among the crews of his previous employer which he knew would be a distraction and he summed it up for me, relating exactly how he had told the boss.

"AYE! I have told Burrows that Bangor's the wrong place as there's only two things that go on there – f****** and fishing. And during the winter... NOBODY GOES FISHING!"

I was shocked, because *NO-ONE* referred to our esteemed Director of Flight Operations by his surname, mind you, Bangor sounded like an interesting nightstop and so it proved. Over the next few seasons of ETOPS flights, our company slipped loads of crews in Maine and the Holiday Inn in Bangor found our custom so profitable that they actually built a third storey on the hotel. As one of only six First Officers in the company who were ETOPS qualified, I spent the next year or so 'on the Atlantic' which was a great experience.

The writing was on the wall however for riotous crew parties and licentious behaviour as increasingly employers tightened up on the regulations as they acknowledged their duty of care not only to their employees, but also to their hotel service partners where the crews stayed. Instances of unacceptable behaviour often resulted in disciplinary action being taken, although this rarely resulted in punishments as harsh as demotion.

There were exceptions of course and there is the famous tale of one young inebriated Captain who forfeited his command for a crew party. It happened many years ago in an airport hotel in Manchester. As a result of high spirits and apparently as part of a 'game', he ended up being pushed into a lift naked by the crew on the fourth floor, who then pressed the button to take him to the ground floor... As the lift doors opened in the lobby, a young family was walking past and a little girl screamed - before he had the presence of mind to cover his modesty with the only part of his uniform which he was wearing – his hat! A return to the right-hand seat for a couple of years was a high price to pay for an evening's frolicking.

So now, is it really that bad and were all the doom mongers of the early nineties right about the way things would be? Well the B757 is still going strong and of the 1050 that were built, there are very few that are not still operating. Fears that they were not 'built to last' have proved groundless, Mister Boeing builds a strong airframe and they will be around for a long time yet.

We still 'have fun' at work, although perhaps not in quite the same way as in the past – some of those antics belong to a more innocent age, before the Health and Safety fun detector was invented. My theory is that it is a perception issue and each successive generation expresses the same views about 'the way things were'.

I suppose if you can say one thing for certain, it is that "nostalgia ain't what it used to be!"

Airline Flying - The Long and the Short of it.

(If you join a big enough airline you can have both in the same company).

Popular misconceptions are commonplace in modern society. For example it is frequently believed that "Policemen are getting younger, vinegar is being watered down and summers were longer and hotter in the old days". In fact the average age of the Police in the UK has increased slightly as officers join later in life and stay in longer. With the passage of time, tastebuds become less sensitive and well recorded 'global warming' gives the lie to the other two false impressions. In a similar way, many pilots have the misconception that "Airline flying is boring". In fact nothing could be further from the truth.

It is true to say that there are differences between longhaul and shorthaul airline flying, one of them being how frequently a pilot has to go to work. In the case of the shorthaul aviator, it is not uncommon now to find that pilots are working nearly a five day week, with two days off. The working day is likely to start early in the morning or finish late at night and in the case of jet operators, the pilots will mostly fly four sectors (flights) per day.

When it comes to shorthaul, low-cost scheduled services; the average sector length is less than two hours. The most efficient and likely profitable sector length for the Low Cost Airlines (LCAs) is between the ninety minutes and one hour forty five mark. Less than this and customers have the option of the train (or even driving), which may be nearly as quick and once over two hours, the aircraft utilisation goes down. To give an example of this, one of the LCAs conducted a feasibility study of commencing flights to the Canary Islands from a northern English airport some years back. It was decided that it would be more productive to use the aeroplane to operate a Nice then a Barcelona flight in the same time frame, when you would see potentially 600 customers as opposed to 300. It must be borne in mind that onboard sales count a lot towards operating profits these days and the more potential buyers on the flights, the more potential revenue there is.

Moving forward from the cabin into the flightdeck, we can see that the pace of life here is pretty frenetic at times and the workload can be tiring. With every departure and arrival, there are separate sets of calculations required, different settings to be made and adjusted to the instrumentation, the navigation aids and the radios. Even the briefings between the crew need to be tailored to accommodate the different factors involved having regard to the weather conditions, the runway in use, taxiway routing, fuel requirements, local noise abatement regulations, you name it, and we do it!

Or at least we talk about it and plan it and think about it and consider it and concentrate on it... no wonder shorthaul LCA pilots talk of fatigue. Some of the multi-sector days can be six sectors and these are often from the smaller bases where there are fewer routes, so it may transpire that you are flying with the same person, doing the same or similar routes for several days in a row. Which is why on day three of this bewildering block of work, whilst taxying out for the fifth takeoff that day, at an airport you have been to several times already, you will be asking each other, "Have we really done the pre-takeoff checklist? Or was that yesterday...?"

On the upside of things it is great fun and there is never a dull moment, however it is a strong and competent character who can withstand such pressure indefinitely. Many of my colleagues in the LCA sector of the market talk about "burnout" and the reasons for this are clear. No matter how interesting and exciting life is as shorthaul jockey, there comes a point in most pilot's lives when they realise they have done enough.

In my case it was seven years and I knew it was time to leave. When I looked around the crewroom, there were very few faces left with whom I had joined and those that were there, like me, had aged a lot. Young fresh faced cadets had become seasoned First Officers ready for their Command, young F/Os had become experienced and competent Commanders, mature Captains had become training Captains and I had witnessed the retirement of some of the most experienced pilots. Yes it was definitely time to go.

A new company and a new pace of life; a change of scene and new routes, with similar airframes can work wonders for your sense of well-being. Many of the routes were longer too with typical sector lengths of four or even five hours – this was 'midhaul'. Some fascinating parts of the African continent to visit, along with some challenging pilot training on the line to contend with, made for a very interesting time. Being a smaller company, the way in which they looked after their people was different also with much more of a personal feel to it all. Certainly when 'Crewing' called you up, they knew exactly who you were and what you were employed as.

Overall the job was easier although the money was slightly less, but there is always this balance for lifestyle in the airline industry. Quite often we flew with the same crew members, so that also had a nice family feel to it and for me it was reminiscent of the early days with the LCA when we only had four aeroplanes and everyone knew each other. The downside of the smaller company of course is that news travels fast and if you make a bad name for yourself, then everyone gets to know about it very quickly.

This is especially true of pilots who have "CRM issues" and they will normally attract themselves a nickname from the rest of the crew. The airline industry is a hotbed for gossip and the grapevine which conducts most of the cabin crew rumours is often referred to as "Galley FM". If they are talking about you on Galley FM as "Migraine Mike" for example, because you give all the rest of your crew a headache, you know you've got a problem!

When you are applying for your first commercial piloting job, most applicants will think of aiming to get the biggest, newest, shiniest jet on their licence that they can. One thing to remember here of course is that large airliners are not built for shorthaul. They are built for long or even ultralong-haul routes where you may be away from home for long periods of time. Many are the times when I have heard pilots complaining about their roster and saying that they are away from home too much.

This is sometimes in the cruise at 37,000 feet when we are flying a widebodied twinjet on a nine or ten hour flight... I look across at them and think, *well what did you expect?* If you don't want the job, then don't apply for longhaul, it's as simple as that. It almost goes without saying that all crews moan about their roster at least some of the time and the ideal airline job for you is the one where you moan least – worth bearing in mind for later. Longhaul flying is certainly not compatible with early married life when you have babies being born and young children to care for; however it does seem to suit some pilots later in life when the kids have grown up and flown the nest.

When planning a career in the airlines in the UK, it still makes sense to apply to British Airways first and see what response you get. The reason for doing this is because you could stay with the same company throughout your whole career and adjust your lifestyle by changing your aircraft type from time to time. In reality the company will impose limits on how often you are able to do this, it could be three years or more that they freeze you on a fleet type.

Unless you enjoy and embrace 'change' in your life, then it would be most beneficial to be able to remain with the same employer, but attain a different working pattern. For example, many of the longhaul crew who operate B747s and similar aircraft out of Heathrow actually reside on the continent – some as far away as the French Riviera and even Southern Spain. Naturally they commute to work from abroad and then fly straight out of UK the next day, which from a taxation point of view can be very advantageous. This is not limited to BA, but also applies to other longhaul airlines that are based in the UK. The only word of caution here is that the rules on taxation do have a habit of changing periodically and not always in the way in which we would like to suit our own particular circumstances.

Longhaul or part-time working is the only way in which you could satisfactorily achieve a long distance commute if you have a young family (and wish to remain married). I have observed in the past what happens to pilots when they try to commute long distances while flying intensive shorthaul and the results are not pretty. It must be remembered first and foremost that it is our individual responsibility to ensure we are adequately rested before we commence a flying duty.

Also with longhaul work it is important to plan ahead and make allowances for how it will affect you. For example, there has been much research into Cosmic Radiation and the longhaul crews are the most exposed to it. Certainly the infamous 'jetlag' will be an occupational hazard (or circadian dysrhythmia as it is known by the medics) and there are strategies which can be used to combat the effects. One of the most common problems and least anticipated however is that when you return from your week long trip to the Far East or wherever and the crewbus drops you off in the staff carpark, it can sometimes take ages to find your car... Top tip; make a note on your mobile 'phone where you park it for when you get back!

I feel the need… *for Speed!*

(We remember Maverick and Goose – but would they be any use flying airliners?)

There's an old Training Captain on the circuit, Captain 'X', who still teaches pilots on Airbus and Boeing simulators, even though he has exceeded the magical age of 65. He is more than a little outspoken in his views, some of which are less than temperate and he is often to be found in confrontational situations with other members of our profession. That being said, on many occasions when the dust has settled and the protagonists have had their say, he has been proved to be right. He has an almost unshakeable resolve and total confidence in his own opinions, "Don't confuse me with the facts – my mind's made up!" He thinks at high-speed and tends to talk quickly too, often shooting from the hip without giving much consideration as to how this may sound to persons of a more sensitive nature.

It never fails to amuse me when one of our mutual colleagues relates a tale of what X did or said, when and to whom. Often I find myself chuckling, when it turns out that somebody was either offended or sincerely upset about X's occasionally ridiculous or apparently unreasonable viewpoint. Of course he is so thick skinned, that after all these contretemps he moves on immediately, but he often leaves a trail of wrath in his wake. He has been described variously as cantankerous, pugnacious or irascible and in fact on occasions he shows the traits of all three personality characteristics simultaneously. The annoying part about it is that he is so often correct in what he says – it's just the way that he comes across which gets people's backs up. He is the perfect example of why the science of Crew Resource Management (CRM) was invented.

Take for example, the vexed question of which instrument presentation is better, heading-up or track-up display? What you normally find is that some pilots will have a preference for one or the other and this is normally fostered by their background and what they have been used to flying with. Anecdotal evidence over the years convinces me that usually it is the less experienced pilots who have a strong preference for one display type.

Contrast this with the views of those aviators who have operated for many thousands of hours with different azimuth displays and who realise that both philosophies have merit. Logically speaking it matters less where the aircraft is pointing (heading), but is more important to be aware of where it is going (track). In X's mind though he is entirely convinced that "heading-up" is much the superior instrument display and happily extols the virtues at great length to all who will listen. This is at odds with my experience and for a while I was having difficulty working out why. After all, as indicated before, logically the aeroplane's track across the earth's surface is what really matters in flying and where it is pointing to achieve the track is simply a function of the effect of wind called drift...

But then it clicked for me. I suddenly realised why Captain X is such a big fan of 'heading-up' displays and has never really got used to flying 'track-up'. I also had a flash of inspiration which put all of his views and attitudes into perspective. My revelation meant that I could see exactly why he sometimes finds it difficult to fit in with the very ordered, disciplined and measured world or airline flying. You see Captain X was originally a 1960s Fighter Pilot. He was what used to be called a WIWOL, which stands for "When I Was On Lightnings".

In the same way as somebody from Texas has to tell you this in the first conversation you ever have with them, WIWOLs will always let you know about their operational type sooner rather than later. Of course the Lightning was so bloody quick and had so little endurance, there never was any drift to consider! You just pointed it in the right direction and it would arrive at where it was headed, very soon. When you have been trained to operate one of these single-seaters in your early twenties, everything else in your life will happen slower until you die – end of story.

So that's Captain X for you; a rounded peg in a square(ish) hole. There was never any drift to think about back then and he's not going to start 'drifting' now. He is quite adept at fitting in where he has to – he has had plenty of practice over the years, but in many ways he is still true to his roots. It is interesting to note that the modern fighterjocks are much less easy to spot and I think this must be a reflection on the evolution of the military's selection criteria. Whereas in the glory days of a young, virile Royal Air Force in the era of the Cold War, there was more emphasis on stick and rudder focused egotists to get the job done, more recently this has changed to needing 'team-players' with other more subtle skill-sets.

From the experience of training many ex military pilots coming to their first airline job, I have found that the younger ones are more ready to accept the multi-crew concept and eager to learn all about their new world. Broadly speaking the older fighter-pilots commonly have more deeply held prejudices about becoming 'Lardy Arse Trash Haulers' as airline pilots are sometimes colloquially referred to and this can have a detrimental effect on their readiness to learn.

Overall though, you have to say with the odd exception, the ex-military aviators make above average airline pilots in less time than it normally takes with trainees from other sources. There are two reasons for this and both are linked. Firstly the military selection, grading and training system means that only the very best applicants will manage to get through to the front line. Secondly, there is no other flying training organisation which can spend money on the same scale as the military (on behalf of the government) in their training of personnel. The sums are simply colossal and the outcome is predictable – the very best pilots in the world will be produced. To every rule there are exceptions of course and these below stick in the memory.

Years ago we had an ex fighter pilot from another nation's Air Force to train onto the B737. On paper he had plenty of hours and an armful of medals from his military career, but he took a very long time to struggle through his Line Training on the Boeing. One step forward and two steps back at every stage and there were some who thought he would never manage to achieve the required standard to be a Line First Officer. His rate of learning appeared to be very slow and at one review meeting in the training department, one of the Training Captains made the sanguine observation, "Bugger me! Those F15s must be easy to fly!" That being said and contrary to the predictions of some trainers, he finally did make the grade and was cleared to the line – we all breathed a collective sigh of relief.

This particular pilot's problem was rare however, because he was blighted by having limited spare capacity for learning, combined with a below average instrument scan and was apparently under-confident. The majority of ex-military pilots coming to the airlines are usually blessed with plenty of spare mental capacity, above average flying skills and bags of confidence. The challenge facing these candidates is one of 'adapting' to their new environment. Throughout their military training and operational phases, the emphasis has been on speed of action combined with frequently solo decision making.

I have lost count of the number of times I have heard the words "Sit on your hands and think about it..." as good advice to eager F/Os who are ready to dive into what they see as the problem and their own idea on how to fix it. Really, the emphasis is more on teamwork and sound collective decision making when it comes to problem solving in airline flying, much more so than a quick response and a snap decision...

A prime example of this is from my own training experience when I was a newbie co-pilot going through my first recurrent simulator check on the B757. Naturally being a confident sort of a chap and having had six months flying 'on the line' I was looking forward to being able to demonstrate my proficiency to the Examiner. It was on the first day and I was the handling pilot flying the 757 through the first turn after takeoff, on instruments, in cloud. Suddenly my concentration on the instrument flying was impeded by the loud ringing of the fire warning bell and red master caution lights which illuminated on the instrument panel!

I looked down to my left and on the centre console between us, the APU Fire Handle was illuminated bright red – we had indications of an APU Fire. At that time the Captain was talking to 'ATC' and looked like he was busy, so I took it upon myself to pull the fire handle and rotated it to discharge the extinguisher, immediately afterwards cancelling the fire warning system. There was then silence in the simulator and not just because I had stopped the bell ringing – the motion freeze had been activated and both of the Captains were looking at me...

"Doh!" Homer Simpson hadn't been invented in those days, but I knew how he felt when he realised he had just made a huge mistake and the family had all surrounded him to tell him exactly how stupid he had been. Basically I had broken every rule in the book of multi-crew operations. While hand-flying the aeroplane, I had (without any consultation with the aircraft Commander) taken it upon myself to diagnose the problem then to decide upon the course of action to be taken.

In so doing I then broke another cardinal rule which states that "none of the major engine controls or any of the Fire Switches shall be moved unless confirmed by BOTH pilots". The main point of all this of course is that while both pilots are conscious on the flightdeck, we should operate as a team, there can be no exceptions to this. In my previous training I had been much focused upon single seat operations and then after doing my commercial licence I was employed in a single-pilot Air Taxi operation, neither of which prepared me well for the multi-crew environment.

It may seem paradoxical in a world where we cruise around at 500+ mph all the time, but 'speed' is just what we don't need most of the time.

1985 Jet Provost T5A – A truly enjoyable aircraft – fast, powerful & very strong...

What *Really* Makes a Good First Officer?

It was once told to me that the definition of a really good First Officer, is one who says on the 'second go-around from minimums at Birmingham' – "I know a really good pub in Manchester!"

It seems there is an awful lot of misinformation out there in the ab-initio flying training world about what essential qualities should be possessed by a "Good" First Officer. Certainly the idea that a First Officer (F/O) should be so concerned about the welfare of the customers that they might be tempted to go walkabout in the cabin is a very scary thought post 9/11. As the majority of airliners are usually operated with only two flightdeck crewmembers, then it is obvious that except for the very occasional need to answer the call of nature – both of the pilots will be fulltime occupants of the cockpit. In concert with the temporary vacating of the flightdeck during flight, there is a very strict protocol to be observed by the crew to protect the integrity of the locked flightdeck door.

Another factor to be considered when leaving only one pilot on their own in the flightdeck is the possibility of sudden and catastrophic depressurisation. Rare as this occurrence may be, one of the basic tenets of our operating philosophy as professional airline crew is to constantly plan for and anticipate the worst case scenario. Thus for example, every six months in the simulator, we always rehearse for catastrophic engine failure, often with accompanying engine fire warnings, at the worst possible moment – i.e. just after Vee One speed, when we are committed to fly, at heavy weight, on takeoff in a high drag configuration.

Whenever we leave the flightdeck in flight, we always ensure that the remaining pilot is aware of the Minimum Safety Altitude so that if it is above 10,000 feet they shall be sure of levelling off from the emergency descent before they hit the mountains. If an F/O is in the initial stages of Line Training, then it is also a good idea to ask them what their first action would be in response to the 'Cabin Altitude' warning if they were alone in the cockpit. If their reply is anything other than, "Put on my oxygen mask immediately!" then we have a little tutorial about the time of useful consciousness at 35,000 feet and the effects of rapid onset hypoxia.

High altitude cruising in quiet and comfortable, modern airliner cockpits can lead crews to a false sense of security. Another common misconception is the new F/O often says something like, "...well of course once I have started the emergency descent, you'll come back in the flightdeck to take over won't you?" Wrong! During the emergency descent, the Captain is likely to be sitting in the toilet with a passenger oxygen mask on, hoping that the First Officer remembers the aircraft is over the Alps and the MSA is 18,000 feet!

Only when the descent is complete can the other pilot regain access to the front office. The tragic events of the Helios B737 accident near Athens a few years ago serve to illustrate the point exactly, where it appeared that both pilots suffered hypoxia and became unconscious, with the Captain actually being out of his seat at the time.

There are other useful qualities which must be learned by good F/Os and strangely enough keeping a record of their Captains' preferences and idiosyncrasies is not one of them. I have known some young pilots even getting to the stage of keeping a little black book of how each Captain likes to 'run their ship'. This is ridiculous, potentially hazardous and entirely at odds with the modern day philosophy of progressive CRM (Crew Resource Management).

Inexperienced First Officers would be better advised to focus on learning SOPs (Standard Operating Procedures) and ensuring that their own line operation when they are acting as PF (Pilot Flying) runs along standard lines, than trying to adapt to what they think an individual Skipper might desire. Fortunately the autocratic Captains of old are a dying breed and the current generation are much easier to work with in all respects. Good CRM nowadays depends more upon open communication between the crew, rather than junior members planning to anticipate which would be 'the next Captain's order to obey'.

There are times however when this can work in reverse to the detriment of flight safety. You could be forgiven for thinking that this situation would not be possible; however I was given evidence of it occurring only a few years ago. At the time, I was flying as a Captain on an ordinary line flight (i.e. non-training) with a relatively experienced and competent F/O. The destination, (Calvi Airport in Corsica) was something of a challenge as the narrow runway was not only pretty short for B737 operations, but it also had a dramatic slope combined with high terrain close by – there was literally only one way in and one way out.

Due to these difficulties, it was designated as a 'Captains Only Airfield' for landing and takeoff in the company's operations manual. We briefed the flight with all of this considered, including the weather which was proving less than cooperative. We agreed that the F/O would operate as PF for half of the outbound leg and then we would swap over duties in good time for me to be the PF prior to descent and for the landing. I would then be PF for the takeoff/departure, whereupon halfway back to the UK we would again change roles. This way we would both fly a landing and a takeoff in the two sectors.

It was on the ground during the turnaround however when he made the point that although I was 'sticking to the rules' not all of the Captains did so. In fact he said that some of them let the F/O carry out the takeoff, contrary to the instructions in the Ops manual. I was intrigued by this revelation and we had an in depth discussion about it – it seemed that some of the less experienced commanders felt that it was unfair on the experienced F/Os to prevent them from the pleasure of a full-power takeoff, downhill on a short runway towards the sea.

I explained that this particular restriction was there to protect both pilots and of course their passengers, with nosewheel tiller steering only being available for the left-hand seat occupant. If something went wrong on the takeoff roll and a rejection had to be carried out, valuable seconds would be lost handing over control to the left-hand seat for "the Stop". This could well make the difference between the aircraft stopping by the end of the paved surface or beyond it. And beyond it lay the blue waters of the Mediterranean...

By accepting the Captain's kind invitation to act as PF for this takeoff, the F/O was jeopardising not only the lives of all onboard, but also the careers of two professional aviators. An example which I raised was that of a technical malfunction that could occur during the takeoff roll, which might lead to a subsequent investigation by the airline management. In this situation it would likely become apparent who the operating pilot was in direct contravention of the SOPs and even though the technical issue might have been handled well by both pilots, the SOP non-conformity could end up as a disciplinary matter.

In the career of an experienced First Officer approaching Command Selection, such an event could have disastrous consequences and potentially delay their command, resulting in the loss of Captain's salary for a year or two. This is why it is incumbent upon F/Os to protect their enthusiastic and well meaning colleagues who sometimes through lack of experience make the wrong decision to allow the F/O to fly the aircraft when it is not permitted.

I recall a situation which happened years ago, while I was a pilot manager at Liverpool when we experienced early morning radiation fog – the first wave of aircraft had departed before the visibility deteriorated. At the invitation of the ATC manager, I was able to monitor the operation of LVPs (Low Visibility Procedures) from the control tower and could see our returning B737s in the radar room making their instrument approaches.

Fortunately the fog started to lift and although technically the airfield was still 'in LVPs' by the time flight XXX started down the ILS, we were above Cat 1 limits. At that time, the SOP for the Boeing fleet was for the Captain to be PF for the autoland which was a requirement following an LVP approach. But I could hear the transmissions from XXX and knew that it was the Captain who was operating the radio – implying that the F/O was flying the aircraft in contravention of the SOP. As a manager, I had a decision to make.

I decided that, all things considered, because the weather was improving so quickly, what they were doing was safe enough although against regulations - I would speak to the Captain about it later, perhaps there was some other explanation for it. When I talked to the Captain however, he confirmed that he had allowed the F/O to make the approach, even though the airfield was still technically in Low Vis Ops simply because it was the F/O's sector as PF and they had not expected the weather to prevent his landing the aircraft.

I opted for the softly, softly approach, sometimes known as 'a word to the wise'. I pointed out the reasons why the SOPs were written for the Low Vis approaches and advised him to have a think about all of the possible consequences if something had gone wrong. He said that he would do so, but I admit to being sceptical as I put down the 'phone. It was one of those moments when you think to yourself, *he didn't listen to a word I said...*

A year later and my suspicions were confirmed when I was tasked to investigate one of our flights that had made an unstable approach and low go-around in poor weather at Luton – it was the same Captain, but a different F/O. The fleet SOPs included more restrictive weather limits for F/Os making approaches as PF and on the day the cloudbase was just on the F/O's limits. The Captain had decided to let the F/O fly the approach, again 'because it was the F/O's sector', but in the subsequent formal interview admitted that he was then distracted by the thought of what would happen at the Decision Altitude if they did not break out of cloud.

He was so distracted that both pilots forgot to select landing flap (Flap 30) and continued down the ILS with Flap 20 set. The call of "Decide?" from the Captain, was answered by "Visual – landing!" by the F/O which coincided with him taking the autopilot out and simultaneously the configuration warning horn blaring out!

The aircraft wobbled and drifted high on the visual profile as the Captain slammed the flap lever home to the Flap 30 gate. Realising their predicament, fortunately he had the wherewithal to shout "GO-AROUND!" while whizzing the flap lever back up to the Flap 20 position. The second approach and landing, flown from the left-hand seat was without incident. To his credit, when I was sent to Glasgow to interview him about the incident, he was the first to raise the subject of our conversation of a year earlier. He was full of remorse for what had taken place and finally I think he understood what I had been trying to tell him.

It was a shame he hadn't listened properly in the first place, however if his F/Os on both those occasions had been playing the game then they would have politely declined his kind offer to imperil their careers.

It reminds me of the old joke about childhood development. It matters less how we behave as kids, it's all about how we bring up our parents – think about it.

Arrival in Jaipur, me and Captain Doug Knights –
you wouldn't believe we had been up all night ...well maybe you would

The Art of Touch.

(Body language is a giveaway. Study it).

If you Google 'Art of Touch' on the internet, you will find many references to websites focusing on exotic massage. Fascinating though these may be, they are not relevant to airline flying and the interaction of the crew, well not at work anyway. What we are discussing here is an examination of the body language and Human Factors elements exhibited by airline crew in the execution of their duties. That phrase, 'execution of their duties' is a very formal expression and is itself an indicator of the highly regulated world in which we operate. What is not so easily understood perhaps by pilots new to the profession are some of the unwritten rules and less obvious codes of conduct which govern how we behave at work.

Some of these rules have been in existence since the very early days of commercial air operations and often reflect the much talked about 'chain of command'. In other words, despite modern CRM (Crew Resources Management) teaching that tends to blur the rank barriers, there is still a pecking order which is observed by crews when they meet outside the flightdeck. This is most easily noted when all crew members are in uniform and therefore the rank of each crewmember is clearly evident. In the simple case of two sets of pilots meeting with each other, the Captains will often greet the other Captain first prior to greeting the First Officer of the other crew. In the case of the F/O, the reverse is true and they in turn will shake hands with their opposite number on the other crew. Note that a handshake is usual, although there are cultural differences all over the world and in certain countries of course it is common to be more demonstrative. I think it is safe to say that it is probably not a good idea if you have just joined a British airline as a new F/O to greet your fellow male co-worker with a big bear hug and kisses on both cheeks...

If it is the opposite sex however, then it is quite normal for male and female pilots who are on friendly terms to demonstrate more than just a handshake, but it is important not to be over-familiar. Kissing on the cheek and an upper body hug is fine whereas kissing on the lips is not. Experience of the manner in which crew greet and touch each other in socially acceptable ways can only really be gained by practice. Of course in the early days of aviation, female pilots were few and far between and even now they are a rare sight in some companies.

I will always recall when working on the Airline TV series and I was training a female F/O (Georgie Hobbs), we had hidden cameras inside the Flightdeck of the 737 while we flew. On the TV programme where Georgie carried out her crosswind landing in Amsterdam, there was a point after shutdown on the ramp when the cameras recorded that we kissed/embraced across the centre console... To many of our colleagues this might have seemed to be a little over-familiar for just another sector, however in reality this piece of film came from another flight some days later when I had just informed her that she had passed her Final Line Check – it was on the ground in Malaga! Who says the camera never lies?

I was amused afterwards though when the film crew producer seemed to be very pleased with the footage and I think this may have been the first time ever that airline pilots have been seen kissing in uniform on the telly. Not a bad result from his point of view. Georgie was an excellent pilot, an above average trainee and just for the record our relationship was entirely proper in all respects. The same could not be said however of a male Captain and a female F/O in another airline where I worked. The poor old 757 Fleet Manager had his work cut out for him when he received a stream of complaints from the Cabin Crew that Captain X and First Officer Y, (who were often rostered to fly together) had started 'locking' the flightdeck door from the inside. This was in the days when routinely the flightdeck door was left unlocked – you could almost say it was a more innocent time.

The word 'innocent' would probably be inappropriate to describe the working relationship of these two professional aviators however, as the Cabin Crew's main complaint was that when they finally gained access to the cockpit, they were made to feel like they had "invaded somebody's private boudoir"! The mind boggles. The Fleet Manager's instruction to the rostering department prevented them flying together in the future and there was never any incident therefore which could have arisen as a result of unorthodox behaviour at work.

Apart from accidentally brushing against each other, we males do not normally touch each other in the course of operating on the flightdeck together. In fact if we do accidentally touch the other pilot's hand or vice versa, the feeling is something of a shock and often an apology is made. As a Training Captain however it is part of my job to make sure that the trainee remembers what I tell them especially if the message is an important one. A good example is when an inexperienced F/O under training, while landing the B757 at Orlando in Florida slid his throttle hand forward and grabbed hold of the thrust reversers. A usual action for the operating pilot one would say, except the important and dangerous part of this was the fact that we were still *airborne* in the landing flare!

I deliberately placed my right hand firmly on top of his and held it there so that he could not deploy the reversers until **after** the main gear had touched down. Needless to say I explained in detail after the event the reasons why I had done so and the grave importance of **not** attempting to select reverse while airborne. I do not think he will forget the incident and I am sure he will not develop this bad habit – I just hope he does not doubt my intentions either...

In the simulator also, touch can be used to emphasise reassurance to pilots who occasionally get it wrong. A comradely pat on the shoulder from the instructor is useful to remind the trainee that we are all human – it says, "Look here's the human touch", literally. The message is one of empathy and sincerity, it says, "I know how you feel chum and I have done the same myself". Often accompanied by, the verbal "let's try that again shall we?" Very occasionally you come across a story which involves inappropriate touching while at work with the airlines. Like the B737 Captain who had a habit of smacking First Officers with the back of his hand while they were airborne if they incurred his displeasure.

The reason that I became acquainted with this particular story was because a type-rated recruit from an Irish airline relayed it to us during his interview to join a low-cost airline that employed me at Luton some years ago. Naturally we were able to assure him that he was unlikely to experience similar poor CRM techniques with his new employer. Apparently the senior Captain was renowned in the company for his behaviour and it even resulted in F/Os threatening to hit him back if he did it again.

Inappropriate touch by a crew member on the ground was exemplified back in the early '90s in the UK during a very busy summer typified by long ATC slot delays. On one such occasion and after significant verbal abuse and under extreme provocation by a male passenger in the departure lounge, the incensed First Officer threw a punch which knocked the punter off his feet!

Needless to say the F/O was arrested by the airport police, charged with assault and lost his job, but there were many crew members who sympathised with his position. It should be noted that as in all industries, physical violence is not acceptable at work and assault of any kind constitutes Gross Misconduct that will likely result in Summary Dismissal.

Which reminds me of the time when I was a Pilot Manager for a great number of pilots; in a previous existence, as they say. Like all managers, most of my time was taken up with very few people and these I referred to in private as my 'Troublesome Parishioners' (or TP for short). One of the Captains in particular was always ready to come into the office and complain to me at high volume about all manner of things that were wrong with the company, the job, the rostering, the crew, the airport, the aircraft, you name it, he'd complain about it.

At times he used to get himself so wound up that he would literally start to rant at the top of his voice, often with his nose only a few inches away from mine. As I was the manager, he saw ME as part of the problem and he believed that I should be fixing it all for him. Well I have to say that we as a company had spent a lot of time and effort trying to accommodate this particular gentleman although to hear him shout, you would think we had done nothing.

As we had an open office policy at this company, nothing was secret in the base office, especially as Captain X would tackle me head on, standing toe to toe in the middle of the room. Of course as one of my TPs, he had also been involved in many adverse incidents with crew, crewing, operations staff, handling agents, passengers and we had almost exhausted the disciplinary process, but he was still employed.

As he appeared to enjoy confrontation with his aggressive manner, I adopted the policy of arguing forcefully on behalf of the company, mainly because a lot of what he came out with was pure subjective bull**** and somebody needed to let him know the truth. The other staff in the office started to get concerned for my personal safety however, when this strategy resulted in him getting more and more angry. The Base Office Manager said,

"One of these days he's going to punch you when he gets all steamed up like that, you need to be careful..." This was after a particularly nasty incident when Captain X had blown his top at me once again in front of everybody.

I looked across from my desk and replied with a mischievous smile and a wink "Oooh, do you REALLY think so...?"

A Figure of Speech.

(Careful what you say and how you say it).

People often assume that because we are airline crews and fly all over the world, then we must be fluent in several languages, such is not the case. Whenever I am asked this, I often jokingly reply that I am only fluent in English, but I can say "Fill 'er up!" in 23 different languages, while talking to the refuellers. The truth is that in reality, it's all about getting the message across and if you can do that with some smatterings of the local lingo and plenty of sign language your job is done.

Often hand signals are the only way in which we can communicate with the ground crews when pushing back or starting engines with a big airliner and therefore it is very important to know which signals to use. The international signal for "Fire!" for example from a marshaller on the ground, is the waving of his hand in a horizontal figure of eight, but surprisingly few of our colleagues seem to know this one. In fact when recruiting pilots for a low-cost airline based at Luton, this was one of our standard questions which is why I am aware of how few professional aviators know the sign. In response to the question, "How can you tell from the marshaller that the aircraft is on fire?" the most common reply was, "When I see him sprinting away at high speed in a state of panic..."

Even though we are trained to communicate with the ground crew via hand-signals, sometimes you cannot beat verbal or audible communication. It is often the case however that to make yourself heard in the noisy environment of the ramp outside the terminal it is usually necessary to shout. The ambient noise levels of this area of the airport are very loud indeed, with air conditioning packs running, airliners pushing back, starting jet engines and the incessant whistling of APUs running.

In the past when trying to expedite the turnround and to let the handling agent know we are ready for passengers, I have found one of the quickest methods on the 737, is to open the flightdeck DV (Direct Vision) window, lean out and give a piercing whistle across the apron. As the handling agent then turns towards us, the universally accepted sign of thumbs up, normally does the trick and pax boarding soon commences.

Talking of DV windows being opened to call the ground staff, reminds me of the time some years ago when the Fleet Manager was travelling back with his young family from their holiday to the Greek islands on one of our airline's 757s. It was the middle of a busy summer of ATC slot delays and many pilots had been working to their maximum hours for months. It was night-time and the main cabin doors had all been closed for some time, in anticipation of engine starting, but nothing was happening.

The Fleet Manager was sat in the forward part of the cabin in row 6 with all the other passengers and could see that the flightdeck door was ajar. This was pre 9/11 of course when the flightdeck door was routinely left open until the cabin had been secured. All of a sudden the Fleet Manager (along with others in the cabin) became aware of a growling, impatient noise emanating from the cockpit, then the unmistakeable sound of the DV window being wound open in a hurried fashion. Much to the embarrassment of the rest of the crew, the clearly audible voice of the operating Captain then came wafting back through the open door with the shouted words, *"LISTEN ****! YOU DO YOUR JOB AND I'LL DO MINE – ALRIGHT!?"*

It appeared that the message was effectively communicated, as very shortly afterwards the engines were started and an uneventful return flight to the UK was carried out. I believe the Manager had a quiet word with the skipper the following day, advising on the potentially negative PR value of such behaviour. No I was not that skipper.

When it comes to PA announcements, the number of stories regarding who said what and when is legendary. Like the famous PA made by one pilot welcoming people to New Zealand many years ago with the words, "Ladies and gentlemen, if you want to know the local time - you can put your watches back twenty years!" Unfortunately for him a senior official of the NZ tourist board was travelling in the cabin and did not see the funny side.

Similar complaints were made on one of the airline military trooping flights, when after climbing out from one of the remote island bases, staffed mainly with males, the Captain mischievously made the PA announcement, "...so all you Island *Princesses* who were SO beautiful yesterday, must realise that you are all now OFFICIALLY UGLY again!" He got into big trouble for that one.

On a serious note though, there is much damage that can be wrought by controversial or risqué comments on the PA and it is important for pilots to realise the potential for dropping themselves in it. I learned my lesson many years ago on a flight to Denver from Bangor Maine USA. When flying long sectors at high altitudes, the atmosphere inside our aluminium tubes becomes very dry indeed. It is common for us all to use moisturiser to protect our facial skin and this particular morning I had run out.

While waiting for the passengers to arrive, I asked the rest of the crew if any of them had any neutral (i.e. non-perfumed) moisturiser I could have a quick squirt of. The message came back that one of the cabin crew at the back of the aircraft had some, so I left the Captain up at the front and trotted down the aisle to the rear galley. Angela was on one of her last flights as she had just found out she was pregnant, but fortunately for me, she had some spare moisturiser which I gladly rubbed all over my face.

Later on while flying to Denver, word came through on the intercom from the Senior Cabin Crew Member in the forward galley (a funny lady called Di), that the stuff I had so gladly smeared all over my face on the turnround was not really facial moisturiser, but was "Nipple Anti-Stretch Cream and all the cabin crew think it's hilarious!" My cheeks burned, despite the anti-stretching agent, at the thought of being the butt of the cabin crew's jokes, but I was determined to put a brave face on it.

As it was my sector, I was making the PA announcements and thought it would be amusing to tell the passengers what a trick had been played on me by the girls down the back. I told the passengers all about being so grateful when Angela had offered me some moisturiser and then I said I felt a bit queasy when I found out that it was Nipple Anti-Stretch Cream used by expectant mothers. I didn't think any harm could come from telling a joke against myself and from the laughter in the forward cabin, I thought it had gone down well. Shortly afterwards, Di called the flightdeck on the intercom again and asked to come in to see us.

She came in and sat down on one of the jumpseats and said that she had received a complaint from a passenger about my PA which mentioned women's bodily parts! I was astounded, but she went on to say that this gentleman had pushed the cabin crew call bell as soon as I had finished my little speech to say that he and his wife were very religious and felt it offensive that I should have made this announcement, he demanded that I make another PA to apologise.

Now I felt bad and the Captain didn't help. When I looked over at him and asked what I should do, he said that I should sort it out myself and he was not involved. Well, I was not going to make another PA to apologise and look really stupid, but I was genuinely concerned that perhaps I had upset somebody, so I asked her to invite him to come and see us – ahh those were the days, when we could have visitors to the flightdeck.

This rather earnest looking young gent came in and I did my best to mollify him, apologising for any offence which my little joke had caused to him and his wife. He suggested again that I make a public apology, but I countered with the fact that the majority of passengers had seen it as funny and did not believe this would be necessary. Eventually after I had virtually exhausted all my diplomatic skills, he went back to his seat and we continued on towards Colorado. I felt miffed that anyone could be so stuffy and was very careful with my announcements on the PA after that – no jokes.

The return flight was uneventful, although I had to put up with all the girls taking the mickey out of me about how I had upset the religious set on the way out. Finally the whole embarrassing saga was over and we were off duty back in the hotel – time for a couple of drinks to wind down after the flight, so we all ended up in one of the cabin crew's rooms. "Well, what shall we drink to?" said I in a loud voice, just thankful that we had not received a written complaint, yet.

The girls all seemed to be in an unusually cheerful mood and Di with a twinkle in her eye said,

"Why not let us drink a toast to... the most gullible First Officer in the fleet!?" At which point there was a chorus of,

"THE MOST GULLIBLE FIRST OFFICER IN THE FLEET!" and they all fell about laughing hysterically.

For the second time in a day, I felt my cheeks burning with shame as I realised I had been conned. It was all a complete wind up and apparently the gentleman passenger was put up to it by Di as a joke. Peter, the Captain had also been in on the act, because while Di had been talking to me she had shown him her other hand behind her back, upon which was written, "IT'S ALL A JOKE!"

I recalled how he spent much of the time looking out of his window for the rest for the flight, especially when the passenger came in and I was trying to talk my way out of it - I didn't realise he was trying not to laugh.

I still smile when I think back to that day and their cheerful faces in that hotel room in Bangor Maine, but it certainly made me more careful about my PAs to the cabin after that. This is especially true if you are going to try and make a public address in a foreign language, or even part of one.

There was a Captain in Easyjet who made the mistake of trying to greet the Spanish passengers from Madrid in their own tongue, but it did not have the desired effect when they came out with, "Ladies and Gentlemen. Buenos Aires, welcome onboard this Easyjet flight to Luton!" Fortunately a positioning Easyjet First Officer was travelling in the cabin and witnessed the mirth with which this attempt at linguistics was received.

In the same company at about that time, there was an attempt to standardise the PA announcements from the flightdeck by the publication of a 'Guide to PA Announcements'. This was handed out to all the crews, but unfortunately to those of us who had already been flying for many years, it told us nothing new.

In fact it became the subject of much derision on the line as it was over the top patronising in tone at times. For example, it criticised the practice of referencing "the present position of the aircraft" to a little town called Limoges in central France. The reason that this town was allegedly used so frequently by the crews was because the waypoint and VOR beacon with the three letter code LMG, is at a significant junction of several airways. *'Do **not** mention Limoges'.*

Sadly, (and maybe predictably) this backfired. Many of the experienced pilots felt that they had been patronised by the supercilious tone of the PA booklet, so the actual mentioning of the small town, famous for its artisans producing some very fine blown glassware increased that summer.

Many was the time when I would be flying with a pilot that had just made a PA, who then finished and turned to me to say in a Basil Fawlty voice,

"I mentioned Limoges... *but I think I got away with it!"*

Even when we were nowhere near that area of France and had already informed the passengers we were passing just to the west of Paris, we were in the habit of adding, that's approximately 200 miles North of Limoges!

Well it kept us amused that year anyway. The moral of the story is, as a pilot manager, you really should be careful what you publish to the line crews.

Uncontrolled Flight Into Terrain (U.F.I.T.)

(So many examples of accidents to choose from here. Pilot Flying? STAY focussed!)

The term Controlled Flight Into Terrain (CFIT) was coined by Boeing engineers back in the 1970s to describe the phenomenon of accidents involving serviceable aircraft which fly into the ground. The humorous expressions "rock-filled clouds" or "Cumulogranitus" (an amalgamation of Cumulus cloud and Granite rock) are sometime heard when people in the industry discuss the subject of CFIT. As aircraft design, engineering and maintenance has improved vastly over the past decades, so increasingly the statistics show that airliner accidents are more often caused by human factors errors. This is what used to be known as Pilot Error and a significant group of these occurrences have been described as CFIT.

Often the human factors scenario leads to a loss of Situational Awareness by the flightcrew, such that they do not comprehend the dangerous situation in which the aircraft is in until it is too late. More recently however there have been several accidents where ostensibly serviceable airframes have flown themselves into the ground in apparently inexplicable circumstances. These I suggest are evidence of a growing trend where the aircraft are lost when nobody is actually in control of the flightpath; these are UFIT accidents where the aircraft is actually not being controlled effectively by either pilot.

Let's get back to basics. Take the simplest situation where we have a crew of two pilots on the flightdeck of most modern airliners. They are now doing the jobs of five crew in previous times when there were additionally a navigator, radio operator and flight engineer in the cockpit. Through advances in technology with automated systems, it has been possible to reduce the tasks of five down to two, but this relies upon the two remaining pilots following standard operating procedures (SOPs) to share the management of the workload and ensure that the safety of the flight is not compromised at any stage. Thus, normally they will fly leg and leg about. One pilot operates as PF (Pilot Flying) while the other acts as monitoring pilot (PM) and then they will swap roles for the next sector. Even the ways in which they communicate with each other has been preordained and the "SOP Calls" are essential tools of the trade for the airline pilot.

The philosophy is simple, PF 'calls' what he does and PM calls what he 'sees'. In practice it works well as a system for keeping both pilots 'in the loop' and strong adherence to following SOPs has long been advocated as a prime measure to promoting good Situational Awareness. For example, on landing PF might call "Manual braking" as he applies the wheel brakes, but PM cannot see this, until the 'Autobrake Disarm' light illuminates, whereupon they will say "Autobrakes Disarmed". On occasions the autobrakes have deselected themselves on landing without the PF intending them to do so and at those times the call from PM "Autobrakes Disarmed" becomes a cautionary warning that they have failed to operate as expected.

The Turkish Airlines B737 accident at Amsterdam Schiphol is a good example of what appears to be a serviceable airliner hitting the ground without intervention from the pilots. Of course it is early days in the investigation of this accident and not all the facts are known, but there is enough information to say that none of the pilots on the flightdeck appeared to be 'in control' of the flightpath. If they were, then they would not have allowed the airspeed to decay to such a dangerous degree due to the actions of the automatic pilot and autothrottle system. Apparently the Captain's Radio Altimeter appears to have developed a fault, (showing close to the ground while still at 1000 plus feet) which lead the automatics to believe that it was time to land the aeroplane – hence close the throttles and raise the nose into the flare. Despite this occurring, the PF should have overridden the automatics and took direct control of the power and attitude to continue safe flight. Why this did not occur will presumably be central to the investigation from here on in – quite likely the Radalt failure distracted them from flying the aircraft. It appears that one of the pilots did take action eventually, but too late to prevent the aircraft hitting the ground.

Taking the premise now that this accident occurred when the aircraft flew into the ground due to nobody being in control we can look at other occasions in a similar way. In 2007 there was another B737 accident in Indonesia, this time the operator was Adam Air and the flight was 574. It was night-time, they were at 35,000 feet (FL350) and there was a failure of one of the Inertial Reference Systems (IRSs). The resulting NTSB accident report states that "both pilots became engrossed in identifying the problem" to the detriment of monitoring the flightpath. At one point when they switched to Attitude mode, it appears that the autopilot was deselected which neither of the pilots noticed. The Digital Flight Data Recorder (DFDR) shows that recovery from the unusual attitude was only attempted when the aircraft had rolled to 100° from the vertical and the nose was pitched 60° down. There was then a major structural failure as the airspeed and manoeuvring loads exceeded the design limitations of the aircraft, but only a minute or so earlier the airliner had been almost completely serviceable.

Perhaps one of the most extreme examples of UFIT (which was classified as CFIT) was that of Eastern Air Lines Flight 401 in December 1972. This was a Lockheed Tristar L1011 which flew into the ground in Florida on a flight to Miami. At the time the flightcrew, two pilots and a Flight Engineer were distracted by a failure of the landing gear indicator bulb which had blown. They believed that the autopilot had been engaged and the First Officer had been nominated as the PF, however it seems that he was drawn into the discussion/problem solving of the blown bulb. None of the crew noticed that the aircraft was descending gently towards the swamp, as it was night and they had all failed to note the ground proximity warning. This was America's first wide-bodied hull-loss accident and at the time caused the most loss of lives – 101.

Helios's ill fated B737 crash of 2005 could also qualify for the category of UFIT, as when it hit the ground close to Athens on 14th August there was effectively no-one in control of the flightpath. At the time, this was a most mysterious loss as it appeared that the aircraft had flown on its intended route and flightplan until running out of fuel. As always there was more than just one factor involved and this was a classic Swiss cheese accident in many ways, but had the PF intervened at an early stage to level the aircraft at or below 10,000 feet during the climb, then it would have been no more than a 'pressurisation incident'. Once again however there was a major distraction which degraded the PF's performance at controlling the flightpath and in this case it was the Altitude Warning Horn.

Without doubt, 'Automation Complacency' is one of the root causes of this modern phenomenon of UFIT accidents and in fact it is exhibited by many of the crews that we see coming to the simulator. An example is the PF who sits there with his hands on his knees and often with his feet flat on the cockpit floor watching the autopilot 'fly' the aircraft. In times gone by, companies used to insist in writing that PF covered the flying controls and thrust levers with their hands and feet at all times below Minimum Safe Altitude (MSA) in cloud (IMC). These days it seems that Flight Operations departments of some operators see less of a need to emphasise that job one of the PF is to 'Fly the aircraft'.

There has been a distinct but subtle change in the demographic make-up of pilots recruited into commercial aviation over the past decade. This has partly resulted from the average airline CEO's obsession with 'low-cost' especially where training is concerned, but also it is due to the lack of ex-military pilots. The much vaunted peace dividend which was the inevitable fall-out of the end of the cold war meant that nations could reduce the numbers of military trained pilots in their armed forces. These pilots were trained when money was no object and their inclusion in the intake for the airlines was always a flight safety asset that was never fully recognised. Add their loss to the fact that commercial pilot training has been carried out 'down to a price' for the past ten years, as companies shrug off the onus of funding onto the trainee and the current situation is predictable.

There is a way forward. Commercial Pilot training needs to be completely revamped and the MPL (Multicrew Pilot Licence) is only part of the answer. This is understandable really because cost is the main reason for the existence of the MPL. Cost to the airlines and cost to the trainees – it is popular from both angles. They (the companies) have justified it from the point of view that it trains pilots in a focused manner for their job as First Officers on jet transport aeroplanes and this holds true to a degree, but it's not the whole story.

Pilots still have to be able to sense when their piloting skills are required to keep the operation safe and if the perceived growing trend of UFIT accidents continue, this is obviously not happening. Pilot training should include plenty of real flying in aeroplanes and even maybe a course in basic aerobatics. I can hear the health and safety lobby's protest starting even now – but remember this could be done in a simulator. Finally there should be a specially designed section of the MPL simulator course which is focused on loss of situational awareness scenarios. In a similar way in which we use windshear profiles in the simulator to get pilots to recognise the warning signs, so too should they be put through some of the UFIT accidents right up to the point where they could make the difference.

Without wishing to add to AAIB's workload, I suggest that it would be beneficial to re-examine the accidents which might qualify as UFIT over the past 30 years or so and then to use this information to re-evaluate the way in which we are training our flightpath controllers.

"Try not to crash...?"

(Such good advice on the face of it and perhaps it should be Rule No 1?)

The engineer looked at me and smiled. "Try not to crash", was all he said as I let the brakes off and the heavily laden B767 started to roll forward under the application of power. As I lined the aircraft up on the centreline, of runway 03 Left I knew this was going to be a difficult takeoff. Johannesburg is 5600 feet above sea level, where the air is much thinner and therefore takeoff performance is more limiting. Add that to the fact that we were close to the maximum takeoff weight of 186 tonnes and the outside air temperature gauge was reading 40 degrees Celsius. Oh and I nearly forgot, we were expecting Windshear on departure. On the face of it, the engineer's words seemed like good advice.

Windshear is one of nature's little tricks which can ruin your whole day when you fly aeroplanes for a living. The effects of rapidly shifting wind speed and direction during takeoff or landing can produce large and sudden deviations in airspeed that are difficult to counteract. Quite often associated with adverse weather systems like thunderstorms, these shifts in wind speed are hard to predict as they are invisible until you fly into them. Unfortunately there is much reliance upon PIREPS (pilot reports) and these are not necessarily authentic indicators of real Windshear conditions. One man's Windshear is another man's turbulence.

I recall many years ago when flying a light, propeller driven aircraft into an airfield that the flying conditions on final approach were certainly sporty, however no worse than moderately turbulent. Looking at the windsock, it was not difficult to see why, as it was in agreement with the Met man's prediction of a strong and gusty wind. While taxiing in to the apron, I was amused to hear the pilot who was now on final approach transmitting to the tower, "Tower, this is XXX, be advised there is VERY SEVERE WINDSHEAR on finals!" His voice had a certain breathless quality to it and he had obviously just given himself a big fright, but his PIREP was a little over the top. In fact there are only two types of Windshear to be reported, either moderate or severe. There is nothing worse than "severe" – so VERY is not an option.

As the 767 gathered speed, I noted that the acceleration was slow, even though full power was applied and the significant speed of 80 knots seemed to take ages to appear. At this rate, it was going to take a week to get to rotate speed. Due to the heavyweight takeoff, the Vr was pretty huge at 160 knots and our takeoff roll was going to require most of the runway to get airborne. The call of "Vee One" came and went. In my own thoughts I said to myself, *there's no going back now...* we were committed to fly.

The thrust levers were hard up against the throttle stops and the N1 (power) gauges of both engines were showing maximum, I could see the end of the runway approaching and thought *this is going to be close...* "ROTATE!" I had already started to increase the back pressure on the control column and now it felt REALLY heavy. I could sense the nosegear unstick and see the pitch attitude increasing - the end of the paved surface was really close now.

The call, "Positive Climb", came when we were only 20 feet off the ground with both the Radio Altimeter and the VSI showing a climb.
"Gear Up!" I replied through tightly pursed lips and then I saw the airspeed start to decay. The synthetic voice started calling "WINDSHEAR! WINDSHEAR!" and the red warning captions displayed on the attitude indicators. I noted that we had barely made 150 feet on the radalt when the Windshear warning started as the airspeed dropped and dropped – I held the attitude close to the Pitch Limit Indicators (PLIs) and hoped for the best. Brief stickshaker warnings showed we were very close to the stall, but now the radalt started decreasing and outside the flightdeck windows I could see the ground getting awfully close.

The pressure from my right arm forcing the thrust levers forward increased, but the engines were already giving their all. The GPWS warnings added their voice to the proceedings with an American accent, "DON'T SINK... DON'T SINK!" Again, good advice I mused while scanning the radalt, airspeed and VSI all at once. 38 feet was the lowest number I saw on the radio altimeter before we finally began to climb again and the airspeed started to behave itself. Eventually we were accelerating and passing 500 feet on the radalt – sheer luxury! Soon we could start retracting the flaps. Phew! Only THIRTY EIGHT FEET! It was time to make a decision.
"Let's go back and have another go - that was too close to call it a success".

I had made my mind up and the engineer working the simulator instructor panel pressed the motion freeze button. Of course that's the beauty of the "Sim", it allows us to live and fight another day when in the real case we might be toast. You could be forgiven for thinking that we were 'playing' here, but there was a real reason for our presence in the simulator.

I had been asked to come and help the engineers calibrate the windshear settings for the machine as in the recent CAA annual approval test-flight they had been pronounced as too extreme and in some cases 'unsurvivable'. This came as no surprise to me as many of the scenarios installed in the programme of the simulator are based on real accidents where the aircraft and all on board were lost in the accident which followed. They were denoted Dallas, Tokyo, Philadelphia etc.

In my discussions with the engineers, they told me that the Training Captains of old, made sure there was little chance of the crews surviving the simulated windshear by using the 100% option on the selection panel. Apparently their reasoning here was that the crews would be scared of going anywhere near windshear situations and therefore they would fly safer. In the modern way of training professional pilots this is known as 'negative training' and is definitely at odds with current thinking, hence the CAA finding fault with a machine which emulates unsurvivable scenarios.

The philosophy now runs with the principle of allowing crews to fly into a windshear event and then by using the correct flying techniques to keep the shiny side up, fly safely away from the ground again. In the simulated takeoff from Jo'burg, we had survived, but only just and we needed to have a little more of a comfort factor here. To prove it, I flew the departure twice more, using the recommended technique and the aircraft collided with the ground on both occasions – just about in the same position where I had missed it by 38 feet on the first one.

By a clever tweak in the software, it was possible to experience windshear on takeoff, but survive. Don't get me wrong here, the dramatic effects of the 'shear close to the ground were still there, but by rigid adherence to the recommendations of the manufacturer in the Flight Crew Training Manual we had climbed away safely. You would still not describe this as 'a walk in the park', as some of the pitch attitudes required feel and look quite extreme, but Mr Boeing as always is there to help us with the little yellow (amber) PLIs on the attitude indicators.

The aim is to select an attitude where the small black wingbars of the aircraft, sit on the bottom of the yellow eyebrows and despite some transient stickshaker indications with full power engaged, this will give you the best rate of climb. The technique benefits from practice of course, because normally when we pilots are alerted by the 'shaker, our response is to push forward out of the aerodynamic stall – at such low altitudes this is not an option... The houses get awfully big, awfully quickly.

It is amazing how time passes when you are having fun and soon four hours had been consumed while we explored all of the listed windshear events on the instructor screen. Some of them, we deleted as they were of nil training value, for example when they produced such a minor airspeed excursion, that there was nothing to confirm a windshear was present.

There were a few which were toned down in severity and all were checked under the worst possible conditions. For example during the approaches, we made certain the aircraft was at or close to maximum landing weight with high ambient temperature and a high elevation airfield.

If all the foregoing proves nothing else, it shows that the authorities are working in the right way to improve training facilities and techniques to enable airline crew to benefit from the experience of flying the simulator every six months during their recurrent checks in a modern, progressive environment.

It is not often that we get time to meet and work with the simulator engineers and I was pleased to be able to take part in some really interesting flying exercises which stretched my poling abilities beyond the norm for some time. In the real world there have been a few occasions when we have delayed our departure until the thunderstorm which has been hovering in the overhead of the airfield has moved away.

The recent simulator experience I had will not make me any keener to get airborne in such difficult weather conditions.

After all as the old saying goes, "it is **always** better to be down here wishing you were up there, than the other way round!"

Have some Respect.

(Learning from the mistakes of others is healthier, but don't forget the departed).

Some time ago I completed a CRM Instructors course as a 'Trainee Instructor' and I was quite proud to achieve the qualification of CRMI (G) – the brackets G bit stands for 'Groundschool'. It's funny, but no matter what experience you have gained in flying aeroplanes as a profession and regardless of how many airlines you have worked for, when you are back in the classroom again with your colleagues as 'delegates' on a formal learning course, all of a sudden you are back at school in short trousers. We often say in our industry that "Flying's a great leveller" and it's true. I have lost count of the number of pilots who tell me that when they have moved to another company, the chap who was their First Officer at 'a previous outfit' is now the Chief Pilot and this is often accompanied by a whole host of reasons why (in their humble opinion) they are not suitable for the job. In this situation, the old maxim applies, "Be careful who you s*** on, on your way up.... because they will do the same to you on the way down!"

Yes, ours is a small industry in many ways, although the instance of your Chief Pilot at the next company having only recently served as your First Officer in your last is a perfect example of how it is possible to leave your past behind when you move companies. It really is possible to reinvent yourself, or rather to start afresh and wipe the slate clean. I remember when I had a change of company some years ago. When I got to the new airline, I was very surprised to see whom they had employed as pilots before my arrival. Looking into the pilots' dropfile drawer in the crewroom made me gasp when I read the surnames along the top of the folders. "Mmmm.... some of the usual suspects here" I muttered and closed the drawer again quickly. There were pilots whom I knew for a fact had been dismissed from their previous employer for incompetence and/or underperformance at flying airliners and yet, here they were again, not only flying the same type for a new operator, but also in management and training positions! Very strange.

But, what has this all got to do with CRM? I hear you ask. Well I will tell you. During the CRM Instructors course, we the delegates, studied in detail many of the accident reports which had human factors playing a large part in the sequence of events which led up to the final result. During our research it became apparent that some of the key players had 'previous form' as Inspector Morse would say, with one of the most shocking accidents being that of a Falcon business jet which crashed, in I think, February of this year while making an approach to land at a high altitude airport in Switzerland. The Captain was a very experienced pilot who had recorded many thousands of hours in his logbook. However the weather conditions were extreme and it was clear from the accident report that they should not have attempted to land. Sadly, both of the crew were killed in the crash, the aircraft broke up on landing and the one passenger, a businessman who owned the aircraft, was severely injured.

When you saw the accident site photos, it was clear that the cloud was very low, visibility was poor, it had been snowing heavily (was still snowing) and the airport is surrounded by high terrain. The delegate on the course who made the presentation of the accident to us was actually a personal friend of the co-pilot who died and in fact it has been his job to break the sad news to the man's widow on that fateful day. Even more shocking than this, the delegate revealed that the Falcon commander had also been in command of another aircraft which had been written off in a landing accident in the Alps some years previously. In essence, the Learjet Air Ambulance which he had been flying at that time tried to land halfway down a short runway at an Austrian military base at too high an airspeed with a tailwind and had run off the end – both the crewmembers had survived. As if this was not enough, the Austrian Regulatory Authorities were highly critical of the operational standards of the Operator and way in which the flight had been conducted. At that time, the Captain was in his early sixties and you would have thought he might retire. In fact some of us made the comment that he was in the wrong job in the first place, but it was a bit late for that. Remember, if you change your company, you can leave your past behind.

For those of us still living however, there are lessons to be learned from all of these accidents and perhaps just as many from incidents which have happened when we have been flying. The course delegates themselves produced many examples from their own flying careers of "The Wrong Stuff" and it was clear that some of us had had lucky escapes in the past. The real point of the course though was for us not only to hone our skills at presenting case studies, but also to engage with our future trainees and facilitate the learning process. We CRMIs are not so much teachers, but more mentors and conduits through whom others can communicate their own message for the benefit of the group. The statistics tell a grim tale. When you analyse commercial aviation accidents from the past 30 years or so, three out of every four of them involve some sort of human factors element or CRM breakdown, which is just horrifying. What is even more shocking is the attitude which is still prevalent among some of the more experienced crew members in our industry: that CRM is somebody else's problem and 'it won't happen to me'. This we have got to change.

In many cases there is an 'error chain' involved which precedes the ultimate disaster and as has been proven by scientific experiment, if you break the chain by removing only one of the elements, the whole sequence of events ends there. I saw a case of this only recently when I was carrying out a Line Check on an experienced crew. Now, as a flightdeck jumpseat occupant, I am acutely aware that I am not part of the legally nominated crew. As such, my status is that of interested observer, but I am not involved in the decision making in the cockpit and I must be very careful what I say. The reason for this is that if I were to have undue influence on what occurs then I could at a later stage (during the debrief) be accused of interfering, which could have a distracting affect and possibly a negative outcome. This particular crew were old hands at flying the 767 and as they made their descent and approach into Kuwait International Airport at night, I was quite relaxed in the darkness at the back of the flightdeck, although I was monitoring the radio traffic on the spare headset.

The ATC controller was trying to be helpful and gave them quite a shortcut in the arrival routing which meant the aircraft was higher than normal during descent and this tended to increase the cockpit workload for the pilots. Then there was an aircraft crossing the track that led to a descent restriction from ATC to maintain the altitude until the other traffic was clear. The descent then recommenced and they were even higher, which meant that the Pilot Flying was using the speedbrakes to make the descent angle steeper. From my point of view this made it all the more interesting as I observed an experienced, professional crew coping well with a changing environment. In essence there was a small chain of factors here which could result in a difficult final approach and landing phase. The 'difficulty' of course would be that the crew might be manoeuvred into accepting shortcuts to the point where the aircraft is high and fast with too much energy onboard to make a normal transition to the landing configuration – in extremis this becomes an unstable approach from which a safe landing cannot be assured and a go-round is necessary.

By now, my senses were fully alert as I sat behind my two colleagues, observing them closely and listening to the interaction with ATC. They were being vectored downwind for runway 15R (Right) which is the normal (SE) landing runway at Kuwait, although it would produce a very long taxi routing after landing. All the navigational/approach aids were set up for 15R and the flight management computer had also been programmed for 15R. Now the speed was back under control, the flaps were being extended and despite the well intentioned efforts of the radar controller, they were going to be neatly setup for the ILS approach on 15R. It was a beautiful clear night and the lights of the city slid silently below the flightdeck windows as they were handed over to the Tower controller. "You are clear to make a VISUAL approach on runway 15 Left if you wish..." offered the controller. I could sense the tension now. All of a sudden, at the last moment and while trying to be helpful, the ATC man had pitched them a real fastball... what would they do now? The Captain looked over at the First Officer who was flying the aircraft and said, "Nah! You don't want that mate do you?" to which the F/O replied, "Whoa! No thanks Boss!"

The Skipper then keyed the mike switch, "Negative Tower, we will continue with the ILS to Land 15 RIGHT. *Shukran*". And that was it. As simple as that, the chain was broken and it ended there – the landing on 15R was a non-event and then 20 minutes of taxiing later the airliner was shut down on the ramp with the passengers disembarking normally. Of course it could have been very different if they had accepted a last minute runway change to a visual landing at an unfamiliar airport at night in a foreign country. They passed their Line Check without a problem and I complimented the Captain on the decision making.

Of course, after many years flying airliners we all get a little blasé about what we do for a living. In fact we also get a little bit hardened to accident reports too and there have been many of these down the years. I did get a timely and poignant reminder on the recent CRMI course from one of our instructors who briefed us all, prior to watching a 14 minute video of an airliner accident which centred around the CRM breakdown leading up to the fatal crash. She said:

"Gentlemen, please remember when you are watching this video that we have the benefit of hindsight here. We are all sat in a classroom watching events unfolding which led to a catastrophic accident in which many people, including the pilots, lost their lives. These were experienced professional crewmembers doing what they believed was their best in very difficult circumstances, just like you have all been through in your own careers. Please.... have respect for them and their loved ones."

Wise words indeed. We must have Respect for the ones who have gone before us, especially when they have given us the privilege of learning from their mistakes.

What Goes Up...?

(Not many light-twins have flown in formation with an Avro-Shackleton).

Of all the laws of physics which govern our activities as pilots, the gravity one never fails. Whether we are moving, hovering, climbing, descending, taking-off or landing we can rely on good old gravity to do its thing. Of course sometimes not all the parts of an aeroplane which commence flight leaving the ground at the same time return to earth simultaneously. You only have to think of the number of times when bits have fallen off airframes while in flight. DC10 cargo doors in the '70s, Concorde Rudder parts in the '80s, BAe ATP Landing gear bits in the '90s and you get the impression that the sky is full of falling debris!

Of course it's not really true, however the fact remains that it all must come down somewhere and fortunately one has to say, 99% of the time all of the airframe returns to Terra Firma in one piece. There are some aircraft that had a reputation for losing parts of the airframe whilst in flight and one wonders whether the Avro Shackleton Airborne Early Warning aircraft of '60s and '70s fame was one of these. This four engine propeller driven bomber was an incredible piece of engineering with its roots harking back to the Second World War and carried the nickname "Ten thousand rivets... flying in close formation!" Perhaps some of them became rather 'loose formation' at times? I actually recall having had the privilege of flying the "Lead Ship" with a Shackleton formating on my aircraft back in 1988 while working as an Air Taxi pilot on light twins in Manchester.

Funnily enough it wasn't even supposed to be my flight, but the company had accepted an air to air filming assignment for a TV News Station at very late notice. I just happened to be in the company offices at the old South Side hangar at Manchester Airport, when all of a sudden there was a big commotion. Due to a breakdown in communication, the RAF 8 Squadron Shackleton had appeared and was now on the ramp on the other side of the airport, across the runway from us, with its engines running!

Now this was a serious issue as the Shackleton crews used to have a massive lead up time to get themselves ready for operations. Whereas other operational types of military aircraft used to have their crews prepared to launch at say "Readiness Five" (meaning five minutes required to getting airborne), the Shack used to have various states of crew alertness including I think something like 5 hours in advance! Additionally, the TV camera crew contacted the Air Taxi company from the ramp on the North side to say they were ready to climb aboard our light twin and *"Where the Hell are you!?"*

The pilot who was supposed to fly the mission turned to me and said, "I've not flown close formation for a long time and I'm not sure if I can do it..." Within seconds we swapped roles and all of a sudden I found myself Captain of an aircraft which was about to fly formation lead with a dissimilar type. The run through the hangar was exciting, but not as exciting as finding the Partenavia PN68 outside with a flat battery! *"GET A GPU QUICK!"* I shouted at the top of my voice to the company engineers who were watching. Soon we were cranking for England and the engine burst into life with a cloud of blue exhaust smoke immediately blasted backwards. Chocks gone and we started taxiing with my oppo working the R/T as fast as he could to get us clearance across Manchester International's busy runway.

I don't recall feeling sweaty palms. In those days we all wore leather gloves when flying the camera ship as it got cold and windy inside, flying with the big back door off the aeroplane, but was that sound in my headphones really from my heart beating wildly? There was a full harness with safety straps for the cameraman so he could move around the freight section at the rear and a headset socket so he could communicate directly with us in the cockpit. Having done most of the preflight checks as we crossed the runway, we had reserved the power checks until the engines had warmed up – *at this rate these would be done as we lined up for takeoff,* I thought to myself as we taxied alongside the huge Shackleton.

Both aircraft were powered by propellers, but in reality that was where the comparison stopped. The little high-wing Partenavia piston twin with tricycle landing-gear was dwarfed by the four-engined, tail-dragging bomber with twin contra-rotating props on each motor. I remember it being very, very shiny and I wondered how long it took to polish all that paintwork. But no time for reverie just now, as soon as the parking brake was applied, the camera team were climbing aboard being briefed by the P2, while the Co-Pilot from the Shack came to my window for a quick brief for the formation on behalf of his skipper.

We must have made a very odd couple as we lined up for takeoff as a formation pair with a five second gap between the times of 'brakes-release'. Power checks being done just before we slipped the brakes, we were soon rolling in a south-westerly direction gathering speed. Behind us the mighty Shackleton roared down the runway and lumbered skywards. We had agreed a speed of 150 knots for the formation and this seemed to be common ground for both airframes – perhaps a bit fast for the Prat and a bit slow for the Shack, but at least we knew our aeroplanes' capabilities. The actual piloting as lead-ship was a non-event in many ways.

All I had to do was to fly as smoothly as possible, getting my co-pilot to call the speeds and heading changes so the RAF pilot could formate on us. He came into position in close formation at 'Echelon Starboard' which meant that he was on our right-hand side and set back a little behind our wing line so the cameraman could get a really good view of the machine. We manoeuvred with Liverpool ATC now so that we were heading northwest and therefore the sun would be behind the lens for the best pictures. There was quite a lot of chatter both from the ATC frequency and on the intercom with the cameraman, but not much between the formating aircraft. Through the open back door I could hear the drone of the engines next door, even above the noise from our own slipstream.

My view was obstructed over my right shoulder, so I couldn't actually get a look at the Shackleton, but from what my chum in the right-hand seat was saying, it was an impressive sight worth seeing. Both the co-pilot and the high-wing were in the way, "I want to see, let me have a look", I said and briefly he took control of the aircraft as I loosened my harness and leaned right forward into the area behind the windshield – the sight took my breath away! Only mere feet away from us, alongside was the Shackleton.

It looked ABSOLUTELY HUGE with shiny dark grey paintwork and ALL those propellers spinning round in the sunshine - it felt they were turning only inches away from our wingtip. The faces in the other cockpit wore big grins and they looked very relaxed, but my pulse rate must have gone off the scale. "THANKS! I have control!" I said on the intercom with as much sangfroid as I could muster, once again concentrating on keeping the wings level and controlling my breathing. *Strewth, that is CLOSE FORMATION!* I thought to myself while trying not to heavy-breathe on the microphone.

"How does it look from there?" Came the transmission from our right wing and I keyed the mike,

"You're looking BEAUTIFUL!" I hoped he realised I was talking about the aircraft. Eventually the TV crew had enough footage and the RAF had used enough fuel – it was time to part Company.

"You're clear to break right..." and in one smooth dark grey wingover they were gone.

From what I heard later, ITV were very pleased with the pictures. My family taped the evening news story, but I never got to see the video film as the tape was a duff one which was used for the recording. That being said, I will never forget that truly beautiful sight of a four engined bomber just outside the window of our little Partenavia on a sunny afternoon. Of course I don't know how many rivets were still together when they got it back to base, I guess they may have lost a few.

This brings me back to the original thought of bits falling off aeroplanes. Perhaps the most extreme example was the Pan Am 103 disaster in early 1989 when a whole B747 broke up in mid-air after the bomb exploded killing all onboard. A good friend of mine, who lived nearby, heard about the event and travelled to the site that night to see what had happened. He is not a morbidly curious type, but has always maintained an interest in aviation – his father and stepfather were both pilots.

From a distance he said he could see the emergency services were very obviously in attendance with a huge fire being tackled by fire engines where the main part of the airframe landed. As he had arrived quietly on his motorcycle through the back lanes he had avoided the police roadblocks and now he set off on foot across the fields in the dark. All of a sudden he came across the remains of an engine, still smoking, in the middle of a field! It was a huge shock. At that moment he realised that this was not the place to be. He turned around and left before he discovered anything more macabre.

Macabre is certainly the word to describe the stories about bodies being found on the flightpath for London Heathrow very occasionally, assumed to have fallen from the main landing gear bays of long haul aircraft inbound from the third world. Of course these poor stowaways don't realise that without pressurisation, they will actually die from hypoxia, well before the airliner reaches cruising altitude. Fortunately with increasing improvements in security standards at foreign airports these tragic events are now much rarer.

On the lighter side, there are some amusing stories about what falls from the sky and one of these was a favourite of mine for some time. I recall when I was much younger; I thought that perhaps the toilets on airliners were simply flushed into the atmosphere. It didn't occur to me then that airframe manufacturers would have gone to the trouble of plumbing in holding tanks full of blue fluid to store the waste products of in-flight catering.

Not all systems work perfectly however and there are occasions when, according to the engineers, the dump valves of the lavatory tanks develop leaks into the service panel area while flying in the freezing conditions of high altitude cruising. The locks on these service panels are well used and not 100% secure... Not a pleasant thought.

This thought probably did not occur to the farmer in Cheshire on the flightpath for aircraft landing at Manchester, who called the police to investigate what he termed "a UFO" which he found, had landed in his field.

When the police arrived, he duly showed them into his kitchen where he had put the UFO for safe-keeping.

In the family freezer, along with the steaks and a shoulder of lamb he proudly showed them a very large chunk of blue-ice!

What goes up... must come down, somewhere!

Training SkyGreece Pilots – author Top Right / Capt Stefan & Capt Dinos with the ladies of SX-VIP

Sentimental Airline Pilots?

(Oh give me a break! It's just a JOB...isn't it....?)

Commercial airline people are not known for their overt sentimentality. In fact they work in such a highly regulated industry that normally cool, factual, professionalism takes precedence over emotional hyperbole. It is refreshing and sometimes surprising then when evidence of our colleagues' more gentle side makes an appearance – I believe this is referred to as being "fluffy".

In fact the very way in which the word "fluffy" is used by crew members indicates that it is an alien concept to most airline personnel. The reasons are manyfold, although chief among them must be that the industry is a very hard-edged business environment in which to operate. This is an industry which thrives on TLAs (Three Letter Abbreviations) for just about everything and which has a language all of its own that is littered with jargon and technical expressions.

From manufacturing, through commercial, all the way to flight operations, there is a continual reliance upon numbers. Everything has either, a part number, a registration number, a stock reference number, a regulatory approval number and even the people are branded with employment numbers. Passenger e-tickets are given booking confirmation numbers, while crew tickets for dead-heading (such a lovely expression) are given locator numbers, which have a similar purpose.

In Flight Operations there are numbers for speed, altitude, direction, weight (mass), while in Engineering it is a numerical feast with digits for every occasion available. In fact it is possible to have a face to face meeting between two airline employees where the spoken words are composed of virtually all numbers or esoteric expressions unfathomable to the outsider!

The abbreviation DOB does not stand for Date of Birth anymore, but Death on Board; Un-Min is short for Unaccompanied Minor; GPU is Ground Power Unit; ASU is Air Start Unit; LIAC is Late Inbound Aircraft when it comes to logging delays (or Code 93); PAX is short for Passengers; PAP is just one Passenger; CDL is Cabin Defects Log not be confused with CDU which is Computer Display Unit; FMC and FMS are very similar, but not be confused and in the same vein, IRS's and IRU's are also very close in meaning...

It is possible that an FTL exceedance or FDM event requires an ASR to be filed which might become an MOR under the company's SMS when the FSO gets involved if they think it should be sent to the CAA. Not all ASRs are managed in this way and that is why there is an SMS there in the first place. (Incidentally don't confuse an ASR with a PSR or CSR they are totally different things).

Talking of FTLs of course brings us to CAP371 and the strictures that it places on crew working patterns in that a crew member could be on SBY, CTBL when called out. It might not be long before they reached their max FDP and went into Discretion which would have subsequent consequences for their Minimum Rest period to follow... Then the engineers are great when they start talking about ADD's and CRS's when it come to filling in the Techlog. Items such as Tyres become WTL, while engines are BSI'd or have MPAs while the MEL and DDG cover dispatch with unserviceable items which are then repaired at 'A' Checks, 'C' Checks or 'D' Checks.

These repairs or replacements are recorded as being carried out IAW, AMM code XYZ-1234 etc. Oh, and when it comes to old father time we really go to town! UTC is fairly straightforward, but then comes ETA's, STD's, STA's, ATA's and ATD's, then we have CTOT's, EAT's, EET's and so it goes on.

In the midst of all this tangled web of communication are the employees, **the people** who make it all happen. Somehow we manage to get our messages across to each other and at times the whole industry seems to run like clockwork – amazing. In fact there have been countless times when we (as a crew) have been rushing to try and get an aircraft away from the stand on time when it really has looked hopeless even up to just a few minutes before STD (Scheduled Time of Departure).

The holds are still open, the cabin crew are still counting heads as the last passengers are boarding while in the rear galley, there is organised chaos as the last catering is being done. The pushback tractor (which has been called for on the radio several times) is nowhere to be seen and the handling agent is making calls in the terminal for the missing passengers who have not yet found the gate...

All of a sudden, the pushback team appear round the end of the pier, as the catering truck pulls away and the rear galley is secured, the hold doors are closed, the last pax appear at the door and are ushered to their seats, the senior stewardess appears in the flightdeck door with a thumbs-up asking "Okay to close-up?" normally while you are halfway through a PA to the cabin and the First Officer is calling for Push and Start on the Ground frequency.

Then the checklists are all completed, and the groundcrew on the headset are saying "Release the parking brake please Sir, commencing pushback, you are clear to start engines 2 then 1..." You look at the clock and it is **exactly on the minute of STD** and you wonder, 'how the hell does that happen?' Incredible, but true, we have seen it many times. There are so many factors which can go wrong to prevent the flight departing on time, but so often we manage to get away just on the minute – it really is very strange.

Yet that also is part of the magic of the industry, in that although there is such a reliance upon technology you can always see and relate to the human factors in the mix. The politeness and good manners of people working under incredible pressure, the private jokes and funny expressions from crews which have bonded together – often they develop a sub-cultural life of their own.

I recall a crew years ago whom I met while downroute and they had all been together for over a week. We worked for the same airline and I knew some of them individually, but I had not been part of their 'gang' on that trip. They had found something incredibly amusing about the expression from the London underground system "Mind the Gap!" and this had become their in-joke. Whenever one of them said it out loud as if announcing it on a tube station platform, all of the rest of the crew would collapse laughing hysterically, this while others of us shook our heads in wonderment! But they were funny to watch.

There is also humour which crosses the divide between different sections of the airline community. Sometimes as flightdeck crew we witness this when talking to the dispatchers or handling agents, maybe even on the headset while communicating with the pushback crewchief. I remember once when we were downroute and we had switched on the red anti-collision lights before engine start on the ramp – there is one mounted on top and one underneath the fuselage.

We could see the reflection of the one above, flashing red in the terminal windows, but I suspected that maybe the lower one was not working so I asked the crewchief,

"Is the anti-collision light working down below?" the answer came back,

"It's On..... it's Off.....it's On.....it's Off....it's.." I interrupted him,

"Oh! Yes thanks a lot Ground, very funny, we're cleared for push and start now!"

But we were still chuckling as we lined up for takeoff. Talking of which reminds me of Dave Williams' experience while he was still flying as a skipper for British Airways on the B767 fleet as they lined up for takeoff one day with *"landing traffic at four miles"* from ATC.

His First Officer questioned him in French out of the blue, "Sur le Croissant?", to which Dave replied "Eh, what?" and the First Officer explained,

"Are you going to take it on the *Roll*...?"

Yes funny times and funny people combined with long duty days and major timezone changes produce an emotional roller coaster of a working life. The great leveller in it all is the flying. No matter what your position, you are a key part of the team which makes it all happen and hence the current focus upon CRM (Crew Resource Management) to get the teams functioning together at a high level as they should.

While flying as a new First Officer on the B757 with my first airline, I had the nervous pleasure of flying with one of the most senior pilots in the company as my Captain. On the return sector an incident occurred which emphasised how well the senior pilot had managed the CRM to make me, as a very junior F/O, feel at home and able to speak my mind.

We were in the cruise and flying serenely above the Alps in the darkness heading back to Manchester when he said to me, "So what's the latest gossip then? You've got your finger on the pulse James, what rumour's doing the rounds on Galley FM?"
"Erm.... Nothing really as far as I know, it's all pretty quiet out there on the shopfloor", was my reply, but he was insistent and was not to be dissuaded easily.

"Go on, you can tell me, I like to hear what scuttlebutt is going around, it helps me to understand if the crews are happy or not, I like to know about the crew morale".

I could see that my stonewalling was not going to be enough and it was true that he was a good boss who liked to stay attuned to the mood of his people. There was one rumour though which had been circulating for some time now, maybe I should tell him...

"Well.... If you must know..."

"*Yes?*" he replied encouragingly, then taking a sip of tea. I took a deep breath.

"The latest gossip is that... *you're having an affair with Emma Cousins!*" I blurted it out, to which the reply from the left-hand seat was spluttering and choking as his tea went everywhere! "*Well you did ask...?!*" I said as he composed himself.

"Nooooo... I know where *that* one's come from, erm we have a very similar sense of humour... and were on a trip together to Florida last year... and...", I stopped him.

"It's okay, you don't have to explain it to me you know, I am sure it's just an unfounded rumour", I said with a huge smile on my face, secure in the knowledge that he would not be asking anymore questions about crewroom gossip on this flight.

So there is humour and humanity throughout the industry too, although it is rare to see it when we are all hard at work trying to be compliant with the regulations, while cutting costs and trying to maximise profit margins simultaneously. I did see evidence of our "fluffy" side recently though while viewing two 767s which were waiting to be purchased by a new owner. They had been delivered from a Middle Eastern airline into the care of an engineering organisation while the sale of the airframes was completed and from an original fleet of 18, these were the last two which had left the airline.

The very last one in fact was Golf Victor, (Vicky) being the last two registration letters of the airframe. The engineer who was guiding us round the airliner pointed out that there was graffiti on the hull in permanent marker pen to mark its last flight from the Gulf State where it had been flying for 15 years. The crew were saying their goodbyes to an old friend and it was touching to see. By the L1 entrance door, on the outside of the hull, there was "*goodbye my love goodbye*" and on the lower fuselage were written lots of warm messages such as "*Goodbye Vicky*" and "*So long Sexy*", "*Thanks for all the service*", "*Good luck!*" etc.

Even the local CAA representative had signed a goodbye message and there were some in Arabic too. The aircraft had been in service with the airline since new, 15 years before and now it was time for a change of equipment, yet it appeared that the machine had developed something of a personality. Very soon of course those sentimental messages will be painted over by the new owner and the aeroplane will start a new life flying between new destinations in a brand new colour scheme.

After all it's only a machine, an inanimate, lifeless object without any capability for feelings or emotions, but just for a little while, it showed the tangible proof of the human (fluffy) side of our industry. It was a good feeling to have witnessed it.

Note: Emma Cousins was not her real name and it was only ever a rumour anyway...

Hull artwork on Golf Victor - see Sentimental Airline Pilots above

"I wonder what it's doing now...?!"

(Have the airline manufacturers & airlines been too clever for their own good?)

"I wonder what it's doing now...?" If I had been given £1 for every time I have heard these words spoken by pilots on airliner flightdecks, I would be a rich man. Normally this question comes from the Pilot Flying (PF) when all of a sudden the airliner appears to be doing something which is not what they had in mind. Often however the 'automatics' are only obeying instructions or responding correctly to inputs from the PF, but if that is the case, then why should the PF be surprised by the result?

The answer is complex and not easy to pin down exactly, but if we take some examples of real incidents that have happened, then it should give us a greater understanding of what is going on. Let's start swimming in the shallow end and take it one stroke at a time. In the early days of airline flying, the rate of technological progress was slow and there was a fashion for the industry to put great emphasis on the pilots being given access to huge amounts of technical information. Commercial airline pilots would be required to commit to memory, large volumes of statistics, limitations and figures during their type rating training courses. For example it was considered essential that the pilots know all the limitations regarding the engines such that they would be able to recite by rote the oil pressure limits, RPM limits and significant facts and figures involved in their safe operation while flying the aircraft. Although this was in many ways a "memory test", the net result was that these pilots had great mechanical empathy with the powerplants and a substantial understanding of the technical aspects of their operation.

The modern trend is definitely away from this and much more reliance is placed upon using automation to reduce the workload of the flying pilot. That is all very well if they understand how and why the automatic systems are functioning, but if not there is a dangerous loss of Situational Awareness developing and potential breakdown in the safe operation of the flight. Take the example of the First Officer who activated and executed a much lower cruise altitude in the Flight Management Computer (FMC) without informing the Captain who was distracted by talking to the Cabin Crew on the intercom at the time. The first that the Captain knew something was different, was when shortly after the entry into the FMC, the message came up saying Insufficient Fuel... The computer did not know that the flight would probably be cleared to climb to the normal cruising altitude later and therefore it assumed that the selected CRZ ALT would be maintained all the way to destination. The breakdown in cross-cockpit communication was complete when the Captain convinced the First Officer that the aircraft had suddenly developed a significant fuel leak and they should land as soon as possible to have this investigated. In this scenario, the major factor which let them down was poor communication between them both.

The phenomenon of 'Old dogs and new tricks' is sometimes to blame for aircraft accidents and incidents where the more senior members of our profession are inhibited to ask the younger pilots for help in understanding the new-fangled technology. Of course this shouldn't happen, because theoretically we are all less hierarchically minded than before and we should not hesitate to say "Please help me, I do not understand..." In the older generation however this is seen as a sign of weakness, perhaps even a lack of moral fibre (LMF) and therefore there is a natural resistance for these old guys to request (or accept) assistance. Fortunately these dinosaurs are a dying breed now, but there are still some in existence and they can be very hard work from the 'training' perspective. They tend to have a reputation among the F/Os in their airline and it is not hard to spot them. I saw an example of this only recently when the Captain under training (quite close to retirement) decided to activate and execute some entries in the FMC which were so quickly accomplished that he accidentally deleted the whole route! My response from the other seat was one of astonishment, I had never seen anyone manage to do THAT before - needless to say he didn't understand how he had done it either.

As we were approaching top of descent, at night in an unfamiliar area, it was not the most comfortable feeling to be in the pointy end of an aluminium tube which was travelling at 500+ mph without any specific directional control. I must admit he did look stunned as he sat there starting at the black hole on

the EHSI map display where only seconds before a nice magenta LNAV track had existed. I said calmly,
"I don't think you INTENDED to do that did you?" I recall that Harry Enfield came to mind when I considered the comedic aspects of our situation. His catchphrase of "Nah! Ya don't wanna do it loike THAT!" would have been most appropriate.

Again, part of his problem was communication - that's the Captain under training, not Harry Enfield by the way. If he had involved me, as the non-flying (monitoring) pilot in his decision-making (route modifying) before he pushed that last 'Execute' button, I would have had chance to intervene and prevent him making a fool of himself, but I was not given that opportunity. Pushing buttons hastily in an airliner is never a good idea and I remember one of my early Training Captain mentors telling me years ago,
"Once a button is pushed it cannot be un-pushed!" In the case of our hasty friend I encouraged him to type the entire route back in himself so that he could have some more practice with the FMC – which was obviously what he needed.

To be fair to the older generation however, the airliner manufacturers are more than partly to blame for the lack of information which the pilots receive - you see it works like this. After the cost of the fuel is taken out of the equation, one of the next most significant costs is crew and especially the training of the crews. Therefore if a manufacturer can convince their potential customers (the airlines) that their airframes require less crew training costs, it will increase their sales. Of the two major airframers, neither is less guilty than the other in this respect. Let's look at two examples.

Firstly, back in the days of yore, when bell bottomed trousers seemed to be quite the thing to be seen in and Ford produced a car called the Cortina which was also pretty cool, (the 1970s) Boeing designed an aircraft called the B757. This was a derivative of the B727 and B737 combined in some ways, as the fuselage cross-section was nearly identical, (stick to what you know) although obviously a lot longer. Very shortly afterwards their new wide-body (B767) was rolled out which, surprise, surprise, had the same flightdeck as its thinner bodied older brother. When it came to type certification, the manufacturer managed to convince the regulator (US FAA) that both aircraft should be considered the same **type** therefore pilots would be able to fly both aeroplanes without having to requalify with another type rating, hence avoiding the expense. In actual fact, although superficially they are remarkably similar, in reality there is only 15% of the airframe which is identical and most of that is the flightdeck! On the B757 you step down into the flightdeck when you enter from the cabin, whereas in the B767 you step up – the reason being that they kept the flightdeck floor at the same height above the ground (13 feet or so) to make them easy to operate in the same way. In practice you have to say it works okay, however it is generally acknowledged that Boeing would not have got away with it these days.

Secondly, when the airframer from Toulouse decided to produce their new fly-by-wire series of airliners, in the following decade - they employed a similar tactic and in fact the A319, 320, 321, 330 and 340 are all nearly identical in the cockpit. Again the airline companies were pleased to see that their crew training costs had been reduced by obviating the necessity for all that crossover training from type to type. The problem is though that a new generation of airline pilots were then coming to "the line" that had been brought up on a regime of much less training and preparation time given to them to do the job.

Simultaneously the manufacturers had designed and built the most advanced flying machines with the most sophisticated automated flight systems, using cutting edge technology about which the crews were informed less and less. For example, which one of us who completed the B757 type rating back in the late 1980s, was told that the 3 Inertial Reference Systems (IRSs) which were the heart of the navigation system, contained a laser ring gyro each that was designed by NASA for the Space Shuttle? I bet most of us found out by accident and under our own research later on, long after we had qualified to operate the type. Admittedly we weren't trying to fly a moon-shot, but we were out over the Atlantic and the navigating principle is the same!

Roll forward now to the end of another decade and the manufacturers have sold many more new aeroplanes, the commercial aviation industry has grown by another huge margin, we are near the end of the '90s and the LCAs (Low Cost Airlines) had arrived! Now the onus for paying for initial type rating training is placed firmly upon the shoulders of the newbie airline pilots who are each facing bills for another £25,000 (on top of the £75,000+ which they have already paid for their licences) just to get their first job. Answer this question. Are they going to pay the extra money for what they consider to be a superior (quality) product from one Type Rating Training Organisation (TRTO) or are they going to opt for the cheapest way to put the type on their licence?

So another generation of under-trained, under-supported, under-financed, inexperienced pilots join the ranks of their previously under-trained and under-supported brothers... But, it doesn't stop there. Oh No! Not by a long a long chalk. Because now the LCAs are growing so fast - again think back ten years - they are desperate to promote from within. Desperate to promote, not simply because *"We believe in developing our people"*, but because "We need to put bums on seats luvvies. No, not in the cabin silly – *in the flightdeck!"* More particularly in the LEFT-HAND SEAT because otherwise their growth will stop and the fleets of brand new Boeings/Airbuses will sit on the ground idle and the all important share-price will collapse (God forbid). Remember, I was there, I saw it happen and no matter what I say about trying to maintain the quality of training etc. in large part the LCAs have changed the nature of our industry forever.

It should come as no surprise that many pilots were promoted to Captain during those years – the latter half of the '90s and beginning of the double 'Ohs - who were really not up to the mark. I do not make that claim lightly and I do not wish to denigrate my profession, nor the many professional, conscientious and competent Airline Commanders out there who would have made the grade anyway. The fact remains that in the period '60s to '80s new ATPLs were lucky to get the first job on a jet airliner and if they did they would spend 5 years in the right-hand seat before being considered for command with a minimum of maybe 4500 to 5000 hours in their logbooks.

By the end of the '90s some turboprop "experienced" F/Os were only in the RHS of the B737 for maybe 6 months then starting their command training, by this time also the total flying hours requirement had magically reduced to 2500 minimum. To make matters worse, many of them would be complaining to their line manager about why they were not being promoted. More than a few times, I saw inexperienced, overworked and under-supported pilot managers who were pressurised into putting forward unsuitable Command candidates for assessment with predictable results. The current airlines' fashion for appointing inexperienced, under-trained managers in all departments (cost saving strategy) is also to blame for the lack of good managers in the right positions from middle management right through to the board.

So where does that leave us? Have they been too clever for their own good? Yes, that certainly applies to the design teams well before the metal hits the shop floor. To design an aircraft where it is possible to misuse the autopilot, such that it will follow a descent rate of 3000+ feet per minute towards the ground when really the PF just wanted it to fly a 3^0 vertical profile is not smart. (Strasbourg Airbus accident) But, then the designers were not to know that the airlines would choose to send a couple of 'old technology guys' on the fast track course to a type rating on the "electric jet" who might not understand all that the 'clever' automatics could do to them. Although the tragic accident at Strasbourg was the result, there were countless other incidents, many of which probably went unreported which did not end up with wreckage on final approach.

'Complacency with the automatics' was also cited as a significant factor in the turboprop accident near Buffalo in bad weather a few years ago. Another example of an airliner being too clever for its own good would be the B757 in the Caribbean which took off with a blocked pitot tube. The airspeed seemed to increase and increase and then came the overspeed warning "clacker", to which the Captain responded by raising the nose of the aircraft higher and higher and h-i-g-h-e-r... Then came the stall warning stick-shaker at the same time – the tragic result is history.

The Turkish B737 on finals to Schiphol whose auto-throttle thought it was landing, so it took all the power off a long way above the ground – mush too clever. Or what about the 'electric jet' that lost all of its electrics in-flight, (yes that's right ALL...) and the pilots didn't know what to do initially because they had never been trained, because the manufacturer had said "it could not happen" – again, too clever by half. The South Atlantic Air France 447 accident report is another sad example and makes for depressing reading.

I have lost count of the new pilots I see on the line who make what appear to be quite arbitrary, or even random selections of autopilot modes while flying the aircraft. I know how that sounds, but it is true and it is really not their fault – it is without doubt the fault of the training/airline system - please refer to all the above. For example, when I am employed in a training capacity on the line and I ask them some questions, only simple ones, it does not take long to plumb the depths of their technical and professional knowledge.

Not all new pilots are like this, just the majority. When I ask them to talk to me about their understanding of VNAV (the Vertical Navigation element of Boeing's glass cockpit airliners) there is not a lot of substance in their replies. I reassure them (what else can I do?) that in truth, it will take them a year or maybe two to understand how VNAV really does work while they "fly the 'plane" through the automatics.

So have the authorities noticed that there is a problem? Well yes they have and a few years ago now a project team called F.O.R.C.E. was set-up to make studies into how changes to type-rating training especially could combat the problems of 'Automation Complacency'. The Flight Operations Research Centre for Excellence is a really great title and an even better acronym and the terms of reference looked great, but where are the results? Where are the changes which may make all the difference to the way in which we are going to train tomorrow's generation of pilots so that they will be more able to meet the challenges of flying the airframes of the future?

Well the Force is not with us yet, it has all gone quiet, but now there seems to be more of an emphasis on a new pilots' licence for pilots to fly airliners called an MPL (Multicrew Pilot Licence). Perhaps this is the key to making sure that our young men and women who fly aluminium tubes around the world at close to the speed of sound in all sorts of atmospheric conditions are well prepared and trained for the future? When you consider the past as described in the foregoing, of course the answer must be more funding, so we should expect this new MPL to cost a lot more. On the contrary, even though when we look back at the reducing funding for proper, thorough pilot training over the past decades, the MPL could be as little as half the price... Somehow I don't think this is going to be the answer.

I would like to say, I think it is going to get better, but it's not. You know all those inexperienced, self-selecting, self-sponsoring, trained-down-to-a-price, young aviators who joined in the recruiting boom of 5 or 10 years ago? Well they should all be getting their commands around now and in the meantime, the aircraft become more complex, yet the pilots apparently don't need to know as much.

Quite frankly it is the stuff of nightmares. When I think about the accident statistics for the next decade as a result of what our own industry has done to itself I literally shudder.

Fasten your seatbelts everybody, it's going to be a rough ride!

Don't Trust Me, I'm a Pilot.

(Because I don't trust you... and I CERTAINLY don't trust ME!)

Commercial Pilot careers take many forms. Going back a few decades the choice was easier because there were distinctly fewer options, in fact there seemed to be only three. Option one; join the armed forces to fly aircraft (fixed-wing or rotary), as a career, after which, when you "came out" you could have an extended flying career in the commercial world and your military experience would be well respected. The second option would be to join a commercial airline as a 'Cadet' pilot. Starting right at the bottom, you would be supported by a major airline to study for your Commercial Pilot's Licence (CPL) after which they would employ you as a First or Second Officer on commercial line-flights.

Finally if you were unable to obtain an entry to either of these establishments, then the possibility was there to self-sponsor by hour-building as a Flying Instructor or similar on light aircraft. Once you had above a magic figure (700 hours rings a bell) then you were permitted to gain your CPL, via the written examinations, which gave you access to the job market. Of course you were still no good to anybody because you didn't have the all important 'Type Rating' of a useful commercial type on your licence. Back then however, when there was a shortage of pilots, the airline companies all footed the bill for this most expensive part of the equation.

According to the wise old aviators, the 'shortages' were cyclical. It was common to hear that the industry went from feast to famine every few years or so. Certainly back in the '80s and '90s this had more than a little truth in it. An example was the shortage of 1988/89 which resulted in a great deal of 'movement' of the labour force throughout the airline industry. Air Europe at that time lost a lot of pilots so gave their people an unprecedented pay increase of something over 20% to stabilise their employee numbers.

Other airlines followed suit with terms and conditions improving in leaps and bounds throughout the holiday charter sector. I remember this period well, because this was precisely the argument I used while negotiating the future package for pilots at the Air Taxi company in Manchester where I was working at the time. At the end of the discussion, which centred around the fact that with the same licence we could all leave the company and fly heavy jets as F/Os, I was pleased to see that there was an increase in salary of 50% or so – not bad for an afternoon's work! Now those *were* the days, when the use of logic and a persuasive argument won the day.

Roll the calendar forward a few years and the demise of Air Europe and Dan Air (among others) brings us to 1991 or so. At this time, if you were out of work as a pilot, then you could be unemployed quite some time – especially as happened to some of the ex-military pilots who were in the process of leaving the service at that time. By the end of the '90s, the industry was short of pilots again due to the stellar rise of the Lo-Cos. Then another bad patch hit us all shortly after 11 September 2001 when many airlines who were overextended and over-crewed took advantage of the depressed trading conditions to thin out the workforce. Perhaps the one sector which rode out the economic storm the best was in fact those same Lo-Cos again. During times of economic downturn, the prestige class of flying catches the cold the worst, while those who still *need* to fly will look for the lowest cost alternatives. Love them or hate them, easyJet and Ryanair have been pretty recession proof since the beginning. They have substantially destroyed the short-haul networks of the legacy carriers throughout the EU and in doing so have spawned many imitators. Some of the imitators have been good, some not so good.

As a pilot, job security is an important aspect – once you have got your first job that is. I recall during the heady days in the autumn of 1988 when I was simultaneously given three job offers. It was an accident of timing of course. You apply to lots of different companies and try to obtain the one job, however like buses, this time they all came at once. Dan Air offered me a position as F/O on the B727 based at Manchester, which I quite liked the look of. Then Orion Airways (in process of morphing into Britannia) offered me the B737 based at Luton and finally Air 2000 called me up with an offer of the B757 based at Manchester. Conventional wisdom then said to take the job offering the newest, shiniest Boeing on the market, so off I went to Air 2000. Seven years later, I had no regrets about my decision, a great airliner and a great company with some fantastic people to work alongside – including the management. (They just don't make DFOs like Neil Burrows anymore).

Now in 1995 I was getting the distinctly uneasy feeling that maybe it was time to leave for pastures new. Although the company still had many good folk in it, some of the best flight operations managers had left and that leaves you wondering if it is time for you to go too. In fact it was a hard lesson to learn, when the newly formed department of Human Resources grew rapidly within the company and all of a sudden forced the new flight operations management team to canvas employees for redundancies. They wanted to make 6 pilots redundant and this had already been incorporated in the next year's financial forecast – it was a done deal. This was strange to us on the line, however not as strange as it came to the managers who were already planning to recruit some more pilots for the following spring. The HR reasoning was that if they obtained 6 voluntary pilot redundancies, this would make the other employees in the group of holiday companies feel better about being made redundant themselves.

In November 1995, the announcement was made and there was a deluge of applications from the pilots! We had been a very well motivated group of professionals who had been lucky enough to have experienced some of the best pilot managers in the industry leading us and now they were gone. Not only that, but the shock of being asked if we wanted to leave the company in a very abrupt way made all of us look for another job. During the next 18 months, the company lost over 25% of its pilot workforce. It must have cost millions to replace us with retraining etc. all because the accountants wanted to save a few hundred thousand.

Which in a very roundabout way brings me to the subject of 'last flights'. Yes, get on with it, tell us about flying airliners - okay well I will. This is a prime example of never let your guard drop, never make assumptions and never TRUST anyone, - especially not yourself - while flying aeroplanes for a living! This day was going to be my very last flight with the airline and I was more than a little apprehensive. Today would be the wrong day to make a really dumb mistake and I knew it. Of course there were distractions and mitigating circumstances – the cabin crew were all playing practical jokes on me and downroute we were all posing for pictures outside on the ramp. No high visibility waistcoats required in those days. It felt good to be posing for photos in a Captain's uniform in the Spanish sunshine after seven years with the airline – I was going to be 'leaving on a high', I thought to myself, but how little did I know?

It was halfway through the two sector day and we were turning the B757 round in Malaga. I had just flown the aircraft in as Pilot Flying and completed a smooth landing and we had planned for an autoland back at Gatwick when we got there. Part of my superstitious attitude to the day at the time made me want to carry out an automatic approach and landing for the last one so less could go wrong. It was the First Officer's PF sector to Gatwick however so I asked them how much fuel they wished to take, in accordance with the new CRM principles which were in their infancy at the time.

The F/O replied with a figure, I gave the computer flight plan a cursory glance over and saw that the figure they had nominated was plenty more than the minimum fuel required indicated. I cross-checked the position (Lat/Long) and the FMC route that was inserted into the Flight Management Computer and the F/O gave a very competent brief on how they were going to fly the departure. With a full load of passengers (233 seats all full) the Senior Cabin Crew member asked if she could close and arm the doors and I said "Yes, I will give them a quick welcome onboard PA..." Something was amiss. I couldn't quite put my finger on it, but something was not quite right. The FMC was refusing to show how much fuel we would have at each step of the route, why was it doing that? Where have the predicted fuels gone to?

"Shall I call for start-up?" asked the F/O and I replied, "Yes please..." but was still thinking about the FMC, I had checked all the entries for it, the cruising altitude FL390 had been put in as per the computer flightplan, I just could not work it out. "Ah well it will sort itself out when it's airborne" I thought to myself and then got stuck into a brief PA to the passengers, "...and we will be flying at a cruising altitude of 39,000 feet blah, blah..." a small alarm bell in my brain said *we – never – go – up – that - high from Malaga with a full load of pax*. My train of thought was interrupted from the other seat however when the F/O said "We're clear to push and start!"

"Okay, panel-scan please and run the checklist!" I sounded more confident than I felt, but everything else seemed fine. The weather was great, the aircraft was perfectly serviceable, the crew were happy, the F/O was good to fly with... but there was something. A few minutes after takeoff and we were passing a few thousand feet in the climb heading north – "we don't normally climb straight to 390 out of Malaga, I am sure..." I said as I looked carefully at the FMC. That would do it of course, if we put too high an altitude in there, the machine would sulk and refuse to display fuel quantities – I put FL350 in as the cruise altitude, there was a slight delay. Now the fuel predictions appeared, but surely some mistake, it was showing a ridiculously low figure at destination, well below our minimum reserves! I was horrified.

MY God! We're going to have to land in Paris to pick up fuel at this rate; we haven't got enough to make Gatwick! How embarrassing would that be on your last flight? An ignominious end for sure! I quickly rechecked the flightplan, all still seemed good and I knew for certain we had put fuel onboard to the figure which the F/O had asked for, so where was the problem? "Ahh! There it is! This is a flightplan for an empty aircraft, the Zero Fuel Weight is 20 tonnes lighter than we really are – that explains it..." When I said this the F/O was mortified and kept apologising, to which I replied that it was definitely NOT their fault, "It always stops with the Captain, he signs for the jet, end of story" I assured them, "now let me show you all the tricks I have learned in the past 7 years of flying these machines about how to save gas!"

I remember the feeling of cold terror which gripped me as I punched numbers into the FMC and cancelled the climb derate "Full Climb Power" said I along the way to let the F/O know what I was doing. Every time I made a change to the FMC route or tweaked the engines or autopilot, there was a corresponding increase in our arrival fuel, but not enough. London Controllers would want us down from our economical cruising altitude too early as we crossed the channel – we would not be able to do that... I cancelled the early descent in the route and gave us a glide descent at a very low speed (minimum drag speed) all the way to a very short final approach at Gatwick. "Shortest possible groundtrack to touchdown" I explained as I executed the changes.

"Please trim the ailerons carefully and we might just make it now, but I will speak to Ops" I went onto the long-range HF radio and called 'Star Fleet Command' – they who had provided us with the erroneous flightplan. I briefly explained the situation and asked them to speak directly to the London Airways Controllers explaining exactly what we needed – "a glide descent from 35,000 feet with nil power on till about 4 miles out on finals for runway 26L". We would be putting the gear and flap down at a very late stage, I checked again the fuel remaining and yes we just had enough to be legal and safe, but no surplus, it was going to be so tight...

The arrival was expeditious with no delay, the controllers were superb and the F/O flew the cleanest approach with minimal drag which I have ever seen – we still did an autoland which performed as per the manufacturer's design. As we touched down on the runway, the 'Insufficient Fuel' caption came up on the FMC again, but I was not worried now. When we taxied in and shutdown, I put the Fuel Remaining figure in the aircraft techlog and guffawed. The F/O asked me why I was laughing and I said, "Well somebody is going to pick up that techlog in the next few days and say, he was a good chap that McBride, he was a 'minimum fuel' man all the way to the end. Little do THEY know!"

When I say to my fellow colleagues these days as we fly along, "Don't trust me, I don't trust you, we don't trust the handling agents, we don't trust the engineers, we don't trust the ops people, we don't trust anybody, but especially don't trust me, because I don't trust me!"

They give me a strange look sometimes, but you see I have trusted people before and whenever you 'trust' people they let you down. They don't mean to, it just happens, we're only human.

My advice is to cross-check *everything* at least twice, preferably from different data-sources and trust no-one! NO-ONE; especially not yourself.

Getting 'Groundhappy'.

(The pitter patter of webbed feet in the crewroom).

I was on the 'phone to one of my ex colleagues the other day and she was bemoaning the fact that she had "been on the ground for what seemed like ages". I have known Sarah for many years and she is not a workaholic – far from it, she very much enjoys her time with family and friends, but her wish to "go flying again" started me thinking. She's actually Cabin Crew, but that is irrelevant where our profession is concerned, at the end of the day she's part of the crew. She was complaining that she had too much time on her hands and was looking forward to going back to work. Her symptoms were irritability with the family and annoyance with life in general – "Yes" I said to her, "you're getting Groundhappy".

Of course it's a sardonic description of a person's state of mind and although I have used the expression many times over the years, I have never really thought too much about the origin of the phrase. Well it must have been since the Wright brothers first flew of course, but I think it is probably much later and comes from a time when flying was considered both stressful and dangerous. Think 'Biggles', think 'Royal Flying Corps'... think 'Attrition Rate' and I reckon we are in the ballpark here. Without doubt that early period of flying history was a dramatic and perilous one, even though technology made great strides forward simultaneously. The 1914-18 War was a proving ground in many ways for solutions to aerodynamic and technical challenges, however the words 'Flight' and 'Safety' had not yet been used in the same sentence. It was dirty, difficult and dangerous work flying rickety old biplanes on the western front. Some of the firsthand accounts of the flying make for disturbing reading.

Apart from the ever present danger of being shot at by the enemy, the pilots of the old SE5As, Sopwith Camels and Pups had to deal with constant diarrhoea. The cause of this was that the engines were lubricated by Castor Oil which worked on a total loss system, thus while the pilot was actually flying the machine, they were ingesting and inhaling a constant flow of lubricant with predictable results! The squadrons of Royal Flying Corps pilots found that the only remedy to this was to use large quantities of alcohol (often Gin) to relax the bowels enough to prevent their anatomical exhaust system from taking priority...

Needless to say factors such as this, the intense cold of flying open cockpit aeroplanes in the winter and the extraordinarily high mortality rate, combined to make the occupation one of the most stressful ever invented. No wonder then, that when a period of particularly inclement weather made 'Ops' untenable, the pilots rejoiced in the relief of being able to stay grounded without appearing cowardly. Of course 'cowardice' was a swear word. In those times of strict formality, discipline and stiff upper lip, it was just not possible to "funk it" without being suspected of 'lack of moral fibre'. It is no surprise then that these young men became 'Groundhappy'.

In fact 'Lack of Moral Fibre' (LMF) was still the mark of an invertebrate or faint heart during the Second World War and was actually a valid reason for removing a serviceman (or woman) from duty. Even as late as the early 1980s when I was in military flying training, some of the older Flying Instructors referred to 'LMF' when discussing students who were not making adequate progress. Certainly if you were facing a 'chop-ride' and the weather was very poor such that flying operations were consistently cancelled day after day, you became 'Groundhappy'. The temporary relief of Mother Nature only delayed the inevitable and soon it became time to face the music... When it came to the Check Flight, either you could hack it or you could not – there were no grey areas here. If you were able to achieve success, in the First World War squadrons they would have said you could "Cut the Mustard" – more recently this expression has become 'Winged It' or 'Breezed It'. In between times of course it was always "A Piece of Cake!"

'Groundhappy' is not a good place to be though, in fact it is an oxymoron, because it is a stressful feeling to have and no pilot is really 'happy' being on the ground. The whole point about being able to fly is that we can *leave* the ground. Our generation is blessed with the ability to defy gravity, through a whole system of laws of physics and the application of technology. The employment of highly trained and skilled individuals who can operate heavier-than-air craft safely and repetitively completes the picture. For a pilot, the true job satisfaction comes from the joy of flight and I have often heard the expression that we are paid for the time we spend on the ground not up in the air.

At a company where I was working a few years back, there was a pilot employed who had not flown an aeroplane for many months. The reason for this was that he was engaged to bring a new 'type' of aircraft to the company to operate on behalf of a customer. He had been very much involved in all matters technical and regulatory, but the airframe itself is not yet certificated after major cabin interior modifications were carried out. All those months he spent in the offices, working on manuals, checklists, loadsheets, technical support documents and the like. He had adopted the nickname "Penguin" when he introduced himself to newcomers and says himself that he is "A bird that cannot fly".

I watched him closely and every time he made this little joke, he laughed, but it was not a joyful sound. He was frustrated, irritated and wingless – he was 'Groundhappy'. When the aircraft was nearly ready to operate and as the big day approached, I sensed an increasing tension. He was gearing up for the big moment when finally he lines that machine up with the runway centreline for his first takeoff in nearly a year. Then he will truly "slip the surly bonds of earth" again and enter his true environment. No longer a Penguin he was going to become a Seagull, an Albatross, an Osprey maybe, but not an Ostrich.

He would soar like an Eagle and with the power of thrust from four jet engines he would be thrilled to return to his home – the sky. Perhaps all pilots should have email addresses which end in @sky.com in fact I know that some of them do and I am sure they are aware of the significance. Because really *that* is where our home is, not here on the ground, doing earthly, surface like, groundy things. The sky is where our spirits surge and literally our hearts sing and in our minds we say "YES! This is what our life is all about". Maybe this sounds a little overenthusiastic and gushing, but you see I have also been 'Groundhappy' in the past. There were times when I had not flown an aeroplane for many weeks and I know that it is not a nice feeling. I had been office bound, 'flying a desk' for months and had not touched the controls in all that time.

Then when I know I have a flight planned I anticipate that it will be such a huge relief to get airborne again. To feel that extraordinary power we have to alter the angle of the earth's horizon with just the lightest pressures of our hands and feet is going to be purely magical. Like a child, I get all giddy inside as if I am planning for a trip to the funfair or amusement arcade, yet I am forced to hide it with mature sounding phrases such as, "Let us consider all the options here", when being faced by a problem in the office from the staff.

Not so long ago, I met an old man who was travelling as a passenger on a private jet as a guest of the owner. When I first saw him and we were introduced, I could see that he was a small framed man, in his early seventies, unshaven and wearing an odd mixture of clothing, a sleeveless sweater (woollen tank top) with a woolly hat on to boot. The hat would not have looked quite so incongruous, had we not been sitting in a very posh restaurant for lunch at a five star hotel in an international airport. He was of Middle Eastern origin and clearly significantly wealthy, however I am sorry to say that I categorised him as an eccentric, mostly because of his appearance. As lunch was served and most of us were involved in the business, we started talking aeroplanes. All boys together, we were soon chatting away like old friends, and then I was surprised, because this particular old boy seemed to know an awful lot about aviating. When it transpired that he had been a *fighter pilot* in the 1960s and 70s with a Gulf State's National Air Force, you could have blown me down with the proverbial feather!

Not only that, but he spoke about all of his training with the Royal Air Force and soon there was so much which we had in common. This little old man had actually been trained by the RAF to fly Lightnings – amazing! To think of him strapping into one of these supersonic single-seaters was an incredible mental image, but of course he said with a twinkle in his eye, "We were young then and not afraid of anything!" I nodded silently and listened intently as he revealed all the intricate details which he recalled with perfect long-term memory to paint a vivid picture of flying these phenomenal jet fighters. No need for camouflage in those days of course, just polished aluminium and the ability to fly at Mach 2 – wonderful.

I remembered that they were one of the first aircraft which could climb vertically AND accelerate, with a power to weight ratio greater than 1:1 – awesome. By the end of the lunch I was enchanted, what a wonderful, special man he was, so unassuming, yet so rich in experience. He served his country for 20 years in the Air Force, before leaving with a high rank and pension to work in business. As a pilot, he had been on the ground now since his last flight, thirty plus years ago. As we bid our farewells to the party on the windy apron, I made a point of shaking his hand warmly and thanking him most sincerely for telling us what he recalled about his flying career over lunch.

As he climbed the airstairs of the brand new Gulfstream to enter the world of luxurious air travel as a client, he turned and smiled at me.

I nodded and gave a casual, mock salute in return and I thought to myself, *'yes he was probably Groundhappy once... but I think he's got over it now!'*

The LPC (Lemon Pie Club).

(Spoil me with some lemon pie...   Yes those Presidential flightcrews are very spoilt)

The flightdeck door opened and the new Captain U/T (Under Training) entered. He had just returned from the forward cargo hold of the big Boeing once again bathed in sweat. Outside the temperature was baking hot – after all this was Africa and in the middle of the day +38°C is not uncommon. He wiped his brow with a handkerchief; the holds have no air-conditioning system.
"Well that's all the bags loaded and I have secured the nets okay, it was a swine of a job, but I managed to close the cargo door without trapping my fingers in it..." He sat in his Captain's seat, his uniform shirt soaking and looked across at me, "you never said I had to work as a baggage handler too!" I grinned back at him and replied, "Yeah... but just wait until you taste the Lemon Pie!"

+   +   +

The world of the corporate jet pilot has always seemed to be a privileged one when it comes to flying for a living. The down side is usually given as being 'on-call' a lot of the time, often 24/7 for a truly Private Jet, which is operated outside of public transport regulations regarding maximum duty times etc. The upside is that normally the terms and conditions of service are very generous. There was a time when I made the transition to flying "Bizjets" and was then engaged in training pilots in this field, most interesting it was too. The first thing I noted was that the actual flying of the aircraft is nearly identical. There are some considerable differences regarding passenger comfort, but we will consider those later. Technical competence and safety are very much top of the list of priorities in both spheres as one would expect, after all we are dealing with high performance jet aircraft, some of which are the size of large airliners. When you are operating at this level in commercial aviation, it is vitally important to get it right.

Unfortunately I do not have the demographics to hand, but I am fairly sure that corporate aviation employs a much greater percentage of older pilots. The key factor here is not just their age of course, but the operators know that with age comes experience and it is that broad base of previous experience which is a major safety element. There are several charter brokers who always ask the operators (on behalf of their clients) about the experience level of the pilots who are planned to operate the flight for them. Normally they wish to see this expressed in flying hours, both TT (Total Time) and hours on type. A further breakdown is sometimes required of whether these hours are P1 or P2. The very rich and famous can be quite fussy and with good reason – if they are paying the piper, they know they can call the tune. They are also generally more aware than the average passenger who flies, about exactly why some aircraft accidents have happened in the past and why there really are no old, bold pilots...

I had the pleasure to be involved in the recruitment of some 'new' pilots to the corporate jet operation and they were moved to say that they were very impressed with the experience levels of the pilots already on the team. During their Operator Conversion Course, we spent a couple of pleasant evenings sitting together talking about previous jobs, former companies, mutual friends and lucky escapes. We were a sight to behold, all that grey and thinning hair, tanned faces etched with the laughter lines of a hundred thousand jokes and large chronograph watches of course. Was it convivial? Certainly. Reassuring? Definitely. Comfortable? Of course! Yes I too am now becoming a 'Silver Back' I guess and I know that I am not alone in being happiest when surrounded by other highly experienced aviators – especially when I fly.

Without meaning any disrespect to the next generation of pilots, it is just simply more relaxing working with experienced professionals who have seen so much before. Flying the aeroplane to a very high standard of accuracy is a given. CRM is almost never an issue because you are sitting in the comfort of a Gentleman's Club surrounded by likeminded gentlemen – all the Silver Back monkeys together! During one of those 'convivial' evenings, one of the new recruits turned to me, wiping the tears from his eyes from yet another well told story and said, "It's brilliant, how did you do it? How did you get all these experienced guys together in one team?" He was genuinely delighted to be joining a team where he knew he could rely 100% on any of the other team members. It was interesting to think that here was a 50 something ex Belgian Air Force Pilot with many years flying the F16 and that was before he came out to operate commercial jets which had been his profession now for more than a decade.

So are the corporate jet pilots really that spoilt? I suppose you have to compare apples with apples and if they are better treated than their airline counterparts, then they probably deserve it when you consider the extraordinary challenges they have to face. Without going into too much detail, the airlines generally have a substantial support network with big shiny flight operations departments to provide 24/7 global cover for the crews who are out flying the line. In the Bizjet environment, often the pilots have to fend for themselves and soon find they can multitask with the best of them. In the smaller cabin jets for example, the pilots are often faced with loading and offloading the passengers' baggage, making all the galley preparations, restocking the bar and even giving the passengers the safety demonstration! On arrival at destination, they often help passengers find their way from airside, after liaising for the transport to meet the correct time of arrival of the flight. Even then their work is not done as many of them are faced with cleaning the cabin of the aircraft too, which includes wiping down all the table surfaces, cleaning the windows, polishing leather seats and hoovering the deep pile carpet. In the case of the large cabin VIP airliner which we were operating, the whole team got involved, but it still took time. There are up to seven cabin crew and maybe three or four flightdeck crew – we would normally carry a travelling engineer to support the operation and sometimes an extra pilot for the longer range operations.

As always in life however, there are compensations for all this extra work which is never put into any pilot's contract of employment. Certainly one of these benefits is the catering which is supplied for the crew. Often the crew have access to first class catering and the quality of the food on offer is truly breathtaking. If you are used to 'airline fare' the difference is astounding. I recall one beautiful moment when I was on the 'phone to home while we were waiting on the ramp in Nice for the passengers to arrive. As we had positioned the aircraft empty to Nice and were then picking up the passengers, we had arranged to load VIP catering on arrival in France so we were all a little bit peckish on arrival. The flightdeck door opened and in walked one of our young ladies with a tray of snacks... My wife still recalls my words of farewell, "Whoah! Sorry darling, I've got to go, the canapés have arrived!" and a fine sight they were too. Of all the nations in the world, perhaps it is the French who take their food most seriously, so when you order VIP catering on the French Riviera, you know you are in for a real treat.

A perfect example of this was on another flight when we were taking some Middle Eastern Princesses from Italy into Barcelona. It was a relatively short flight, but the flight attendants provided an awesome lunch, complete with silver service and this can take time. Just as we were about to commence descent the senior flight attendant contacted the flightdeck to ask "how much longer 'till landing?" I informed her that we had around 30 minutes to go, to which she replied, "Is it possible we can have another 10 or 15 minutes we are still serving the food?"
"Yes, no problem at all, you've got it" was my cheerful response, to which the other Captain on the flightdeck looked at me and said "You're kidding, right?" I smiled and shook my head. As I was operating the radio at this time, I called the controller.
"Marseilles Control this is XXX we request another 15 minutes airborne please? We can take up a holding pattern if you like". There was a pause before a rather surprised Frenchman replied, "Erm, XXX what is the raison for the dee-lay Monsieur... do you 'ave a problem?"
"Negative Marseilles, this is a VIP flight and our passengers have not finished their lunch!" Now he knew and he responded as any Frenchman would.

"Oh! But of course Monsieur, that is not a problem, I will inform Barcelona control and they will coordinate the 'olding for you". Sometime later, the cabin crew had finished their service and called us on the interphone, "You can land in twenty minutes if you like" and all was well. I pointed out to my colleague that he had just joined the airline where the cabin crew tell us "twenty minutes to landing".

Now I know what you are thinking, what about the Lemon Pie? Well this came about during a series of Head-of-State flights when the new Captain I was training was expressing surprise and pretend horror at some of the duties which we had to perform to keep the show on the road. Whenever he came across yet another unpleasant and un-pilot like function to be performed, he would say something like, "You never mentioned this at the interview..." and my response became the standard, "Well... we didn't mention the Lemon Pie either... and believe me the taste is to die for!" Needless to say this went on for several days and unfortunately Lemon Pie was not one of the desserts loaded by the VIP caterers for the airports we visited until we landed in Paris Le Bourget from the USA.

Once again much elbow grease and hard work greeted us here. I was pleased to see that the new Skipper pulled his weight and got stuck in with the rest of us – very gratifying. After departure from Paris heading for Africa, once we were in the cruise and the passengers had been fed, the flight attendants came to serve our lunch. The crab seafood starter was a delight and the main courses were all delicious, then the 'piece de resistance' – The Lemon Pie. My man had two helpings and his facial expression changed as the angelic pudding melted in his mouth – he had died and gone to heaven!

Now he really was a member of the LPC.

Shoot the Pilot...?

(The BAD old days. Yes they really knew how to play the blame game then).

I recall a little while back now, when I was doing a Flight Operations management job, walking into the Flight Ops control room the day after the airline had experienced a serious incident. It was not a new type of event – in fact it had happened many times before with various airlines. The aircraft took off and the crew were unable to retract the landing gear... yes you guessed it, the undercarriage ground lock pins had been left in! Well naturally you are unable to fly very far or very fast in this condition, so they returned to the airport and landed again ten minutes later.

Apart from a suitable amount of embarrassment among the operating crew and the maintenance staff who dispatched the airliner, no damage was done and nobody was injured. It was a mistake, (a human error), which fortunately resulted in nothing more than wounded pride. The follow-on from the incident was that there was an Air Safety Report raised by the crew and an investigation carried out by the Air Safety team to establish the facts and analyse the cause.

Of course what normally happens is that the Ground Engineer should remove the Ground Lock Pins before flight and additionally the pilots should check these have been removed during their preflight walk-round. Neither of these two procedures occurred as they should have done, so the pins were left unnoticed. The memorable part for me though was when I walked into the Ops Room and was greeted by the Ops Supervisor who was obviously aware of what had happened the night before. He approached me with a twinkle in his eye and I knew instantly what he wanted to talk about.

"So you heard about the turnback of Flight XXX last night...?" he asked and I could tell he already knew my answer. I was instantly on guard because I know that it is all too easy to judge people's flying skills standing at the bar in the Flying Club. In a similar way, some of our earthbound colleagues in the airlines succumb to the temptation to judge first and ask questions later. I was therefore rather cautious with my reply.

"Yes, I heard about it", I shrugged my shoulders, "what can you say? There but for the Grace of God go all the rest of us". He looked at me and could not resist smiling as he responded.

"Shall we shoot the Pilot and hang the Engineer? Or shall we do it the other way round...?" At this I laughed out loud, it really was not what I was expecting to hear and it was genuinely funny.

"No Andrew! Those were the BAD old days! We won't be hanging, or shooting anybody. We will find out why it happened and then put into practice the lessons we can learn from the incident and inform all the other crews so it doesn't happen again". He was clearly very pleased with himself at the effect of his little joke and I still chuckle to myself even now when I think of it.

Was it really like that in the bad old days? And another question to ask, is 'how far back do you go' to see what it was like before the words 'No' and 'Blame' were put together in the same sentence? The answers are "Yes" and "Not too long ago!" I can certainly recall when a Fleet Captain (Pilot Manager) at an airline in the '90s was variously known as 'Darth Vader' or 'Prince of Darkness'. These titles were not undeserved it seemed, if the crewroom gossips were to be believed. He was renowned for pulling pilots off the line and getting the metaphorical gallows ready in his office on the top floor for when they were to come for an interview with him. This was in the days before 'Human Resources' was invented. Innocent until proven guilty... What? Don't make me laugh! It reminded me particularly of the story about the Army Colonel who was scheduled to carry out a disciplinary hearing, shouting from his office desk through the open door, "Wheel the guilty bastard in Sarn't Major... AND HIS LYING FRIENDS!"

The same attitude of presumption of guilt pervaded this particular airline fleet at that time and the culture always comes from the top. Literally a climate of fear existed and all of us line pilots felt very uncomfortable in the presence of this gentleman – that's the Fleet Captain, not the Army Colonel! Well, in fact it would not matter, one could have deputised for the other without anybody noticing the difference.

I was travelling back from holiday on the flightdeck jumpseat once (with the permission of the Captain) and as I opened the flightdeck door I saw that it was Lord Vader in the left-hand seat and an experienced First Officer in the right. In fact I always got on quite well with the Fleet Captain, I guess because I was reasonably competent at my job and not easily intimidated by senior managers. He joked, "Oh! If I had known it was YOU, I would not have said Yes!" (A reference to his authorisation being sought for jumpseat travel). I replied.
"Well... if I had known it was YOU flying the jet Captain, I wouldn't have ASKED!"

As I took my seat and strapped in, they were calling for start-up and pushback, but something was wrong. The atmosphere was ice cold and not just because of the air-conditioning packs being set too cool. Although the flight was not supposed to be a 'Check', it turned into a Line Check of the worst sort and by the time we reached our home-base the First Officer was an emotional wreck. The more mistakes he made, the more the Captain barked at him and the more the Captain barked, the less competent the co-pilot became. I felt really sorry for the guy, but as I was not a member of legally nominated operating crew I just sat silently on the observer's crew-seat and cringed.

In the cruise, I tried to defuse the situation a little by some cheerful chat about what we had done on holiday etc when the Captain asked me, but the First Officer looked completely miserable. Worse still it was his PF (Pilot Flying) sector on the way back, so he was demonstrating his flying skills while under extreme scrutiny from the left-hand seat. I watched in silent horror as the F/O listened to the Automated Terminal Information Service (ATIS) and it was broadcasting a Non-Precision Approach (NPA) with the ILS Glidepath out of service... Oh? This was not good news, but sadly in his haste to respond to the Skipper's "Get the weather!" He omitted to write down that it was a Localiser only approach and in fact I don't think he even registered it while listening to the broadcast. I was caught in a trap. It was clear from the way the Fleet Captain reacted (with raised eyebrows) that he knew all about the LLZ approach – in fact it had been on the Notams but the F/O had forgotten. As the F/O turned away, the Captain gave me a conspiratorial look which I correctly interpreted as 'Keep quiet Jim and let's see what happens...'

What was I to do? I thought through all the various scenarios and even considered trying to pass the co-pilot a slip of paper warning him of the imminent disaster for his career – but it was no good. At the end of the day, I resolved that I would ONLY be able to 'interfere' legally if the flight was to become unsafe. In the meantime I had to sit and watch as the entrapment unfolded. Inwardly I groaned as the aircraft intercepted the localiser and the F/O armed the autopilot. There was clearly no G/P signal showing and the ARMED caption meant nothing. We would fly level straight through the point of final descent. I thought, 'this could be a go-around' and then felt sick inside. Why didn't he note the ATIS remark "glidepath out of service", but that was history now. How far would the Captain let it go...

I knew from my Flight Instructor days that it is important for the QFI to let the student pilot make the mistakes up to a point and then to correct them so they can learn the lesson, but this was a public transport flight with paying passengers onboard? And we do not DO failure management 'on the line', only in the Simulator – now it was my turn to feel miserable. At the time I was a junior Line pilot and this Skipper was MY boss, Arrrgh, what to do? The distance clicked away and the airliner was still flying level for what seemed like ages – we were fast approaching the final descent point, he didn't notice. There was then a broad hint from the left-hand seat,

"Where is the glideslope? Should you not be able to see it by now?" No response from the co-pilot – oh dear... The Captain continued, "Did you really listen to the ATIS properly?! We should be carrying out a LOCALISER ONLY APPROACH!" Now there was a reaction.

"What?! I don't understand...? Whoa, *wha...wh..?*" The Training Captain had seen enough by this stage and he realised that as we were still in cloud it was necessary to carry out some sort of instrument approach to get visual for the landing. He shouted in a loud voice.

"START THE DESCENT MAN... GET ON WITH IT! *VERTICAL SPEED DOWN!... RIGHT - I HAVE CONTROL!"* The poor First Officer had now turned to jelly and the Captain reached across and was putting the landing gear down himself, while operating the flaps and dialling the autopilot with the V/S mode to get the machine descending rapidly. We were on the centreline and still above Minimum Safe Altitude, so I could still keep quiet legitimately. It was a perfect example of lack of Situational Awareness for the First Officer who had been behind the aircraft from the start, but it was a dramatic way in which to be shown it by a Training Captain.

Fortunately we had plenty of height as we broke cloud and even though it was clear we were very high on final approach, the Captain made some smooth 'S' turns, gliding with full flap and gear down to get us in the groove by five hundred feet to go. The after landing scan and taxi-in were carried out in frozen silence. When Mister Boeing ordained that a quiet flightdeck was the aim, I was sure this was not what he had in mind.

By the time the engines were shutdown; I was unstrapped and briefly said my thanks for the jumpseat ride home. I was off like a 'Robber's dog' up the airbridge and into the terminal before starting to breathe easily again – what a horrible experience.

The poor old F/O was suspended and had to go back to the simulator and then through another Line Check before he was allowed to fly the Line again. The Fleet Captain continued his reign of terror for a considerable period to the detriment of several careers. That particular co-pilot never got offered a Command with the airline.

Do you know it's a funny thing, progress in our industry. Sometimes it is a case of two steps forward and one step back, while at other times you actually feel we really are moving in the right direction. Certainly this is true in the area of 'Flight Safety', which has evolved over the past few decades.

Now in most progressive companies there is a well established "No-Blame" or "Non-Punitive" culture. The funniest thing though, is that it has taken us so long to realise that this is truly the ONLY way forward.

After all we have known it for many, many years and I can prove it for you in an ancient proverb…"*To err is Human, to forgive is Divine*". Think about it.

You know when you've really made it as a superstar -
when you can have a proper Christmas Tree in your own private jet.
Bizjets don't come much bigger than this one.

Captain Jack Daniels.

(JD and coke anyone? While we watch the sun go down over Ahmedabad).

Captain Jack was one of the old school. He had spent 16 years in the Royal Air Force flying for Her Majesty and then another 20 years flying airliners on charter holidays to and from the UK. He had been a 'Skipper' for a very long time and honestly I think if you had removed Jack's cynical gland from his body he would have died. He had flown just about every charter jet airliner that had ever been built and was a naturally gifted pilot. The Boeing 757 was just another jet to Jack, but to me at that time it was like a spaceship! I was what they called 'bright-eyed and bushy-tailed' then and I worked as Jack's co-pilot flying the bucket and spade brigade – British holidaymakers going abroad.

In the early days I used to fly a lot with Jack, it was not a huge base and the pilots generally all knew each other. Sometimes the rostering was not very imaginative and you found yourself flying on similar routes at similar times with the same crew for what seemed like weeks on end. I remember coming into work one summer evening as the sun was going down and Jack was the captain for a night flight to Dalaman. He greeted me with, "Ahh! I see you're on the Turkey part of the roster... like me". That was Jack, never at a loss for a one-liner.

Perhaps it was later that night, or another night like it, that we were flying together passing Belgrade and the young female ATC controller kept asking different aircraft for their indicated Mach number. Probably she was working on longitudinal separation by ensuring that airliners at the same level did not infringe the distance minima, all Jack said was "Humph! She's doing a Mach number survey". Which I thought was quite amusing at the time. In fact he was a funny man, if you managed to look past the cold exterior and (at times) acid tongue. He was a very gifted aviator, but he was a non-standard one and that was really the big issue.

In many ways the management used to love him because they reckoned he earned his salary back in only a few months by the fact that he burned less fuel than any other captain in the company. Of course this was in the days before Flight Data Monitoring had grown into the science which we have today. We are going back 20+ years here in the days before Safety Management Systems, Error trapping, CRM and 'Health and Safety' came along. In those days the definition of an unstable approach was not as clearly defined as we have it now, where an airliner must be in the landing configuration, on centreline, on slope, on speed with correct power applied by one thousand feet on finals. 'If not then a go-around must be flown' – that's what it says in most airline flight operations manuals these days.

The reasons are clear; too many airline accidents occurred either because pilots continued to try to land without sufficient runway left to stop or because they undershot the threshold and hit the ground too short. We should always aim to touchdown at the one thousand foot point with an airliner – this then gives plenty of latitude for error and keeps the operation safe. Of course this was not challenging enough for Jack and in his eyes it burned too much fuel. When the weather was right, with a clear blue sky and you could see for miles and miles, I saw Jack carry out a deadstick (glide approach) landing to touchdown at the thousand foot point on the runway in the 757 *and the thrust levers remained completely closed from top of descent!* It was an awesome performance and a demonstration of near perfect judgement of the energy levels required as he decided when to deploy flaps and gear to slow the aircraft down for landing. Not only that, but I saw him do it on consecutive days; it was no fluke – he really was that good!

There was a downside to flying with Jack though and it was this. He wanted to do everything as fast as possible and the cabin crew always joked that you would never be late home with Jack. There was no doubt about it, he was a strain to fly with in the flightdeck and all of us newbie co-pilots hated it. Only later did I analyse why I hated flying with him and really it boiled down to two things. Firstly he was non-standard, not just in some of the things he did, but in *virtually everything* he did while flying; and secondly he used to pressurise his co-pilots below 10,000 feet. I recall that when he was acting as Pilot Flying he used to do everything so quickly that it was hard to follow what he was doing.

So instead of it being a proper two crew operation, the poor old FO was left wondering what was happening. Jack would get so far ahead of the aeroplane that there would be a huge chasm in the flightdeck and pity the inexperienced First Officer whom he had left behind. It was different once you gained more hours on the aircraft and became used to the operation though, because then at least you could mentally 'stay with him' in the headlong rush along the airways. The expression 'he didn't suffer fools gladly' could have been written specially for Jack, but if you got up towards his level of operational speed, then he had respect for you and even bothered to include you in some of the decision making process.

An example of this was when he was acting as Pilot Monitoring on an approach in good weather to Alicante airport on a flight from Manchester – the FO was flying the approach. At about 10 miles out on finals for Runway 11, he dialled in the ADF frequencies for the Runway 24 approach back at Manchester – a completely non-standard thing to do. The First Officer who was flying the aircraft said to Jack "What have you done that for?" to which the reply was,

"Just getting ahead of the game... we are going to Manchester next". The FO quickly reached down and deftly swapped them both back to Alicante Runway 11 frequencies,
"And why have you done THAT?" Said Jack irritated that the FO could react so smartly. Immediately the response came from the right-hand seat.

"Well using your principle, we're rostered to come here again tomorrow!"

Of course the stories about what Jack did and when on the line were legendary and many were second-hand. However I really was there at Tenerife one night and we were taxiing out in another 757, from the Gatwick fleet when we heard the Manchester flight arriving on the radio. It was a beautiful night, ideal for a visual approach onto runway 08, downwind, right-hand pattern over the sea. Jack's voice came over the R/T on the tower frequency announcing their arrival into the visual circuit and in the background of the transmission was the overspeed clacker in the flightdeck!

"*Clack, Clack, Clack...*Visual downwind, call you on finals, *Clack, Clack, Clack!*" Now the overspeed clacker is set to trigger at 350 knots low level, so that must have been the speed they were coming downwind at. The Captain I was flying with and I laughed so much; we were still chuckling hours later during our arrival into Gatwick.

There were numerous events which Jack was called into the office for and a common theme appeared to be that on several occasions he would carry out the takeoff before the Cabin Crew had given the 'Cabin Secure' message to the flightdeck. There was none of that "Just two minutes for the cabin", on the R/T to the tower as you approached the holding point with Jack. Oh no, if it was a choice of a delay for traffic coming onto finals at 4 miles or accepting an immediate departure, then we rolled! Needless to say the sight of Cabin Crew hanging on to seats in the aisles as the aircraft rotated was probably a little disturbing for the passengers even then. These days there would be a major enquiry.

Was he safe? That is a question I often got asked by other pilots when I tell 'this is what Jack did' stories. The answer to that is a definite yes. Not only safe, he was brilliant. Once you got used to the way in which he operated and got up to speed with using the automatics, although exhausting, Jack was great to fly with - but still non-standard of course. I remember him on a flight from Malta in the early hours of the morning (still dark) and we had just reached our cruising altitude. He started to get some Jeppesen airways charts out from the aircraft flightbag – this was novel. I didn't think I had ever seen him use a chart before. He was so completely familiar with every route in Europe, it seemed superfluous.

He began to open the charts out fully, and then tuck the edges into the surrounds of the flightdeck windows, when it literally *dawned* on me. The sun would be coming up in an hour or so and he didn't want to be disturbed from his slumber. Because slumber he did in the cruise, he could hardly stay awake on the way home to Manchester where we were based. Once at top of climb out of 'funny place' and heading for home in the early hours, he would ask nonchalantly, "Do you feel okay? Can you take the radio for a bit while I have a kip?" of course, in those days I was so excited to be flying in an airliner cockpit, I could never sleep anyway, so I always answered yes.

He would then push his seat all the way back to full recline, put his headset on low volume over both ears, close his eyes and he would be gone. The sun would come up and it was just me and the controller – hardly any other traffic around. Mach .8 at 36,000 feet is a lonely place to be when there is just one of you flying along as the sun comes up behind you. I used to look over at him, snoring away and I thought to myself, *I will never be like you.* The man's flying skills were brilliant, but his people skills? Well that was another story entirely. I guess he had just done too much. Too many nightflights to the same destinations; too many sunrises in flightdecks all over the world; too many x-ray security checks; too many staff car parks, tired after a nightflight looking for where you left the car... but, that was ...another flight! *'Oh come on! It must be around here somewhere?!'* Well anyway, I distinctly recall thinking to myself; *I will never be you Jack Daniels.*

Fast forward now to the end of '95 and I was still flying the same aeroplanes with the same airline, but I had been a captain myself for a couple of years. Maybe I had done too many nightflights to the same destinations... At top of climb out of Tenerife on the way home to Manchester, I said to the FO, "Are you feeling okay mate? Can you take the radio for a bit?" I knew nothing more until top of descent, when he shook my shoulder and said, "Here James, it's the weather for Manchester, landing on Runway 24 this morning". I was shocked. Oh My God! Have I really become like him!? I said to the FO, "That's it, I have got to find another job, I have become Captain Jack!" he didn't know what I was talking about, so I explained. Within a day or so I had resigned and was soon on my way to fly Boeing 767s as a Captain for Alitalia on the contract with Ansett – and that WAS the best job in the world at that time.

Funnily enough I did come across him again, many years later and several time zones from the UK in Ahmedabad while operating B767s for Air India on another wet lease contract. You see Gujarat is a dry state and alcohol is not openly sold there, but is allowed discreetly for westerners under strict liquor licence rules. Normally as airline crew on short stopovers, we were unable and unwilling to make all the complicated bureaucratic arrangements to buy beers, or whatever, so we didn't bother.

Some bright minded individual, who obviously enjoyed an adult beverage after flying; did go to the trouble of making an informal arrangement however, which served us all very well. As we checked into the Crew Hotel in Ahmedabad we could obtain access to alcohol in a charming and discreet manner by asking the right question of the staff behind the desk.

They would then carefully bring out a large, specially labelled cardboard box. Inside the box, wrapped in layers and layers of plastic carrier bags was a large bottle of spirits which when mixed with Coca-Cola, made a very pleasant sundowner to be enjoyed in good company on the roof of the hotel, prior to visiting the ground floor restaurant for one of the best curry buffets in the entire sub-continent.

Well that contract is long since gone as Air India got their act together and managed to train enough crews to fly all the new 777s they bought from Boeing.

However if you ever stay in Le Meridien hotel in Khanpur, Ahmedabad and fancy a drink, simply ask the desk clerk, **"Is Captain JACK DANIELS in the house?"**

PS. Of course 'Jack Daniels' was not his real name, but it's how I like to remember him. I think he would have liked it too if he had ever known about it. Perhaps in a funny sort of way, Jack did me a favour really, because from that moment of revelation while flying charter 757s for Air 2000, I knew I just HAD to go. Some people never know their moment and maybe hang on too long in the same position.

Testing Times.

The amazing thing about aeroplanes generally - and airliners in particular - is that they very, very, rarely go wrong. In the past few decades, technical advancement has not been limited solely to R&D (Research and Development), but also to all aspects of maintenance and engineering. Of course even though the modern aircraft are computer designed and even computer 'flown' before they are actually built, there is still room for good old fashioned gremlins to appear. Even the largest aircraft manufacturer is not immune to this phenomenon.

There is still plenty of need for real 'test' flying however when it comes to proving that the aeroplane functions as it is supposed to. This is often required when an airframe changes ownership or when it has undergone certain types of maintenance, particularly involving changes to the flight control surfaces. We have all heard stories about aircraft where mistakes were made in the rebuilding of them such that the flying controls did not act in the correct way, but I never expected to see it myself. Until one day I was asked to carry out a testflight of a light aircraft for the owner. I made time to receive a very comprehensive briefing from the Civil Aviation Authority, which covered all aspects of light aeroplane testing and I had plenty of flying experience including aerobatics. I was already familiar with the aircraft and had a good relationship with the engineer who had carried out the rebuild of the plane which had been imported from the USA.

It was a lovely little machine really, fabric wings and tricycle undercarriage with quite a high powered engine, so theoretically it should have had good short-field performance. Exactly how good, I was to find out later... There should not have been any commercial pressure regarding this job, but as luck would have it the owner who imported the machine for reassembly had now secured the sale of the aircraft and was keen to get the money. It was winter in the UK and the weather was not playing the game. It was one of those periods when the skies were leaden, even when you could see them.

There was really poor visibility trapped under a layer of thick cloud with little chance of a change of airmass. The air was still for day after day and we would need at least some good visual conditions to go testflying. Add to this the fact that the aircraft had been reconstructed at a grass strip in the middle of the countryside and the first flight was also a ferry flight to take it to another airfield with grass runways which were waterlogged. Every day I checked the weather and every day the owner was on the 'phone to me trying to persuade me to fly the aeroplane. He did not seem to see the weather reports in the same way as I did and more than once I was at pains to explain to him carefully that it was just not possible to do what he asked.

I distinctly recall one particular 'phone conversation when he said to me, "Why aren't you going today? It is what they call VFR isn't it?"

I laughed at his description of the clag which I could see outside the window of the hangar and said, "Yes, but ONLY if that stands for Very F****** Risky!"

I am a great believer in the old adage that it is always 'better to be down here wishing you were up there...' So in the main, I am happy to wait for the weather to improve before we fly. After one of the longest periods of socked-in conditions that I have experienced for a long time, eventually there was a change in the air mass and we had a large Atlantic depression come through the UK from west to east. Never had I been so happy to see a cold front, I can tell you.

We went through all the documentation carefully together; me and the engineer and I checked all the duplicate inspections had been done. He was actually a PPL holder himself and a keen aviator too, so he volunteered to accompany me on the testflight. I have got to say that from the pilot's point of view this is the MOST reassuring thing the engineers can say. It is worth so much more than any documentation or assurances of airworthiness from any other source. When the engineer who actually built the darn thing puts his life on the line with yours, then you can be sure he believes 100% in the quality of his own work! In fact thinking back now, I cannot recall many times when the engineers have not wished to climb aboard for the testflight, whatever machine it is.

With regard to our little classic aeroplane, we had done all the checks and lined up for the takeoff run from the top of the field. This particular grass strip has a pronounced slope on it, so we invariably took off downhill, virtually regardless of the wind conditions. Today, the wind was actually blowing quite strongly up the slope, so an uphill landing would have been tricky. I had been quite careful about setting up the trim for takeoff, especially in the light of the fact that we had not flown this aeroplane before – in fact nobody had done so for 14 years, so this was quite an event for us. With full power applied, there was negligible swing and with only two of us onboard, the acceleration was rapid indeed. I had the control column forward to lift the tail and very slowly she reacted to the control forces. 'Wow, this machine's tail heavy' I thought to myself as all of a sudden passing about 40 mph we were off the ground with me still pushing hard!

"Well this IS a new experience", I said to the engineer on the intercom as I pushed hard and continued winding tailplane trim to try to keep the machine level. I had never before had to push the control column forward and keep pushing during the takeoff. The acceleration was now quite slow as we were climbing rapidly with a high nose attitude, as I brought the power back, the nose attitude lowered, but we lost height and hardly gained any speed.

I settled on a compromise of lots of forward pressure on the elevators and not quite so much power. We were flying, but it was not a pleasant experience – "It feels like *somebody* has put the tail on upside down!" I said grimly to my colleague, looking across at him – he appeared most uncomfortable.

"Here you try and fly it!" I shouted, handing over control to him. As I did so, he had not anticipated the forces involved and the nose pitched up dramatically, the speed fell away and we nearly stalled. I took control again and we had to decide what to do. A return to the airfield of departure was not really an option as the wind was out of limits and one of the closest potential destinations was the planned airport for arrival to the main engineering base. We decided to head for there as this would be (commercially) the most preferable. I was still pushing hard as we came in to land about 40 minutes later and we taxied in towards the big hangar with relief that the experience was over. The engineers were relieved that we had completed the delivery flight although not much of the testflight schedule had been achieved.

In fact when they checked the controls later, it seems that the screwjack which has the aeroplane longitudinal trim control on it, really had been fitted upside down and therefore it was not possible to trim out the forces on the tail. The aircraft was 'tail-heavy' all the time and we only just had enough control authority to actually fly it straight and level. Before the ferry flight, we had both been asked by various friends if they could come along for the ride - we had two spare seats in the back after all... Fortunately we had resisted the temptation to 'bend the rules' and carry passengers on what should have been a test-flight. If there had been passenger weight in the rear of the cabin too we would never have made it, pure and simple.

Thinking back on this event now with the benefit of hindsight, although the mission was accomplished in that we delivered the aircraft to where it was supposed to go, I did make one big mistake and that was this. The control forces were really abnormal and the manufacturer had never designed the aeroplane to be flown with such out of trim forces to be applied to the flying controls. This included all of the levers, linkages, pulleys, cables and so forth.

For me to have opted to fly past a couple of large airfields that were open with excellent facilities was really dumb when it could have shortened the time that the extreme forces were experienced by the airframe.

The only reason I can think of is that I was conscious of what I thought the owner might say about a diversion. These were early days in my flying career and I have learned a lot since then.

With FO Tom Carter and one of our coolest VIP customers

Scared of the Dark?

From the rear cockpit, his voice was gravelly over the intercom in the headphones of my flying helmet as I started the engine of the BAe Hawk T1A advanced jet trainer. "Now remember, I'm an old man and we just want to have a nice quiet nightflight with no unnecessary *excitement*, d'y'hear me?" I smiled and replied briskly, "Yes Sir!" It was a good night for flying with calm wind and excellent visibility. Although there was total cloud cover with a base of 4000 feet or so, the Metman at the briefing assured that the tops were only 9000 feet and above that was clear sky. It was nearly a full moon too, a 'night flier's moon' so we should get a reasonable visual horizon for our sortie. Shortly after we were airborne, with the gear and flaps away and climbing up towards the cloudbase, I heard the familiar, "I have control" growled in my ears, so I relaxed and let him take over.

He checked the airspace was clear above us with a call to the military radar unit and then I felt the nose of the Hawk pitch upwards to a steep angle - soon we were in the thick grey clag. Solidly on instruments now, I felt my eyes drawn to the large Attitude Indicator in front of me with regular glances to and from the other major flight instruments – Selective Radial Scan. As we had built up plenty of speed beneath the clouds before we pulled up, this energy had been turned into vertical speed and rapidly increasing altitude – the VSI was off the scale which only read up to 6000 feet per minute.

BOOF! We appeared to shoot out of cloud into the black sky above studded with a million twinkling diamonds – Cor! How beautiful was that? There was still loads of speed and our climb angle must have been about 40 degrees or so, "Let's have a look around shall we?" he grunted from behind me and immediately I felt the aircraft roll through 360 degrees so we could see all around us. The tops of the clouds were uniform and exactly where Mister Meteo said they would be 9000 feet above sea level, we were way above them now and the sensation made you feel a bit giddy as you looked way down to where they lay.

"Just a couple of Aeros eh?" and with that the cockpit rolled inverted and I felt increasing 'G' force as he went for a half-Cuban, I began to giggle, "Wow! Aerobatics at night? What fun?! Old man my arse!" Standing Orders forbade aerobatics in the dark, but then with such a moon and being VMC on top of the clouds with a beautiful horizon, it wasn't *really* dark was it? More rolls and loops then he had, had enough, "You have control!" came quite suddenly and I grabbed the control column and trimmed the ship out straight and level, I noted we were around 15,000 feet now and cruising at 350 knots indicated. We were heading northwest and in the distance I could just make out the light of another aircraft at around the same altitude, "Let's see who that is?" came the growl. So I pushed the throttle open and pointed the nose towards the solitary light source...

+   +   +

Statistics prove that flying at night carries significantly more risk than operating aeroplanes in daylight. Even with all of our sophisticated navigational aids and advances in lighting technology, we cannot get away from the fact that the night makes things much trickier at times. The old joke goes that "the aeroplane doesn't KNOW it is dark outside" which is a bit like saying, "the aeroplane doesn't KNOW it is flying over water", when you are halfway across the Irish Sea...

While I was learning to fly, I distinctly recall that some of our instructors got very twitchy when they were tasked to teach us how to fly after the sun had gone down., Although they were at pains to point out that "It's just like flying in daytime really and there is nothing to worry about". When later on I became a QFI myself, I realised why we said these things to our students - because we were told to! In all the patter manuals, instructors' guides and wherever else it always advised us to put the student at ease, because night-flying is dangerous enough without having the trainee paralysed by fear while they are supposed to be learning the trade.

False horizons; distorted distance judgement; apparent movement of stationary light sources; spatial disorientation, you think of it and the scientists will name it for you. It is possible to prove some of the effects yourself without ever leaving the ground, for example if you sit in a completely dark room and just have one tiny light source visible over the other side of the room, then without any other visual cues, the mind will play tricks. If you stare at the light, after some time it will appear to move. Not only that, but it is impossible to say how far away the light is without any other visual references to locate its position in space.

There are other dangers too and not just from the Human Factors angle. An old buddy of mine went to the USA many years ago to build his 'night hours'. At that time, you needed a minimum of 100 hours nightflying in your logbook to attain a commercial licence. He had only recently left the military and had very little night experience at all, although he was highly qualified and proficient military aviator who had flown all sorts of military hardware. With several thousand hours in his logbook including helicopter, 'fast jet' weapons delivery etc. he felt that perhaps the licensing people could have made an exception for him.

He was still 60 hours short, but had a job offer waiting as soon as he had converted to a civilian licence. He enquired if there was any restriction on the type/size of aircraft these hours needed to be logged in and was told he had carte blanche. So being a resourceful chap, he travelled to one of the southern states in the USA and rented the cheapest, oldest, dog of a Cessna 150 he could get his hands on. He had decided to do the 60 hours in two weeks!

Well it did not take long for my mate to realise that flying single-engine at night over areas of territory which could be anything but flat was a potentially lethal activity. He was experienced enough to realise that should the worst happen and the engine quit, he would have nil chance of making a survivable forced landing over open country with no lights. He came up with a plan that if he was gliding towards the ground, then he would wait until the last second before impact before pulling the stick all the way back and stalling the aircraft, such that the massive deceleration forces would be taken nearly vertically at a relatively low speed. The flying school was quite used to seeing the funny English chap turn up at dusk to rent an aeroplane to drone round the sky for a few hours every night and left him to it when they closed up for the day, with the instructions to note the Hobbs engine meter reading for the airborne time so they could bill him appropriately.

He soon realised that the engine meter on the Cessnas would register even on the ground at a high idle RPM and after a few nights of 'real' flying decided to limit his exposure to the risk of engine failure by sitting in the aeroplane on a deserted part of the taxiway with the engine running for a few hours. This also had its perils because not only were the aircraft cheap to rent, they were also carrying lots of defects, such as unserviceable parking brakes... To work around this, he would have to hold the toebrakes with his feet for a very long time.

It was boring 'work' and he took a book with him at night to help pass the time. Naturally the jetlag took its toll and whilst sat there with the constant drone of the engine and the heater on with a nice warm cockpit the inevitable happened - he fell asleep. His feet relaxed on the toebrakes and the result was predictable. He woke up with a real shock to find himself "in the cockpit of an aeroplane flying along, in pitch darkness and suffering apparent moderate turbulence". (His words). What he didn't realise was that the machine had left the taxiway at the first bend and was now bumping along on the grass. He said he nearly wet himself when he looked at the airspeed indicator showing zero! Fortunately as he was about to slam the throttle open he saw the altimeter was also showing zero.

With no damage done (apart from to his central nervous system) he spent the rest of the week running 2 aircraft per night for a few hours simultaneously, with the wing tiedowns still in place at their parking spots– he considered this to be a much safer option. Within two weeks had reached his target and left to take his rightful place as a pilot with Big Airways. So much for reducing the dangers of nightflying in light aircraft.

The ASI was showing nearly 400 knots and we were level at Flight Level 150 as I watched the oncoming light. At first there had been just a single, steady white light, now as we bore down on him, there was the flashing red anti-collision light also and I could see just a shade of a red wingtip navlight... How far away? So hard to tell, but my QFI in the back could see the signs as we steamed in towards the unsuspecting aircraft. He was flying in the open FIR straight and level minding his own business.

There was an oath in my ears and all of a sudden "I HAVE CONTROL!" Immediately the throttle was slammed shut and the speedbrake was deployed, but it was not enough. We looked like we were on a collision course, I braced myself. *"GRUNT!"* in my headphones again and the nose pitched up; we were rolling up and over the top of him. We could see him now quite clearly silhouetted for a moment against the lighter part of the sky below it was a Royal Navy Sea Harrier! My old gentleman instructor in the back seat was enjoying himself hugely as we completed the barrel roll right over the top of the other guy's canopy – I was in heaven!

The Navy pilot reacted quickly. It must have been a real shock for him to have a Hawk rolling round the outside of the window seemingly only a few feet distant with red anti-colls blazing away while he had been sat there fiddling with his radar or whatever he had been doing. He rolled fast now, diving to the right, but my man was just as quick. We were on his tail about 5 or 10 metres behind and in dogfighting terms he was a dead man for sure – I whooped with delight in the front seat. This really was "The Business"!

The 'G' started to increase again as he tried to out-turn us, but he had no chance and we were both diving in a spiral towards the clouds. An expletive came from behind me, "OH F***! HERE'S HIS MATE!" I twisted right round in my seat with helmet hard up against the canopy and looked back over my shoulder – WHOOPS! Another Sea Harrier was *right behind us* with his flashing wingtip lights showing he was right in there on our tail, he meant business – the hunter had become the hunted, we were toast...

Panting noises now came through the intercom as the exertion of the chase lead to extreme evasive action; we rolled left really hard and pulled straight down. The suddenness of the manoeuvre was so violent that we broke loose from the chase immediately. I called radar on the R/T for recovery to base, it was time to go home now. I was still breathing heavily and absolutely fizzing with excitement as we taxied in quietly to dispersal fifteen minutes later.

"SIR! That was... WELL... it was errr, JUST AWESOME!" I said with deep respect. His voice was quiet and calm by return, perhaps a little like Dumbledore of Harry Potter film fame some years later. All of a sudden he was just a little old quiet professor – an unbelievable transformation. "Now remember McBride, we had a nice quiet nightflight and we hardly saw another aircraft in the sky, don't forget!"

These days nightflying in the commercial world is still deeply satisfying in many ways, but never quite as exciting as I have known it in the past. When asked what my advice is for pilots who are planning to start nightflying I reply, "Get yourself a good torch!" Which I guess is about as much use as somebody who asks for a good tip being told, *"Never stand behind a reversing car!"*

Of course there are other good tips, such as "Never stand up in a small boat" and that old classic "Never put your fingers in a closing door!" Well you get the idea anyway.

1986 Tactical Weapons Unit – BAe Hawk.
"The aeroplane doesn't know it's dark outside".

Altitude Above You... and other proverbs.

(Please don't try this at home – it could ruin your whole day).

Traditionally there are three 'most useless quantities for aviators' and listed in no particular order these are, 'Runway behind you, Altitude above you and Fuel in the bowser'. There is no doubt that having a huge length of runway in front of you, in either landing or takeoff mode in a flying machine is very comforting. This requires little explanation, but the other two proverbs perhaps bear closer investigation. In fact there is a loose association and it is related to the 4th Dimension – time. More specifically when flying aeroplanes there is such a thing as 'thinking time' and this is an important element of the decision making process when managing a flight. A good example is that of a friend of mine who was training on Jet Provosts back in the early 1980s with the Royal Air Force. He had a heated debate with another 'baby pilot' as to what was the quickest way to get the aircraft into a vertical dive from level flight. Bear in mind in those days we were all encouraged to explore the full capabilities of each aircraft type that we flew. Of course there were those students among us who wanted to *really* push the boundaries...

+   +   +

The altimeter was showing 14,000 feet and the airspeed was a cool 240 knots. Outside the canopy was mostly blue sky above with some scattered cumulus clouds around – they resembled lumpy cotton-wool. The solo student pilot thought to himself *'Always cotton-wool, why do we always think they are like cotton-wool?'* He shook himself out of his reverie however and started concentrating on the flying of the machine again. The old JP3 was described as a Basic Jet Trainer and was pretty easy to fly, although the QFIs always seemed to complain about the lack of performance. To the students there was plenty to think about in the early days, but as they became more familiar with the aircraft and the way it handled they started to feel comfortable in its operation. *Familiarity breeds contempt?* Well, not that particular 'C' word exactly, but let's say Complacency. The pilot made another call on the R/T and received a negative answer from the RAF controller, "Negative, Uniform X-ray XXX, the circuit is full, continue to HOLD until advised".

Well another proverb comes to mind here, because the devil really does make "work for idle hands" and when you are training to be a fighter pilot, life gets pretty dull when you are told to fly a holding pattern... Of course the worse thing was that the 'hold' was not published, so creativity took over. The aircraft was at medium altitude in the open airspace above the beautiful Yorkshire countryside on a relatively sunny day. After completing some checks from memory, the pilot started some clearing (visual) turns to prepare for aerobatics.

Pulling up into a wing-over with 'G' falling away around the top as the wings banked through just over 90 degrees and the ASI getting really slow (around a hundred) and then down the hill the other side – *'ooh, lovely'* he thought to himself as he surveyed all the altitude beneath him. 14,000 feet is just over 2 miles to the ground and it seemed a *very* long way down at that time. Loop followed roll and barrel roll followed loop, with 'half-cuban' following barrel roll and vertical roll with stall-turn following 'half-cuban' and so on until he had exhausted all the aerobatic manoeuvres which he knew. Still at 14,000 feet with a little over 200 knots indicating, he recalled the conversation which had taken place a couple of hours previously in the crewroom that morning and having assured that there was nothing beneath the aeroplane, he rolled completely upside down and started to pull the joystick back hard... He counted aloud in his oxygen mask, panting as the 'G' loads increased briefly, "One Thousand, Two Thousand, THREE THOUSA..." the aircraft was now in a vertical dive in just less than 3 seconds, exactly as he thought it would be.

The acceleration was dramatic however and now the airspeed had literally shot up with the altimeter unwinding at a phenomenal rate! Instinctively, he closed the throttle and hit the speedbrakes – NO EFFECT, she was going down like a train and the noise level was incredible. The thought *"Pull-out!"* Went through his mind briefly, as again he increased the backward pressure on the control column and positive 'G' increased. The wind noise over the canopy was louder than he had ever experienced it and with so much speed, 5G was rapidly reached on the 'G' Meter. Grunting hard now to try and combat the effects of blood pooling in the legs, he tensed his abdominal and leg muscles *really* tight, he started to lose his vision. A grey mist descended over his eyes and now he couldn't see the 'G' Meter anymore. In fact he could not see any of the instruments at all, but the wind noise was still there in his ears, he unloaded the wings slightly and got some sight back briefly only to see **5,000 feet** on the altimeter and ***STILL GOING DOWN!*** "ArrrrruugHH!"

Grunting and panting he pulled harder and now it was nearly black, he knew it would not be long before he lost consciousness at this rate. His own 'G' tolerance put him at 6G maximum for a few seconds and then he would be gone and he had nearly reached that point. He knew he would lose his hearing last of all. But now she was slowing down, he could hear the rush of air subsiding slowly as the nose came up and the aircraft responded to the stick. Pitching up all the time, 4G became 3G, (grey mist coming back), then 2G now and he could see the altimeter and... it was finally *climbing, PASSING 2,000 feet – **YIKES!*** He felt nauseous at how close he had come to impact with the ground. There were several cute expressions in fighter pilot circles for this such as "Buying the Farm!" or "Tent-pegging!" Yes, he had *'nearly bought it'*- he was cold and shivering at the thought. The R/T interrupted him "Uniform X-ray XXX is cleared through initials for the run and break, call 'Initials'".

Speedbrakes away; throttle increasing and now he turned towards the initial point for the airfield and commenced the run-in for the break. Anybody watching from the ground would have perhaps wondered about the very 'weenie' run and break which they witnessed as the Jet Provost made the turn onto finals for landing, but then *they* had not seen what had occurred just a few minutes before!

+   +   +

Altitude is a vital commodity for flyers and when you run out of it, the aircraft has reached the surface of the earth again. If this is done in a controlled manner, it is referred to as a landing, and if uncontrolled it is a crash. Certainly that has happened many times in the past and I recall my dad telling me about some of the things he witnessed while he was with an RAF Typhoon Squadron in the Second World War. He used to say that one of the most difficult manoeuvres was "three upward rolls", carried out from low level. By 'low', I think he meant tree-top height and I now know he was referring to vertical rolls. Of course each aircraft has its own flight envelope which must obey the laws of physics and although all pilots are at different skill levels, they will only be as good as the airframe after a certain point. The story which sticks in my mind was that of a Spitfire pilot who tried three upward rolls over an airfield which my dad was stationed at only a few days before the end of the war.

He said that by this time the pilots were getting "browned off" through lack of targets and little action compared to what they had been doing for the previous weeks and months. He said the aircraft came in very fast and pulled up hard into the vertical over the centre of the airfield and started to roll. He said they all started counting aloud, "One..... T.w...o......... T.h...." but the Spitfire had run out of airspeed and the aircraft stalled and fell out of the sky. He said he was sickened by the thought of the waste of a young life and all that went with it. I was deeply moved by the story and although I have no other details, (such as squadron, registration, date, location) I believe it to be a true account of what he witnessed on that day.

+   +   +

It is also sad to think that it takes us so long to learn some things in life. Like 'Altitude above you', which is SO important. It was certainly vital to the Rolls-Royce display pilot David Moore flying Spitfire RM689 at British Aerospace Woodford on 27th June 1992. He ran out of altitude while pulling out of a loop during his low-level display and hit the ground in front of the crowd. The fatal accident report summarised that a lack of recent display practice, combined with heavy fuel-load, high ambient temperatures and too low/slow when he started the loop were to blame. They say that if he had another 60 feet of altitude on the loop entry he could have got away with it...

Coincidentally this was the day when we flew our first display in the vintage Beech 18 (Southern Comfort) at RAF St Athan in South Wales – I remember it was 32 degrees Celsius, the Beech is very 'heavy on the controls' to fly and we were soaked in sweat in our flying suits after we had finished. We had a good display, but just before leaving St Athan we heard the sad, sad news about David Moore (RIP). With the rest of the crew of Southern Comfort we flew home in virtual silence on the intercom. It was a sobering occasion for us all, but for me in particular it struck a chord.

We often think 'there but for the Grace of God go I', but in my case it really was true. I was very thoughtful about it for a long time, but kept coming back to the fact that I had learned my own lesson about having enough altitude back in 1984... in a Jet Provost Mk3A over the countryside in Yorkshire!

I got away with it, but only just. Not for nothing did the older pilots used to say to one another cheerfully, *"Try to keep the Shiny Side up!"*

Losing It.

(Sharp faculties are a given for pilots, but when they deteriorate...?)

I remember thinking to myself, *'This is hard work'* as I struggled to get all the instruments to behave themselves while flying the B737 down the ILS approach. Of course this was after we had experienced a catastrophic engine failure which had blown apart the combustion chambers of the left motor and seized the core of the engine just after V1 speed on takeoff. Being heavyweight hadn't helped, with the reduced climb performance much evident, but my own rusty handling skills had made the situation worse during the initial climb-out with the strident "BANK ANGLE!" Audible warning shouting at us, as I had failed to anticipate the rudder requirement to keep the wings level...

+   +   +

Degraded performance by pilots while flying can be from a variety of different causes. Fatigue comes to mind – the Mangalore crash in India is a good example where the Captain seems to have been asleep for most of the flight (evidenced by the loud snoring sounds on the CVR). He then went on to fly an unstable approach which lead to the accident, ignoring the poor Co-Pilots' pleas for him to Go-around.

Inadequate training is another reason for poor performance. When recruiting airline pilots, many companies use a simulator evaluation session to decide if a pilot is worth employing and in the past I have been involved in many of these assessments. Virtually all companies/organisations plan for each candidate to have a minimum of 30 minutes as PF enabling a proper assessment of their abilities. In reality, after you have done quite a lot of these and carried out hundreds of Line Training flights for new pilots, it is possible to tell within 5 minutes whether they have 'got it'. But our job is not about taking things for granted nor assuming that we know what to expect; we are tasked with 'carrying out the mission', which is why we very rarely cut short the half-hour session. Of course sometimes you do need to use the whole period to ensure that you have all the evidence you need to back up the decision which you have made as the assessor. What we are assessing in these situations is not just Attitude, it's not simply Preparedness – we are judging 2 qualities really and they are closely related. We judge Competence and Performance.

After doing lots and lots of these Sim sessions, unfortunately most just blur into one and after some time only a few really stand out. At the end of the day there are only so many ways to either fly an instrument procedure properly or cock-it-up. One of the most memorable performances which I witnessed took place in a B737 Simulator at Heathrow several years back. For this particular company, we (the assessors) were required to brief the candidate, set the Sim up then hop into the Captain's seat while the candidate sat in the right-hand seat to fly the aeroplane. So aswell as being 'part of the crew', we also had to make notes on how the flying was going. I remember that this particular young gentleman was quite tense at the beginning, so I mentally prepared myself to spend the next 30 minutes trying to get him to perform at his best. Cards on the table here, nobody wants anybody to fail, least of all the assessor. So all of us spend a lot of time putting the candidate at their ease and trying to produce the best possible environment for them to shine. On this occasion, I remember that I put even more effort into this than normal, so that by the time he was strapped into the hot-seat he was as ready as he would ever be.

Despite a careful brief, which had been preceded by extensive, detailed briefing material, things started to go wrong the moment we were airborne. Massive over-controlling, combined with an erratic approach to instrument flying lead to some spectacular unusual attitudes even before we had got the flaps away. It is quite difficult to behave in a rational manner with normal vocal tones when the 'aircraft' is being flown in a bizarre fashion, but somehow I managed it. In our line of work we talk a lot about "unstable approaches", but I had not before see an *unstable departure*! Half of my brain was checking out where they might have put the hidden camera if this was one of those wind-up TV programmes, but the other half of me knew this guy had a really serious problem. During his first ILS approach, he had major challenges in tracking the localiser and glidepath and we went from full-left deflection through to full-right a couple of times while we were supposed to be flying level at the last platform altitude before we commenced descent on the slope.

There were some prompting calls from my side as monitoring pilot, such as "Glideslope alive!" and "One-dot low!" through to "One dot HIGH!" and thereafter "FULL fly down!" – at which point he over-reacted and pushed the control column hard forward, pulling the thrust levers closed as he did so...

'Now THIS will be interesting!" I thought to myself as the 737 bunted nicely into a fairly steep dive. The glideslope came... and the glideslope went, as we barrelled on down towards Mother Earth. *'Holy Sh...!'* thought I, *'we are going to get the GPWS shortly!'* and indeed we would have done, except for one thing. I had left the cloudbase at 400 feet above the ground on the instructor's panel and the visibility was about 2 kilometres. So we popped out of cloud into murky Vis and immediately he raised the nose of the aircraft, sort of levelled off and started looking out of the window. He was looking for the runway! Bearing in mind that we had been way off the extended centreline even before we commenced our final descent – there was going to be fat chance of seeing it. I called "Speed, Speed!" as the Air Speed Indicator fell to dramatically low readings and we were quite close to the stall with full-flap and the gear down while he stuffed on loads of power.

Of course with the underslung engines of the B737, this gave a massive pitch-up moment and we re-entered IMC (cloud) again. I was astounded by the technique being displayed here; I had never before seen this kind of approach to instrument flying. Eventually I took pity on the chap and said "I have control" and hit the total freeze button. There was a big sigh of relief from my seat as I managed to breathe again for what seemed the first time in minutes, but when I looked across at the candidate and he looked back at me there was just a sort of puzzled facial expression with a vacant look in the eyes which I found very disturbing.

"Well... let's try that again shall we?" I said trying to be cheerful and repositioned the aircraft back to a 12 miles final position on the ILS localiser. As he settled down again, I made a couple of brief notes and then gave him a bit of a pep-talk. Usually you would resist doing this, but I felt that he needed every advantage if we were going to get anything meaningful out of the session. He said he was ready and appeared to absorb the training input, so when he reaffirmed he was ready, I released the freeze.

"Full-left... Full RIGHT!", localiser was swiftly followed by "Glideslope ALIVE!" and then virtually a repeat of the first attempt. Worryingly, there was no improvement and we ended up again at around 400 feet above the ground over featureless virtual terrain with gear down and landing flap deployed going round in circles. *'It really is my fault'* I thought to myself, because IF I had not left the cloudbase so high, then we would have at least had a prominent Ground Proximity alert warning and then maybe we would not be in the situation of driving the aircraft aimlessly in circles looking for the runway. When setting the simulator parameters up, I had been trying to be kind, because I know how hard it is to make the transition from Instrument Flying to Visual Flying as you break out of cloud – so if the base of the cloud, is higher it gives the pilot more time to make a stable transition and gives a greater opportunity for a successful landing.

Eventually I stopped the sim again and gave him a third attempt, this time with more briefing about where he had been going wrong. Now I really studied his instrument flying and noted that he was making the tyro mistake of 'chasing the needles'. As soon as he noticed one parameter coming adrift he fixated upon that, to the detriment of all else – literally 'he had no proper instrument scan'. My summary contained these very words and I was completely honest when I stated that I found it hard to believe he actually held a valid Commercial Pilot Instrument Rating. So here was a classic case of poor performance due to a lack of basic training.

+   +   +

As pilots get older, normally their increasing experience more than makes up for slowing down of reactions and deteriorating faculties due to age, but there are some cases where the onset of the ageing process becomes very evident. On a few occasions in the past, I have been unfortunate enough to witness the degraded skill level due to a combination of lack of recency/approaching retirement and as an examiner I have had to be the one to break the sad news to a senior gentleman or two that their performance was no longer up to the required standard to be considered safe. In modern language, they could be described as "Losing it".

In my case in the Simulator, plain old fashioned 'rustiness' from lack of recency was the reason for my struggling to achieve the required standard. Of course everything is relative and in fact my performance was assessed as 'above average', but for me, I had to work very hard to get it there. I know I breathed a sigh of relief when the Proficiency Check was over and I candidly said in the debrief, "It's so sad guys, because I remember a time when I was really quite good at this and now I feel I am losing it".

Too much time in the office tends to blunt the flying skills and perhaps there will come a time when I must decide it's time for me to stop active flying – I would like to make that call myself rather than be told by somebody else.

Flightless Birds - and Other Animals.

(Squawking sounds – but no flapping sounds...)

I have written before about the pilot who was nicknamed 'Penguin', because he spent so much time on the ground that everybody thought he had forgotten how to fly, but this was not the only flightless bird I have known in my flying career. I recall there was a manager at a previous company who was known as 'Ostrich' and you can imagine why he got the name. The poor chap could not make a decision to save his life. Whenever difficult problems arrived at his door, he would try to bury his head in the sand until they went away.

His antics were reminiscent of Major-Major, the character in the book 'Catch 22' who would leap out of his office window to evade callers so he too would not be required to make a decision. That being said, of course we have to recognise that we live and work in an industry which is populated by predominantly proactive, enthusiastic, smart individuals who enjoy working together in productive teams to produce positive results.

In the normal course of events, the most gifted, smart and well connected employees manage to progress fastest in their careers, but occasionally a 'duffer' rises through the ranks and achieves a position which is above their capabilities. There can be various convoluted reasons for this happening, but one of the ugliest of these is nepotism. When this happens, I have noticed that there is a form of subtle retribution which takes place among the 'smart set' who have not achieved such lofty heights themselves. Overnight, the duffer gains a nickname which is normally less than complimentary and tends to highlight their shortcomings for all to see...

Often it appears that the nickname is related to a particular animal or bird and this of course adds to the amusement value when related about somebody who is supposed to be in a position of power. For example, in an airline I used to work for, I overheard some of the junior line pilots talking about the latest activities of one of the very senior pilot managers.

This gentleman was renowned for sending out patronising memos to the pilots and generally making blunders which upset the more senior members of our profession. Let's face it, the job of being an airline pilot is pretty grown-up, so they tend to take offence when they are treated like children. That being said, even I laughed my head off when I heard they called him **Eeyore!** A.A. Milne has a lot to answer for by creating a character as dumb as an Ass.

I also remember being moved to a fit of giggling when I heard about a lady pilot in another company and the nickname she had earned for herself. Her recruitment and almost instant promotion to Captain had been achieved by the fact that her husband was a very senior man in the hierarchy. This process had not been a smooth one and the opinions of quite a few experienced Training Captains had been ignored in order that she might attain the much coveted left-hand seat. Now in the early months of her new command, she managed to prove that nepotism is not always a good thing, as there were several instances which demonstrated her lack of experience and unsuitability for the job. I confess I did scratch my head when I heard the nickname and asked "But why do they call her **that?"** to which my informant gleefully revealed.
"Well, you see Captain, **'EMU'** is an ugly bird and she can't fly!"

In some ways I should not have been surprised really, because pilots are always using 'bird' metaphors and similes. During commercial operations, plenty of paperwork has to be completed in order that the airline can track the progress of flight operations. Not only the company of course, but also the regulator (the CAA or national equivalent) requires that certain documentation is carried and filled in by the crew in the course of their duties. One of the most important of these forms is called by various names, depending on the company, but is actually the same form. I have known it to be called "The Journey Log" or "The Operations Return" (ubiquitously abbreviated to "Ops Return" of course).

The best of all names is the *"Captain's Voyage Report"*. This last one harks back to the origins of the commercial aviation industry when 'Airliners' equated with Ocean going Liners – wonderful! Now *they* were proper Captains, those bewhiskered gentlemen who were in charge of thousands of lives as their huge craft crossed the globe. In addition to all the facts and figures about the flight, there is a section on all of these report forms for 'Captain's Comments' – a space where a narrative can be written with feedback from the aircraft commander in order that the airline operations personnel can make improvements. It was while working as a manager in a low-cost airline that I recall seeing one of the best of such reports ever and again it contained a bird metaphor – not once, but twice.

The flight had been delayed from Luton by *"a comedy of errors by the ground-staff - the result was a 'Baggage ID' due to inability to reconcile how many bags had been loaded on the aircraft!"*. This happens only rarely, but when it does, it means that all of the baggage has to be offloaded onto the ramp in a long line and then the passengers (who by this time have already boarded the flight), are required to get off the aeroplane and identify their own suitcases which are then reloaded into the cargo holds. For the crew, this is a tricky exercise to manage and tends to make their day much longer, often leading to grumpiness in the flightdeck once they finally get airborne.

There was a continuing theme in the Skipper's report as the flight arrived in Barcelona, was parked on a remote stand, then neglected for ages as no transport had been booked for the passengers and generally *"a very long turnround due to Manana syndrome"*. When the flight was ready to depart according to the author, *"ATC refused to give engine start clearance because the flightplan had not been filed!"* The last words of his report were a joy to read as the obviously frustrated Captain gave full vent to his feelings in a most articulate manner. *"It is impossible to SOAR LIKE AN EAGLE, when you are operating from a **TURKEY FARM!"*** Ahh yes, they don't write them like that anymore.

I confess that I try hard not to upset the support personnel on the ground as I have witnessed Captains in the past make the error of showing their feelings too strongly with negative results. I recall when one Skipper became so irritated with the slowness of the baggage loading on our aircraft he took it into his head to "go downstairs and have a word with them". The result was very nearly an industrial dispute when he became involved in an argument with the chief baggage handler. No doubt his use of the phrase *"I could train a F****** Monkey to do the job better!"* did little to calm the situation. It was only the timely intervention of the Dispatch Supervisor which prevented a robust physical reply from the aforementioned primate that could have had a detrimental effect on the Captain's Medical category.

Flying airliners can be quite stressful at times and the temptation to be less than diplomatic is sometimes irresistible - the last word must go to Shane. He was a larger-than-life character who I worked with several years ago. He was an American Pilot who had flown C5 Galaxies for the USAF and then for some convoluted reason ended up flying Orange 737s for the Big Easy. He was a New Yorker originally and was an excellent pilot – in fact I would say he was one of only a few naturally gifted aviators I have ever met. The trouble with Shane was that he would often speak before thinking about the effects upon the listener...

It was a dark Christmas Eve and it had been snowing hard. Belfast Aldergrove had been closed on and off throughout the day for snow clearance. An easyJet 737 came onto the tower frequency from the approach controller – he had been vectored onto final approach and was now descending on the ILS through a snowstorm. This was another delayed flight which was destined to be the last of the day as the weather closed in once more. The tower controller's voice came over the airwaves,

"Easy 636. Expect late landing clearance, we have the Bird Scaring unit on the runway".

"...Erm... Roger that, Easy 636". There was a long pause and then a strong New York accent came on the air.

"*Jeez guys! Whatcha lookin' for... PENGUINS??*"

Astraeus Airlines B737NG.   *September 2006*

Count Dracula Calling...

(Ah yes; the Evil Count meets his HR match in an interview).

Statistics prove that the worst way to select the right person for a job is with a one-to-one interview. From the assessor's perspective they will only see one aspect of the person being interviewed and therefore their assessment cannot be anything but subjective. Not only will they probably choose the person/people whom they 'like' the most, but they may discard other potentially valuable applicants who could do the job equally as well if not better. There is no doubt about it; if you are assessing people applying for a job you must leave a lot of your own baggage behind. This obviously includes any personal prejudices too. Remember there are laws which prevent discrimination on the grounds of race, creed, colour or sex by employers. If you are tasked to provide judgement on the suitability of people to work for an employer then you have a duty to act in a lawful way to protect the company from possible subsequent litigation.

Many companies use a selection "panel" of three people to do the assessing and this produces some good results. Normally one will ask questions, one will take notes while the third member of the panel checks things like licences and logbooks. Certainly as a candidate you can expect a panel of 3 assessors if you are applying to the likes of Big Airways etc. although smaller companies do things slightly differently. Whatever the make-up of the assessing team, their main focus must be to predict accurately whether or not a certain individual is the right choice for the position which is vacant.

I recall very well the story of Captain Gregarious who turned up for his interview with Air 2000 for the position of Direct Entry Captain on a large Boeing Airliner. Now it must be said that Capt Gregarious, (whom I flew with several times after he got the job), was a larger than life character and a **very sociable** person. So sociable in fact that in the morning when he arrived for his interview, he was suffering the "Mother of all hangovers" (his words not mine) and so he sat cross-legged, sideways in the chair with his head in his hands having explained to the interview board the reason for his "condition". Apparently they all thought this was hilarious and in fact it was viewed by the all male selection panel of senior pilots as a favourable quality. For the benefit of anyone thinking this might be acceptable in these politically correct times, I would advise them to bear in mind that this was in the late 1980s. Selection boards for airlines have now changed completely, such that not only is there usually a senior HR advisor on the panel, but also in some cases there may not even be a pilot among them...

This could come as a surprise to many professional aviators, but pilots are actually a very expensive resource and not all of them have the right qualities to enable them to provide a positive contribution to an interview panel. The reason for this is clear, the skills required to pilot an aeroplane are completely different to those needed to carry out Human Resources (personnel) functions. Evaluation of pilot applicants' technical skills is best left to a formal technical quiz which will give an objective result, rather than adhoc questions which tend to be less scientific.

There is another test which has a reputation for intimidating prospective candidates and this is the Psychometric Test. It is an advanced form of Personality Test and often comes in the form of a structured question paper which has multiple choice answers – i.e. tick the box A, B, C or D which best applies. The interesting thing is that for this particular part of the assessment process, this is the one element where the candidate knows all the answers. All the questions are about "What do you think?" And in the revealing of the personal likes and dislikes, the applicant tells the story of their personality. It is important to understand that personality and behaviour are different, although they are linked. Individual behaviour patterns and trends are often reflections of personality, but whereas behaviour can be modified, a person's personality is pretty much set once they are into their twenties.

To make things even more confusing, there are several alternative methods for classification of personality, but from the point of view of the pilot applicant this is irrelevant. The main thing to focus on is the actual 'test' itself. One of the most common Psychometric tests consists of hundreds of short questions which rely upon a quick response from the person being tested. The theory goes that if the person has only limited time to think about their answer, they are more likely to give a genuine reply.

From experience as an assessor for a major airline in the past, I can testify to the integrity of the personality test as being a very good indicator of personality type. In broad terms, the commercial aviation companies are looking for very stable personalities who are slightly extrovert in their outlook on life. They should be good at social mixing and this is often evidenced by their being good team players. This ensures that they are easy to work with and are likely to integrate successfully and smoothly into a new company. Yes it is all common-sense stuff really and that is quite a good description of the science of 'Psychology' – common-sense with fancy titles.

+   +   +

Looking at the whole thing from the candidates' perspective there has been quite a significant change in recent years in the way that the actual interviews are conducted. As mentioned above, the interview part of the process is only one element and now there is a range of tests and measures which have to be undertaken to be successful. In days gone by, you could expect a nice cosy chat with an interviewer who may have been accompanied by one or two other members of the panel and the questions would have been all fairly normal. "Tell us about your schooldays"; "Talk us through your career"; "What sort of sports and games do you play when not at work?" However this is not a very scientific way of filtering out the undesirables, so the HR specialists have been hard at work and have come up with the "Competency Based Interview".

There are a few things you should know about the Competency Based Interview and they are these. Firstly each question which is asked in this structured interview is carefully designed to elicit information (evidence) that you have a particular competence or skill. Also, all the questions which are asked at every interview are the same and therefore there is a set standard or benchmark against which you are being judged. Although you do not know what the questions are going to be, you can do a great deal to prepare yourself in advance.

For example, you need to practice speaking in response to somebody asking you a question and your answer needs to be more than just a few words. You will be asked to give examples of what you did specifically given a precise situation which you may have faced in the past. The interview team are not interested in your opinions or what you might do if you faced the situation in the future; they want to know what you ACTUALLY did in the past. Notice the emphasis on YOU. Yes YOU as a person, an individual, not YOU the team. Your answer needs to tell the story of what you did and it needs to be convincing. Why? Because it will be 'scored' on the validity of the 'evidence' which you give.

Here is an example of how a CBI question is constructed – this one is assessing the competency of Leadership. **"Describe an example of a time when you had to co-ordinate the work of other people".** You can see straight away that the assessor wants you to tell them a story of what you did in the past – they are looking for a specific example. They are not asking if you THINK you are a good leader or what in your OPINION makes a good leader, they want to know what YOU DID. They will also have a couple of sub-questions which they can use to help draw the answer out of you and to encourage you to talk more if you start to stumble.

They may ask, **"What were you trying to achieve?"** or **"How did you go about organising the work?"** And these may help you to give the evidence they are seeking. An important point to remember about all of this is that even though it may seem like the scientists have got together to put you under the microscope, nobody actually wants you to fail. I can tell you from experience that it is much easier in your role as assessor to have a candidate who is happy to provide nice compact answers to all of your questions. Practice is the key here. Do not take the attitude, **"Oh I'll just go in and Wing-It!"** because believe me, you **will** come unstuck.

They will ask a nice simple question and you will say the wrong thing and they will write down your answer...ahh? Did I fail to mention that? Yes ALL of the answers which you give to their questions will be recorded. While one interviewer asks the questions, (which come from a set list) his/her partner will be writing down your answers. They will tell you that this is just because they have a record of all the interviews afterwards with which to compare, however there are other good reasons also. For example, perhaps after the interview is over you feel that you were the victim of discrimination and therefore wished to make a complaint about the conduct of the way in which you were treated.

From the notes of the interview which they made at the time and with your knowledge and permission, they have the evidence to defend their conduct and therefore protect their company from groundless (time consuming and expensive) litigation. So do your research, find out all you can about the assessment process which will be used to check your suitability for the job and prepare yourself well with as much of the material on the market that is available. I was reading the other day that somebody has produced an interactive DVD for the purpose of making you practice your interview answers in front of a panel of interviewers – great! This is just the sort of thing you need to do to prevent yourself *from saying something stupid or ill-advised* during the interview. You can never be over-prepared for these things.

I remember with acute embarrassment an incident which occurred to me in a CBI some years ago when I was being interviewed for an important managerial position with a company. I was asked by an HR specialist, whom I knew well, a question which caught me off guard.

She asked me how I thought people whom I managed would describe me...?

"Well..." I stumbled for an answer, "I know that maybe some people consider me... erm..." Searching for the right word, "Draconian...!"

Doh! I watched in silent horror as she wrote down, **'He says they call him DRACONIAN'.**

Of course it's laughable now, I mean how ridiculous?

Little old, **fluffy** old me, being thought of as like Count Dracula...? Hah! What utter nonsense!

Author with other members of the Lemon Pie Club
Capt Stefan, Leanne, Amanda, Emma & Beki

Troublesome Parishioners.

(There are times when the 'good Vicar' must have the patience of a saint).

It is interesting when you think about managing airline pilots. After all, on the face of it, they perform one of the most technically skilled and highly regulated professional jobs in the world. Perhaps more visibly than all of the other professions, peoples' lives are literally in their hands by the hundreds on a daily basis. Of course the same could be said of brain surgeons and other top jobs, but normally here it is a case of one at a time.

So you could be forgiven for thinking that the management of groups of such highly trained, specialist individuals would be a very cerebral process – not so. It comes down to 'people are people' and in fact the same maxim applies throughout the whole HR arena. As a people manager, 90% of your time is taken up with managing 5% of the people. In these politically correct times, it is sometimes risky to categorise or label people, for the ever present danger of being called a discriminator lurks around every corner, but as a busy manager I recall that I needed to have a name for the folder on my computer desktop containing files relevant to my particular 5%. In some ways I saw myself as a vicar for my flock, I had to call them something and so my folder was called *'Troublesome Parishioners'.*

+   +   +

When I applied for the job of Base Captain to manage fifty airline pilots, I made a point of calling a very experienced manager to ask him what he thought the job entailed. He told me that a Base Captain's main role was "holding hands and wiping noses"! I thought this description was a little trite, but I refrained from saying so as I held this particular former boss in the highest regard. That being said, I recalled these very words on many occasions while I was administering to my flock. There appeared to be no end of ways in which the pilots I was responsible for could misbehave.

Whether it was to be caught out using staff travel to go on trips abroad when they were officially off-sick or being caught in bed with somebody else's wife, a minority of the pilots were always up to something. There were times when certain pilots requested specifically not to fly with other pilots – this was something which we tried to avoid as it put extra limitations on an otherwise highly stressed rostering department. Exceptional cases occurred however, like the time when one of the Captain's wives (a company Stewardess) ran off with a First Officer! She didn't run very far however, as all three continued working in the same base and there was the distinct probability that they could be rostered to fly together... Obviously this was an extreme situation where there was a danger of a major verbal, maybe even physical dispute occurring in-flight. All of them were put on opposite shifts to ensure separation, but there were still some frosty moments when crews met on the ramp during aircraft handovers.

+   +   +

Although we were very busy as Managers in a rapidly expanding company, we always took advice from the HR department, but I have got to say occasionally they were less than helpful to us. Like the time when I called to ask what to do when I found one of my pilots had actually been on a holiday using his Staff Travel concessions on the airline while he was on long-term sick. For me - and on behalf of the other hard working pilots in the base - this was too much. I could hear my heavy breathing down the telephone as I called the HR department in headquarters and spoke to one of the senior HR advisors – "Surely we can fire him?" It was an open and shut case in my eyes. "Here we are in the middle of a busy summer flying programme and we are all busting a gut to get the job done with pilots doing maximum duty hours and some of them hitting fatigue limits and this... this..." I searched for a civilised word to describe him, "...this JACKASS! Thinks it is acceptable to go on holiday to the Riviera while he is on long-term sick leave?! UNBELIEVABLE!"

The lady on the other end of the 'phone could sense my frustration I think and so she replied extra calmly, "Well I know it seems wrong James, but you see you didn't say where he had to be off sick did you? If you had confined him to the UK then it would be easier to deal with..." I

was nearly exasperated, I blurted out, "Yeah well I didn't think he was up for travelling very far as he was allegedly off sick with STRESS!" To which her calm reply was,
"Actually, a holiday would be quite good for stress..." my grip on the receiver tightened as I considered my own stress levels.

It was some time later that I managed to cool off and consider the matter. "Bah! So much for HR advice!" I said to no one in particular. Yes it was true; this specific pilot seemed to have outwitted the system. He had been off with stress, had a holiday (several holidays I later found out) been to see the CAA doctors who had removed his medical for a while, then he got it back and finally 'dragged himself back to work' to continue having personality clashes with all and sundry on the line.

I lost count of the number of reports from handling agents, ramp staff, crew and passengers whom this clown had upset – the folder on my desktop was growing larger. Each time however he just got away with it, such that although there was a lot of circumstantial evidence and second hand, anecdotal reports of his misconduct, I couldn't quite pin it on him. It was obvious to me that we would have a long game to play here before we could complete the process as per HR instructions (and they had been quite specific about it – we had to be fair and consistent at all times as managers).

Then one day I thought I had him banged to rights. He was now back at work and we had received a very fresh report of his misbehaviour – this time he had been caught out, "swearing and shouting abuse at some disabled passengers onboard the aircraft..." *Oh yes!* I thought to myself. *Thank you God, I know this is the one incident which will do it finally – this has GOT to be Gross Misconduct?* I immediately asked to see the rest of the crew who had been on the flight with him the previous day. Apparently he had taken over the aircraft and there were two disabled (wheelchair) passengers who were right at the back of the airliner cabin waiting for the ambulift crew to help lift them off the aircraft and take them to the terminal. They had been waiting a long time when Capt Stressball came along and shouted at them, with rude and abusive (possibly foul) language.

So much I got from the crew at the front of the aircraft, but what about the actual words he used? They were too far away to hear properly, they just saw him waving his arms and shouting at the disabled people. I knew from experience that a full word by word account of the incident would need to include a transcript by a witness of his actual words. There were two cabin crew who had been in the rear galley at the time and I asked for them to come and see me. We sat down together and I got my notepad and pen out.

"Now... take your time ladies and tell me in your own words and from your recollection what the Captain ACTUALLY said to the wheelchair passengers. Don't rush; take your time we need to be absolutely sure what he said to them". Cat outside a Mouse hole in the skirting board I waited, pen poised at the ready...

"He was VERY angry", one of them said, echoed by the other one. "OOH YES, the Captain's face was BRIGHT red and he was shouting at the top of his voice".

"Yes", I said patiently, pleased with what I was hearing, "and what did he say?" this was it. He had, had it coming to him a long time, now I was going to have a real, first hand eye witness account of unacceptable, rudeness and abuse to customers and DISABLED ones at that. Let's see HR explain THIS ONE away? The older girl took a deep breath and related...

"He said, 'It is a BLOODY DISGRACE! I have told them about the stupid b*****ds who drive the ambulifts before! They are *ALWAYS BLOODY LATE!* I am **SO SORRY** that you have had to wait for them as usual. So sorry for the inconvenience!"

I put my pen away with a big, long sigh... They looked at each other, then at me.

"Is that it Captain McBride? Can we go and report for duty now?" They looked at me expectantly - aware of my disappointment.

"Yes ladies, thanks for popping in to see me and have a good flight won't you", I said wearily as I thought ...*not this time then?*

Our Office Manager was called Sarah and she was a very hard working, dedicated employee; plus she embraced the low-cost philosophy with a passion. I always knew she could be relied upon to monitor the actions of all of my parishioners while I was away from the office and especially their expenses claims. Every month she checked the company 'phonebill for all the Captains' mobiles to ensure that there were no 'discrepancies' or abuses of the system. Although it was infrequent, there were a few pilots who tried to 'unblock' their company mobiles to allow free dialling. Of course these were easy to spot from the itemised billing system we used. One of my Troublesome Parishioners was Captain Corelli.

Sarah pointed out the magnitude of his company mobile calls and we knew he had found a way to unblock his 'phone the code would need changing and to do this we would have to access the handset. I wrote him a nice memo and put it in his dropfile in the crewroom.

Dear Captain Corelli,
The normal bills for our Captains are in the region of £30 per month and your phonebill was £200 for last month alone. It appears from the itemised bill attached, that the company mobile which was issued to you has lost the call-barring mode which restricts the user to company approved numbers only.

When you are next on duty, kindly drop by the office and I would be pleased to restore this particular function to your company mobile.
Yours sincerely, James McBride, Base Captain.

Strangely enough there was no response from Captain Corelli and over the period of the next week or so I tried on several occasions to contact him – he was being very elusive. However I did notice that he had picked up his mail in his dropfile, so he knew I wanted to see him. I tried to call him on his mobile when he was not on duty, but as soon as his 'phone rang, it cut-off straight away, almost as if it was done deliberately, I sent him emails with no reply...

"Oh I am sick of this!" I said very unprofessionally in the office one day, "Sarah can you please order a new company mobile for Captain Corelli and when it arrives I would like you to terminate his old one". Two days later it arrived in all the brand new packaging, complete with new Sim card. My plan now was to leave it for him in his dropfile as I knew he checked that every time he came in to fly.

As I was checking out the new company mobile, I turned it on to make sure that only the company operational numbers were available. In the 'settings' menu and after selecting 'options' I chose the edit function for the greeting message which displayed on the screen when the 'phone powered up - this was the first thing Captain Corelli would see when he switched it on.

In capital letters I wrote "I WILL TRY NOT TO BE NAUGHTY TODAY!"

More Lemon Pie Club flying, this time with Capt Stefan Kondak –
who is possibly the best pilot in the world according to my daughter...

Will it be today...?

(Voices in my head and the reason why I stopped Air Display flying).

I looked at the ASI, 130 mph, not QUITE enough airspeed but "Just enough", I judge aloud. Now with both hands firmly on the control column, I push hard to one side – FULL AILERON. She rolls upside down (of course) and then slowly continues to roll round the horizon, but sluggishly as the speed drops off and the aircraft 'dishes out', we miss the sea by a narrower margin than I would have wished and climb away. "Sloppy and mushy" I think to myself, angry that I made the mistake. I normally only do the roll at 140 minimum, why today did I not climb away and bin it? *"Early in the season I guess",* comes back the answer from the little voice in my head. I know from experience that when we start the season it takes a few airshows to blow away the cobwebs from the previous year...

+   +   +

In 1999 when I was doing the filming with LWT (London Weekend Television) for the Airline series on ITV, they featured some flying in the Harvard in preparation for the Air Display season. The aircraft was a 1942 North American T6D with a 600 horsepower Pratt and Whitney radial engine. It weighed a ton (or at least felt like it when you were taxiing around on the grass) and had great stage presence. In fact if you were going to use any old aeroplane as an 'on-screen character' for a TV programme, this was one of the most accurate bits of casting ever. Getting into the cockpit was always a bit like climbing up the side of a ship and the similarity was not just in the size and colour of the fuselage compared to the hull of a destroyer (both are grey and rather slab-sided), but in addition, the rivets of both hulls protrude from the sheet metal!

The Harvard, or Texan as it was called by the USAF, was mainly employed as an advanced trainer of fighter pilots during the Second World War. The size and handling characteristics of the T6 were ideal preparation for pilots to fly the large, high-performance single engined warbirds of the 1940s. In fact it gained an enviable reputation as one of the world's greatest training aeroplanes, just like the Stearman and Tiger Moth of similar era. There were issues with the Harvard as a Trainer though, because the handling characteristics were definitely unforgiving beyond a certain point. Put quite simply; it had a vicious stall. When the wing reached the stalling angle, the sudden loss of lift was dramatic – it literally fell out of the sky! Even a competent, experienced airman would need perhaps 1000 feet of altitude to recover from a clean stall and a stall which was carried out with gear down and flaps extended would need much more...

Imagine the scene back in the early 1940s with tyro pilots tottering round the circuit with a 'downwind leg' flown at maybe only 800 feet – a stall during this phase of flight was always fatal. Of course aviators are a cynical bunch and the old joke went around among them that *"The reason for the Harvard gaining the reputation as being a 'great Trainer' is because it'll kill anybody who can't fly it!"*

So it was not without a few reservations that I undertook my first Harvard flights back in October 1991. At that time I had a dream; to fly all the big piston singles of WW2. The only way to achieve that was to start by flying the Harvard. Fortunately I had plenty of tail-dragger experience, so that first hurdle was not a stopper for me. I had instructed on De Havilland Chipmunks for several hundred hours and even flown the type with the RAF Air Experience Flight too. Also I had flown the Pitts Special for several hours practising aerobatics in Florida, so I knew all about how to use my feet on the rudder pedals to keep the machine under control on the ground. My day job at this time was flying Boeing 757 airliners and we didn't normally use our feet for much unless we had an engine failure in the simulator. I thought I was pretty much ready for the Harvard, but those days flying circuits at Blackpool were hard work I can tell you.

I did make progress however and over the next few years I managed to reach a level of competence which was quite pleasing. The solo aerobatic display made way for a formation display with dissimilar aircraft types and gradually I managed to feel very comfortable flying my way through the summer airshow season. In the good company of likeminded individuals, we made a formation display team which demonstrated the beauty and grace of these 50 year old flying machines to good effect. It was always a rush in the spring to get ready for the first display however and often I felt that we arrived in a big panting hurry at the start of the season.

Winter activities precluded flying the machines as mostly maintenance actions were performed then and of course the weather was rarely kind to us in the UK. The display was practiced several times before the first show, but there is really no substitute to recency when flying aeroplanes – especially when the technical skills have to be demonstrated to a very high standard in front of a large audience.

Lined up for takeoff in the Harvard G-JUDI on a sunny Sunday afternoon with the canopy locked in the open position, while only a matter of feet away was the crowdline was my idea of heaven. The reason for the open canopy was the same as for all the piston engined tailwheel fighter aircraft, in that if there was a takeoff accident and the beast turned upside down, the pilot had a better chance of the fire services getting him out. With the canopy closed, there was no chance – a sobering thought indeed.

Over the next few years, each summer passed quickly as we learned the craft together, I and the rest of the air display team. We were a happy band of travelers who met regularly with lots of similar folk at airshows around the UK and near continent. Of course accidents happened and it was with great sadness that we watched some of our friends and colleagues take-off never to land back on again. In 7 years of display flying I saw quite a lot of them go and after some time, it tends to prey on the mind. I have never been one for morbid thoughts and generally speaking have usually been described as an optimist by my peers, but successive losses take their toll. There were a few funerals to go to and more than once I used to question whether it was worth it.

The dream was still alive though and I spent a lot of time imagining myself at the controls of a P47D Thunderbolt or a Spitfire, maybe even a Hurricane! I might have been an ex-military pilot with lots of tailwheel time and large airliner in the logbook too, but in the pecking order of display pilots I was an apprentice. I still needed to learn the craft, so I patiently and studiously practiced the arts in many different locations and with all sorts of weather, runway combinations. Wheeler landings gave way to three-pointers, the runways which I could operate from got narrower and shorter too. Cross-wind takeoffs and landings in the Harvard became easier with time and the Aeros display became slicker. Because the controls are so heavy in the T6, I used to fly it with both hands gripping the control column. Soon after takeoff, with the airframe clean (gear retracted and the flaps up) I set 'climb-power' and left it there. With the throttle and prop pitch levers screwed with the friction set tight, they did not move, so I could focus on the flying controls themselves. Of course, every aerodynamicist will tell you that with climb-power set, the aircraft will either accelerate or climb as the energy level builds. What we did here was to manage the energy level such that speed was converted to altitude and back again for the next 8 minutes.

Grunting and panting as I pulled and pushed my way through those summer displays, often I came out of the cockpit with my flying suit soaked in sweat on a hot day. As mentioned before however, the feeling was incredible! Climbing steeply after takeoff to 1500 feet, a wingover then coming rushing back down the 'hill' with airspeed building rapidly gave me 230 mph for the first loop at crowd centre, then half-cuban and barrel roll and tight 360 before the hesitation rolls and so it went on. The big radial growling away just in front of the cockpit window and the tips of the prop making that buzz-saw sound as they went transonic are vividly etched in my memory even now.

Grunting hard as the 'G' built up in each of the vertical manoeuvres, I pattered my way through the display. Sometimes I even caught myself talking to the airframe, down at the bottom of the slope, looking up, PULLING UP and GRUNTING, PANTING, the nose now through the vertical... over the top of the loop... "Come on old girl, you can do it, **grunt**, come on, **COME ON JUDI!**" It was so good when the manoeuvre came out right and with energy to spare we entered the next one, but this did not always happen.

I distinctly recall one of the wives of an experienced display pilot telling me, "...and please, please don't do a barrel roll too low in the Harvard!" She knew a thing or two about low-level Aeros as she had watched more than one pilot 'tentpeg' on the pull-out from a barrel roll. Good advice indeed as I recall very nearly doing the same myself one year – there was an awful lot of 'green' in the canopy as I exited the barrel and only then did I realise how close I had come to fulfilling her prophecy.

Then in quiet moments I would think about the accident... *my accident.* The high-speed crash, which would be the result of my making a mistake, doing high performance aerobatics in a fifty year old aeroplane. After all, I think to myself, it seems to happen to everyone else after enough time has passed, so why not me? The accident will not happen slowly, I know it. When you are displaying at very low altitude at 200+ mph, it is going to be quick. I consider my Display Authorisation – I am cleared to perform aerobatic manoeuvres down to 50 feet above the ground. The margin for error becomes smaller as the altitude decreases – the high speed is a comfort though, as the controls are firm and the aircraft is responsive with aerodynamic energy in abundance.

All the comfort factors in the world cannot reduce the risk enough for some of us. We know intellectually that increased exposure to risk is quite simply that – the likelihood of an occurrence becomes greater on the balance of probabilities. When I first became a father in '95, I managed to rationalise the fear of an accident and carried on flying displays, but after my son was born in '98; and seeing a few more pilots 'buy the farm, I started to think about mortality and 'the risk' a lot. Eventually I decided to retire before it was too late.

With each air display, I begin to get déjà vu. They all start the same way. A large stopwatch on the cockpit coaming, canopy locked open, engine sounding good, smell of hot oil mixed with new mown grass from the airfield, holding her on the toebrakes with the stick held back against the buckle of the safety belt harness... the clock is ticking and counting down the seconds now to the start of the display – only 8 minutes timed from 'brakes off' all the way through to touchdown again.

I am watching the clock, I can hear the ATC controller in the headphones, the sun is shining – blue sky above, I give another sharp tug on the lapstraps of the harness until it feels painful... I blink and think of the kids...

Suddenly I am cold, very, very, cold and then the same old question comes into my brain, the voice sounding really hollow inside my head.

But it IS my voice, it IS me speaking... "...*Is it going to be today...? **Will it REALLY be today?***"

Definition: A 'Stall' is a reduction in the lift coefficient generated by an airfoil as angle of attack increases. Airspeed Indicator in MPH? Yes Sir, she's an American Airplane!

Author with Harvard G-JUDI practising for Display Season,
1993 Anglesey, N Wales.

"Could Do Better...?"

(A continuing theme in my school reports and I am not alone).

Although from a purely linguistic point of view the expression *"Could do better"* is an unimaginative description of a student's performance, I recall that it was a recurring theme in my own school reports. I am the first to admit that I was not the easiest of pupils to teach, but I do not remember any specific reason why the teachers were so dismissive of my academic talents. In reality of course, "Could do better", was an inadequate description of a student's performance and on reflection I think it was more accurately a damning indictment of their teaching skills...

Fast forward a few years and I found myself in the classroom situation again as a student. This time however I was at CTC in Southampton during my Core Course to become a Training Captain on Jet Airliners. The year now was 1998 and I was engaged (and fully committed) to the huge growth of one of the new generation of short-haul Low Cost airline companies. The Core Course is a highly intensive foundation course lasting one week and mostly it is classroom based, but there is a flightdeck simulator also. I find the course challenging and stimulating in equal measure. As I sit there among my colleagues from different companies, I learn of their past experiences and I realise that although we are all from different origins, we are now at a similar level in our professional flying careers. We are a small group of 8 and have all been selected by our employers to become trainers.

One of the skills we learn is the art of Writing Reports. We are all instructed to write in printed capital letters, which although takes longer, has the added benefit of giving the author time to think clearly about the composition of the text. While we practice our techniques in the classroom, I am reminded of an incident which occurred years earlier during my own training. I had just finished a training sortie and was in the process of being debriefed by my military instructor. Military flying training courses 'take no prisoners' and the debrief was always a tense time. He was in the midst of writing the report in my training file while I waited for him to finish. The "Student's Training File" was a document which was treated with almost as much reverence as the Military Pilot's Flying Logbook, so to interrupt him was unthinkable. Instead I sat quietly and tried not to fidget while outside I could hear the distant whine of jet engines being started up as other aviators took their turn on the flying programme.

My instructor paused mid sentence, almost as if he had only just realised I was present and looked across the table straight into my eyes. It was as if he was searching for the right word as he asked, *"Are there two P's in appalling?"* There was laughter in his eyes then as he observed my reaction – Hah! What a joker!? Later I confess that I was to use this trick myself to break the ice and to good effect to reassure an under-confident trainee pilot. I used to look up from writing the report, pause for dramatic effect and then ask them, *"How do you spell abysmal...?"* It had me in giggles every time.

In 1998 however, we were taught to do it properly and the acronym which was given to us then was C.A.P. – nice and easy for us hard working Line Trainers to follow – a real tool of the trade.

C stands for Commentary; which is a short descriptive précis of the observed performance, which also records the various environmental factors such as Weather conditions, ATC, technical malfunctions (non-normal occurrences), passenger issues etc.

A is for Appraisal; which is the judgment part where the deficiencies of the trainee can be commented upon and recorded. Not only the negative aspects of the performance, but also the positive and it was always emphasised to us that we should try to sandwich the bad news with the good. In this manner, the student is much more likely to be receptive of the constructive criticism which must inevitably be given. A balanced critique is what we should be aiming for here. Of course the mistakes which are made by the trainee are acceptable provided they are prepared to learn from them. In fact one of the most difficult aspects of flying training is how far to let them go before correcting the mistake... When you are airborne and travelling at a few hundred miles per hour in a jet airliner weighing many metric tonnes, this can be a tricky call.

P is for Pointers; which are aimed towards improvement. A good trainer will be able to analyse the faults in technique and procedures then advise them on how to improve (raise their game) to prevent making the same errors again.

A poor trainer is easy to spot and their report writing is clear evidence in this respect. The words "Could do better!" are not going to help the poor trainee to improve at all. It simply hints at latent ability which has yet to materialise. In a similar way I recall a report written at a military training academy back in the early '80s which was so negative, the last sentence read "...*and I suggest that we would not breed from this Officer!*" Fortunately we have not yet reached the stage of sterilising our fellow human beings whom we judge not to have reached our standards. Talking of standards reminds me of the words used in one young pilot's training file when the instructor wrote, "*Flying Officer XXX continually sets himself particularly low standards, which he invariably fails to achieve*". Imagine reading **that** in your training file? It would be enough to discourage anybody!

In my first year as a Line Trainer on the Boeing 737 with the rapidly expanding Low Cost Airline, I think I must have flown nearly the full 900 hours permitted by law. In fact one of the rostering officers called me over one day while I was in easyLand (as the headquarters of the airline was called) and informed me that I had completed 864 flying hours – nearly all of it was line training. The job of an airline Line Trainer is one of the most difficult positions and in many flights there are stressful periods, where high levels of concentration are necessary to monitor the flying situation and balance the training inputs at the same time.

If a trainee becomes overloaded ('maxed-out' as it is known in the trade), then they start to lose their grip on the flying and things can rapidly take a turn for the worse. In an extreme case, the Trainer has to take control, both of the aircraft and maybe the radio communication also and coax the trainee to get back into the game. While making instrument approaches in bad weather at busy international airports with high intensity ATC workloads, this is not for the faint hearted!

At the end of the day though, it is important to build the trainee's confidence and raise the standard of their performance. Often I would use the written report as a method of doing this by reassuring them of the positive elements of the flying while being judged against a backdrop of tough environmental conditions. Humour is always a good way to win people round to seeing the world in a better light, so phrases such as, "*On arrival at Amsterdam Schiphol, the weather was as overcast as East Enders*" can be helpful. Another of my favourites when writing about the severity of icing conditions in cloud which we flew through, was, "*The Engine Anti-ice was On and Off like Pavarotti's fridge light!*"

There were important points to be made also. I recall flying with a fairly experienced First Officer (Co-Pilot) who had just joined us from another airline where he had been operating the same equipment (B737s) – sometimes these guys were the hardest to teach as they were resistant to the idea of learning new SOPs (Standard Operating Procedures).

Many was the time when they liked to give the impression that they did not need any 'training' inputs, because they were already 'trained'. Up to a point this was true, however each company has standards which must be maintained and the training system at my airline did not compromise. Eric (not his real name) would not listen to me however and I found that he wanted to gash it and not to follow our quite strict procedures including the SOP 'calls' which the pilots make. His casual, 'Cowboy' attitude did not impress me at all and over the period of a few flights, I gradually raised the tempo of criticism to little effect. I finally wrote in his training file a report which ended with the words,

"Eric's previous employer appears to have accepted lower standards of operating behaviour than his current one. This casual attitude is not acceptable here! It is time to sell the Ten-Gallon hat Eric and put the spurs away. If you wanted a Cowboy outfit, you should have asked for one for Christmas!" Now that got his attention! Lo and behold, over the rest of his Line Training he really got on the right message and passed his Final Line Check with flying colours.

Another time I was teaching a young Australian F/O who had a habit of jabbering on the radio, seemingly not appreciating the need for short, precise transmissions here in Europe. I think he probably needed the dictionary when he found I had written in his report, *"Jabbering on the R/T is unwise, unsafe and unprofessional. You should aim to be Punctilious without Persiflage!"* Anyway, I know **he** got the message, because he became one of the sharpest pilots on the R/T in the whole base.

Sometimes though it is years later when students actually appreciate the true meaning of their written report and I cite an example from my own childhood. Like I say, I was not the easiest of pupils to teach, however one teacher in particular found a way to cope with the stress and frustration of instructing a difficult child when they wrote in my school report, *"James's examination position this term of 29th out of 31 pupils in the class flatters his true ability in this subject..."*

I smile as I re-read it all these years later and I say one word ***"Quality!"***

(P.S. The subject to which my teacher was referring was English!)

Fighter Pilot's Breakfast.

(Top Tip; For trouble free crew hotel residency. Do not build a pyramid of empty beer cans on a hotel balcony handrail four floors up...)

Napoleon Bonaparte knew a thing or two about Human Resources, evidenced by his attitude to nutrition for his soldiers when he famously said *"An army marches on its stomach".* Certainly under-nourished troops would be a liability in the battlefield and he knew it - what a shame then that some contemporary airline managers are resistive to learning the lessons of history.

+   +   +

They say breakfast is "the most important meal of the day". When you consider that normally the human body has been inactive for many hours before this, with a steadily reducing blood sugar and without receiving any fluids or foodstuffs, you can see the reason behind the argument. When you also think about the nature of the job which airline and other commercial aviation crew perform, it is a worry that some of the new breed of low-cost operators seem to neglect to look after their operating personnel by refusing to provide food onboard for them to eat. Of course this is in the interest of saving money, but the cost of the food is not really the issue here as much as the expense of into-plane delivery as they call it – often this is much greater.

I recall many discussions at my former lo-co airline when the crews were told by 'the management' that crew-food was not required and in fact was envied by the office staff who complained that the pilots and stewardesses were spoiled. "After all", they said "the admin staff have to buy their own food when they come to work". Which was not really a valid comparison because as the crews were quick to observe, *"It is not so easy to 'pop-out' for a sandwich at 35,000 feet!"* Well of course the argument rumbles on even today with some of these companies and if you will excuse the pun the crew-food issue is a real bone of contention.

Naturally if you start an airline without this particular specific condition of employment, then there is less to negotiate away if you wish to reduce the terms and conditions of service. Back in the early days of an Orange low-cost airline there was a concerted effort to remove the crew-food from the contract, but those of us who were there at the time sincerely believed it was important enough to resist this. In fact when the original order for the new - 700 (New Generation) Boeings was put together, the specification was planned to be without any ovens in the galleys. Needless to say, those of us who were out in the front line knew exactly what that would mean. Once a series of new airliners were delivered to the company without ovens and accepted to be operated by the crews, it would not be long before the current fleet had their ovens removed as being 'not required on voyage'.

It was touch and go for a while and you have to put it all into perspective. The trouble for the managers at that time was they only had just a few Line Training Captains who were doing ALL the Line Training for the new joining pilots – in fact there were three of us. We were literally flying all the hours God sent and in reality there were not enough to train all these new 'drivers (airframe)'. Although it should be remembered that the average line pilot would expect to fly only around 470 block hours per annum, we Line Trainers were always up around the 900 hours a year. We already knew how it felt to drive on hard for week after week of maximum effort and eventually as computerised rostering was refined to take advantage of every angle – so did all the rest! So in essence we knew how important it was to have hot food accessible to the crew during arduous conditions of duty – thank God we stuck our necks out and held out for the 'perk' to be retained.** By contrast when we took over another airline we found that they were all taking their food to work with them, which is all very well, but what happens when you get called at four in the morning from standby? I suppose you should then be stopping on the way to work at an all-night garage to pick up something with 'Ginsters' written on it...?

Somebody asked me recently to sum up my seven and a half years in low-cost airlines. Now consider flying multi-sector days, five days a week while the rate of company growth seems to be like an exponential curve. I thought for a minute and said that "On balance it was like trench warfare really, you occasionally gain a little ground, lose a lot of people (pilot attrition) and sometimes have to retreat in the face of overwhelming odds. Yes, muck and bullets pretty much sums it up!" Bear in mind in the first 18 months of operation after gaining our own AOC, even though we started to receive brand new aircraft one a month, we lost 40% of the pilots... I knew why. They (the leavers) just couldn't stand it any longer. They wanted so much to believe in the product, but it was such an incredible shock to the system – especially as ALL of these people had been used to working for real airlines where everything was managed nicely with a surplus of staff who cared for all the needs of the personnel on the line.

Now in the new world as I began to realise, when you looked to the rear from your position in the trenches, there was nobody back there to support you! A few years after this when I myself reached the dizzy heights of Pilot Manager with the company, I was often required to give a short welcome speech to the new joining pilots – the majority of which were still coming from the traditional operators. I started the talk with the message prepare yourself for a culture-shock and I ended the dissertation in much the same way. In between start and finish, I emphasised that they were about to enter a company which employed some of the finest, most highly trained professionals it had ever been my privilege to serve with and I meant it.

The analogy with the First World War was perhaps a little harsh, because there were many, many times we had a lot of fun flying together. For example I recall in the early days of the company when we started operating the new route to Barcelona – wonderful city. It just so happened that because of rostering difficulties, our crews were always spending overnights in Barcelona and in the course of the next few months the crews were expelled from 3 hotels in the city... Only 2 of these were the crews' fault though. On the third occasion it was because the company had not paid the bill – honestly, it is true!

I was assured that the pyramid of empty beer cans, which had been built carefully outside on the handrail of the fourth floor balcony of the hotel at the top of Las Ramblas was an amazing sight to behold. However, it was never the intention of the crew, that it should fall noisily in the early hours of the morning onto the occupied parked Police car in the street far below... Fortunately the Barcelona nightstop was 24 hours long so that there was plenty of time for the crews to recover from the partying and to be safe and legal to operate the next afternoon. Put into context – this was the end of the naughty nineties now and everybody realised that quite literally *"Time"* had been called on the bad habits of the past. Excessive partying and alcohol consumption had long been associated with pilots and their cohorts. Maybe it was a form of stress relief perhaps combined with the easy access to cheap duty-free supplies, but aviators the world over built a reputation for themselves. The bad old days were perhaps typified by Tom Wolfe in his iconic book 'The Right Stuff' which was ostensibly all about astronaut training back in the sixties. I recall he described with graphic precision the extra-curricular activities of the fast-jet pilots of that era as they pursued a fast-living existence which consisted of flying and drinking and drinking and driving and drinking and flying etc.

Even in the early eighties there were echoes of the past in the behaviour of some military pilots. In those days if you were spotted by the squadron boss drinking late at night, his only admonishment were the words "you won't be flying solo tomorrow will you?" and that was it! There was no other suggestion that your faculties might be seriously impaired by the lingering effect of alcohol being washed out of the system.

There was a time when we used to joke about it all and say things like *"This morning I had a Fighter Pilot's Breakfast... two aspirins and a cup of tea!"* But the world sees things differently now and that joke is not funny anymore. Maybe the industry has finally grown up.

** This was at the end of 1998. Andy, Robin and I were prepared to resign unless hot crew-food was retained. The Line Training programme for the whole fleet was at that time being carried out virtually by us three alone, so the managers took the 'easy' option.

Inaugural easyJet flight from Liverpool to Cologne - 22 June 2004
(Ray Farley photo)

Getting Lost.

(A vital part of the learning to navigate process & the amusing "basic flying rules").

Being 'temporarily unsure of position' while airborne is rapidly becoming a thing of the past. In fact it is a worry to think that this generation of pilots will not have experienced an essential part of navigation training – getting lost. Let me explain.

+   +   +

Over the past century since the Wright brothers did their thing at Kitty Hawk Sands in North Carolina USA, there have been many famous cases of pilots losing their way. We are not talking about moral compasses on layovers here, but more closely associated with the real thing. From misreading the map, forgetting to start the stopwatch, putting the drift on the wrong side, miscalculating the magnetic variation (and applying this to the heading), misidentifying waypoints, we have made all the mistakes possible while navigating our way across the earth's surface. Not only have we made our mistakes, we have also learned so much from them and one would like to think that we became better aviators because of it. Becoming totally reliant upon automation, blindly following the lead of the computer is the road to Hell in our profession and there have been so many instances of this over the past decades.

As each particular technological advance is made, so it seems that correspondingly we lose yet another skill. This point was made to me very clearly while working for a rapidly expanding low-cost airline in the late 1990s. One of our B737s departed from Luton, but returned from airborne after less than 30 minutes because the crew had suffered a "failure of the FMC" (Flight Management Computer). They declared a Pan Call to ATC and required much support from the controllers to arrive at the departure airport again... Those of us not involved in the incident were left scratching our heads about why they had not continued the flight with navigation aids in the old fashioned way? Bearing in mind that the EFIS equipped B737 was fitted with twin VORs, two NDBs, two ILS systems and all these aids were serviceable, the only thing they had lost was the moving map display, they could have flown across Europe if necessary, 'beacon-bashing' as we did in times gone by and they were only trying to find Belfast Aldergrove!

Three little letters have rocked our world now – G.P.S. Theoretically we can never get lost again. We have a moving map display in front of us that will never lie... It is, as they say, a "God's eye view" of our position in space and what an arrogant way of thinking that is?! Just like the boys who all of a sudden forgot how to navigate their B737 cross the Irish Sea when the computer generated map failed, I fear we will see much worse episodes of pilots getting lost in the future. You see these guys actually trained on aeroplanes which had only the very basics of Nav Aids and when they arrived in the flightdeck of the Boeing it was their first time using an Inertial Navigation System which provided the FMC with Lat/Long info to power the HSI (Horizontal Situation Indicator) – so they should have been able to manage. Now we equip the tiniest powered flying machines with information technology which is far superior to what NASA was using to navigate the Apollo moon-shots, so when these pilots reach the large commercial jets they will have seen nothing else at all.

They will not have known the gut-wrenching fear which comes from knowing that you have lost your way while you are navigating while flying the aircraft. I myself have done it several times and it is never pleasant. For me, one of my most memorable cock-ups was at low-level in a BAe Hawk up in Scotland. It was such a beautiful, sunny day in the Glens, that I was quite distracted by the scenery and managed to misread the stopwatch by one whole minute. With an indicated airspeed of 420 kts, one minute becomes 7 nautical miles and seven miles later than I should, I turned through 90 degrees into the wrong valley - oh dear! Within a very short space of time, the topography made no sense and I kept trying to 'make the map fit the ground', wishing it would all come good again. Naturally this was a waste of time and very shortly afterwards I pulled up out of low-level and aborted the LL Navex so that I could fix my position properly with radio navaids. Although I did not think about it at the time, as I was rather busy tuning and ident'ing the VOR etc, the famous phrase *"You've never been lost until you've been lost at Mach 3"** would have been very appropriate at this point.

This was a salutary lesson for me that while travelling at 420 knots only 250 feet above the ground, it is always wise to keep your wits about you. Of course in some ways the actual 'Navigating' part of the operation becomes easier the faster you go - providing you do not misread the clock. Due to the fact that at 420 kts there is very little 'drift' – you just point the jet and it will go there. Maximum Drift is easily calculated as being windspeed divided by TAS expressed in NM/Minute. 20 knots of wind divided by 7 miles per minute = 3 or thereabouts. So even if the wind was all across (the track) the maximum difference would be three degrees. Wind from the North? Mag Track 270°? IAS 420kts? Steer 273° and job done.

Being sure of your position is a relative thing of course. I recall later on in my military flying training when I was navigating a Gazelle Helicopter at 120 kts at low-level on another pleasant afternoon and my QHI asked me to tell him where I thought I was. My reply was that I was "enroute between the last waypoint and the next, about halfway along the track" – flying 'heading and time', we would get there soon. For him this was not good enough and he said, "So you are LOST then!?" I took a deep breath and looked out at the beautiful countryside we were passing over, before pointing out to him "No Sir we are not lost, I can see Plymouth in the distance with the coastline and on the right is Dartmoor, behind us is Exeter, we are somewhere here" – I stuck my gloved thumb on the map in the area of our location on the trackline – "...and very shortly I can tell you our precise position as the next waypoint goes under the nose!" Sure enough only a few minutes later, the tiniest of bridges over a small river came into view and we made the turn on to the next track.

What I was not aware of at the time, was that the basic rotary squadron instructors used to deliberately make the student use a small, nondescript feature as a waypoint so that they would miss it, get lost and then be able to prove the point that we should choose unique easily identifiable markers for navigation. Normally this worked a treat and the 'studes' all learned a valuable lesson. In my case however, I had been trained to deliver low-level bombing/strafing runs at 250 feet, doing 420kts to find 'a plank over a stream' in all sorts of weathers, so I was not going to fazed by 120kts in a chopper on a sunny day. I had already been lost 'big-style' several times before in my flying training and now I knew that above all else, there were two factors to focus on – heading and time. Flying a really accurate heading is vital in raw data navigation and having made all the calculations, believing the clock is also essential. Yes there are other skills, such as constant assessment of whether the aircraft is on track or going off it etc, using prominent features as reference points and these are added to the navigator's toolbox shortly after they learn the importance of the first principles.

Now our young aviators are learning other skills – *like finding the switch which powers the GPS system and then blithely relying upon it to do its job without fail.* I cannot help but feel that they will not have seen as much along the way to being professional pilots as the older ones did. Perhaps it is the price we pay for progress that the next generation in all walks of life are dumber yet smarter than their predecessors. The IT generation of pilots are with us now and it is not even easy to convince them of the need to crosscheck the FMC position with raw-data VOR. Naturally they do not know Morse code anymore because they have never had to learn it properly. When you ask them to check the ident on the beacon, they spend ages looking for the three letters written on the map so they can see the dots and dashes next to it... So the latest generation of drivers (airframe) will be fine if all the systems work okay, but their basic skills will not be there when they need them most. So maybe when it all turns to s***, they will run out of ideas and make the wrong decisions?

Here's an example for you. Very recently I was flying across Europe at cruising altitude and heard a UK Charter Airlines aircraft declare a Pan call and "divert due to a generator failure". No seriously, these were the radio transmissions which we heard and both I and my colleague on our flightdeck were left scratching our heads. It appeared that the XXX was at cruising altitude and was looking for descent with a Pan call on the ATC airways frequency – we could not work it out. Why divert for a single electrical generator failure, with a modern airliner when you have two other sources of AC power, i.e. the other engine genny and the APU? The crew sounded quite calm as they put out their Pan call which was reassuring, but even more impressive to us was that the eastern European controller knew what a "Pan-Pan" R/T call was! Of course it *may* have been that the aircraft had dispatched with an unserviceable APU, but what are the odds thereafter against getting a further generator failure in-flight? *Infinitesimal* is the word you are looking for here.

My colleague and I were left shaking our heads and wondering if the latest generation of pilots were really so short of ideas that they immediately diverted when something went wrong. Don't get us wrong here, if this really was their only remaining source of AC power, then the book says divert to nearest suitable airfield ASAP, but we came to the conclusion that it wasn't. Also if they had only one remaining source of AC, the R/T transmissions would have been so much more urgent. The other worrying aspect for us, was that this was a UK crew operating with a reputable UK carrier – they should be the best in the business (or nearly so) – so what about the rest of them? What about airmanship, good situational awareness, staying ahead of the aeroplane, effective decision making processes, modern CRM? Are we now losing all these skills as automation takes over? Staying ahead of the aircraft is a major part of our job as pilots and when you are initially learning to fly it is also one of the most difficult things to do.

I leave you with one final thought and I apologise for not knowing the author of the (very amusing) "basic flying rules".

Rule one and two combined state; **"Try to stay in the middle of the air, do not go near the edges of it..."**

**"You've never been lost until you've been lost at Mach 3" – Paul F.Crickmore, Test Pilot.*

Playing with the kids on a Santa Flight for easyJet 2004   (Ray Farley photo)

In flightdeck B737-300 Geneva 2003 - with FO Wayne Connor (Ray Farley photo)

Fallback Position.

I have always assumed that there is an obvious answer to the question, "From where will come the next generation of pilots?", but recently I have had cause to view things rather differently. From my perspective, flying aeroplanes and getting paid to do it is pretty close to being in heaven. Call it 'kid in a sweetie-shop' or 'pig in you know what', but it has been a highly satisfactory career choice all the way for me. It has always been a vocational thing, either you have it or you don't – it is not something you can acquire or learn. It has to come from somewhere deep inside the person, not so much cerebral as cardiac. In short it comes from the heart.

In the case of my own children, I have never over-encouraged them to want to fly. My opinion has always been that it must come from within them and so far, I have to say, they have shown scant interest. There was a time a few years back when my young son came to ask me 'how long' it would take him to become a pilot – my heart skipped a beat. I was more than a little excited at the prospect, but realised that I had to play it cool (Dads are usually SO uncool). So I gave him what I thought was a suitably positive response without appearing to be 'gushing'. Later on while discussing the incident over dinner with his mother, I found it difficult to restrain my enthusiasm as I told her what he had said. She tried to let me down gently when she informed me of the reason for our son's new found interest in aviation as a career. "It's only because you have just flown Manchester United round the Far East for two weeks!" True enough he was mad keen on football and this was his favourite team. I was crushed.

In the intervening years, the subject has hardly been raised and whenever anyone has asked me if he intends to follow in his father's footsteps, I have been sensible enough to reply in the negative. He has always seemed much more interested in computers, mostly through virtual gaming of course, but there have been indications of something more serious about the technical side. A couple of years ago we were having a conversation alone together about schoolwork and where it might all lead to. It was along the lines of, "Why do I have to learn all this stuff? It won't be any good to me when I leave school and get a job".

This at the tender age of 14 is either an indication of how lazy he is going to be, or how far-sighted he really is. He made some typically teenage flippant remark such as, "Well if I don't make it in I.T. *I could always fly aeroplanes*", to which I guffawed and said, "Dude – you are NEVER going to be a pilot". He looked at me genuinely surprised and said slowly, "No Dad, THAT'S my Fallback Position".

Well I was stunned! Fallback Position? Really?! Is THAT what our profession has been reduced to now... a F-F-FALLBACK POSITION!? I couldn't speak. I just walked away – of course he didn't seem to notice, well the guy's a teenager, why woul

All those long hours of study, all the late nights, and the pass or fail examinations, the Morse code (ugh!) The aviation law exams, the do or die scenarios. The continuous assessment by Senior Examiners, Training Captains – (even now), every six months in the simulator for our proficiency checks. The constant monitoring of our performance by the CAA. The competitive scramble for jobs when our airline goes bust. The constant fear of failure (however slight) and the repetitive medical examinations which we have to pass to "Class One" standard. Then there are the REALLY challenging days when the weather, technical, ATC and passenger problems all conspire to try to prevent us flying. All of this for a profession which the class of 2012 call a Fallback Position? Unbelievable! Even now two years later, although I have calmed down, I still cannot comprehend the attitude.

I always assumed that every little boy was like me, mad about planes. Always interested when anything to do with flying came on the TV, happy to tag along with the family whenever there was a visit to the airport in the offing – either to drop off or pick-up, it didn't matter, I would get to see some JETS! Where did I go wrong? Did I make it look too easy? Let's face it; he has got the wrong idea about what I do to pay the mortgage so it must be my fault. Some kids are keen to fly. They appear inspired by the thought of "slipping the surly bonds of earth" which is encouraging that there may actually be enough new joiners to crew the airliners of the future. In my case, perhaps I played it too cool, probably I didn't "big it up" enough (teenage speak), I should have made it seem more like fun. Yes that's probably the reason, by the time my son was born, I was flying for the airlines and when I left the house with my flightbag and uniform with gold stripes on it that clearly did not equate with FUN. Similarly when I returned from 'work' sometimes and he would see me arrive, tired, jet-lagged and smelling of 'Eau de Boeing', that didn't look like FUN either.

What a pity he couldn't have seen how it was in the beginning. He never saw the banter in the crewroom with your mates – the parties in the mess. Learning to fly high performance aeroplanes and take them close to the limits – certainly close to your limits as a pilot, then later heading towards the performance limits of the machine. He never witnessed the fantastic experience of learning aerobatics in a clear blue sky, thousands of feet above the earth's surface. The joy of flying through your own slipstream on the pullout from a loop; the exquisite pleasure of flying a smooth, round barrel roll and then converting the speed into height; pulling up high for a nice 90 degree wingover; a quick check on the T's and P's round the top then down the hill again to build up speed for a four point hesitation roll... Yes this was all fun and more besides, but he was never there to see it. Nowadays what little hair I have left has plenty of grey in it and I guess when you are 14 you just can't see grey haired old guys doing the fun thing.

There is a real concern though that in our state of the art, futuristic, E-this and i-that age, the youth of today are not much interested in going flying for a living. Evidence the new TV advertisement by British Airways which seems to be an admission that the job just isn't sexy enough anymore. I found the images fascinating – especially Concorde, how we miss her now she's gone?! Literally a crying shame and we shall never see the like again in our lifetimes. Recruiting enough young aviators is obviously a struggle for the major carriers, I would say and finally the prophets are being proved correct that eventually demand would outstrip supply. All of the Middle East giants are advertising and training hundreds frantically to keep pace with the vast number of aluminium tubes they have ordered for delivery over the next decade. It will get worse of course, because none of the airlines prepared themselves properly for the famine, so they are busy poaching applicants from each other with lots of roadshows and full page adverts in the back of Flight.

When trying to find the reason why there are fewer potential pilots now I postulate that perhaps our generation is to blame for the current situation. Obviously we have all been witness to the erosion of the terms and conditions such that no school leaver would want to do it for the money anymore. In the good old days you could work for fifteen or twenty years as an ex-pat pilot and retire comfortably with a pot of gold, but that ship has sailed. The romance and glamour has gone from the job, with thousands of new-age lo-co crew members all calling each other "mate".

There was a time when an airline Captain would have been referred to ubiquitously as "Sir" by everybody on the airside ramp in whatever airport you cared to name, but no more. The security situation has taken its toll also, with all crews required to run the gauntlet of petty minded jobsworths on a regular basis. Without forgetting who is most at risk of terrorist acts onboard the aircraft, it should not be forgotten that it is *the pilots who have control of everybody's safety* while in flight simply by flying the machine. So when we talk to our sons about the job we do and the deterioration we have seen over the years, maybe it should come as no surprise that they get the message it is not all it was once cracked up to be.

Now I realise that I am as much to blame myself when I recall the informal career advice sessions which have been held in our house. When my son has asked me in the past what he should do to get a good standard of living in a comfortable working environment after leaving school and making his way into adult life, I have been consistent with my replies... be a Divorce Lawyer!

And if you don't succeed in law, then perhaps being a pilot would make quite a good "Fallback Position" – *Hey maybe the kid's got brains after all?*

VIP B737 on left base for RW22R at Nice Cote d'Azur airport

The Obituary Column.

October 2011 saw the demise of two men who had a profound influence on the lives and thinking of many people for a very long time, Muammar Gaddafi and Steve Jobs. Although the contrast between these two singular individuals could hardly be greater, there were similarities also. Both of them were extremely wealthy; both touched the lives of millions; both were leaders who were followed by thousands of people and both of them also connected with our world, 'Aviation', but in very different ways.

+   +   +

Through the development of touchscreen technology among other things, Steve Jobs gave us user-friendly interactive hardware which has greatly enhanced the safety and efficiency of powered flight. He will be remembered for being a visionary and product minded CEO who led a great team of people to deliver the Apple computer, iPod, iPhone and iPad. No doubt he will be sorely missed by his family and friends, many of whom were also his working colleagues. His gift to aviation will live on and provide great benefits to pilots now and in the future. More than that though, the example of how he lived his life has proven to be inspirational for a whole generation of Americans who will now go forth in the spirit of Steve Jobs to push their own boundaries and achieve their potential in all areas of their own lives. He was a highly entertaining and effective motivational speaker. An example of Steve Jobs' philosophy is easily appreciated with some of his memorable quotations, one of which was; *"Your time is limited, so don't waste it living someone else's life. Don't be trapped by dogma - which is living with the results of other people's thinking. Don't let the noise of other's opinions drown out your own inner voice. And most important, have the courage to follow your heart and intuition. They somehow already know what you truly want to become. Everything else is secondary".*

Contrast this with Gaddafi, the self-styled 'king of kings' (Sic) who also made many speeches, one of which to a female audience, contained the words; *"Women must be trained to fight in houses, prepare explosive belts and blow themselves up alongside enemy soldiers. Anyone with a car must prepare it and know how to install explosives and turn it into a car-bomb. We must train women to place explosives in cars and blow them up in the midst of enemies, and blow up houses so that they can collapse on enemy soldiers. Traps must be prepared. You have seen how the enemy checks baggage: we must fix these suitcases in order for them to explode when they open them".* Let us not forget that this was the man who gave us (among other things) the Lockerbie bombing of Pan Am 103 and the tragic murder of WPC Yvonne Fletcher shot from the Libyan Embassy while on duty outside in London. One has to ask, "Who will mourn the passing of Gaddafi?" - a rhetorical question to which we all know the answer.

+   +   +

Although it may seem bizarre, we do actually have much to be grateful to the ex evil dictator for in regard to Aviation Security. Without his evil intentions towards the west which resulted in various acts of terrorism sponsored by his regime, the advances in baggage screening for weapons and explosives would not have advanced so quickly. We are now fortunate in our industry to have the most effective security systems in place and for these we should be thankful. There is no doubt that without the pressure of need to develop the technology in body-scanning, explosives detection, passenger profiling and the like, many more lives could have been needlessly wasted in the intervening time since December 1988. It is to be hoped that although the actual bombers themselves have not been brought to justice, the families of the 270+ victims will find some closure with the premature death of the main instigator of the atrocity.

The heightened threat of terrorism in our industry has also been responsible for a complete change in the way we operate. Whereas in the old days, our paying customers would be viewed as our friends, they are all now seen as a potential enemy. Indeed we as crew are seen as suspicious even when we try to clear ourselves through security screening to reach our normal place of work – the aircraft. Many of us that know what it was like in the rose-tinted past, now look back on those days with fondness and I admit that every time I bend down to take off my shoes for the security people, I mutter "I cannot wait to retire" under my breath. For all that though, overall fewer innocent people have died and for this we should give thanks.

Funnily enough, I actually offloaded myself from a commercial flight a few years ago as a passenger entirely because I did not like the look of the passengers. Now I know how stupid THAT must sound, but it is true. I was in the queue at the check-in for a low-cost operated scheduled flight, when I was struck by the appearance and apparent origin of the majority of my fellow travelling companions. I asked myself, "Is this Dodgy-Airways I am flying on?" But when I looked at the board over the check-in counter apparently not.

What I had failed to appreciate however was that Viking Airways had regular flights from Manchester to Athens and from Athens to another destination in the Middle East - not only that but their fares were ridiculously cheap... Doubtless it was the 'value for money' aspect of the ticket sales which attracted both myself and the other passengers to use the airline, but there the similarities ended. As I stood there in my suit and tie, on my way to work, I realised that I was just about to consign myself to be sealed in an air conditioned aluminium tube at 37,000 feet with nearly 200 other souls, some of whom standing quite close to me were rather smelly. Not only that but there was the unmistakable smell of exhaled stale alcohol fumes in the air nearby which further heightened my level of concern.

Now don't get me wrong, I am not given to snobbery and I am quite used to travelling in economy, however I do have discretion and I am supposed to be employed as a decision maker, so I gave the matter some thought. Looking forward to the front of the two queues of passengers, many of whom appeared rather more casually dressed, I noticed that there was a delay with the check-in of some of the people. Two very smartly dressed officials on this side of the check-in counter were deep in discussion with a couple of young gentlemen and their passports and travel documents were being examined very closely. It was clear that I was not the only person interested in the origins of the passengers. Well, I thought about it for a little bit longer and although I was not formally told who the smartly dressed officials were at the front of the queue, I have seen enough Special Branch officers in my time to recognise the breed. I now considered the urgency of my own travel needs.

Well, I was wanted back in the office in Athens, but due to the power of the internet, I can do plenty of work remotely from other locations, so that would not be an issue. Also I thought about all of the disruptive passenger incidents I had ever been close to and/or involved in with my previous companies – many of these had resulted from the negative aspects of poor communication between ill-educated people, combined with alcohol when artificially trapped in a confined space all together. One more visual sweep by myself of the people in the queue, confirmed that there were apparently few brain surgeons present, nor any Maths professors, so it was time for me to go. As my bag was not checked in, it was not an issue.

I walked away and called my company's travel agent to say that I was going to miss the flight and could they please find me another one – easy. There was nothing tangible, but the whole situation had a bad feeling for me, so I made a sharp exit and left. Afterwards I did check the flight tracker system and this particular flight seemed to operate entirely normally – a slight delay to departure of 10 minutes or so, but nothing untoward. The fact remains that even though nothing actually went wrong, there were certain elements of a potentially dangerous situation present and I recognised them. Quite simply I wanted no part of it and I would do the same again under similar circumstances. These days in fact I am more discerning about which carrier I will get on and there are some with whom I choose not to travel. Maybe that sounds odd coming from somebody within the industry, but then again perhaps it is understandable. If you were a hairdresser by trade would you go to a barber called Sweeney Todd for a wet shave?

Finally, I did think (just before I left the queue for the flight I offloaded myself from) about all of the passengers on flights like the ill fated Air France 447 lost in the South Atlantic. How many of them had uneasy, sixth sense feelings while waiting to check-in?

I know that much of it is just silly superstition and I am also aware of the scientific structure of the aviation industry which includes the very real statistics regarding safety. Commercial airline flights really are the safest way to travel on the accidents versus distance basis – much less risky than crossing the road in most countries, UK included.

+   +   +

Which brings us back to our two deceased, world famous gentlemen. It is interesting to note that they both preferred private jet travel to scheduled airlines, but then if we had the money wouldn't we all?

Mental note to self, 'must buy more lottery tickets!'

An Apple a Day.

A while back I hurt my foot playing table-tennis against my son and was walking around with a bit of a limp for a few days – you could say it was a Sports Injury, although this would have been stretching things a bit. He said to me, "Dad, why don't you go and see a Doctor?" my reaction of horror surprised him. **"No way mate, us pilots try to stay away from the medics whenever possible, they can pull our Medical!"** (I am not allowed to call him dude anymore – that is reserved for friends only).

+   +   +

In our business I have often heard it said, "We are only as good as our last Proficiency Check and our Last Medical" and the meaning of this truism is self-explanatory. A successfully completed Licence Proficiency Check (LPC) validates the ATPL and it is the Licence *and* Medical which are the vital parts of a commercial pilot's meal ticket – without one of them, the other is no good. It is a legal requirement to have both original documents with you when you fly for a living and there is no way round that.

It comes as no surprise then, that most pilots view their Examiners both medical and technical with a certain amount of mistrust. Either the Training Captain (TRE) or the Aeromedical Doctor (AME) could potentially be responsible for the ending of a dream career. In the case of the former, at least there are ways in which a pilot can better their chances of success, by preparation for the LPC with practice and study. The revision of knowledge and rehearsal of techniques are of great value prior to going into the Simulator every six months and definitely have a positive effect on performance. All very well for the flying part of it then, but what about the medical?

In many ways we are the unwitting recipients of the results of the genetic lottery when it comes to which of us can pass the Class One medical. In fact I recall the advice of professional aviators who recommend that any potential student for a commercial pilot's licence undertakes their Class One aviation medical as a first step. It is no good committing yourself to spending thousands of pounds in aviation training if there is no future due to some obscure medical condition. Back in the day when I was teaching PPL students, I remember one of them went to the extreme of getting himself tested for HIV and when that came back negative, he then felt able to commit himself fully to his CPL course. Needless to say he also made some radical changes to his lifestyle to protect his new investment...

+   +   +

When it comes to performing well in the AME's consulting rooms, there are some things which can be done to help your chances of passing the tests. I will admit to having a habit of memorising the bottom line of letters on the eye-test chart on the wall behind the Doc' when I sat down for the initial part of the medical – in fact I still remember the first 4 letters A – M – O – T... Then a few minutes later I could 'read' them from the other end of the surgery with confidence. This went well for a few years until one day the AME brought out this funny little stick gadget which he put on the bridge of my nose and which had tiny, tiny writing on a little block which he placed at an impossibly close distance from my eyes – "Ah! The game's up Doc".

When it came to hearing tests though, things were easier as my not so young AME put a lot of store in the 'whispering test'. By this he would sit at his desk at one end of the room and I would stand at the other end. He would then whisper words which had nil connection which I was required to repeat back to him like "Dakota...Jersey...Smith..." naturally it was an advantage to remember them for the next time as he always used the same ones! I used to sometimes whisper back my answers to him, to which he replied "Pardon? Say again..?" It was with a sense of mischief once that I explained to him that this test was going be self-defeating eventually as his own hearing deteriorated with the passing years and thus his whispers would become louder – and so it proved.

Monitoring of pilots' hearing does not solely rely upon subjective human examinations though and the AMEs have some very nice audiometry equipment. Judging by the appearance of the 'Cans', (headset earpieces) most of these machines seem to date back to the 1950s and this was certainly the case in the armed forces. As military pilots it was expected to observe a steady decline in hearing function (especially high frequencies) over the years of our service due to continuous exposure to high levels of noise associated with operating close to jet engines. Also, being in the military subjected a chap to quite a lot of loud 'bangs' at various times and from a range of sources. We were all taught at an early stage that hearing loss due to high noise levels is both cumulative and permanent – ear protection is a must.

Testing of military pilots' hearing was done by placing the candidate in a soundproof box and then asking them to put on the headset while holding a button on the end of a wire. "While you are hearing the sound of the beeps, keep pressing the button", were the instructions to us and we then kept very still and held our breath... Tiny, tiny beeps could be heard through one ear at a time and they seemed to come in groups of... seven? Yes definitely - there were **SEVEN** tiny beeps and then it went on to the next frequency, but not only that, they got fainter and fainter as they went on. *'Oh this is good... so I just keep counting and holding the button down for what seems like the correct period of seven beeps – hmm? That should help a lot!'* At the end of a pilot's military service, all are required to complete an exit medical to ensure that their medical condition is recorded. I believe this is to prevent retrospective litigation for compensation which is logical. When I was given the results of my audiometry test, the Chief Petty Officer was very impressed as he said, "Bloody Hell Sir! You could get a job as a whistling guard-dog!"
"Thank you Chief", I replied politely as I took the certificate and headed for the CAA.
It appeared that my own hearing had actually improved during my military service...

+   +   +

This apparent shyness from pilots towards the medical profession is nothing new as anybody who has read the story of Chuck Yeager breaking the sound barrier will tell you. He did so at that time while suffering an injury (broken ribs) from falling off a horse two days previously and was in a great deal of pain as he strapped himself into the Bell X-1 above Edwards Airforce Base -

he knew that if he went to see 'The Doc', he would have been grounded. There have been countless other examples since then of pilots self-medicating and 'soldiering on'. In the general scheme of things it is good to not be a hypochondriac when working as a professional pilot, but this can go too far. The last thing you need in your career is an incident of incapacitation at the controls of an aircraft, although this is a scenario which all aviators are trained to deal with.

When I was managing pilots at a certain low-cost airline, we did have an incident where the Captain of the crew became *partially* incapacitated while they were flying back towards their home base. The First Officer suggested to him that they should divert to another airport enroute with the FO taking over control, but the Captain vehemently disagreed. It seemed that the more senior pilot had some form of food poisoning and was in a bad way, but refused to admit incapacitation. The upshot was that they arrived safely back into Luton, but when they parked on stand the Captain collapsed unconscious and had to be taken to hospital by ambulance – he survived and made a complete recovery a few days later.

After the flight and during the subsequent investigation, some of my fellow managers said that the First Officer should be disciplined for 'failing to insist to the Captain' that they divert and that 'command' of the aircraft should revert to the right-hand seat. I was of a distinctly different opinion however because the situation was not a straight-forward incapacitation; it was a partial. This meant that the aircraft Commander, although debilitated, was conscious, lucid and refused to divert the flight or give up control of the aircraft to the FO. Fortunately the rest of them saw it my way in the end and the FO was praised for the support he gave to his Captain during a time of great stress. In fact we all agreed that the flight would have been in more danger if the co-pilot had been put into the position of flying single-handedly into an unknown foreign airfield.

+ + +

When it comes to hiding information from the medics, you can go too far. Witness that there have been airliner accidents in the past, where evidence suggests that one of the pilots (usually the Captain) had suffered a heart attack shortly before losing control of the aeroplane. This has usually happened at a critical phase of flight, either on takeoff or during landing. In one of the reports I read a few years back, the Captain (and all onboard) actually survived when he declared to the other crew-members that he was unwell with chest-pain and they turned back after takeoff. Later it transpired that he had in reality had two heart attacks – the first of these had been in the terminal BEFORE the flight – at the time he had dismissed it as a bad case of indigestion.

There is a middle ground here - I know lots of pilots who have streaming eyes and runny noses in the summer, but allegedly have *never* suffered from Hayfever...

The moral of the story must be that you should try not to drop yourself in it if you don't have to, but there will come a time in your career when you have to admit your human frailty.

Hazardous Henry.

We can all think of instances when somebody well known to us has behaved in a manner which seems at odds with what we would usually expect of them. In most forms of employment this might provide for an embarrassing moment or a difficult social situation for colleagues to deal with, but in our industry it can literally be a matter of life or death.

+   +   +

You see a lot of what we do as professional aviators depends largely on positive interaction with other human beings, often with crew members on your own aircraft. The successful outcome of every commercial flight is not down to any single individual, but the concerted efforts and teamwork of probably hundreds of people. Some teams working together are potentially more important than others and when it comes to the aeroplane's crew, the mutual cooperation is absolutely critical – hence the reason for modern Crew Resource Management (CRM). Unlike any other form of transportation which operates to move people and materiel around the surface of the Earth, flying is three dimensional. It also happens much, much faster than anything else we have seen before. Take the train for example. They can be pretty quick and can carry hundreds of tonnes of freight and/or hundreds of passengers, but they are destined to follow prescribed paths both laterally and vertically all the time.

A passenger jet is like an airborne train, however the following of the intended vertical and horizontal path is really down to the individuals onboard and the decisions they make. We know that it is far more complicated than this alone of course, there are so many different variables that sometimes it is really a wonder that any commercial flight departs and arrives on time at all. In spite of all the difficulties, the system works and regularly we see airlines achieving brilliant schedule results. This is not happening by chance. For every eventuality, there is a mitigating course of action to protect the schedule. Think about what happens when a booked passenger fails to arrive at check-in for a particular flight. Quite simply if they do not show up for check-in they are listed as a "No-Show" and the flight proceeds without them. Similar procedures are in place at the boarding of the flight – if a passenger fails to arrive at the gate in time for the scheduled pushback, their baggage is identified and removed from the cargo hold, then they and the bags are "Off-

Loaded" from the passenger manifest. So much for the abnormal behaviour of the customers, but what happens when it is a member of crew?

In the overall scheme of things, "Crew" as they are known, turn up for work on time and do their jobs to the best of their ability. Although there are various anecdotal tales of misbehaviour by crew members at hotels in various parts of the world, generally they are a conformist, rule following group with a highly developed sense of what is right and wrong. It is all the more unusual then, for them to behave in an abnormal way. As a manager of people you do seem to develop a list of the usual suspects. These are the names which keep cropping up again and again, such that when you pick up the 'phone in the office and the other end says, "I want to talk to you about Capt XXX", you automatically think, *Oh no! What has he done NOW!???*

There are also crew names which you associate with normal quiet, predictable behaviour and one such pilot was ubiquitously known as Hazardous Henry, simply because he wasn't – he was renowned for being one of the safest (if slowest) operators in the base. Capt Henry would always be ontime for work and usually fairly well presented and well prepared. One day he arrived in the crewroom for the preflight briefing and appeared in a bit of a state. Unshaven and with his uniform looking a mess, Henry seemed to be very preoccupied as the crew went through their preflight briefing and did not pay attention to the planning for the flight. Suddenly he looked down at the floor beside him and said to the Co-Pilot, "Where's my flightbag?"

Having driven over two hours from his home to get to the airport, he had done so without the most essential part of a pilot's equipment, the flightbag. This extra large briefcase contains much more than just an aviator's lunch (although in some low-cost operators there is that too), but also his licence, passport, often crew ID and many more professional tools of the trade without which we believe we cannot operate. The fact that Henry had been so preoccupied as not to have noticed his omission, speaks volumes for his state of mind.

Although I was the Base Manager, I arrived as crew on an inbound flight and was informed by eager ramp staff that "A First Officer has off-loaded the Captain!" which was a new one on me, but when told the rest of the story, I realised what had happened. Quite simply Henry had some stuff going on in his personal life which meant that he was under external stress to the point where he found it impossible to concentrate on his work.

As his Manager it was up to me to 'do something' and so I went off to find him – he was really upset and felt he had let everyone down. We sat together privately in his car in the staff carpark and he told me the story of what was kicking-off at home. I was quite upset for him too; we all go through stuff at times which we should leave at home when we go flying. Nobody is immune.

My advice to him was quite simple, "Henry, go home mate. Take as much time as you need and when you are ready, come back to work. Don't feel under pressure to do that until you have got everything under control and your life is back on track. What you have to remember is that this operation is huge and we have loads of people who can cover your absence, it's really not an issue. Although there are hundreds of flights every day in the programme, there are thousands of crew all over the network to run it. You have a very good employment history and no-one will ever complain about your absence, it is for a situation which many of us have been through before. Now get out of here and don't call me till you're ready to come back flying again!"

Three weeks later, Henry was back in action and good as new. He had dealt with all of his problems without any need to worry about the roster and he was a changed man. He still maintained his nickname among the crew however, (he never moved any faster) but carried on flying safely to a happy retirement.

Many years before this, I had myself been a co-pilot with a Captain under stress, but in his case this was his normal state of mind. Well when I say normal, it was part of his persona which had been accepted by the rest of the base in which he was employed. On one night charter flight to Palma, his behaviour became quite extreme as he was shouting across the flightdeck his views about *"F****** Spanish Controllers!"* while I was transmitting to Barcelona ATC on the radio. I am sure they heard this maniacal outburst in the background and maybe that would account for our two hour slot delay after we arrived in Majorca! To get back to Manchester we had to fly north again through Barcelona airspace – oh dear!

"Oh dear!" was probably not what was said afterwards by the Spanish lady dispatcher who was abusively addressed at high volume by Capt Stressy when she came to visit our flightdeck to talk about the slot delay. She had a face like thunder as she left the cockpit and if she didn't burst into tears walking down the steps, I would have been most surprised. I did try to calm him down a bit by pointing out some of the positive aspects about the delay, "Well at least we can eat our crew meals in peace on the turnround..." but at every turn I was silenced by another transmission of vitriol.

To say I was 'cheesed off' having to fly with this joker was an understatement, but I tried to just let it all flow over my head and act in a calm, supportive manner. Bear in mind that this was in the days prior to the invention of CRM as a science. In the past I had been a Psychiatric Nurse so I was experienced in the use of de-confliction techniques to try and bring the situation down a little. Humour was no help, although I tried that too and all the cabin crew were afraid to enter the flightdeck in case they got their head bitten off. I resolved that somebody had to have a word with him, but not now; after we get back. Not here, downroute; where he was blowing his top at everybody - we were "ALL BLOODY INCOMPETENTS". Like the rest of the crew and the delayed passengers in the terminal, I wanted to get home to

Manchester – if we ended up having a row here in Palma that might not happen tonight...

His scathing remarks to the passengers on the PA about *"Barcelona Air TRAGIC Control - who cannot organise a piss-up in a brewery!"* probably didn't win him many friends among the English speaking Spanish Nationals in the cabin. In the flightdeck, sat next to him, I winced when I heard him say it. Generally it was one of the most fraught and unpleasant flights I ever had to operate – I can remember all the details even now some 25 years later.

Finally we landed back in our home base and got off the aircraft. As his usual practice, he did not wait until all the crew were ready, he told me to get my stuff together and we headed off to the terminal separate from the Flight Attendants. After passing through crew clearance at the Customs office we were once again walking outside towards the crewroom and he lit up a King-size cigarette. Inhaling deeply and blowing the smoke out with satisfaction, he stated, "Well! That seemed to go all right!" I was incredulous. I assumed he was referring to the appalling flights and his bizarre behaviour, but I had to check if I was correct.

"Do you mean the flights to Palma and back which we have just done tonight?" I asked.
"Yes" he replied, "of course I do, I was just saying, I think it went okay under the circumstances...". He looked at me and waited for me to speak, *'well here goes'* I thought.
"I think you should have a good think about how you appear to other people XXX"
He clearly did not comprehend, so I continued,
"you see downroute you were exhibiting *all the signs of mental instability* and you obviously find this job stressful. Please. You need to be careful or somebody is going to report you..." I trailed off. The look on his face told me all I needed to know about whether he agreed with me or not.

We didn't continue the discussion and when the rest of the crew caught us up, they didn't mention it either. I wondered if I should speak to somebody in the management about it, but I came to the conclusion that it wasn't actually dangerous when we were flying, provided that I stuck to all the standard challenge and response calls and refrained from saying anything which could wind him up.

Funnily enough I learned about a year later from one of the Fleet Managers that Capt Stressy himself had gone to the Boeing Fleet office the very next day to make a formal complaint about ME! Apparently I (as his FO) was "not showing the right attitude and was being negative".

Needless to say the fact that I was not informed for about 12 months and even then only found out in a bar, told me how the managers felt about him.

Author & Pitts Special S2A, Florida 1990. Awesome aerobatic aeroplane. Loved it

Another Red & White machine, not quite so manoeuvrable, but loved this one too

Nuns and Lapdancers.

As you can tell by the title of this piece, young people's career choices can sometimes be literally 'poles' apart...

+   +   +

Similar to the bewildering choice of employment being made available to all sections of society, even within one profession there are different routes to be taken. For example there are many different forms of professional aviator and these can be roughly broken down as follows. Firstly there is a military or civil split and thereafter come the specialisations. Of course in some areas there is overlap and there are opportunities for pilots to move through the specialisations at different points in their careers. Military pilots tend to be much younger than civil professional pilots on average and many commercial airline pilots have been military aviators in the earlier stages of their careers.

It is true to say that the chance to join the armed forces as a pilot have shrunk in recent years as most western governments have taken advantage of "The Peace Dividend" offered by the end of the cold war. In the past 12 months we have even seen UK armed forces pilots being made redundant before the end of the their training in the interest of cutting cost.

By the same token, fewer ex-military pilots are arriving to the commercial operators to begin their second career and this at a time when the industry is expanding once again. Some years back the pundits were forecasting 15% year on year growth, but that was before 9/11 and then the 2008 global financial crisis. Currently the most optimistic experts are indicating single figure growth rates, but the significant fact is that the industry is still growing. This leads us to the predictions of pilot shortages for the commercial airline industry in the near future.

From the perspective of one of the older generation of current pilots, I can say that it is not so much the quantity of new recruits required which bothers us, but more importantly the quality. I distinctly recall the formative days of a low-cost carrier when we were busy recruiting and training greater numbers of low-houred CPL holders than ever before in the history of British commercial aviation.

At first the quality of the young 'airframe drivers' was quite good, in fact from one particular training source it was very good and those young F/Os of the late 1990s went on to become senior management and training personae in their own right. They were highly disciplined and well coordinated, eager to learn and easy to train. From personal experience, I remember that in many ways, "us Training Captains - we really did have it 'easy'".

The crunch came when the supplies of highly suitable young men and women began to dry up, then we noticed two things. Firstly the average age of the new trainees steadily increased and the length of time it took to get them up to the required standard extended markedly. There are some mature aviators who seem to take certain pride in the fact that they "have never had to go-around in my whole flying career!" Certainly when I began Line Training at the low-cost carrier, I could even have said that myself, however at the end of 7 years I had actually logged 5 go-arounds and most of these were in the latter part of the period. The reason for the go-arounds were mainly due to either an unstable approach which was not recognised by the trainee or sequencing too close behind an arriving or departing aircraft. Again, this situation is sometimes difficult for a trainee to manage. A basic tenet of learning to flying high performance aircraft is the ability to recognise and learn from your own mistakes. From the trainers' point of view, it is necessary for us to allow the trainees to make the errors and to recover from them and it is that judgement call from the training captain which is critical.

Of the 5 go-arounds in the B737, a couple of them were particularly memorable and the one which first comes to mind was when we were making an approach to Luton airport's runway 26 at night. The trainee First Officer was flying the sector inbound from Barcelona and I was aware that he had struggled through some of his Line Training sectors, especially in regard to landing the aircraft at night. Landing consistency is quite a common problem in the early days. Prior to descent I briefed him in detail about the 737 landing technique and we also discussed the issue of crosswinds. When I got the ATIS, the latest weather report contained a wind report which gave an element of 5 knots crosswind.

Bearing in mind that he had flown 20 sectors already in his line training, only 5 knots crosswind should be do-able. I pattered him through the initial approach and onto finals, prompting occasionally to ensure he selected the gear and flaps in good time – the last thing he needed was a hot and high approach tonight... Eventually we were set up nicely on finals, fully visual from 10 miles out. He disconnected the autopilot and autothrottle so he could fly the aircraft manually. I had recommended him to go manual early in visual conditions in order to get a good feel for the aeroplane – up here at two thousand feet or so you could sense the drift as the nose of the aircraft was pointed into the wind.

He lost the centreline a couple of times, but with some verbal coaching from my side he managed to get it back on the localizer and I was pleased to see he had taken my advice about keeping the power changes to a minimum. When flying large jet transports, the fewer changes in thrust the better on finals because every thrust-lever input either up or down requires a consequent re-trimming of the stabiliser. The most stable approaches are the ones where the pilot sets the power to a datum and flies the jet with little change thereafter.

Now as we got closer to the runway, we were through the one thousand foot point and ATC had cleared us to land. I could see from the control column movements that he was indulging in some over-controlling and advised him to make smaller inputs, but then I could feel the rudder pedals moving first one way, then the other. The localiser beam started to slide sideways again, but this time it was because he had turned the nose of the aircraft straight in line with the runway... *Oooerr... this is not looking good...* I said to myself, while aloud I encouraged him with "Centreline... Speed Speed..."

Now we were approaching 500 feet above the ground and it was clear we were off to the downwind side of the extended centreline of the runway, he was pedalling away on the rudder pedals to no good purpose and it seemed he had run out of ideas. Looking across at his face, it was clear he had maxed-out and 'the hard-drive was full'. It was time for me to take control...

"I have control!" I called in a loud voice and instantly he released the control column and rudder pedals as I immediately banked the aircraft into wind, reduced power and tried to regain the centreline for a landing.

Damn! I've left it too late, even I can't land the bloody thing from this position! Went through my mind and a fraction of a second later I called, "Going Around, FLAP FIFTEEN!" simultaneously hitting the TOGA switches, raising the nose and advancing the thrust levers, the power of two CFM56s surged in reassuringly.

Clack, clack, clack went the trim wheel and I heard the flap lever moving sharply to the Flap 15 gate, but no other sounds from his side. A quick glance and I could see we were now climbing rapidly away from the ground, so I called *"Positive Climb! GEAR UP!"* and he came alive again and brought the landing gear lever smartly into the "UP" position. I hit the transmit switch at the same time *"Easy XXX. Going Around..."*

We flew a quick circuit to the south of the airfield and within a few minutes we were back onto finals with gear down and landing flap set. The crosswind was still there, so I gave a pattered demo of a night crosswind approach and landing while he followed through lightly on the controls.

The epilogue to the story was that he went back to the simulator for a training session to practice, doing night, crosswind landings in the B737. When he came back to line training a week later with restored confidence and well honed skills, the remainder of his line sectors were completed in record time. He was cleared to the line as a junior First Officer and fast forward a few years, he got his command on the type in the minimum flying hours possible.

+   +   +

When it comes to career choices, it was clear that my young friend had made the right one, although his initial training on the Boeing had not been entirely plain sailing.

In fact he had been heavily influenced by his father who was also an airline pilot before his retirement. All of which leaves one interesting question in my mind...

What influencing factors would make a young lady become a 'God-botherer' instead of a night club hostess?

Born to be Mild.

(British holidaymakers going abroad – don't you just love 'em? I still shake my head and smile when I think of this one. It was so funny).

It was an easy Sunday out and back charter flight from the UK and we were approaching top of descent; destination Alicante. The weather was gin clear all along the Costa Blanca coastline and we would get some lovely views of the beaches as we made our final approach to land on runway 29. Yes everything in the garden was rosy and I should have known it was not going to last... My reverie was interrupted as the cabin crew call chime sounded twice in the overhead panel and as the monitoring pilot; I gave the R/T to the FO and answered the intercom. "Hi it's James in the flightdeck?" The senior stewardess answered back hurriedly, she sounded stressed. *"Captain! We have a problem with some passengers' behaviour and will need to call for the Police to meet the aircraft on arrival..."*

+   +   +

I think it would be true to say that the vast majority of Airline Pilots are fairly civilised individuals. They neither seek confrontation in their everyday lives, nor do they deviate much beyond the bounds of normal civilised behaviour. In fact some of the best pilots I have ever flown with are rather shy retiring personalities, who are more focused on the technical aspects of the job and shun anything to do with dealing with the passengers. As a breed, you would not say we were 'Born to be Wild' that's for sure. Naturally there are a few exceptions, but mostly we are rule following conformists who enjoy pushing buttons for a living. Additionally, it is a remarkably safe occupation; certainly we always think in terms of being more at risk of accidental death or injury while driving to or from the airport. The profession is interesting, but I suggest not hugely challenging once you have reached a certain level of operational competence and settled into flying a specific type of aeroplane.

The above statement really does not apply during the early days of learning to fly airliners though. Back then, I distinctly recall being terrified of making PA announcements to the cabin and did not want anything to do with the passengers. For me, learning to actually fly the big shiny jet was enough thank you very much and I wanted the least amount of distractions possible so I could get on and do it to the best of my ability. With the passage of time, more flights and increasing confidence in all aspects of the job, your vision tends to widen.

With this increased situational awareness comes the ability to encompass more in your line of sight without the need to be so task focused – a perfect example of travel broadening the mind if you like. You are able to extend your nervous sensitivity to cover the entire machine, right out there to the wingtips, through the cabin, round the hydraulic systems, along the fuel-lines, through the engines, entwining with the electrical system... Well you get the idea anyway. Not only are you able to confidently extend your consciousness to control the whole of the flying machine, but you also start to think ahead of the airplane, visualising and planning the descent, approach, arrival phases of flight all the way up to parking at the gate. Eventually, if you do it long enough, the whole thing becomes much easier and therefore we should please forgive those of our very experienced brethren who describe their job as 'hours and hours of complete boredom, punctuated by moments of sheer terror'. They are only being humorous really.

After a while, especially once you change seats and take command for the first time, you are conscious that all the crew look to you for leadership. As Master and Commander, you are their 'rock' and in times of crisis, they need to see a firm hand on the tiller as the ship is buffeted in heavy seas. So it comes to pass that occasionally you have to confront that minority of passengers who insist on misbehaving onboard your aircraft. In the old days of course, it was possible to leave the flightdeck while airborne and deal with them face to face, but since 11th September 2001, that option is no longer available to us. In fact normally if there is any disturbance by disruptive passengers in the cabin, the flightdeck armoured door is immediately deadlocked for the remainder of the flight.

If we are going to have a melee in the cabin it is MUCH better to have it on the ramp with the doors open and the airbridge attached than at 35,000 feet. Several times in the past I have been advised by 'the Number One', (old name for Senior Cabin Crew Member), that some passengers during boarding have appeared intoxicated and potentially disruptive, singing and swearing etc. At which point I ask their advice on whether he or she wants to travel with them. If the No 1 says "OFF", then I immediately call for the airport police and security to remove them and their baggage from the aeroplane - I never disagree. The reason is that THEY (the SCCM) are THE expert when dealing with the punters and I would always go with their assessment, even if they appeared to be erring on the side of caution.

There are other times when they suggest that I 'come and have a word with them' before departure and at these times I have a few well chosen words on the PA which I use. The full effect is best achieved by standing at the front of the cabin in uniform, with the microphone and delivering a clear warning in loud, slow, English, regarding misbehaviour onboard the aircraft which will NOT be tolerated, assuring that if this warning is ignored the police WILL meet the aircraft on arrival and "*YOU WILL BE ARRESTED, for endangering the safety of an aircraft!*" On the very few occasions when I have had to do this, I have never experienced ANY trouble during the subsequent flight.

Needless to say I have got over my earlier stage-fright and these rare incidents liven up an otherwise unremarkable flying day. The point to remember here is, they are ALWAYS a minority of miscreants and the 'right-thinking majority' of passengers totally support the actions of the crew. In fact once I have given my "YOU WILL GET ONE WARNING ONLY... THIS IS

IT... THERE IS NO SECOND CHANCE!" speech, there is usually a reassuring round of applause from our shallower-end of the gene pool customers as I disappear back into the cockpit.

+   +   +

But today? Why today with no warning whatsoever? On a lovely, peaceful Sunday-afternoon-happy-holidays type flight to the sunshine? I was quite bemused until another intercom call from the forward galley when I was informed of all the circumstances. Before taking action to call out the Police, I needed to know the exact nature of the incident. Apparently two young girls, 18 or 19 years old, had been winding up two older females in the seats behind them to the point where (fuelled by alcohol) one of the middle-aged women behind, grabbed the girls by the hair and issued death-threats which were overheard by the cabin crew – unbelievable! It started with a reclining seat argument which developed into a proper row, insults were exchanged, offence had been taken and physical violence was now a real possibility.

"What did they actually say and did *any of the crew actually witness them saying it?* Please be specific", I was using my slow, deliberate tone of voice, the one which my kids hate to hear at home. The SCCM replied with confidence.
"Well, yes I heard her say it myself, she said, *'when we get to the airport terminal I'm going to f****** kill you!'"* Now I was convinced and replied quickly, "Oh yes! That's a threat alright, we will have the Police meet the aircraft and I will speak to all the passengers as we taxy in to stand after landing".

It was clear that if we detained the older women for say half an hour talking to the police at the aircraft, then the younger girls (who said they had no intention of making a formal complaint) would be able to pick up their baggage and do a runner from the airport to their hotel. So we radioed ahead to the handling agent at the airport. "Please have the police meet the flight on arrival at the gate we have two disruptive passengers onboard who have been using threatening behaviour..."

In the flightdeck we discussed the situation in detail and decided this was the easiest way to handle the event – after all, we didn't really want anybody to be arrested on a sunny Sunday afternoon. Basically we would detain the two older females who would be embarrassed in front of the rest of the passengers, get the nice policeman to give them a good talking to and then they would be able to go and enjoy their holiday like everybody else. It would be the equivalent to an informal caution, the problem would be solved, the young girls would be well away and then we could get the aircraft turned round and be on our way with no delay – perfect! Little did I know what would happen next...

As we taxied in, I made a formal PA to the cabin instructing all passengers to *"remain in your seats with seatbelts fastened as the police will be boarding the aircraft at the gate".* This usually gets their attention and sure enough nobody moved. We parked the aircraft on the stand and quickly whizzed through the shutdown checklist so I could get out into the cabin. Jacket on, (full uniform carries authority – yes even now) I am in the forward galley with the entry door open, then I am leading the police officers to the row of seats where the older women are sitting. It is true to say that the coppers were not looking inclined to actually DO anything and who could blame them? Sunday afternoon police duty at Alicante airport in very early summer must be one big snooze of a job. Arresting two middle aged English holidaymakers was not in their afternoon siesta plan at all.

That being said, we removed the two ladies firmly from the aeroplane so the cops could talk to them at the side of the airbridge while the rest of the passengers disembarked. There was a river of humanity flowing past us as we (the SCCM and I) talked with the two Spanish police officers and the two disruptive passengers. I noticed out of the corner of my eye, two very relieved young girls scampering briskly up the jetty into the terminal. Now the women were protesting their innocence of course, however I was determined they would not wriggle out of it so easily and prompted the Senior to give the police her account of what she saw and heard in the cabin, including 'the death-threat'.

The older and more inebriated of the women now became very aggressive, not only towards the SCCM, but also to the senior police officer which was a surprise. If she'd had any sense, she would have let it go, apologised and we could have all moved on. The B737 cabin was empty by this time and we were keen to turn the aircraft round and get on our way home. Now she was in a belligerent mood, swearing and shouting, she suddenly grabbed the sergeant's uniform, but he was having none of it and whipped her wrist into an armlock with her head down bent over double! Two seconds later, with handcuffs on, she was out of the airbridge and being marched unceremoniously down the steps to the waiting police car on the ramp below by both police officers. We were all agog.

+   +   +

"Senor Capitan. You write statement in station of police". The senior policeman was a little out of breath as he had run back up the steps of the airbridge; I turned to the SCCM and the First Officer who had now joined us.

"Get the aircraft ready to go, then board the passengers, I'll be back in ten minutes".
I shared the back seat of a second police car to the terminal with the other woman who turned out to be the younger sister. I advised her to try and get her aggressive older sibling to calm down and apologise to the police before they threw her in jail for a week, but she said it was impossible. While I wrote

a brief statement in one office at the police station under the terminal building, I could clearly hear 'the accused' berating her captors at full volume in the office next door. It was so amusing, I almost burst out laughing at some of the stuff she was coming out with; maybe she was more drunk than she had appeared before.

Meanwhile, I nearly managed to keep my 10 minutes promise to the crew and in fact we departed Alicante on schedule. I was right; the views of the Spanish coastline were spectacular from the flightdeck as we climbed towards cruising altitude. The normal background sounds of the CVR during the sterile climb were punctuated by sounds of intermittent giggling from the two occupants – most unprofessional!

+   +   +

In my report to the airline of the incident which I wrote later on the Captain's Voyage Report, I stated, *'When last seen, Mrs X was very likely going to be charged with assault and/or affray, probably by the police officer to whom she constantly referred as "F****** Big Nose!"'*

Kissing Frogs.

(They say you've got to kiss a lot of them to find your Prince...)

There are two distinct schools of thought when it comes to the assessment of piloting skills. On the one hand they say there is no such thing as a 'natural pilot', while on the other they say the Baron Von Richtofens of our industry are born to be 'Aces' from the start. Over many years of training people to fly powered flying machines, I have deliberately tried to keep an open mind on all aspects of the profession. I must admit though to starting off with the cynical view that the best aviators are trained, not born and for a very long time this has stood me in good stead.

+   +   +

Well that's okay as far as it goes for Flying Skills, "Keep the wings level and pull the stick back... watch... the houses get smaller", etc. but the funny thing is they say you can *teach* people CRM (Crew Resource Management). Now here is a really different arena and one which is guaranteed to keep a room full of Training Captains in heated debate until the bar opens. If we assume that peoples' personalities are pretty much 'set' by the time they reach their early twenties, then surely there is only so much you can do to modify the way in which they interact with the rest of the world and in particular their working colleagues.

I well remember one individual, a 30 year old First Officer who was reviled for being difficult to work with by every person in the airline. No matter that he had received at least his fair share of CRM 'courses', he was still hard-work to sit next to for a long flight. For some reason he just wanted to prove himself right about everything and to everybody, which is an irritating personal quality in itself, but then even when you tried to communicate with him, he would come across as arrogant or even downright rude. One example was when I was returning to the B757 as Captain having been away from the type for some years. We were in the simulator together and it appeared (to me anyway) that he was trying to highlight any errors which I made to the instructor sitting at the console behind us.

I would like to think of myself as a very patient person and certainly I try to embrace all modern teachings of CRM, but my patience snapped at one point regrettably when he pushed it too far and questioned my judgement in a way which suggested that he was trying to score yet another point against me in front of the instructor. The subject was the Passenger Evacuation Drill for the B757 which was in the checklist and, from experience, I had known many crew, cock this up on many occasions while trying to do it all from memory.

Of course it is a vitally important procedure to do quickly, if the aeroplane is on fire and stationary on the ground after an emergency landing or abandoned takeoff, however it MUST be done correctly if we are to reduce the numbers of casualties. Many is the time in the Sim, (myself included in the past) when we have called "Evacuate! Evacuate..." on the PA to the cabin, but have omitted to shut down one or more of the engines... Predictable results would be that any escape slide which was deployed in front of an RB211 would be sucked into the intake and any slide blown from behind the engine would subject descending passengers to burns from exhaust. Not clever.

At that time, the drill was a 'memory item' for us Boeing pilots, but some of us had already started briefing that, in reality, we would carry out the procedure as a 'read and do' to make certain we didn't make any mistakes. The time element would take maybe only 30 seconds longer to do it this way, but at least we would be completely sure as we ourselves slid down the slide after the passengers, that at least the engines were shutdown. The Spanair MD83 landing accident at Liverpool which I observed many years before was a case in point. After the passengers and crew evacuated the aircraft, the engines were still running five minutes later when the Emergency Services arrived on the scene... Well my young colleague started saying in a loud theatrical voice "...*but Captain,* I think you'll find that this is a *memory item* and we should do it by *recall*..."

At this point I looked straight at him and sharply interrupted him with, "Listen Pal!! When you fly with me, in MY flightdeck when I AM IN COMMAND...YOU WILL do it as READ AND DO, END OF STORY! IS THAT CLEAR!!?"

Needless to say there was a new understanding between us from this point on, although I have never had to use such means before nor since. In the remaining time in the Sim together I simply adopted a very direct style of communication, which I would not usually have done at all. "DO THIS... DO THAT... DO IT NOW!" etc.

The funny thing was that less than 12 months later, Boeing changed the QRH such that the Passenger Evacuation Drill was printed in bold letters on the outside back cover of the checklist with clear instructions that this was a "Read and Do" procedure. It goes without saying that they had obviously taken heed of the feedback from the senior Training Captains who had actually been doing it this way themselves from a long time previously.

There is an important learning point here for junior First Officers in the simulator and that is this. Never try to get one over on the other pilot, even if they are the same rank as you. This applies equally to when you do the job for real in the aircraft; we should never try to points-score against our team-mates. The ultimate danger of this is not getting your head bitten off by a much senior colleague, but that there is a real potential for CRM breakdown to the level where flight safety is seriously impaired.

The court case involving the two Flybe pilots a couple of years back is a perfect example of the wrong stuff where our profession is concerned and stands as a lesson to us all in ensuring our egos do not get in the way of our good judgement. Thinking back to my own outburst in the simulator all those years ago, perhaps some people would say I should have reacted with more tolerance but, (and it's a big but here) my junior colleague was unreasonably disrespecting the chain of command. Over the previous days in the simulator training, I had already exercised my tolerance, to the point where my patience had been tried to the limit and this FO was actually becoming a hazard to the safety of the flight. The proof of the pudding was the fact that in the debrief, the instructor agreed with me; he also criticised the FO's behaviour.

Okay, so this guy was a Frog and I happen to know for a fact that he never really improved while he was with that same employer. The question is how do you find a Prince? Well, first they say you've got to kiss a lot of Frogs...

+   +   +

I must admit that I have had the great good fortune to have flown with a few Princes in my time and I don't believe that they became minor royals because of their training – it was always natural. One such man was Captain Bill (not his real name) whom I first met back in the early 1990s while flying charter 757s. From the information I had received on the airline rumour network, Captain Bill had come to our company straight from a mainline scheduled operator. As such, his flying pedigree was very sound, albeit that I suspected he might not have much of a sense of humour.

Naively at that time, I made the assumption that because of his previous airline he would be a serious sort of a chap. Nowadays if I have learned anything at all, it is simply that it is dangerous to make pre-judgements of people, but in those days I was not so smart. At crew check-in for the flight, I greeted the stranger with a cheery "Hello" and made some sort of joke; this received nil response. The tall smartly attired Captain was similarly poker-faced, not only through our preflight briefing process, but also during the long walk out to the aircraft which was waiting for us on the ramp. In those days we didn't use crew transport at Manchester, the DFO said it was better for our health if we walked...

I tried to lighten the mood on several occasions with what I thought were witty comments and observations, but the responses I received were monosyllabic to say the least. In my mind I thought to myself, *'Phew! This is going to be a very long day. This guy's obviously a Frog'*. Once in the flightdeck and while the passengers were boarding, I busied myself preparing the FMC (Fight Management Computer) for the flight and resisted any further attempts at humour. Simultaneously Captain Bill sorted out his paperwork and set-up the navigation aids for his departure – he had already told me in a very deadpan way, "I will fly the outbound sector as Pilot Flying", in reply to my question about how he wanted to run the flights. My impression was that like the Atlantic Barons of a previous era, he was really saying to me *"You'll be lucky to get a sector lad!"*

While we were going through our preflight preparations in almost complete silence, the very attractive young Stewardess from the forward galley brought us in some tea and then left the flightdeck, closing the door behind her. I thought, *one last chance here...*

"The Soup Dragon looks alright today doesn't she...?" To which he stopped what he was doing and turned to face me with a big frown. By the look on his face I expected to get a complete lecture on the stupidity of making flippant remarks to my elders and betters when I would be better engaged in concentrating on the professional aspects of flying airliners... *'Whoa! A bollocking, here it comes...'* I thought. He took a deep breath, before replying with a twinkle in his eye and slowly nodding his head in agreement with me.

"Yes... but, they ALL make your d**k smell you know...!!"

+   +   +

There are not many times I am left speechless, but this was one of them. What an outrageously crude thing to say...? My jaw dropped and must have hit the flightdeck floor, I sat there mouth wide open, totally shocked! Of course he immediately cracked up laughing on his side of the cockpit at my completely stunned reaction and before a minute had elapsed I was laughing too – tears running down my cheeks. He was too funny for words, my Frog had turned into a Prince.

Tears ran down my cheeks again only two years later, as I took the phone call which informed me that Bill had died suddenly in an accident. On a beach, in a freak mishap in the surf, while on a crew layover: a total tragedy for all his family and friends. There wasn't a dry eye at his funeral which was attended by more crew from the airline than I had ever seen gathered together before. The very moving sight of his distraught girlfriend drinking neat vodka from a half-litre bottle at his graveside, while being supported by two of our colleagues is one I shall never forget.

Yes, Captain Bill was a Prince alright. Not only was he a professional aviator and a very skilful pilot, he was also one of the nicest Captains to go away with. Whenever you met him with his crew downroute, they were all in high spirits most of the time – playing games with each other and laughing their heads off.

When I think back to the joke he played on me, I still smile and shake my head, but mostly I think of how lucky I was to have known him and flown with him – it was a life enriching experience. It also taught me not to make assumptions.

For example, I used to assume that Americans don't have a real sense of humour, but that was before I read what was written by one of them about the United States Air Force... **_"The perfect record of the USAF – They never left one up there!"_**

With B767-300ER at Liverpool – 2006   ***(Ray Farley photo)***

Monument to Love.

(A tale of three alternates)

The lazy fan dangling from the ceiling of the VCR (Visual Control Room) at the top of the ATC Tower in Ahmedabad didn't seem to be having much effect on the temperature of the airspace beneath. It certainly wasn't cooling me down as I reflected on my experience of the past 24 hours. Outside it was forty degrees and down below on the stinking hot ramp was our B757, loaded up with passengers and fuel ready to depart for Agra, an Indian Air Force military base in the north of the country. I knew the AC packs were working overtime to keep the cabin cool. Slowly I turned my gaze towards the ATC Supervisor again, he was speaking to me.

"...but Captain, you and your aeroplane must go to Agra, you have filed a flightplan and you have got an ATC slot-time to meet and we cannot avoid this..." he tailed off as he realised his words were having no effect. My voice was very controlled as I replied to him.

"Mister Pradesh, we cannot depart from Ahmedabad without the latest weather reports for Agra and I have stated this several times. We diverted here yesterday because we could not land at Agra due to very poor visibility. We could not make an instrument approach, how do I know that this will not happen again today?" He was not happy I could tell. *Silly Englishman won't get out of my face.*

"Captain, I am already telling that Agra is Military's Airport and this weather report is not available. It is classified secret information and we cannot get it for you – they are very strict with the secret informations".

Now the latest excuse they gave me was that they were too busy - the B757 was the only live movement on the ramp below. I looked again at Mr Pradesh and the assistant who was sitting next to him at the Tower controller's position. I decided to try another tack. I suggested, "Look why don't you get your assistant to telephone Agra Airbase to ask them for the weather report on the telephone?" At which point the assistant picked up the telephone, turned away from us both as if he was having a very important conversation and Mr Pradesh immediately came back with – *"Can't you see he is too busy!?"*

I was staggered and shook my head as I responded, "But he wasn't busy until I suggested it –he wasn't even on the 'phone!"

I sat down on the scruffy, rickety old couch at the back of the VCR and said, "Well it looks like we're staying then! I say, any chance of a cup of tea old chap?" I smiled at him in what I thought was a disarming manner.

+   +   +

In reality the fun and games had commenced in Antalya, Turkey two nights before, where myself and the crew had picked up the jet. We were the relief crew, taking over in the middle of the night for a long distance charter flight from Gatwick to Agra. Why Agra? Well it's just down the road from the Taj Mahal one of the architectural wonders of the world and a huge draw for tourists to northern India. So in the middle of the night, we joined the aircraft on a snowy ramp in Turkey and ordered the de-icing trucks. There was plenty of snow and ice all over the airframe from taxying in through a snowshower and deicing took a while, but then the completion certificate finally reached the flightdeck. We were eager to get going, it was another long sector to India and the turnround seemed to be taking ages. Finally we called for push and start and my young colleague in the right-hand seat started to run the overhead panel scan ready for engine start. He was hesitant as this was one of his first line training flights, so I had to be patient. On the two jumpseats we had a travelling engineer and a 'Safety Pilot' – another First Officer who monitored and supported the FO under training. It was a full house and it was going to be a long night.

It was shortly after the second engine had been started, that we had a call from the cabin intercom and the Safety Pilot responded for us as were still busy watching the engine instruments as the RB211 stabilised, "don't forget the engine anti ice" I said to remind our trainee to turn this on now. Half an ear was listening to the brief conversation on the interphone and I was not impressed when I heard, "Please tell the Captain there's still lots of ice on the right wing..."
Immediately, I asked the SP to pop back into the cabin to check through the windows and it was an anxious wait while he did so. He arrived back in the flightdeck.
"Yes she's right, one of the passengers noticed it and there's loads of it still there!" He looked disappointed. My professional façade slipped just a little bit with my verbal response, "Bugger! We'll have to go back on stand!"

After a brief explanation to the cabin and negotiations with Air Traffic – we arrived back on stand, shutdown the engines and waited for the deicing team to come back. It all seemed to take a very long time, but finally we were airborne, ice free and climbing towards the Jewel in the Crown. If the weather forecast for destination Agra was not good, the number one alternate airport Delhi was much worse – vis down to 200 metres in fog. So during the preflight planning we ensured that we loaded fuel for the other two alternate airports too – better safe than sorry... The second alternate was Jaipur; a small regional airport to the west of Agra and the third alternate was Ahmedabad in Gujarat province – rather a long way away from Agra to the southwest. I remember saying to the other two pilots at the preflight briefing, "We'll take the fuel for the third alternate anyway, but I've never heard of anyone needing to go to their third alternate..." Me and my big mouth!

Flying through the night, we started our descent just after dawn and coincidentally when the early morning mist and fog in that part of the world is usually at its worst. On the radio we heard that Delhi was closed due to fog - 75 metres visibility and no improvement in sight. We asked Delhi ATC several times for the Agra weather, but they had difficulty getting it (top secret military base of course...) So we checked Jaipur weather to make sure our number two alternate was still open – yes it was fine; we continued our descent. Cleared descent to flight level one five zero and then handed over to Agra approach. On contacting the Agra military controller, he immediately requested our endurance and sent us to take up the hold. Hmmm... this is novel. I thought. Holding at fifteen thousand feet is an unusual procedure – then it became clear why. The visibility was too poor for us to commence the SRA (Surveillance Radar Approach) and the minima for this type of approach is very high. It was interesting to note while flying our big circles in the sky that we could actually catch a glimpse of the runways every now and again vertically, but the slant visibility was really bad and not getting any better.

We checked the fuel and I asked the Safety Pilot to get the latest situation with Jaipur on the second radio – Delhi ATIS still gave 75 metres and they were closed. Judging by his facial expression when he handed me the note of the Jaipur weather, I knew it was not good news. *JAIPUR CLOSED – NIL PARKING DUE DELHI DIVERSION AIRCRAFT!* We had been holding for around 20 minutes now and the weather was still bad below – *hmmm only Ahmedabad left then...* I looked at the computer flightplan yet again and asked him to get the latest Met report for Ahmedabad – he came back with the news that the visibility was okay 3000 metres or so, but now it was decreasing – Yikes! There was then a quick discussion between all of us in the flightdeck and the decision was made, I said sharply to the FO, *"Tell them we want a climb. Direct Track Ahmedabad!"* As he was calling ATC on VHF 1, I was reprogramming the Flight Management Computer for our new destination – hmmm... just enough fuel, let's hope the weather holds up...

The radar to ILS approach at Ahmedabad was fine and we then taxied in to a very large empty ramp to be greeted by Indian bureaucracy at its finest – three hours to get us and the passengers through immigration and then on our way to hotels. At the end of all this the crew needed a minimum 16 hours rest period before we could report for duty again, which brought us to the following afternoon and the stand-off with ATC.

+   +   +

By the time I sat down on the scruffiest couch of the Indian Subcontinent, I had spent the best part of two hours trying to get the weather briefing for Agra without success. They gave me everything else including the flightplans, weather charts, fuel receipts, handling and parking invoices to verify and sign for and various copies of the passenger manifest. Apparently they all wanted to keep the Agra weather a secret on behalf of the Indian Air Force! After a cup of quite dubious sweet tea in a plastic cup and several firm statements from me that I was not moving and "We like it here in Ahmedabad, we had a lovely curry buffet last night and I think we'll be staying another night!" Eventually Mr Pradesh gave in. He called Agra on the secret phoneline and I spoke to the airfield Met Officer myself and got the latest actual – it was good enough to go.

+ + +

As we made our initial approach, Agra ATC took us right past the Taj Mahal at quite low altitude and the sight alone was worth waiting for. On the small dusty civilian ramp, we bade farewell to our passengers and then waited to welcome onboard the homebound holidaymakers who had been delayed a day and a half. I made the welcome onboard PA in the cabin centre aisle with the microphone so that all the passengers could see me. "Ladies and Gentlemen welcome onboard and we apologise most sincerely for the delayed arrival of our aircraft which was supposed to come yesterday. Believe me we really tried to get here, but the poor visibility defeated us. We'll be on our way to London shortly, but please spare a thought for your crew who do feel rather hard done by. We had to divert to Ahmedabad in Gujarat province which is dry – so after our extra long 16 hour duty yesterday *we've had over 24 hours with no beer!*"

Carlos the Jackal?

(Please don't leave me and my passengers sitting next to the bomb officer...)

I looked down at the policeman and shouted, "LOOK! I don't think you really understand our problem here Officer. I don't care about your STERILE AREA, WE are IN RANGE of that suspicious device and we need STEPS for the passengers and we need them now! WE HAVE GOT TO GET THEM OFF AND INTO THE TERMINAL..."

At this point I was leaning a long way out of the flightdeck window of the Boeing 737 and felt as if I could reach down and grab his lapels. I looked back again at the large black suitcase abandoned on the empty concrete ramp and tried to judge the distance by eye. *Was it 20 metres or 30...? Too bloody close whatever!* came to mind. I am not an explosives expert, but I do understand the potentially destructive effect of even a small amount of high-explosive material when there is no blast protection. Looking back across the bare concrete ramp to 'the bomb' on the taxiway, I had a very clear picture in my mind of what would happen next if the damn thing went off...

+ + +

The day had started reasonably well, with all the crew reporting for duty on time. The weather down in Naples, our destination airport was fine and there were no technical problems reported with the aircraft. As usual with this airline, it was a Line Training Flight, but as the First Officer under training had already completed plenty of sectors, this should not provide any added challenge to the day. I know it's an unkind thing to say, but I have heard it on many occasions, when Line Training Captains talk about operating airliners as "Single Pilot, with interference". The implied meaning being that in reality they would probably be better flying the aircraft on their own, than having an inexperienced co-pilot with them who is on the back side of the drag curve and with whom they have to explain all of their actions. To be fair, this should only be appropriate in the early stages of Line Training, when they are finding their feet, or should that be wings, with enough frequency of flights, the trainee makes progress quickly. Of course it has to be that way, because Line Training really does mean just that – training pilots to fly the line in revenue service and that means with passengers onboard.

Anyway, as I looked across the briefing table at my young colleague, he seemed 'bright and alert', so we should be fine today. Also I already had a chance to look at his training file – mostly good reports, no sign of "inconsistent landing technique" or other indicators of poor performance. Yes it was going to be a good day today... (or so I hoped). Together we discussed the routing and the likely anticipated standard instrument departure and arrival. I have found from bitter experience that the sooner you get the trainee focused on all the expected elements of the upcoming flight the better.

One of our problems as pilots when we start to fly a new type is that old chestnut, *getting ahead of the aeroplane*. The trainees who can do this soonest have the easiest ride through Line Training and therefore everything that we can do as trainers to help this process is good from all angles. It even starts when we are driving to the airport, when we can see which runway is in use for takeoff and which for landing. Having spare mental capacity is a positive by-product of good Situational Awareness and this has been identified as one of the most important non-technical skills required by pilots. Not familiar with 'Situational Awareness'? The clue's in the name!

As part of preflight preparations we spent a few minutes with the cabin crew talking to them about the expected weather and confirming that they had completed their Safety briefing. This is also the time when I take the opportunity to introduce myself and the FO to the rest of the crew and vice versa. Although ours was a small crew base, there appeared to be an almost constant turnover of staff, so it was not uncommon to find a new face among the cabin crew.

As a captain, I had learned long ago that you only have a few minutes to get to know your crew and this can pay dividends later in the flying day, especially when things don't go entirely right. Although UK airline crew are all trained to very high standards, the differing personalities among the people can make a difference to how they react to situations. Often, once we all leave the crewroom together, this is the last time we see some of the cabin crew for hours on a long flight. It's always good to know who's "got your back" as the Americans say. When you think about it; they are also at the point of product delivery to the customer – in some ways as pilots we only facilitate that process.

We all left the crewroom as a group and made our way through the terminal – this meant that we had to pass through the customers on the way to the gate where the aircraft was parked. It had just landed from a previous sector so we were taking over a 'hot-jet'. With only a limited amount of time to turn the aircraft round and get it ready for passenger boarding, it is often frustrating to us as pilots when the two crews greet each other. There are hugs and kisses all round, especially among the cabin crew. Often this can be a protracted affair and we have to strike a balance between cordiality and potentially delaying the departure of the flight. Today was no different and once we had made our customary greetings to the other flightdeck crew, checking if there were any defects they had experienced on the inbound flight, it was time to get down to business.

+   +   +

It never ceases to amaze me that airline flights manage to depart just on time when there are literally dozens of individual elements which can lead to a delay and so it was on this particular day that I made the call on the intercom to the pushback crew chief. I keyed the mike and said, "Flightdeck to ground, we are cleared to push and start, the parking brake is set" I looked at the clock, one minute to schedule, very nice.

"Release the parking brake please", came the reply.

"Parking brake released" was my response. Thinking - *how many times have I said that?* There was a soft jolt and then we started moving backwards as we felt the tractor pushing a 60 tonne tricycle. I knew that from this parking position we would have to wait until they pulled us forwards again on the taxiway before we would be cleared to start engines to prevent blast damage to the security fence behind us. It was just after they started to pull us forward that the crewchief called again on the intercom, the urgency and confusion in his voice was clear. "Hang on a minute Captain, don't start engines yet, there's a bloke out 'ere on the taxiway...!?" All movement stopped.

+   +   +

"Never a dull moment", I remarked to the young First Officer who was looking at me questioningly. I wanted to sound reassuring to him, but I knew this was out of the ordinary. Obviously to the groundcrew this "bloke" was not supposed to be there, which meant only one thing in our highly regulated and security conscious world... An intruder, possibly with malevolent intent! Then I saw him, marching past the aircraft on the left-hand side, a large man, swarthy complexion, in a long black leather coat, swinging a large black suitcase. He was walking quickly, purposefully, gesticulating and shouting. Now I saw the reason for his hurry, he was being pursued by one of the security staff from the nearby security gate under whose barrier he had ducked. The security officer with his bright high visibility waistcoat grabbed hold of his arm and between them they then held the suitcase.

"Whoa! Possible terrorist right here on the taxiway! Tell the tower please" I said to my young colleague, who couldn't believe his ears, he replied with,

"What makes you think he's a terrorist?" to which I responded shortly,

"Because he looks like Carlos the flipping Jackal and he's fighting with a security officer!"

The scuffle continued, but now the security man had got hold of the suitcase. In our world and in this situation, this means a suspicious device and with one mighty swing, he threw it along the ground down the taxiway, fortunately away from us. I tensed myself for the explosion – it did not come. Within two minutes, the security officer was joined by an airport Police 4x4, then another one, from which jumped armed Police officers with large machine guns. They were pointing the guns directly at the man, shouting at him to get down, but he was still resisting and I recall saying, "This is not good. He is going to get shot in the head!"

But within a few seconds they had used a Tazer to subdue him and all of a sudden he was on the deck with four of them on top of him. The only part of his anatomy which was accessible was his neck above the black leather coat, so that Tazer shot must have been extremely painful, but better than a bullet. A couple more minutes and he was transferred apparently motionless into the back of one of the vehicles and they were all gone! Leaving us parked next to a potential bomb on the taxiway... Strewth!

"Flightdeck to ground...? Would you be so kind as to pull us back on stand please?" I was relieved to find that I was still in control of my voice and said to the FO, "After landing and shutdown checklist please". That way I knew that nothing would get missed in the switchery.

I don't recall the wording I used on the PA to the passengers, some of whom may have witnessed the blue flashing light display outside, but I made sure that it was delivered in as slow and controlled a manner as possible. The main thing here was to prevent anybody from panicking and blowing a slide – I certainly didn't want screaming punters running amok on the apron. Which brings us some thirty minutes later to my shouted conversation with the Policeman on the tarmac. We had been trying to get some assistance for the previous half-hour, but ATC simply said that "Terminal Two has been evacuated as there is a security alert in progress..." to which we replied, "Yes we know that, we are sitting here too close to the suspicious device for comfort thanks!"

In exasperation, it was only when I informed the Police Officer that if he didn't organise a set of steps in the next five minutes I would order the crew to blow the front service door slide to evacuate the passengers, that we were finally taken seriously. Two hours later, a controlled explosion by the army bomb disposal team scattered two weeks' dirty washing all over the tarmac and shortly after that it was business as usual.

(P.S. The poor guy that was the cause of the terrorist alert, was actually mentally ill, however nobody knew that at the time. Remember this was shortly after the July 7th terror attacks in London 2005 and in reality he was lucky that the police did not shoot him; everybody thought he had a bomb – including me!)

Aerial view of Monaco while climbing out of Nice Cote d'Azur in VIP B737. Note to self – must buy more lottery tickets...

Old Dogs and New Tricks?

(Age plays a part in the issue of spare mental capacity and situational awareness).

"Three thousand feet. We are cleared to THREE. *Do you understand? Put THREE THOUSAND in the altitude window!"* His hand moved slowly towards the switch on the autopilot MCP, meanwhile the 737 was still barrelling along at 240 knots at 5000 feet towards baseleg for the ILS approach. He dialled in 4000 and his hand moved away without pressing the level change button. Still, we trundled along at 240 knots, in level flight, burning fuel, getting higher on the profile, too fast, too high... *'My God, I have seen enough'.* My heart was pounding, I had never been in this situation before, THIS was unacceptable, the trainee was UNRESPONSIVE, was he incapacitated? I looked across at him and said in a very loud voice.

"I WILL NOT fly the Boeing 737 single pilot, GET OUT OF YOUR SEAT and change over with the Safety Pilot. AMANDA! Get in the bloody seat and DO IT NOW!"

+   +   +

The weather was nice, some broken cumulus at 4000 feet, but clear below, we were in the final stage of our descent into an International airport in the UK and the ATC traffic situation was light. It should have been an easy sector; we were on our way back from Lourdes (Tarbes) after all, so we even had a celestial advantage... and yet... I was worried. The trainee in the right-hand seat was seriously under-performing and he was actually supposed to be the Pilot Flying (PF). Theoretically, all I had to do (as PNF) was to operate the services promptly on his command and then run the checklists as appropriate for the situation, but it was not like that.

I was having to prompt him for configuration changes, heading, speed and altitude changes. In addition to doing the R/T work, I was actually having to tell him which buttons to press on the autopilot mode control panel. I was thinking, *'This is not good, really not good at all, certainly not after 40 sectors of Line Training...'* And it was true, this guy had done just over 40 sectors of Line Training and he was still travelling round with the safety FO on the jumpseat, which was a damning indictment of his operational effectiveness. Usually we can dump the safety pilot after maybe 10 sectors even with a slow learner. The criteria are that the Training Captain can be certain the trainee could land the aircraft safely in the event of the Captain's untimely demise – not a nice thought, but a practical one.

Now I was sat next to a trainee First Officer, aged 42 years, new to type, albeit with plenty of hours in his logbook from previous aircraft, but it appeared he had reached the limits of his mental capacity. I looked over at him and he was just staring straight ahead, seemingly oblivious to all the inputs from the instrumentation and now more importantly from the Air Traffic Controller... "Starwing 352, descend to Flight Level 70, reduce speed 220 knots", the instruction was clear and precise. I repeated the vital information.
"Roger, descend Flight Level 70, speed 220 knots, Starwing 352". From my right-hand side there was no response, so I said to him, "Flight Level Seven Zero, slow down to two twenty!" Slowly his hand went to the control panel and changed the digital display, too slowly, but he was doing it.

Now we ran through a bit of turbulence as we penetrated a cloud layer and I saw the altimeter passing 10,000, so I called "Flight Level One Hundred" as per the SOPs – which is the prompt then for the PF to respond with altimeter crosschecks... nothing. I put the landing lights on and called again louder "FLIGHT LEVEL ONE HUNDRED!" this time there was a mumbled response, the words all out of sequence, but we had effectively done an altimetry check, "SLOW DOWN!" I called again, as the speed was up around 280 knots and legally we should be 250 or less below 10,000 feet in UK airspace – also ATC were hoping for 220... I prompted again, "You WILL need the speedbrakes to get the speed off". This is a perennial problem when ATC order us to go down and slow down at the same time, not an easy thing to do in modern jet airliners as they are all very slippery in the clean configuration.

The mission had not started too well some hours before, when the trainee had reported for duty with a safety pilot in tow. When I looked at his training file, it was apparent that even after forty something flights, this gent could not be trusted to land the aeroplane safely on his own. Yet all the comments from previous Trainers appeared quite mild, with hardly anything very critical having been written – very strange. The female First Officer who would be sitting on the flightdeck observer's seat for today's flight was well known to me as an above average experienced 737 pilot and we had operated together as a crew before. If she thought it odd for the 40 sector man to still need a babysitter, she was too professional to say so. She simply assisted and guided him through the preflight preparation in a discreet way as he was in a different crewroom to the one he usually operated from.

Clearly the signs were there from the start and our destination airport today in south western France was not familiar to him either, so I opted to fly the outbound leg as PF, so he could 'play himself in'. PNF (or Monitoring Pilot) is usually an easier role and allows students who are not yet up to speed to gain confidence by watching how the job is done without great expectations on their own performance. That being said however, the PNF duties are important to the overall effectiveness of the crew. Modern CRM being what it is, the support and possible intervention of the monitoring pilot is a vital element to ensuring the operational integrity of the flight as I was to prove later on.

"Starwing 352, continue descent. Altitude 5000 feet, QNH niner, niner, eight millibars and turn right heading zero five zero". I repeated the instructions back and started setting the altimeter to the 998 pressure setting, I called across to the FO, "Altimeters!" and he turned to look at me with a blank stare. *Not good, really not good.* I said to him "You need to set QNH, 998..." Simultaneously I realised that he had not set the altitude window on the autopilot either or turned right on the heading bug... "Hey! We need a heading of zero five zero!" and then he moved to the panel and the airliner responded. *Way behind the aircraft, WAY too far.* "I'll give you the approach checklist" I said cheerfully; much more cheerfully than I felt.

As trainers we know that the workload for the crew increases during the descent and approach phase, therefore we often try to prepare the trainee to be ready for it. There are lots of different techniques which we can use to help the learning process and plenty of tricks we can teach the students to give themselves more thinking time during the critical phases of flight. Even so, a lot does depend upon the trainee and their learning rate, which brings us to the question of age versus learning capacity. Sometimes I think of it like the hard-drive becomes full. As one of my very senior colleagues put it when we flew together years ago, "You will notice that I have a huge memory... It is just that it is *very, very short!"*

Now we were instructed to descend to 4000 feet and given a left turn towards the baseleg for our destination. The R/T was clear, I had checked that he could hear it okay, he just had a problem with listening. Not only that, but this time I had to point at the switch and make a down signal with my index finger at the same time. The modern CDA (Continuous Descent Arrival) is not over-generous with time to react before the next descent instruction comes and we really needed to go down now. "Yes and the heading too!" Another prompt required from me. *This is getting ridiculous. We are supposed to be a two crew operation.* I could sense the Safety Pilot's staring eyes from behind me on the jumpseat, no doubt she was as worried as I was. Now, before he had set the altitude window in the MCP, the next descent instruction came, "Starwing 352 *descend* altitude 3000 feet and call Approach One, One, Niner decimal Four". Which was where we came in...

The subsequent approach and landing were uneventful with the Safety Pilot in the operating seat and after the flight I filed an ASR (Air Safety Report) to the company's Flight Safety Department as we do not normally carry out a crew change on the approach to baseleg. Needless to say the debrief after the flight took a long time and I went to great lengths to give the FO an in-depth analysis of the two sectors. He said that nobody had ever done that for him before and I suppose that may have been part of the problem. Perhaps some of the previous Line Training Captains had been too kind to him about his performance in their feedback. This can be a result of the pay to fly regime, where trainee pilots are paying for line training packages and therefore they get treated like a customer in some ways.

+   +   +

As the saying goes, it is not possible to teach old dogs, new tricks. Never was this more so than in flying training and I have witnessed it many times. Frequently I have been asked for my opinion about what age should be the cut-off point for entry into our profession, bearing in mind that now, more than ever, people can "pay to fly" as professional airline crew.

I would say that if you are over the age of 30 when you are thinking about starting on the road to an ATPL, then you should think about it VERY carefully before you commit yourself – it could go horribly wrong and you could be left with £100,000 debt and sweet nothing to show for it.

If you are 40+, then I would advise you to forget it. I am sorry to be blunt, but some of us will always tell you the truth, that's what we're paid for.

Roger the Cabin Boy.

(Humour at work? Well yes it has been known :-)

When Kenneth Williams playing Julius Caesar; delivered his immortal line; *"Infamy! Infamy! They've all got it IN FOR ME!"* (Carry On Cleo, 1964), little did he know that this would be judged the funniest one-liner of all time in a 2007 survey conducted by Sky Movies. There were some other noteworthy finalists in the top 10 and one which will be familiar to all potential airline pilots was Leslie Nielsen's, *"Surely you can't be serious?"... "I am serious, and don't call me Shirley",* (Airplane the movie, 1980). Being 'serious' is actually a part of the job description for personnel engaged in flying airliners.

We live in an increasingly regulated world with more complicated and restrictive Health and Safety legislation impinging on modern life than ever before. Individualism of any description is being inexorably eradicated, such that any examples of 'non-conformity' are cited as potentially dangerous – everybody must conform... This is more apparent in Commercial Aviation than every other part of the transportation industry. In the training of commercial airline pilots, there is huge emphasis placed upon the use of 'Standard Operating Procedures' (SOPs) and the almost religious following of checklists in their entirety. This holds true for not only the emergency checklist, but includes the methodology surrounding even the normal checklist which is used in everyday flight profiles. The separate checks which form part of the actual list are either, challenge and response or read and do, but even the read and do ones should be read aloud by the monitoring pilot to ensure that the flying pilot is able to stay in the loop.

One of the advantages of conducting freelance (consultancy) training and examining for several companies, is that it gives you a very broad view of the industry. Literally we are privileged to be able to see the good the bad or the ugly at firsthand as we operate on/in the flightdecks and simulators across the sector. In some airlines, the training department take this to extremes and are very prescriptive with their SOPs. I recall several years ago doing some Type Rating instruction on behalf of BMI Baby for pilots converting onto the B737 and was amazed at the level of detail which their Flight Operation/Training department went into describing what each pilot should do and when.

My trainees (experienced pilots from other airlines) were similarly mystified as to why a company would go to such lengths as to even describe precisely when each pilot starts his/her stopwatch on the takeoff roll. The reason which I came up with eventually was that this had been a reaction to the British Midland B737 tragedy when the crew had shut down the wrong engine. The human factors of that accident make for grim reading and the outcome was a disaster for our profession with 47 lives lost and hundreds more deeply affected. If as a result, the Flight Operations Management team over-egged the pudding thereafter we can forgive them for that.

In the case of Emergency Checklist usage, the instructions from the manufacturers are quite specific. Not only do they detail who reads the documents aloud and how (pausing during times of high workload etc) but they even say, *After completion of each checklist, the pilot reading the checklist calls, "_____CHECKLIST COMPLETE".*
A pilot new to this sort of disciplined environment may be forgiven for thinking that no deviation from 'the rules' is permitted, however this is not true. In every example of a manufacturer's Emergency Checklist, there is a caveat to warm the heart of every aviator. In plain language is written; *The flight crew must be aware that checklists cannot be created for all conceivable situations and are not intended to replace good judgement. In some situations, **at the captain's discretion,** deviation from a checklist may be needed.*

So I can imagine many people at this point (having read this far) thinking "Surely you can't be THAT serious ALL the time?" Indeed you are correct, there have been lighter moments in aviation and in fact there still are. Just like Hollywood, we have a wealth of material from which to choose some great one-liners. So before the 'forces of dullness' engulf us all forever, allow me to describe a few favourite quotations from the recent and not so recent past; starting with the apocryphal story of the military pilot whose last radio transmission, just prior to hitting the ground, was *"Cancel two late lunches!".*

A truly classic one-liner, the first time I heard this, it was told as a Phantom F4, but in reality I suspect it has its origin from the world of RAF/RN Canberra flying back in the 1960's (360 Squadron maybe?) In a similar vein there is the story about the US Marine Corps pilot who was trying to land a Cobra helicopter with a flight control problem. As the cab was sliding down the runway with sparks and bits coming off it, ATC asked if he needed assistance, to which the immortal reply was *"Don't know... we're not finished crashing yet!"* Perhaps further back in time the equivalent witty riposte was from an RAF WW2 Pilot stepping out from his airframe after a landing accident. As the fire-trucks screamed to a halt at the crash scene, his reply to the question *"What happened Sir?"* was a very polite, *"No idea... I just got here myself!"*

The humour is not limited to Military pilots however. I recall some years ago one of our instructors at the flying club where I worked part-time in Liverpool was recovering from the south under a Pan call with a rough running engine... there was only the *one engine*. With reduced power, he was flying quite slowly at 1500 feet, but asked Liverpool ATC for a climb, to which their reply was "G-XX, you realise that *above* 1500 feet is Manchester TMA airspace, please explain why you need to climb?" to which he came back with *"Well, I believe the river Mersey is rather cold at this time of year...?"*

In the USA too, commercial aviators are renowned for their GSOH. Heading down the eastern seaboard towards Florida once, I heard an airliner being asked by Boston Center about their intermittent transponder readout, to which a laconic drawl was heard to say, *"Ma'am, that ain't nuthin'. In this old ship we consider ourselves lucky to be PRESSURISED today!"* Then there was the time when an early B737 lost an engine on takeoff in the States. No, they *REALLY* lost an engine, as it separated completely and fell off the wing. The tower controller's voice was quite shrill as he assured "_____ *you're clear to land on any runway, all runways are available to you!"* and the transmission from the cockpit was, *"That's nice... You'd like us to land on a RUNWAY?!"*

Perhaps the funniest incidents in aviation come from the differences in cultures combined with the challenges of translation from one language to another. An excellent example of this was a few years ago when I was on the flightdeck of a B767 in Air India colours heading towards Mumbai from Heathrow. We were scheduled to arrive at just around the same time as the British Airways Jumbo, also from Heathrow. This was coincident with the timing of the published closure of the main runway (27) for resurfacing work and switching to the shorter runway 14.

In our case in the B767, we knew that runway 14 was a bit more challenging as the approach is over Juhu, often with a tailwind for landing and the landing distance is reduced, but no real drama. It was clear from the concerned tone in the voice of the British Airways pilot however, that he really didn't fancy making an approach to 14 in the B747 if he could get the full length of runway 27, the main one. He gave his ETA to the Mumbai controller and it was just a few minutes before the runway was due to be closed... surely they would see the sense in keeping it open for the Jumbo? The B747 is a big beast to be landing with a tailwind on a short-ish piece of concrete. If that was me I would like to know too, so I could plan the descent approach and landing.

"Mumbai Control this is Speedbird 139, our ETA is 0655UTC... what runway can we expect for landing please...?" The response was quick.
"Roger. STANDBY Speedbird 139..." Minutes passed and we were all interested now to know the answer, our aircraft was approaching top of descent, just ahead of flight BA139.
"Speedbird 139, this is MUMBAI Control..." In our cockpit we all looked at each other.
"Yes go ahead please Mumbai... Speedbird 139" Whoa, here it comes...

"SPEEDBIRD 139....... you may EXPECT runway 27... OR runway 14...!"

That was brilliant! So funny! Exactly what he did *not* want to hear – there ARE only two runways at Mumbai. In our B767 cockpit we all laughed so loud we did not hear the reply from Speedbird – *Welcome to '!ncredible India'*

Even as a training captain or examiner there are comical moments, especially when the operating crew are old hands. Some of the pilots with whom it is my privilege to work are so competent that it is sincerely a joy to watch them; they have so much spare mental capacity, they even have time to banter while getting the job done. I recently witnessed the following chitchat as the two B737 pilots were finishing their second day of the proficiency check. The Captain was actually doing his right-hand seat check which should have been tougher, but he made it look easy - as the engine ran down, there was hardly any increase in bank angle as the 737 climbed away from the runway. The FO was reading the emergency checklist out loud and they seemed to have so much time.

"Engine Failure Shutdown checklist. Point One. 'Do an engine shutdown only when flight conditions allow'" He looked across the cockpit with one raised eyebrow.
"Erm, we don't have a choice" Replied the captain in a matter of fact tone. The FO grinned back and then proceeded,

"Noted. Then Point Four says 'IF conditions allow: Run the engine for three minutes at idle thrust'" They both looked at the engine gauges of the failed engine – it was dead.
"Hmm... that's not something we can do either..." They agreed and continued with the drill; actioning the items in perfect harmony like the pair of old pros they really were.
"The Checklist Finishes, **'Plan to land at the nearest suitable airport'**" Stated the FO.
"Now that's a very nice idea", said the skipper with a smirk, *"call the Senior Cabin Crew Member to the flightdeck".* After briefing the cabin crew, they continued to action the checklist items in a similar manner, with an air of professional nonchalance.

One of the checks required them to inhibit the function of the Ground Proximity system for a reduced flap, single engined landing, but the FO accidentally misread the checklist and referred to it as the;
"Ground Proximity Flap INHABIT switch" Well, that caused them both to giggle and for me to smile sat behind them in the darkness. There were a few subsequent references to the misnomer. Finally they were well down the approach to land with the old skipper flying a superbly accurate ILS on one engine - certainly there seemed to be no doubt about the successful outcome.

At five hundred feet on finals they broke cloud and the runway was dead ahead, the captain was preparing himself for the single engined landing.

He gave the command to the monitoring pilot as if it was an SOP call... **"Zero the rudder trim....and... Roger the Cabin Boy!"**

*Author with friends demonstrating a VIP airliner for a customer
Elisavet, Olga. FO Alan Fisher, Capt Chris Harris & Depi*

Whinge and Fly!

("Ours is not to reason why. Ours is but to Whinge and Fly!" ANON.)

It will no doubt seem strange to newcomers joining our profession that any of us should have reason to complain. If you look at the popular view of airline pilots, as portrayed by the likes of Leonardo diCaprio in the film 'Catch Me If You Can' as he walks through the terminal in his bright shiny uniform with aviator shades, surrounded by Pan Am Flight Attendants, then what's the problem? The problem is that it's just a job. No, not a glamorous acting career like Leo's, but a proper job. We don't get commission on the box office sales; we receive 'flight duty pay', sometimes called 'sector pay'. We are not expecting to be treated like on screen heroes or prima donnas, we are part of the team that gets the job done. We are sometimes in receipt of Per Diems, which, as the name implies are payments per day for our time downroute away from friends and family – probably Leo gets something similar when he is working on location, although on a bigger scale.

So, first things first, anyone entering our profession with stars in their eyes, needs to disabuse themselves of the notion that they will live happily ever after. It's a rough ride to get to any sort of stable, secure position as flightcrew with a well respected airline – or even one that's not respected... Let me try to explain with some examples of what we're talking about here. The first one is that when your current airline goes bust and you spend months on the beach waiting for another ship, it's only around two weeks into your next job with the new airline that you find yourself moaning about the walk from the staff carpark. Seriously, this happens and I have heard it many times. Similarly you will complain about "My Roster" and how *"unfair"** it is. (*Note: you can substitute the words *busy/heavy/so many nightflights/iniquitous/unstable/evil*, here as you feel appropriate).

+   +   +

The funny thing is there are some who whinge more than others. When I was working as a busy Pilot manager for a well known low-cost airline, I had quite a few of them. I recall that there was one experienced B737 Captain who always used to give me (and other managers) a hard time about how badly treated the pilots were by the company. Of course my job was not just to manage people in a disciplinarian sense, but much of my time was taken up with welfare issues, so I listened. In fact listening was the main function required when dealing with Capt Victor Over. So he used to regularly call me up (as I was one of the senior managers) to let me know how the frontline troops saw things. This in itself was ironic, because I too was on the frontline for the flying programme. As a manager, theoretically I was supposed to operate one day per week and the rest of my time would be 'office' days.

As I finally calculated my flying hours after 7 years, I had logged just over 3500 block hours on the line, most of it Line Training or Checking. That equates to something more than one day per week and did not include Simulator, but let's not go there. Anyway, you get the picture, even though the troops were hard pushed, we managers sweated just the same. I recall that every 'phonecall ended the same way. Capt Over calmed down having sounded off at somebody, I had listened and made the usual empathising noises, then I promised that I had notes of his issues and would do my best to change things for the better. At the same time I asked for his patience and support while we tried to build a better airline. Eventually his stress levels went through the roof and my platitudes were not sufficient anymore and he decided he "couldn't wait any longer!" so he resigned in a huff and went to another company. I was genuinely sorry to see him go; he was a skilled pilot and a very effective Commander.

Imagine my surprise then, when a few years later I myself joined another airline as a Training Captain on Boeings only to find that Capt Over was now one of MY managers! I was pleased to see him and the feeling was mutual. We both commented on the dynamics of the new situation and the reversal of roles. *"Never s*** on anyone while you're on the way up..."* came to mind. As I settled into my new role and loved every minute of being back in command of a widebody, longhaul, airliner it tickled me to realise that Capt Over had not changed. He used to call me regularly on the 'phone to whinge about "how bad" things were at this airline and "what a complete mess" it was etc. etc. I remember stopping him mid-sentence once and saying, "Hey! Victor, give me a break fella. YOU'RE the manager here; I'm supposed to be able to whinge to you! YOU fix it". Sadly, history repeated itself and before long "the bloody crewing department" screwed him over one time too many and he was on his way out again. I just hope that eventually he finds peace with a company, maybe he will.

+   +   +

Contrast this situation with one of my First Officers back at the low-cost airline base in Liverpool who never complained. He was an ex-military pilot with a young family and he was universally popular. Not only among his peers, but also with the cabin crew who had great respect for the fact that he got on with the job without creating any drama and never bad-mouthed the company or his colleagues behind their backs. Solid guy that he was, it was a really tough call when he was offered his first jet command. The base would be overseas, with no likelihood of a Liverpool Captaincy arising any time soon... He simply shrugged his shoulders, smiled and got on with it. He looked after his family as best he could by commuting home as often as possible (no staff travel in those days) and waited patiently for his turn to come up in his home base. Sure enough his patience was rewarded after more than a year and he is still flying at Liverpool seven years later albeit as a Captain on the Airbus. He is well thought of by all the crew and managers alike – he's a diamond. As his former boss, I am still so proud of him.

So, from one First Officer who was the easiest of people to manage, let's consider a First Officer called Wayne. Wayne was one of THE best pilots I had ever flown with in either seat. The fact that he joined the company as an FO was misleading in some ways, because he had originally been a heavy-jet Captain with the US Air Force in his previous flying career so he was bound to be exceptional. Although he was technically brilliant and blessed with above average flying skills, he was from New York... and it showed! In fact I first heard about him well before he arrived in our base where I would be his Base Captain. My 'phone rang and it was the rostering department who wanted to make a formal complaint about one of our Liverpool based FO's because he had already been over-familiar and rude to them on the telephone. I was intrigued, who is this guy? He had not come to us yet but still, the next day another call came from a training manager to warn us of "this Dickhead Yank who criticises everything". He would be joining us in the near future. Alarmed that any one person could have ruffled so many feathers in such a short space of time, I put myself on the roster to fly with him as his Training Captain in some of his early Line Training sectors. I would make sure he knew how his new boss expected people to behave in this base.

I should not have worried, as I was delighted to find he was a superb pilot and a professional aviator on the flightdeck - respect. Of course he did have a larger than life personality and this combined with his incredible honesty made sure that he was not over-popular with some of our overstretched management team – not everyone got his sense of humour. Also they found it difficult to cope with his frequent whinging about his roster and annual leave arrangements. However even I had to sympathise with him, when he came to see me one day in the office, only six months after arriving. He started the conversation as he barged in through the door with his loud American drawl, *"James! Ah'm gonna invite you to mah F****** Funeral!"* In his hand he held his roster and on the page it showed day after day of four sectors flying out of Belfast – our newest base. For sure, if anyone worked as hard as that for a month they would be dead. I studied it carefully after my reply of "Slow down Wayne, take it easy and let's see what we can do here..." and then followed it with, "...go and do your flight today, leave it with me and I will find a way to get you a couple more days off in the month". Almost spot on 100 block hours in four weeks was no joke - they were planning to fly him to the maximum!

I called the rosterers and talked it through with them. Certainly we were critically short of First Officers in Belfast and they were adamant that, "There is nobody else James", so I took a decision and told them to turn 2 of my office days into flying days and I would operate as an FO instead of Wayne while they put him off duty – that would give him a break. They couldn't argue with this and begrudgingly they made the changes - he must have seriously cheesed them off. Naturally Wayne was pleased and grateful when I told him later that same day. Wind the clock forward two weeks to the Aldergrove ramp in Northern Ireland where I was struggling with the high workload in the right-hand seat on a quick turnaround. As a management pilot I was busy answering the company mobile and stuffing paper-towels round the leaking DV window on the right-hand side of the cockpit to stop the rain coming in - we were in one of our 'Classic' B737s.

I looked outside; the rain was torrential and relentless as it can only rain in Northern Ireland. Huge puddles of standing water covered much of the apron, all the groundcrew were soaked. I thought of Wayne somewhere in downtown Belfast on his 'day-off', probably having a pub lunch with friends. The Captain I was operating with came back into the flightdeck from the walkround dripping with rainwater. I said to him, "Just give me a minute Skip, I will do the loadsheet and calculate the Takeoff Performance for you".

And at that very moment, an SMS message appeared on my mobile from Wayne's number... it said; **Yo Buddy! Ya using 'WET' figures today huh? ;-)**

I showed it to the other pilot and we laughed our heads off, "*Cheeky Bastard!*"

Freight Dogs.

(It is not a derogatory term, cargo pilots call themselves this).

The times when the ferries were on strike in the Irish Sea was always good news for a company like ours. The 'high-value adhoc charter' is the lifeblood of the Air Taxi company's finance department. So it was, that we formed a small group of spectators, standing outside the hangar to watch the takeoff, having just finished loading the aircraft with urgent car-parts for a customer over the water. It is fair to say that it had been a "rush job" from the start when we got the call from the freight forwarding company. Once the mission had booked, the engineers immediately stripped the interior of one of our executive large piston twins and the pilot started his flight planning. This included the loadsheet and due to maximum payload restrictions, the shipment would have to go on two flights.

The forwarder said he would send the car-parts in two vans so that we could get the first flight underway as soon as possible. I looked out towards the runway now as the sound of the engines reached us, they were at maximum power and my colleague was starting his takeoff run. The van driver was standing next to me and I said to him, "When is the next van coming?" He looked at me blankly, the roar from the runway was louder now as the heavily laden machine thundered along, halfway down a 10,000 feet piece of concrete and still firmly on the ground. He replied.

"There is no second van, that's all of it!" I was horrified. *Holy S*** it's twice overweight!* No wonder it was still on the ground and now it was out of sight as the runway dipped away from us...

+   +   +

There is a short video on the internet called FE's Lament (FE standing for Flight Engineer of course) which can be accessed via the Freight Dogs forum on PPRuNe. I was a little bit sceptical about the title, but it really is a great piece of film. It shows the life of the "Freight Dogs" as they are known in a very amusing and yet poignant way. I think it should be required viewing for every young commercial aviator because so many dismiss the idea of flying cargo aircraft as being an undesirable part of the industry. In reality of course there is plenty not to like about it. There is a lot of nightflying and strange airports combined with some very challenging assignments often to areas of the planet which feature heavily in the international news channels on TV. The aeroplanes are usually converted passenger types which have gone beyond being acceptable for carrying people and often they appear as airborne HGVs – bright and shiny they are not. The positive sides are many though and include some of the best flying adventures you could ever dream of. Seriously, if I was planning a career as a commercial pilot, I would like to spend some years of it flying freight.

I remember once being given a guided tour of an Anglo Cargo B707 which was in Monarch's hangar in Luton. It was while we were waiting for our B757 to be made ready that my skipper decided to show me round one of his 'previous commands'. With the permission of the engineers, he walked me round the exterior, pointing out all of the interesting bits pertinent to the type. It was when we got to the engine intakes that I had a shock. At the time he was waxing lyrical about "Ahhh! These lovely old Pratt and Whitney JT8Ds..." and all I could see was that the front fan appeared to be damaged beyond repair! There were chunks out of some blades, while others looked bent and twisted – surely this was a scrap motor? No, he insisted, this was 'normal' – well I was quite taken aback – but all four engines were the same. Then we climbed the rickety ladder to the front left entry door and went inside.

A yawning dark chasm greeted us where the passenger cabin used to be. On the roller floor for the freight pallets was piled a whole load of interior bits which had yet to be reunited with the rest of the airframe. Turning left then, we entered the cockpit and to be honest it didn't look any cleaner in there than the freight bay. Of course he didn't appear to notice, because he was still revelling in reliving his memories, I remember saying to him, "Peter, please don't touch anything, you'll get filthy". But this fell on deaf ears as he reached into one of the recesses of that dark old flightdeck and came out triumphantly with a long piece of corrugated plastic piping which you would find on any household vacuum cleaner.
"Look!" He cried, "THIS is how we cleaned the cockpit in the old days" and reached up to the ceiling to open a small circular hatch which had been designed for Astral navigation – it was straight out into the open air. The Navigator in times gone by would take some sort of starshot with his sextant through this aperture, but as the navkit for the aircraft was upgraded, all it was used for was for hoovering the flightdeck floor – unbelievable! As long as the aircraft remained pressurised, it worked a treat.

My own experience flying freight had been with light twins and at the Air Taxi company where I worked, there was a regular night-mail run. Unfortunately when the contract had been agreed with the Post Office, the amount of mail which we could carry on the route had not been calculated very carefully, so we were committed to taking off at Max All Up Weight every night. In fact we had to recalculate (and reduce as much as possible) the allowable fuel load to absolute legal minimums to take the mailbags. For a young pilot doing his first commercial flying job this was something of a challenge to say the least.

Our route took us over the Irish Sea, which in the depths of winter can be a tricky place to be flying through the weather. When I first joined the company, I asked one of the senior pilots what it was like flying the mailrun and he grinned and said, "Not so bad really, you get to read a few letters..." I was never sure if he was joking or not. Mind you he used to do so many mailflights they used to call him 'Pat'. Heavyweight takeoffs at night in bad weather are no fun at all and you need to be on top of your game to get it done safely. On the types we flew, the performance on one engine was so marginal, that in reality if you had a major loss of power on one side a controlled descent was likely to result – not a nice thought.

But the engines kept going and we kept flying and only rarely did we have to cancel a service due to technical problems. There was one night however when I experienced a real issue with fumes in the cockpit shortly after reaching cruising altitude with the mail onboard. The smell was that of fuel (avgas) and in the dark I couldn't see where it was coming from, but the stench was almost overpowering and I kept opening the little DV window next to me to get some fresh air. I looked at the options and decided that as I was halfway between my departure airport and Manchester (our home base), it was as well to carry on and land there – at least we had engineering cover.

Although I did not believe I would pass out, I certainly felt dizzy, so I mentioned this fact to the radar controller and stated that as I had 'fumes in the cockpit' I was requesting a diversion to Manchester. When asked if I was declaring an emergency, I replied "Negative", but given the circumstances, I should not have been surprised when I saw all the blue flashing lights on the emergency vehicles waiting by the side of the runway as I came into land. The landing was not one of my best, but I was just happy to get the bird down in one piece. After landing I was able to open the crew door next to my seat and get loads of air in the cabin – wonderful. I felt better almost instantly.

Arriving outside the hangar, I shut down the engines and went and spoke to the fire and rescue crews. After taking some details from me, they were stood down and returned to the fire station across the runway. The Chief Engineer was waiting at the hangar also, having been called by the handling agents and together we surveyed the problem. The avgas was coming from the fuel pressure gauge supply pipe behind the instrument panel, a tiny hole spraying the floor. While he made the repairs, I brewed some coffee for us and before long I was airborne again to deliver the mail. If the same happened these days, then I think I would want to be checked over by a doc prior to flying again, but this was 1988 and things were different then.

+   +   +

Things were certainly **different** for my colleague in his overloaded aeroplane as he struggled to gain altitude after leaving the runway at Manchester on the day of the ferry strike. We all breathed a collective sigh of relief as we saw the silhouette of the machine in the distance clawing away from the ground, both engines giving 100%.

Needless to say there was a subsequent investigation and overweight checks of our aircraft by the engineering team. Significantly, these revealed nothing unusual which is a testament to a very strong airframe.

Finally there was a reduction in the charter price for the freight forwarding company as only one flight had been necessary to shift the load for them so they were very pleased indeed. Meanwhile all of us pilots learned to check and double-check what was being loaded onto our aircraft before we committed to fly.

P.S. The only time I saw a flatter climbout was when we watched a WW2 Catalina PBY takeoff from the same runway – that didn't climb very well either. Or the heavyweight Rosenbaum DC8 freighter which used to regularly fly out of Manchester as the "Rosie 101" callsign – allegedly they used to recalculate the available payload to use up the rest of the runway. When that ship went out, everyone held their breath in Air Traffic Control! Fortunately with the curvature of the earth...

Truth or Dare?

(Gambling, Gaming call it what you will, but the stakes are high – it's peoples' lives).

There is a game called "truth or dare" which is usually played by teenagers at parties. The person asked the question is honour bound to give a truthful answer or they have to perform a 'daring mission' (also known as a forfeit) with potentially embarrassing results. Now you may wonder what this game could possibly have in common with flying aeroplanes for a living, well the philosophy is sort of tied in with the fact that "there are no old, bold pilots". You see there is a really special place in our world of commercial aviation. It is a place where only truth really matters. A place where above all else, we should be true to ourselves and our colleagues. A place where literally we have potentially a life or death choice and our approach to this place should not be undertaken too lightly. It is also a place where some of us could be tempted to play 'truth or dare'...

+   +   +

Believe it or not, one of the favourite pastimes when downroute for airline pilots is walking. Not hiking or anything sporting, but just going out for a walk in the fresh air. It is one of the enjoyable parts of the job in some ways, where we get the chance to go out walking in a totally different world from the one we have just left. One such time, many moons ago as a First Officer, I was out with my Captain and we were walking in the USA just past the airport we had landed the day previously. It was in Bangor, Maine and the area is pretty rural. As we walked towards the undershoot for runway 33, my colleague looked around and said, "Yes, I would be happy to do it here, there are no really big trees, so it would be okay to go down a bit lower on the ILS".

I was surprised and also horrified at what he was saying, but thought maybe that I had misinterpreted, so I needed clarification.
"Sorry Dave, just correct me if I am wrong, do you mean that you would go below Decision Altitude even if you were not visual?" He could tell that I was not happy and now he started to look a bit uncomfortable, but he still wanted me to agree with him.
"Well... you know, not MUCH below, maybe just a few seconds...?"

I was right to be horrified, here was a professional guy who, on the face of it was just like me, but we had come from different backgrounds. I had been trained in the military for my instrument flying and he had not had the benefit of the disciplined approach to how we should treat Decision Altitude. Quite simply, if we reach the end of the instrument approach and we are still in cloud, (not visual with the runway) then we abort the approach and climb away from the ground, end of story.

It's a manoeuvre called a go-around and there used to be pilots in our industry who prided themselves on the fact that they had nearly reached retirement age without having had to go-around even once in their career. No seriously, there really were a few of these dinosaurs in the old days and I had just met one while out for a nice country walk. I said quite bluntly that what he proposed was something which I could never agree with, it was illegal and dangerous. The only time I could imagine having to 'bust the minima' for the instrument approach would be if it was our last gasp of fuel prior to running out of gas...

This set of circumstances is incredibly rare of course, but they have been known. One such incident was Avianca Airlines flight 52 coming in on the ILS at New York JFK back in January 1990. They carried out a go-around from the approach, but didn't even have enough fuel to climb away and shortly afterwards crashed in Long Island. The aircraft was a Boeing 707 – imagine that, a serviceable four engine airliner in modern times running out of fuel? Coincidentally, I met a retired airline training Captain recently who brought up the subject of this accident when he said that he had known the pilot who landed the airliner just before Avianca made the ill fated approach. In his own words, this pilot used to tell the story about how he had 'cheated' on the minima for the ILS and 'just got in' - becoming visual with the runway **below** Decision Altitude. At the time we all agreed that if this were true, it was a heinous crime which was completely unacceptable and might have lead the following aircraft to believe it was possible to make the approach safely.

I then retold the tale about our instrument approach into Palma Majorca while doing Command Training with a First Officer on a B737. The weather forecast had been poor even before we took off from Liverpool so my young colleague had sensibly decided to take some extra fuel. We would be able to 'hold' for around half an hour on arrival before having to go to Barcelona if the weather was still as bad and we were delayed making our approach. During our descent off the coast of Spain it was apparent that the low cloud and bad visibility were still present at destination, so we took up the hold at 15,000 feet.

This was good because we knew now that we could hold for even longer than 30 minutes as the jet is much more economical at higher altitudes. The captain under training seemed to be making all the right decisions and I was quite comfortable sat in the right-hand seat playing the role of supportive First Officer. He had briefed the passengers; set up the holding pattern; made sure we had good weather at Barcelona (our first alternate airfield) and then got the speed under control to use less fuel. I asked him what his plans were now as aircraft commander (if it really was his decision) and he told me that we had another 15 minutes holding remaining and then we would have to divert to Barcelona – I agreed.

Just then another flight arrived into the holding pattern above us, it was a charter jet, another B737, not UK registered, but from a foreign operator with a good reputation. They asked for the latest weather from ATC and then said they would like to "try an approach" – at which point they were given radar vectors by air traffic and left the holding pattern. In our flightdeck we were listening intently to the radio as they made their approach and landed – maybe the cloud had started to lift already...? I looked across at my young 'Captain' and said, "Now what Skipper?" with a smile on my face. He checked the fuel again – it was right on limits - and said.

"Okay we try ONE approach and if we don't get in, we go straight to Barcelona". Playing devil's advocate, I asked him what he thought about 'delaying at Decision Altitude' – he looked directly across the cockpit at me and frowned, "No Chance!" to which I replied,
"Good man. Just checking. I agree". We were of the same mind. We informed ATC and were given similar vectors descending towards the area west of the island. We knew that the previous landing 737 had been carrying out exactly the same ILS approach as ourselves, so maybe we could get in – they didn't appear to have had any problem with it after all. It crossed my mind at that point, *hmmm...were they playing truth...or dare?*

At Decision Altitude, I called "DECIDE!?" and he called "GO-AROUND FLAP FIVE!" We saw absolutely nothing outside the cockpit windows! Even though our aircraft dipped slightly lower due to momentum we were still completely in thick cloud as we climbed away. We headed straight for Barcelona and obtained a straight in approach to land – we had our minimum fuel onboard, but not much more. In fact I asked him on final approach what he would like to do if we had to make a go-around due to an obstructed runway and his reply was quite simply,

"TELL them MAYDAY! And demand a short visual circuit to final approach again". I nodded and said,
"Okay Skipper, you're the boss". I looked out of my window and smiled to myself, *yes the boy is learning – good.*

As a training exercise in Command Decision making it could not have been a better set of circumstances and to my immense pleasure, my new Trainee Captain performed brilliantly. But as reassurance that our profession is maintaining high standards of operating it was a sad day from my point of view. In fact Palma airport weather did not significantly improve for another two hours after we made our first approach to runway 06L and nothing would convince me that those pilots had made an honest decision.

Which brings us back to the Avianca flight on that fateful night in New York. If you look at the accident report for Avianca 52, there were many events which lead up to the end game. Although not being visual at Decision Altitude was not one of them apparently. Windshear was a major factor on short finals, when the aircraft experienced such turbulence below 500 feet on finals that the approach was destabilised to the point where allegedly they almost hit the ground short of the runway. Perhaps Avianca's truth or dare moment was much earlier when they should have declared their fuel status to New York ATC clearly so that everybody knew what the situation was. By the time New York became aware that the aircraft was critically short of fuel, they had already lost one of the four engines on the go-around.

+   +   +

Truth or Dare...? Me? Well I'm a bit of a scaredy-cat really. You see, I've done a few go-arounds in my time and I may do some more before I retire. As for 'daring' – well we all take risks in our lives at various times, some of us enjoy what may be seen as risky sports, but when we are at work flying airliners it is a time for truth and safety.

Just to be sure we don't forget, that 'special place' is always there for us waiting to test our integrity. Arriving at Decision Altitude, on an instrument approach, with nil visibility... that's the moment of truth.

Hitting the Wall.

(Some more barriers will have to come down to improve safety record in Far East).

When Asiana flight 214 struck the seawall short of runway 28L at San Francisco International airport on 6th July 2013, there was a collective and immediate assumption within our profession that fuel-icing with a resulting "double engine flameout" was a possible cause. The similarities between this hull loss and that of BA038 at Heathrow were quite striking. Both aircraft were Boeing 777s and both accidents occurred on short finals in good weather conditions after a longhaul flight; however we really shouldn't jump to conclusions...

+   +   +

There were significant differences about the way in which the aircraft was being flown onto final approach. In the case of BA038, they were following the ILS for runway 27L when they experienced their major technical malfunction. AAR214 was cleared for a "visual" approach to land on runway 28L, but this approach was initially higher and faster than usual. The Glideslope element of the ILS was out of service and this had been Notam'ed since 1st June 2013, however the Localizer portion was still usable and the PAPIs (Precision Approach Path Indicator lights set at 3 degrees to assist with visual judgement for landing) were also serviceable prior to the approach. They were subsequently damaged and put out of service by the accident debris. Theoretically then, the pilots should have had enough aids and guidance on the day to carry out a safe visual approach to make a normal landing.

Much has been made in the media of the handling pilot's relative inexperience on type (allegedly 43 flying hours), but this is simply another contributory factor and not a real cause. It has some relevance, but I believe it will not be considered of great significance when the final NTSB report is published. It is easy to speculate on any aircraft accident, but it is almost always a series (or chain) of errors, omissions, failures and events which culminate in those final seconds before destruction of the airframe. The experts in the field of aircraft accident investigation have identified that this chain typically contains between 7 and 11 separate elements/errors for almost every accident which has been studied.

Having been involved in flying airliners for a living for more than a few years now, I can say for certain that one of the toughest jobs for an airline pilot is to fly a visual approach. That may sound strange, because when we learn our craft taking baby steps on little flying machines with piston engines and as few as three wheels as opposed to 16 or more later in life, all of our approaches are made visually.

The supposed black art of 'Instrument Flying' (or IF as it is known in the trade) comes much later and is more difficult in theory. Later, after a few years in the profession, your perspective changes and in fact flying the dials is a great game to master – just do it by the numbers. These numbers become your friends. You always have digital assistance and you don't even have to look out of the window – great! Our Instrument Flying skills are essential for flying in all weathers.

Now we come to the crux of the matter. Things change when you get on to flying airliners. The happy relaxed world of the flying club is a distant memory and those blue sky days... did you dream them? Now it is all the serious stuff, crew report times, minimum rest periods, maximum duty periods, FTL's and OM-A's. The flying is still there though that is a constant, and the challenge of learning to fly bigger and more powerful machines than before is as much a drug as anything else in life; but the regulations... well they are endless it seems.

The majority of the flying now is by numbers and the 'automatics' are used almost continuously to carry the load of operating hour after hour, on a daily basis. Nearly every approach to land is by use of the ILS at the major airports and therefore we rarely get the chance to fly a 'visual' approach. There is a worry about the deterioration of basic flying skills among pilots who fly over 90% of their flying hours on autopilot and this is a valid concern, however it is not only their locomotor faculties which are degraded.

I recall when I started to fly into Orlando McCoy airport back in the 90's after crossing the Atlantic with hundreds of people in the cabin who wanted to see Mickey Mouse. In those days, I was sitting in the right-hand seat as First Officer and often we would be asked by ATC "Confirm when you are visual...?" To which many of my senior colleagues would say,
"No, don't tell them yet!" The reason being, that if you informed the radar man/woman that you had "Visual Contact with the 'field", the controller would immediately hand you off to the tower frequency and leave you on your own to establish the aircraft onto final approach. Now this is a busy time for the crew and is known as a time of high workload. The aircraft needs to be slowed down and the configuration changed for landing. It is certainly a time when modern CRM techniques with good cross-cockpit communication helps to keep everybody in the loop and ensure that a stabilised approach is flown to the runway.

For me, this was a valuable lesson in my career. Here I was flying with some of the most proficient and experienced Boeing airliner skippers in the world and they were reluctant to remove the safety net too early. During a busy summer charter schedule, these guys would think nothing of flying to the Greek islands in the middle of the night and carry out a Non-Precision approach, which can be a really tricky thing to do, but here in 'the land of the free' on a sunny day with no high ground around they were not keen to go visual too early – interesting.

There are exceptions to the rule of course and there were some Captains who would be only too happy to fly a visual approach to relieve the tedium of having to fly all approaches on the ILS. One such gentleman was my Captain on a beautiful summer night as we flew to the island of Malta. During the approach briefing which he gave at top of descent, he mentioned that if possible he would like to get a visual approach to land. As he flew the final part of the descent over the darkened island coming in from the northwest, I could see there were little patches of scattered clouds around, but in the main the sky was fairly clear and the air traffic situation was light. We were probably around 4000 feet when he said with an insouciant air,

"Tell them we're visual please". As soon as I had made that radio call, we were given clearance for a visual approach to the runway, but we were a long way from the airport. The Captain pointed out to me where the airfield lay and as he had been here before several times I trusted his judgement – in addition I had the moving map display in front of me which said we had miles still to go downwind.

Now we got busy with the Config. change, slowing down, deploying flaps, getting confirmation from the cabin crew that the cabin was secure for landing, landing gear down etc. During this period the Monitoring Pilot has much to do, so when my PF (and aircraft Commander) called confidently "turning baseleg"; it was on his side of the cockpit, so I assumed he had a complete visual picture of the runways and the airport. We rolled into the turn and I saw the harbour lights of Valetta only a couple of thousand feet below as we hoovered in over the top, but more importantly I looked again for the runway lights and now I could see we were far too close – he had turned too early!
"Are you sure you've still got the runway visual Jack...?" I queried in a matter of fact tone, although the concern in my voice must have been evident. Too late he realised his mistake and so did I.
"Oh F***!" He cried, "Tell 'em we want an orbit! Tell them we will self-position back onto finals again! OH BOLLOCKS!" So with the blessing of the tower, we flew past the harbour again in a big wide circle with the gear and flaps down, heading for a proper final approach now – the passengers must have had a lovely view.

At least he had the good grace to laugh about it afterwards and in my case as a junior FO, I learned a valuable lesson about calling "Visual" with the airfield when it is not truly in sight. I also learned that you shouldn't rely completely on the judgement of the pilot in the other seat no matter how experienced or competent they appear.

Finally I realised that as the PM, I should have been more proactive earlier on in the proceedings and questioned the point where he started to make the baseleg turn. If I had noticed the 'distance to go' versus the altitude at that time, I could have made a timely intervention and prevented him from embarrassing himself. In our case of course we are westerners and embarrassment is not a big issue when we cock-up an approach. In some cultures of the world, the teaching of modern CRM techniques comes up against the proverbial brick wall.

When it comes to analysing what went wrong at San Francisco on 6th July when the tail section of Asiana 214 took out the seawall, my bet is that there are more barriers which still have to come down to improve flight safety in the Far East.

P.S. There have been many occasions since then, when I have witnessed firsthand in airline cockpits what can go wrong with what should be the simplest approach in the world - believe me the permutations are endless.

Capt Snagalot.

(There was a Captain with this nickname at one of the bases – you wouldn't want it).

It is funny how many aircraft defects seem to occur on the last sector of a series of commercial flights. It could be just coincidence of course, but it is uncanny when the aircraft seems to know that it is on the way back to the hangar where these faults can be remedied, so it lets the pilots know then...

+   +   +

It would be true to say that the vast majority of pilots are good employees who turn up for work ontime and try to do a good job whilst they are there. They are highly motivated individuals who produce a high quality performance in all aspects of their working lives and are often very flexible on behalf of the company. In the main this has got to be over 95% of the group as a whole. What is interesting however is that there is a tiny minority who don't fit into this category. These are the ones who stand out and are often very difficult to work with. They can be the bane of an airline crewing department's life and tend to make all of their colleagues lives difficult too.

Not only that, but they can cost a lot for the airline to cope with, especially in regard to how they operate the company's aircraft. Often these individual's behaviour is adversely influenced by poor morale among the operating crews out on the line. There was a well known case in the airline industry back in the 1980's when a whole group of an airline's pilots started to carry extra fuel everywhere they went. Not just a little bit extra, but seriously large amounts of the stuff. The BAC111 fleet of this airline had suffered more than most as the company expanded and bizarrely the pilots thought that by causing commercial harm they would be able to assert how valuable they were. For every extra tonne carried by an airliner, it results in a higher fuel burn of approximately 5% per tonne per hour.

Of course it is very much the prerogative of the Aircraft Commander how much fuel should be loaded for any given flight and in many airlines; there is very sensitive management of this issue. Imagine though that all of your fleet of 15 airliners were all carrying extra fuel unnecessarily everywhere they went? The fuel bills would be enormous!

It is not only the carrying of extra fuel which can have an adverse effect on an airline's fortunes, but also the decision making of the pilots, in particular the Captains who decide whether to operate with an aircraft defect or not. Although the regulations are all in black and white, as we know in life, not everything is quite so simple. For example there is latitude for interpretation of the regulations by individual Captains as they see fit on the day. One case in point here is the situation whereby an airliner is reduced to only one source of AC electrical power by the occurrence of a defect or defects.

Remember that the aeroplanes are all built with redundancy in mind such that with all systems like, hydraulics, electrics, flying controls etc. there is always one backup system if not two. In the situation of the AC power sources, there is an APU at the rear of the airliner which can provide enough electrical power to continue safe flight and then there is an AC generator on each engine. If you are unlucky enough to lose an AC generator from one of the engines, the solution is very simple – start the APU, job done! Of course we are guided by our abnormal and emergency checklists in the solving of technical problems and as the name implies (Quick Reference Handbook – QRH), these lists are there for use when time is short.

In the QRH for the airliners I have flown recently, it specifically states that if there is only one AC power source remaining, then the Captain is advised that he/she MUST land at the "*Nearest* suitable airfield". Here we have a problem because "nearest suitable" is open to interpretation. If the airliner is heading for a destination airport in London and is cruising overhead Paris at 35,000 feet, then should they land in Paris or London? Which is safer? Either way, it's going to take 25 minutes to descend from cruise altitude with the help of ATC and in that time our crew would have covered a lot of miles.

If you go by the literal interpretation of the regulations, then there is a strong case which states the Captain should declare the intention to divert into Charles De Gaulle – this would surely be the nearest airfield. It is not difficult to imagine the problems for the airline caused by an unscheduled diversion and also the extra workload and stress for the crew and passengers onboard. Perhaps the crew are unfamiliar with operating into Paris and maybe this factor combined with coming to the end of a long duty day could lead to forming two of the errors of an error chain which could result in an incident, or worse?

It is a relief to know that the manufacturer is wise enough to put a simple caveat in the QRH. In black and white it clearly states in words to the effect, that the checklists cannot be written to cover every eventuality, failure or combination thereof. Nothing in the QRH prevents the operating Captain on the day taking such action/s that they consider are safest to protect their aircraft and passengers. Having been involved in observing, training and checking crews in their failure management processes for many years, I personally have seen many different safe solutions for the same scenario. 'There are lots of ways to skin a cat'. Provided that the end result has a safe outcome for the flight and that this is not in any doubt, then who are we to criticise?

+   +   +

So we could have a situation here where a particularly 'off-message' Captain who feels that the company have mistreated him in some way could make the entirely justifiable decision to divert the aircraft into Paris. Nobody could argue that his/her interpretation was anything other than correct, "It said NEAREST suitable in the QRH..." However the financial cost for the airline would be into thousands of pounds compared with continuing the flight to London. Perhaps the crew would go out of hours after reaching Paris and be unable to operate another sector, the hundreds of passengers may need to be given hotel accommodation while the aircraft is repaired, maybe a replacement aircraft would be flown in to pick them up – the permutations are endless.

There is another side to the coin however and that is when a Captain and or their crew make strenuous efforts to help the company by in their own minds being very flexible, but to the detriment of their careers. A famous example of this was that of a newly promoted longhaul Captain on a wide-bodied twinjet who elected to continue to destination with only one remaining AC power source. Remember that he had only recently achieved his first command on a large airliner and this is a really important stage in any commercial pilot's career.

The aircraft had a previously recorded defect (Snag) which was acceptable for flight and that was an unserviceable APU which the crew were aware of prior to departure. This is a not unusual occurrence and is acceptable to be "carried" as an ADD (Acceptable Deferred Defect). Now although the known APU defect was not a 'stopper' in itself, it did provide an extra layer of vulnerability, because one of the levels of redundancy was now removed. At cruising altitude and after a couple of hours into the flight, one of the engine driven generators gave up the ghost and after completion of the QRH drills, they were now down to one...

The Captain elected to continue to destination as he believed this to be in the best interest of the company and the other pilot went along with the command decision. The problem was that they had to cross the Bay of Bengal to get to Singapore, some 1600 miles away! In the middle of the night – doh! Needless to say the poor guy lost his command within a day of his arrival – fortunately the remaining engine driven generator carried on providing electrical power for the rest of the flight.

What was significant in this case was the fact that 'the other pilot' on this flightdeck was actually quite a senior First Officer who had previously had a lot of jet command time with other employers in the past. He had been passed over for command with this airline and it is more than likely he felt aggrieved by this. In the end it did him no good either, because the Flight Operations Management decided he was more than partly to blame for the unsafe decision to continue.

Which all goes to show that ours is an interesting profession, with more potential pitfalls than you can shake a stick at. There are times when pilots fill the aircraft technical log with faults and defects of the aircraft which some may deem petty, while at other times pilots operate with faults which increase the risks to an unacceptable degree.

In the case of the first pilot, with his list of minor defects filling the Techlog, he might gain the nickname from the engineering team which reflects what they think of him – "Captain Snagalot".

Somewhere in the middle lies the safest place for your career and your passengers.

Self Preservation Society.

(Good old fashioned British methods for keeping yourself safe).

We were the only aircraft on the ramp, which in itself was a novelty. Also my young colleague and I were in a relaxed mood, having had a very easy flight down to the Canaries from the UK. We were both experienced and confident on the type (B757) and neither of us was under any external pressures. The turnround had been completed in good time and the flight was running ahead of schedule, the sun was just going down. In short, things were going great...

But you already know what's coming don't you? Something which could upset our whole day maybe. We had let our guard down and now as we had started the second engine (the left one) Air Traffic called to ask if we were "Ready for taxy?" It was clear they wanted us to get out of the way as they planned a runway change ahead of the next arriving airliner. I looked over at the First Officer and said "Tell them 'Yes', let's get outta here".

So were immediately given clearance to taxy and that is when I SO nearly wiped out the groundcrew on the headset beneath the aircraft! You see in the distraction of ATC calling on the R/T and us discussing the runway change, we had both forgotten that our crewchief was still connected to the airliner on his headset. There was one final link in the chain and that was the airliner parking brake. As soon as that was released then the groundcrew guy would be at extreme risk of being run over by a one hundred ton tea trolley...

+   +   +

Much has been made of a pilot's self preservation instincts when flying aeroplanes. After all, statistically they are always 'first on the scene of the accident' so it is not unreasonable for them to be very concerned about the prevention of these events. When it comes to commercial airline pilots, we are all part of the same breed in many ways; after all we are trained in a similar way and operate to and from similar places. Working on the first premise of "Try not to crash...", combined with such basic advice as, "The sky is a big place, try to stay in the middle of it!", we pilots learn ways to refine our flying skills and abilities such that we gain valuable experience which helps to make us fly safer.

This means in practice that we develop lots of good habits and tricks of the trade over the years which help to increase the margins of safety while not necessarily over-complicating the operational environment. The KISS principle is often referred to, (Keep It Simple Stupid) which is a well meant expression to emphasise that none of us has to be smart to be safe. KISS was never intended as a derogatory term for flightcrew, although I have seen more than once it being misconstrued as such. If folks wish to imply that I am something of a mental pygmy just because I like to keep things simple and safe in my everyday working routines, then I am not in the least bit offended by that.

An easy example is that our company Standard Operating Procedures (SOPs) often dictate that we only switch on the aircraft Landing Lights AFTER we have been cleared for takeoff on the ground preflight. Now in the hurly burly of a busy air traffic situation as we are running through the remainder of the checklist, getting "cabin-secure" on the intercom from the forward galley; crosschecking the instruments, while being conscious of "Landing traffic at four miles" – you would be amazed at how often that gives us the confidence to be sure that; "Yes we were cleared for takeoff" before we hit the GO levers. We don't need to ask ATC again (doh!) and it removes any nagging doubt. If we religiously never put the Landing Lights on until and unless we have been cleared, then all will be well. Some of us also employ the belt and braces method, which is once we have been cleared for takeoff (or landing when on final approach) I use the windshield grabhandle as an additional reminder. If THAT is flipped up out of my line of sight, then it is further reassurance that we have been cleared for our takeoff or landing.

There are hundreds of these things we do almost subconsciously these days, like making a specific note of where your car is parked in the airport staff carpark before you leave it for a week or two on a longhaul trip. I used to leave mine with a little coloured flag on the aerial so I could spot it from afar, but then the flag blew off so I adopted a different method. Seriously you would think it was easy, but so many times you come back after a trip and go straight to the row where you think you left it... but that was last time, or the time before that. A note on my mobile phone calendar or diary does it for me now. There's nothing worse than dragging your TravelPro (the BIG longhaul suitcase) round the parking lot in the rain, feeling half-dead with jetlag looking for your car.

Fuel imbalance when you are flying? Now there's a good one. You see from time to time, maybe because the centre-tank pumps on one side are more powerful or efficient, we get left with an imbalance between the wing (main) tanks when the centre tank empties. In simple terms it helps to fly straight if the aircraft is balanced and also means less drag because we don't have to use rudder trim to offset the imbalance of ailerons. So we carry out a process of effectively transferring fuel from one wing to both engines – this is called 'Crossfeeding'. On large airliners small amounts of fuel imbalance, say a couple of hundred kilos is neither here nor there, but if it gets to 300+ we usually do something about it on the narrow-bodies.

There was a famous case of a B737 crew who opened the Crossfeed valve in the cruise, (feeding both engines from one wing) then forgot all about it until the imbalance went so far in the opposite direction, the autopilot disconnected and the aircraft nearly rolled onto its back! This extreme case served to remind us all of the importance of NOT forgetting that we have the Crossfeed valve open, so now you will see crews setting egg timers; starting stopwatches; putting the normal checklist in a visually obstructive place; altering the displays on the navigational instruments; using little post-it notes; etc. etc. – ANYTHING to prevent them imitating the original crew's mistake.

On the ASIs of the classic airliners there are little white plastic speedbugs round the outside. These are used as indicators of the different important speeds which we need to refer to from time to time – for example "Vee One" (V1) and "Rotate" (VR) speeds. As these vary with the weight of the jet, then the speeds will also change for a given set of circumstances. In the Boeings there are 4 bugs to set and usually there is a spare bug – total of 5 round the outside of the instrument. Many is the time that I have seen pilots setting the 'spare' at the 80 knots position, so that they can see 80 more easily. It was once recommended to me that I don't do this, because if one of the critical bugs breaks off, then we would have to use the spare to replace it. If I had been used to always seeing a white marker at the 80 position, this would be a cause of distraction at a potentially critical phase of flight (i.e. Just before takeoff). Good advice indeed and good practice.

+   +   +

On the aircraft which I currently operate there are many times when it is parked for some days and while secured, the landing gear pins and pitot covers are fitted. We have a strict policy of ensuring that every time the gear pins and pitot covers are fitted by the travelling engineer, these must be inserted as an open entry into the aircraft Techlog. (All open entries are closed before flight). This is the place where our worlds meet and interact – those of the pilots and the maintenance crew. It is a very formal place, a legal document no less and therefore it cannot be disregarded or trifled with. It is sacred ground to any of us that think deeply enough about it and therefore it is also the ideal place for the reminder to be given to the operating Captain prior to his signing to take over the jet for flight. In common with many other Commanders, I will not sign-off the Techlog until every other item is completed/signed up. That way my crew will hopefully never take an aircraft airborne and be unable to get the landing gear up (pins still locked in place).

Many years ago when I was learning my craft as an airline pilot I used to ask questions of my senior in the left-hand seat while I was operating as their First Officer. Always keen to learn, I used to observe what they did and in what sequence in the normal course of their flying activities. Nothing special you understand just trying to pick up the good habits and spot the ones I didn't wish to acquire. One of the old hands I used to fly with was quite specific about his use of the taxy lights on the B757 – he always said it was for his own protection, but it also protected others. After engine start, he never released the parking brake without first putting both of the taxy lights on. His reasoning was that this is a significant warning to others on the manoeuvring area that the aircraft is about to move under its own power...

+   +   +

Back on the ramp in the dusk of Arrecife, we had been cleared to taxy and all of our checks were complete. I switched on the taxylights and immediately there was a scream on the intercom in our headphones from the ground 25 feet below...
"CAPTEEN I AM STEEL HERE!! NO TAXY. NO TAXY! PLEESE!?" I looked at the other pilot and we both knew instantly what had happened – yikes! That was close. Needless to say I was very, very, apologetic to the crewchief on the intercom, but at the end of the day one of my self defence mechanisms had worked and worked really well. I had not released the parking brake and therefore in reality there had been no incident, but it so easily could have been a complete tragedy. Yes, we are the self-preservation society, but in doing so we do preserve others too.

With thanks to the soundtrack of the film 'The Italian Job' (1969). "We are the self preservation society..." Funnily enough the coach accident at the end of the movie is partly caused it seems by the star (Michael Caine), distracting the coach driver while standing next to him. These days there is a little sign on PSV buses and coaches reminding passengers not to stand forward or speak to the driver while the vehicle is motion.

Friendly Fire.

(When Donald Duck, Fred Flintstone and Scooby Doo get together, you just know that's not going to be a sensible conversation... and so it proved).

I was feeling more than a little hot in the Scooby Doo outfit, which was no doubt part of the reason why I was pushing my fluid intake. Looking across at Fred Flintstone, I really envied him. Now *that* would have been a good way to keep cool on a tropical summer night, bare legs, a short, thin, animal print dress with serrated hemline and sandals. The 'Cartoon Characters' cocktail party had been going strong for some time, but the United States Army Major (masquerading as Donald Duck) was clearly troubled. After all "US Inc." did seem to be taking a hammering on a global scale.

During those days, everywhere you looked on TV, the news channels would carry reports of attacks on US Military forces in all the lousy corners of the world. You could see it from the viewpoint of a regular US Army Major and he was making his feelings clear, "But waahh duh thay'orll hate us so much? Ahh mean we're jess tryin' to do our job of policing the wurld's trouble zones. *Thay is jess makin' targits outta us..."* He tailed off, with a puzzled look.

Maybe it was the wrong time for me to make my contribution, but I wanted to reassure him. Of course I should have chosen my words carefully, but the effect of half a gallon of 'Mojito', put paid to that! I started well enough by reasoning that; "The fact there is so much 'incoming fire' actually validates the presence of the armed peace-keeping force. I mean without it, the locals would just be trying to kill each other". He looked at me and I could see he was starting to get it – "so really you ARE doing a good job Major and we should all be grateful to you for that". He was still concerned about the 'incoming' though and he said so.

"But Hell! Thay's sending RPGs and Mi-ssahls, Mortar Shells and like, all sortsa' small arms fire at us – WHY'd they do that?" I replied confidently, of course it was clear to me.

"No Major, you're looking at the situation from the wrong angle. You see they're not shooting AT you, HEY! They're SORT OF shooting FOR you. You really shouldn't take it the wrong way. I mean...." I struggled now for the correct phrasing to use to get the message across and did not find it. Unfortunately, there was a general lull in conversation all around us as I blurted out... "WELL LOOK MAJOR.... being that you're in the US ARMY, you MUST be familiar with the principle of FRIENDLY FIRE....!?"

+   +   +

It is a strange phenomenon, but working as a civilian, flying military trooping flights with airliners is a very satisfying activity. It is hard to explain, but somehow you feel like you are making a very positive contribution to the stability of mankind. If you believe that mostly the elected governments in the democratic part of the free world are doing their best to nurture a peaceful environment for all, then even when they send their armies abroad, you have to consider there is a humanitarian mission involved also. There is also another part of the job which appeals and that is the fact that we are a separate team from 'the green machine'. Our reporting lines and activities do not come under military discipline in quite the same way, so it feels much more relaxed. You notice it first in the preflight briefing phase when the military Met-officer delivers a very structured and thorough briefing of the weather conditions enroute and those to be encountered at destination. This is different to the way in which we usually carry out a briefing when we are on our own – then it is often a case of the First Officer having read all the Met and Notams in advance giving a brief summary to the Captain of how it's going to be.

Then there are the multifarious rules and regulations regarding the operation of military flying machines which are contained in strange sounding publications such as the 'Flying Order Book' or 'Air Staff Instructions'. Often these do not apply to our civilian airliners, but then at other times inexplicably they do. For example at a military airbase a few years back when we were running behind schedule with our B767, we asked for the passengers to be boarded at the same time as refuelling was to take place. The answer was a negative. "But this will save time and be more efficient" we reasoned with the Duty Officer, also known as 'The DAMO'. He explained to us lesser mortals, "It is because it's not safe d'you see Sir...?" as if we had not realised the serious health and safety implications of refuelling with passengers boarding an aircraft at the same time. This perceived risk resulted in the strict military regulation, which must be observed even by civilian aircraft. Needless to say we were amused by this and replied, "Well you had better get on the 'phone to Heathrow and tell them to stop it, because it is happening there hundreds of times a day. Oh! And while you're at it, call Paris De Gaulle and Schiphol too – if it is *THAT* dangerous, millions of passengers are at risk every year!"

Most likely it is a hangover from the time when high octane Avgas was the fuel being used to power large piston engined aircraft and perhaps there was a danger of spillage from the fuel bowser. Trying to get a puddle of Avtur (aviation jet fuel) to ignite is not easy and requires a special set of circumstances. Certainly it won't happen on a cold, wet and windy apron in England during the winter. On the whole though our interaction with the military personnel was very cordial and they seemed to appreciate that we come from a different operating environment. We were fortunate also in not being required to operate into any really hot zones with our relatively fragile airliners. My brother tells a great tale about going into a war zone airfield as a passenger at night when they switched all the cabin lights off just as they left cruising altitude and the airliner made a very steep descent into a forward operating base. Recently the large insurance underwriters have become more risk averse with regard to airliners so when we fly trooping missions, it is usually to an interim location just over the border from the conflict and our 'passengers' are then transferred to military transporters.

Another bonus when flying the troops is that they are incredibly well behaved. In contrast to flying with the airlines we nearly never see a disruptive passenger whatsoever, but there is the exception which proves the rule. One night departing from the UK, I was called by the Senior Cabin Crew Member into the forward cabin while boarding was being completed. There at the forward entry door was a Senior NCO in uniform swaying from side to side and slurring his words as he tried to explain that he didn't like flying... I spoke with him for a minute or so.

Although he was keen to do his duty and board the flight, clearly he was inebriated to the point of being a danger to himself or others. I explained to him slowly and carefully, that I was very sorry, but we could not take him. All the time I was conscious of the fact that our little vignette was being observed by the senior officers of the forward cabin and therefore I was very polite in my dealings with all involved. This particular NCO had made a very serious error of judgement and was about to be subjected to the military discipline system, such that he would learn the error of his ways – he didn't deserve a lecture from me too. As he went back down the steps to the airbase being supported by one of the groundcrew, I felt very sorry for him.

Nobody wants to go to war and I guess he had tried to solve the problem with too much Dutch Courage.

Meanwhile we got the aircraft secured for our nightflight across half the globe towards the Middle East. Once again there are some interesting protocols which need to be observed as local Military Aerodrome procedures differ slightly from the civil world, but eventually we were airborne and climbing into the familiar airspace of the London TMA – the comforting lights of the capital twinkling below. In a matter of only nine hours or so, we would be landing shortly after dawn at a little known airbase on the edge of the desert to disembark our troops for them to go to war or keep the peace whichever way you see it. In the darkness of the flightdeck up front it is business as usual at cruising altitude as we crosscheck our navigation, monitor the aircraft systems and record the weather at various enroute airports from the Volmet transmissions.

Dinner is served at our "non-smoking table for two, by the windows" and we eat in relative silence. Tonight's flight is not the usual light-hearted airline sector which we are used to. The date is the middle of December and our thoughts are of spending Christmas with our families. We know that our passengers will not be home until the spring, maybe some of them will not come home at all... It is a moving experience doing trooping flights, in more ways than one. As we taxied off the runway after landing the outside air temperature is already 30 degrees Celsius and the large hazy sun has hardly risen. Yes today is going to be a hot one. I pick up the PA microphone and I wonder what to say, as we trundle slowly towards our parking spot on the dusty concrete ramp. There are sand coloured military vehicles and personnel everywhere.

"Ladies and gentlemen, this is the Captain speaking... Welcome to _____ Airbase where you will transfer to military aircraft for the final part of your journey. My crew and I know the difficult and dangerous job you do for our nation. On behalf of all of us we are grateful to you for doing it. Keep safe, look after yourselves. We wish you good luck in your deployment and we look forward to seeing you all home safe and sound early next year. God Bless you all". The mood of our hard working cabin crew in the cabin was similarly sombre and they told me afterwards that there was absolute silence until the seatbelt sign went off.

Meanwhile back at the cocktail party at the military airbase in the tropics. Probably the fact that the US Major was dressed as Donald Duck and I looked like a large dog from a popular cartoon defused the situation. The senior army officer and Base Commander standing with us roared laughing at my unintended gaffe. They all thought it was very funny; in fact by that stage we thought absolutely everything was funny! Thankfully it was not the diplomatic incident which it could have been. As the night went on however, it became clear that the real name of my character should have been *"Scooby Don't!"*, but THAT as they say, is another story ☺

Unstable Approach

(An easy way to flush your career down the toilet, that's for sure).

They say in our business that the first year of your command as a new airliner Captain is one of the worst. By that I mean that it produces so many new learning experiences for inexperienced commanders, that you are constantly finding yourself making decisions in situations which you have never faced before. Certainly I recall one night coming back into Manchester on the B757 when I was presented with a unique set of circumstances. I had been upgraded to Captain only a week before and this was one of my first line flights since cleared to operate in the left-hand seat.

In the right-hand seat was a very experienced First Officer whom I knew had recently been 'passed over' for command, so for this two sector nightflight it had already been an exercise in diplomacy for me. I was still at the stage where I couldn't 'give away landings' (to the First Officer) therefore I was required to be the handling pilot for the first 20 sectors after successful completion of my command course. As we descended from cruising altitude I could see that the vertical profile was quite steep and then this situation worsened when the ATC controller gave us a short cut towards final approach. Throughout all of this I could see that my colleague was doing his best to cope with the descent, but that he appeared to be behind the aircraft and was exhibiting lack of situational awareness. While we were heading downhill, I did make some helpful inputs, like "You're going to need speedbrakes mate..." while we were descending, but his reactions to events was very slow.

Although I cannot remember all the distances (to touchdown) versus the altitudes, I just recall my horror when I first saw the airfield. We broke cloud at 12 miles out on the extended centreline with only Flap 1 set and I felt the airport was in plan view! *My God,* I thought, *what a cock-up?!* I tried to sound relaxed as I said, "Well... as I have got to do the landing anyway, I'll take control now, shall I...?" The look on his face told me all I needed to know. He knew that he had screwed up the descent for me and had only just realised his mistake. The thought, *Hmm, probably why you failed your command assessment then...* went through my mind, as I put my hands and feet on the controls, *oh THAT feels better...* disconnected the autopilot and called, "GEAR DOWN!" in a loud voice. *Oh boy – THIS could be my first go-around – Oh s***! How stupid will I look?*

I immediately started large S-Turns to increase the track miles to touchdown, at the same time I had the speedbrakes out all the way, with gear down, thrust levers closed and now calling for more flap too. Of course at Flap 15 (or greater), the speedbrakes have to be stowed as the airframe buffeting is too much, but it was a relief to see the speed come below maximum speed for Flap 15 anyway! We still had 10 miles to go, but I could see it was going to be 50/50 whether we could get the height off in time. I also knew that an orbit (to lose height) was out of the question, because Manchester ATC are sensitive about night-time visual manoeuvres ever since the Airtours B767 flew down Wilmslow High Street (downwind) at 1000 feet. The trouble was that was 1000 feet on the altimeter with QNH set, so in reality they were only around 700 feet above the ground and it was 1 o'clock in the morning! Apparently they set off more than just the car alarms in this wealthy Cheshire town and by the next day the Captain's career had been adversely affected.

We had ten miles to run, but I still didn't know if we could make it, to be stable on the approach by 500 feet on finals. There is a cute trick which I was shown years ago (thank you Capt Alan Blake) whereby you wind down the autopilot control panel altitude setting to zero. Literally you just dial in all the noughts in the window on the glareshield panel and then you check where the green predictor curve moves to on the EHSI (moving map display) – so you are now saying to the flight director system, "Okay guys, now show me where we will land at *this* rate of descent and *this* airspeed in *this* configuration?" You have to remember it is instantaneous and will only react to the set of parameters it sees at that precise time – but it is a great guide to see if you can make the runway... I looked down and the green arc on the EHSI was settled on the runway itself – *Yikes!* It did not look good, at this rate, we would land halfway down the two mile strip of concrete...

The aviation press has recently been reporting the dismissal of a Southwest Airlines B737 Captain after a landing accident at New York's La Guardia airport this summer. From the details available it appears that the Captain (who had been the non-handling pilot), took control from the First Officer on final approach at a very late stage, 400 feet above the ground. She then tried to land the aircraft, but in the process, landed nosegear first which resulted in the nosegear collapse, aircraft off the runway and the subsequent post landing passenger evacuation. Reports say that the touchdown was at an attitude of 3 degrees nose **down**, which if true is remarkable. Normally a B737 airliner would have a pitch attitude of around 3 degrees nose **up** for the final approach and then around 6 degrees for the touchdown, with maingear first. No doubt about it, 3 degrees **down** would be dramatic. The fact that the nosegear collapsed is no surprise because this part of the undercarriage is just not designed to take such a load. Mister Boeing builds a strong airframe and the maingear can accept an awful lot of punishment (I have tested it personally on occasions) but not the nosegear. No Sir, that is built much lighter and should be treated with respect.

For example, many years ago (we're talking early 1990's) there was a time when Air 2000 was being pressured by the Board of Directors into going to Funchal, Madeira with the B757. The flight ops management were saying, "It's not safe..." but the Board of Directors countered with, "Well Air Europe go in there with their B757s, so what's the matter with you lot?" Legend has it, that a crucial meeting on the subject was scheduled for Thursday in the diary one week hence, when the BoD would be demanding answers to tough questions about Funchal and the Flight Ops Managers would be on the spot.

On the Tuesday of that week, Air Europe had a hard landing with their B757 at Funchal which punched the nosegear up into the hull! The bill for damage was over a million dollars. Needless to say the Air 2000 management meeting was cancelled...

History was to repeat itself several years later in New York JFK, when one of the Alitalia B767s which we had been flying on the Nordstress Contract had a hard landing after all the experienced 767 contractors had left and the new fleet were being operated by Italian pilots. Again it was nosegear damage that led to the aircraft being repaired in a hangar at JFK airport by a special team from Boeing. It was such a shame because those aircraft were brand new when they were delivered in '96 – the repairs took months. From memory, I think the landing accident occurred from an approach via the Canarsie Approach for runway 13. This was a particularly tricky approach to the runway which had to be flown with precision and only by visual references at the end to a curving final turn to the landing. I know that people used to go on about the old chequerboard approach at Kai Tak in Hong Kong, but I think the Canarsie RW13 approach could be worse and I have flown both. Again, this was another occasion where a go-around manoeuvre would have probably been appropriate.

Which brings us to Southwest and if you look at the history books, you can understand why, as a company they are very sensitive about pilots continuing to land after an unstable approach. In March 2000 at Burbank California, Southwest Airlines flight 1455 made a "hot and high" approach to land, touched down halfway down the runway at far too high a speed and went off the end straight through the barriers and stopped just short of a Gas Station. It was a miracle that there were no fatalities, although two cabin crew were seriously injured. Both pilots on that occasion were fired after the investigation found them to be negligent and culpable.

In the recent landing accident at La Guardia in July, the firing of the Captain was not a surprise and the fact that the First Officer was sent for 'further training' is similarly understandable. The one big question for me and many like me remains. "Why did they not go-around?" For the Captain to take control to land at 400 feet on finals is pretty much unprecedented, however if the approach has been flown so badly by the FO, then perhaps it could be justified. But there is another issue.

The SOP for the airline will have industry standard stable approach criteria and this will state that the aircraft MUST be stable at 500 feet on finals or a go-around MUST be carried out. In the case of Flight 345 the approach must have been unstable before the Captain took control, therefore the most correct course of action would have been a go-around, but the Captain chose to take the risk that they **might** pull off a safe landing from this position. If I was the Flight Safety Manager at Southwest I would be asking the difficult questions of the Flight Ops Management right now about what sort of 'culture' is being run, whereby an experienced Captain feels compelled to take a risk, rather than take the safe option to go-around.

Back in the sky over Manchester in the B757, things were looking a little better. The big 'S' turns had helped and the green predictor curve was now definitely **before** this end of the runway. I had stabilised the aircraft with gear down, Flap 30 and thrust levers still closed – we had a good rate of descent and passing through 4 miles on finals I could see we were going to land okay.

We were fortunate also that there was a good 15 knots of headwind down the runway which helped all the way. As 500 feet on the radalt came up, we were on speed, on glide, on centreline with gear down and landing flap and the power was set for final approach. It had been a close call and taught me another lesson about when to take control as a Captain – do it early!

Crew Transport.

(More dangerous than flying aeroplanes for sure).

It was the end of a long trip, late at night and we were all tired. You could see it in the faces of the junior cabin crew as we all heaved our longhaul suitcases once again into the back of yet another crewbus. *I guess the reason is that us 'older ones' probably look tired all the time or maybe we have developed more stamina over the years. Yes that's it, more stamina. We have done this SO many times before...* Eventually the crew baggage was all aboard and we were on our way. I noticed that the wipers were also tired on this particular crewbus and were having difficulty clearing all the snow from the windscreen... In a similar way, the snowploughs had experienced difficulty in keeping the roads clear from the airport and much snow and ice was still contaminating the road surface. Although the driver seemed to be driving carefully, he lost control of the bus as it rounded a corner and we lurched sideways towards a bank of snow. As this was happening in slow motion and we braced ourselves for the impact, I heard a voice from the crew in the back call out, **"...I always said we'd die on crew transport!"**

+   +   +

I know they say "flying is dangerous", but statistically we as crew are all more at risk of death or serious injury while driving to or from the airport. The same goes for our passengers of course and there is a wealth of data to support this. Unfortunately in our cost conscious age, where it seems that the bean counters are running the airline industry, there is a tendency to go cheap on everything which does not carry an 'airworthiness' tag. For example; crew transport. I recall there was a UK airline which was carrying out a new series of flights to Goa in India some years back. One experienced Captain who arrived there was horrified to learn that the transportation for the crew consisted of a 20+ year old bus with no safety equipment onboard and the crew forced to sit with a pile of 25kg hardshell suitcases stacked up right behind their heads, with no restraints.

If the bus had crashed suddenly at only 20 mph, half the crew would have been decapitated! On the return journey to the airport, he refused to allow his crew to board the assigned crewbus, but elected to rent three taxis instead. When he submitted the expense receipt to the relevant department back at base in the UK later, he was told, "Well it IS a third world country you know!" He refused to be put off by this and countered the statement with the observation that, "the established airlines are using modern buses with safety equipment, including cargo restraints for the baggage".

In reality there is a duty of care incumbent upon all Flight Operations Managers to look after their people. Put simply, the cost of their replacement is huge, not only in monetary terms, but also in humanitarian value. When managers acknowledge that 'people' really are their number one resource, then we can know they have really 'got it'. Of course when we make decisions about how, where and when to transport the crew for operational purposes in support of the all important flying programme, there is a balance to be achieved. Logistically it might be very expedient to position the crew to the aircraft at the last possible minute and avoid the cost of an extra nightstop the night before they are due to operate, but this is not always going to work out.

In some charter airlines recently I have even witnessed a move by the 'crewing department' encouraging First Officers under training to 'self-position' for a duty at a far away airport and to 'self-position' home thereafter. In some cases, when the distances are large this is clearly not safe. Usually it is associated with companies who employ FOs on a 'Pay to Fly' basis and is a disturbing phenomenon. One such company which was based in the UK has since ceased trading and good riddance. It just goes to show that even penny-pinching methods such as this will not save an airline which has the wrong business model anyway.

It is one thing to make arrangements for crew positioning when things are going well, but when things go wrong – it is an entirely different matter. An example of this was the accident which occurred on 3rd September 1999 at Glasgow airport in Scotland. The Cessna 404 Titan had an engine failure shortly after takeoff and the subsequent crash landing resulted in the tragic loss of six airline crew onboard plus the two operating pilots. There were several factors involved in the accident, but one of the changes which the airline made, was to decree that no future crew moves were to be permitted with Performance Category C aircraft. They were not alone.

Several other airlines placed this restriction on their crewing departments at the same time. Of course hindsight is 20/20 as they say, but could this not have been foreseen in advance? Those of us pilots with experience operating these 'light-twins' were always keenly aware of the marginal single-engined climb performance. I have clear memories of being the operating Captain of PA31-350 Chieftain aeroplanes departing Manchester back in the late 80's with full airline crews onboard - destination, London Gatwick. It was invariably at night and often in bad weather as we roared off down Runway 24 at Max All Up Weight, with my right-hand jammed hard up behind the throttle levers willing the engines to keep going. Maybe it was safer than it felt, but I don't think so.

When considering the concept of crew movements and their safety there are two words which come to mind – Risk Assessment. I know this may sound dull, but it does not take too much imagination to visualise the adverse consequences of getting it wrong. Think about what happened recently to the two Turkish Airlines pilots in Beirut, taken hostage by some militia outfit with political ambitions. This was not years ago, it was only a matter of months back and they work for a National Carrier! There was some comment on the internet by people who seemed to know, that their employer does not have a good track record of looking after their crews – maybe this was justified? Who knows?

Certainly it is unwise to take things for granted in remote locations and there is so much which can be done by an airline's managers to safeguard their crew in both Hotac and transportation. Unfortunately many companies now seem endorse an adversarial approach to managing crews and this must change. The first principle and overriding mantra should be, **"They are our number one resource",** and everything else will follow suit. At face value there will be a cost to this strategy and it will be clearly apparent, but it would only take a little research by a smart HR employee/manager to prove that the downstream benefits totally outweigh the extra expense in booking good quality hotel accommodation for example. The up-market hotel serves higher quality food and beverages which are prepared in cleaner kitchens, so the hotel guests suffer less food poisoning.

There are exceptions which test the theory of course. Nobody would cite 'low standard of hotel accommodation' as a causal factor in the food poisoning of the flightdeck crew which nearly took the top off the Penta Hotel at Heathrow back in November 1989. As a result there was a court case which ended with Capt Glenn Stewart being found guilty of endangering persons on the ground. Tragically Captain Stewart later took his own life as a consequence of the incident.

For those of us with a keen interest in Flight Safety, the reports of the approach and go-around make fascinating reading. Not only that, but it also affirms the theory that every accident/incident is the result of an error chain composed of between 7 and 11 causal factors. In this case, the food poisoning suffered by the two pilots and Flight Engineer was critical to what happened on that day.

Getting back to crew transportation, I recall in the early days of starting with a low-cost airline when I made a very big mistake. After reporting for duty early in the morning at Luton for a simple Geneva and back, we learned that the aircraft had diverted to East Midlands airport – Luton being fogged out. A crew move was organised with a local taxi firm which provided a 'people carrier' at short notice to take myself and the other four crew up the motorway in advance of the passengers.

Naturally there seemed to be great commercial pressure to get the job done and for our crew to be transported as quickly as possible so we could operate the flight. As we took our seats inside the vehicle, my nostrils picked up the scent of stale cigarettes surrounding the driver who appeared to be unkempt. Not only that, but after a while I could smell alcohol on his breath and even though I was seated behind him the smell was quite strong. My mistake was in not asking him to stop the vehicle and let us all out – he continued driving us to East Midlands and during the two hour journey there were several near misses on the road.

+   +   +

Meanwhile... as the crewbus slammed into the snowbank on the outside of the bend, it was clear that we were all unharmed and apart from being shaken by the experience we were all very relieved. In response to the *"dying on Crew Transport"* comment, we all roared laughing – it was a genuinely funny moment.

Soon after this we entered the warm and familiar lobby of the Holiday Inn at Bangor Maine. Then not long afterwards were ensconced in the hospitable surroundings of Pete and Larry's bar, watching the snow fall outside the windows whilst singing along with the live band to the Rodeo Song, the lyrics of which are far too rude to print here...

(B747-100, G-AWNO, BA 012, BAH-LHR, 21 NOV 89, 27R at LHR. Google "The Rodeo Song" and you will see what I mean).

What Goes Around...?

(It is always interesting to meet your old students and see how they've developed...)

I had been dozing for most of the early part of the flight, but after a couple of hours in the cruise, the seatbelts sign was illuminated as we were jolted around by some CAT (Clear Air Turbulence). From my seat in the cabin next to the window in row 4, I had a very nice view of the Swiss Alps as Captain 'Mike' the aircraft commander, made a reassuring PA about 'the bumps' and how long they were expected to last. He finished off by updating us all on our early estimated arrival into Manchester, including the latest weather which I only half listened to, until the bit about "...and the wind's gusting up to 45 knots..." *Damn, I wish I had listened to the rest of it now; THAT doesn't sound good!*

+   +   +

There is an old saying that "What goes around, comes around", which I interpret to mean that we will all see the consequences of our actions at some stage later in life. I have often had the experience of flying as a passenger on a commercial airliner being flown by somebody whom I have trained to fly in the past. At first I have to say it did feel a bit strange. People have often asked me am I not scared to be 'down the back' without being able to influence the outcome of the flight in any way? But that is exactly the point – I have absolutely no control over events when my position is 20 metres behind the cockpit and the armoured flightdeck door is locked.

This is entirely proper of course as I am flying as a passenger and not part of the legally nominated crew, so I take my seat and chill-out. Generally I have to say I have no qualms at all when I recognise the voice on the PA, "This is your Captain speaking..." but I do occasionally have a wry smile to myself when I think back to when I first flew with the very mature sounding Capt 'X' while he was line training as a young First Officer. Maybe I was teaching him the intricacies of achieving an efficient VNAV descent profile in the B737, or guiding him through the apparent maze that is the FMC, (Flight Management Computer) during his early days on the type. At first it seems that this magic screen has been designed to confuse and confound new users with its multitude of pages which all appear the same...

I may even have been a training captain during his (or her) Command Upgrade course and no doubt we will have been concerned then with guidance on Command Decision making. After all, the actual job of flying the jet is taken for granted at this point in an airline pilot's career – or at least it should be. It is often said among our profession, that to make an easy transition from right-hand seat to left, the candidate/trainee should be able to fly the aircraft almost without thinking. Their main job now is learning how to 'manage' the operation as they move from being 'flight-path controller' to 'flight-progress manager'. Too often in the past, have I seen quite experienced Co-pilots who sincerely believe they are ready for *their* command, when in reality it is a step too far for them at that stage in their career. For whatever reason they simply can't hack it and it would be a mistake to put them forward for a command upgrade course.

In most airlines now there is a difference between command assessment and command course – as the names imply, one comes before the other. Sometimes when I was managing pilots, they would return to our base having been for their assessment phase with their tail between their legs and it was my job then to build their confidence back up. I used to counsel them and advise that they "shouldn't think about it like failing your *actual* command course, which is a terrible thing. It was only the assessment stage and you've got to put it behind you and move on. You will get another opportunity to make a good assessment in the near future. Everything happens for a reason".

There was a time in our rapidly expanding airline though when we were *really* short of Captains and there was a major push to get as many experienced co-pilots through as possible. Once the pilot management team had trawled through the list of FOs who had been with the company for some time, we then started to review the recent joiners. This was based around the premise that perhaps some of these pilots, who were recruited for the right-hand seat, would (under different circumstances) have been given a Direct Entry Command. The list proposed by the training department included one FO whom I felt lacked the right amount of relevant experience.

So I called the Chief Trainer to discuss the issue with him. I said to him that our 'search for stars' among the new intake was based upon the idea that maybe some of them had been recruited for the wrong seat (Captain sits LHS as you know). In the case of this guy, Mr 'X', he was light on hours/experience, quite young and would, in my view, benefit from 6 months to a year flying as a Co-Pilot with our airline. My training department colleague on the 'phone was most insistent that this pilot would be okay to go through the course without a hitch. He emphasised that the FO had been, "above average in the simulator". I was not convinced and said so quite clearly, but I was then informed, "Well, I HAVE TOLD HIM he's going to have the Command slot now!"

There was a long pause between us as this piece of news sank in. Technically and legally, the young FO had enough hours to make the upgrade, but I had a hard time visualising him in command of a B737 on the line. With all the route network expansion it was a very tough operating environment for new pilots. The airline was definitely short of skippers and now if my view was to prevail as Flight Operations Manager, the FO would be informed that we (the company) had changed our collective mind. Naturally he would be terribly disappointed and upset; he might even file a grievance under our HR policies against the senior Training Management... *Hmmm, what to do?* Suddenly, my mind was made up and I said,

"Yes, okay then, I will support you on this one, but please check with me in future prior to informing anybody of their promotion. I am still uneasy, but as you have told him, I will back you up. We need to make sure he is given all the training management support which he needs to be successful". The FO successfully passed his Command Upgrade course and joined the company as a Line Captain. Sadly within his first year of command, he made a very wrong decision while taxiing which resulted in a badly damaged airliner, fortunately nobody was injured. The repairs to the aircraft took months. Perhaps I should have been more resolute – who knows?

+   +   +

Needless to say this was not the same pilot who was aircraft commander for our approach into Manchester and as I sat in Row 4, I reviewed what I could recall about Captain Mike. The last time I had flown with him was back in the year 2000 when I had been Base Captain at Liverpool. I distinctly remember him being one of the most diligent and professional aviators in our base. Not only that, but he was blessed with above average airliner handing skills, albeit that this had been on a B737 while now he was flying an A320. During the descent, the seatbelt signs were put on early and the cabin crew carried out their duties securing the cabin quite a long way out from the airport. As we descended into thick cloud and the turbulence started, I could see why they had been keen to get strapped into their crewseats so long before we landed.

There were significant thumps, bangs and shocks felt in the cabin, which gave rise to quite a lot of verbal disquiet among the passengers around me. That being said, I knew Capt Mike would be flying the aircraft at Turbulence Penetration Speed. I looked around at some very frightened faces and felt guilty that I was unable to share my knowledge of just how safe we were in the hands of this particular skipper. *Oh yes, he was BLOODY good!* I mused as another series of violent shocks ran through the airframe and now there was the sound of vomit bags being used also. Outside my window, the cloud was impenetrable and would be like that until we broke out onto final approach for Runway 23R, abeam Audenshawe reservoir. *Ah good, now I know where we are, about 8 miles out and the wind is straight down the strip.* From previous experience, I remembered the turbulence on short finals was worst in Manch if the wind was blowing over the terminals from the West. *Maybe it will be smoother as we get closer? It is from the southwest after all.*

But instead of abating, the rough air got worse and now we were pitching and rolling almost continuously, the sharp changes in engine thrust being clearly audible as the auto-thrust system tried to cope with the conditions. Maybe it was manual thrust by this stage. The sound of more vomit bags being used. *Oh dear... gusting to 45 knots?! Probably a good chance of windshear in this lot, we're at around 800 feet I reckon...* then suddenly the sound of a lot of power being applied and the sound of the gear being retracted, we were climbing away.

What goes around? WE'RE Going Around! The cabin crew made a nice clear PA informing everybody and assuring that "the Captain is rather busy just now, so he will talk to us when he gets a moment". *OH YES! He will be busy alright, there's plenty to do in that little room at the front during a Go-Around manoeuvre. Lots of flashing of shiny levers, switches, cross-cockpit calls, R/T calls, checklists, confirmations, affirmations of intentions and so it goes on. Hmmmm... NOW what will he do?*

I did not have to wait long for my answer as we turned right-hand downwind in a 'short-pattern radar circuit' at about 2500 feet altitude in rough air, just at the cloudbase, for another approach. Still the turbulence, still the vomiting and still the sounds of jet engines accelerating and decelerating outside the fuselage in response to fluctuations in the speed. The second approach was no smoother and now I felt I knew what was coming. *It MUST be a Windshear Warning this time and I bet that's why he went around the first time too...* Sure enough a couple of hundred feet lower this time, up went the revs, up went the gear and up went the cabin deck angle – our second Go-Around. The gentleman next to me was looking distinctly uncomfortable by now, so I thought I would try and reassure him with some humour. In the noise I had to raise my voice a little as I showed him my watch.

"The Captain said we were going to be EARLY! I bet he doesn't say that again anytime soon hey?!" He laughed and agreed with me. Now we would be diverting to the alternate airport. *Hmmm... Liverpool, Birmingham, East Mids?* As the aircraft stabilised at 5000 feet or so, Capt Mike came onto the PA. He sounded very professional, confident and reassuring. Good man, I was proud of him. *One of my boys.*

There was no doubt in his voice as he ended with, "Ladies and gentlemen we will be landing at Birmingham in 15 minutes time, thank you for your patience". The resulting approach to Runway 15 was clearly no walk in the park as the wind was blowing hard across and just about on maximum crosswind limits.

That being said at least it was smoother and therefore no windshear warning. After landing and as we taxied clear of the runway, there was a heartfelt round of applause in the cabin, including enthusiastic hand-clapping from the gentleman sitting in 4F.

+   +   +

Note1: *In most airlines' Standard Operating Procedures (SOPs) it is written, that "after two Go-Arounds at intended destination airport due to bad weather, <u>a third approach may not be made unless</u> there has been substantial improvement in the weather conditions".*

Note 2: *Turbulence Penetration Speed is that speed which is recommended by the manufacturer as the best IAS to fly the aircraft clean (no gear or flaps) for smoothest ride quality. This will protect the aircraft structure from potential damage and will give the passenger cabin the smoothest ride.*

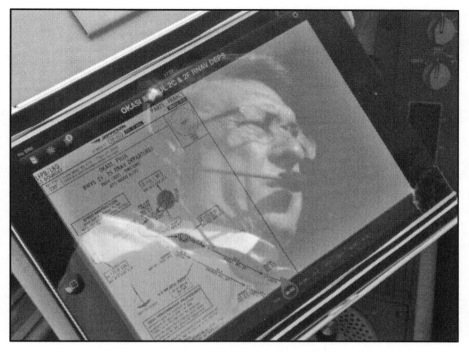

The Lemon Pie Club is looking forward to using iPads for navigation - once approval is granted

Never to be found?

"An airliner has been lost from radar and all radio contact including transponder and ACARS ceased simultaneously". This was approximately the first report of the disappearance of the Malaysian B777 airliner which reached us all around the world. On the face of it, I am sure we all thought the same thing. *A sudden, catastrophic, structural failure of the airframe at cruising altitude.* This could be the only cause for such an instant and permanent loss of all comms. It was only later that we all started to become aware that this was not a "usual" aviation disaster.

+   +   +

These past weeks we have lived through the greatest aviation mystery of all time. Although sharing some similarities with the loss of Air France 447 in the Atlantic Ocean back in 2009, the disappearance of flight MH370 has confounded all the experts from day one. At least in the case of AF447, they knew approximately where to look and very soon after the airliner went missing they found floating wreckage including bodies which assisted in the determination of the most likely location where the aircraft entered the sea and broke up. Additionally from the last ACARS transmission, the BEA (French equivalent of the UK AAIB) could define that the aircraft could not have flown more than 40 nm from this position, taking into account predicted flightpath etc. Eventually the major remains of the AF447 hull was discovered at 13,100 feet deep by sideways looking sonar which picked it up on a flat part of the ocean floor.

In MH370's case, if the airliner really is in the part of the Southern Ocean where the teams have concentrated their search, then the location is even deeper by possibly another 2,000 feet and the underwater topography has been described as similar to the Himalayas. It has to be said there is much less likelihood of anything being found by the present range of robot submarines with their advanced sonar systems, even if they can get down to these depths.

Perhaps one of the most incredible aspects of the search for the Air France aircraft was the employment of Bayesian Mathematical probability principles to predict the most likely area where the crash site could have occurred. Even though the BEA were working on a primary search zone of radius 40nm, this was still a huge piece of ocean. The statisticians at Metron (US company) were asked to use Bayes' law** to re-examine all the known data and search results thus far and to guide the search teams in the right direction. Interestingly, during the first round of calculations and analysis of the search to date, the Metron team assumed (like everyone else) that the Flight Data Recorder pingers were still operational and transmitting during the period when the initial passive acoustic search was carried out.

The main focus (like this time with MH370), had been on the battery life of the radio beacon transmitter – 30 days plus or minus a few. This meant that they discounted a large area which had been 'swept' by the towed array passive sonar listening devices. It was another year later, when the BEA asked for a review, that the team started again from scratch and this time challenged all the previous assumptions. "If" the ELT location devices on the FDR/CVR had NOT been working when that area was searched, then that would change the picture completely. Indeed this was the case and within a week of a new search being carried out, the wreckage was found.

+   +   +

So much for the brilliance of great minds and the application of scientific process. One of the least attractive aspects of the greatest aviation mystery of all time has been the deplorable standard of journalistic reporting. Without doubt the worst example of this has been the US news channel CNN with their consistent sensationalist and insensitive broadcasts throughout the search for the aircraft. They seemed to have had a deliberate policy to go after the commercial 'ratings' by trying to attract as many viewers to the channel as possible, culminating in widespread condemnation from all sides.

The caption on one of their *"inside a real flightdeck B777 simulator"* pieces was totally puerile. Perhaps you have seen it already? Underneath the visual images from a B777 flightdeck with supposed expert aviators giving their opinions, was the wording, *"DEVELOPING STORY:* BOEING 777 WILL STRUGGLE TO MAINTAIN ALTITUDE ONCE THE FUEL TANKS ARE EMPTY". Unbelievably dumb! Do they really think stuff like this can be classified as "News"?

That being said however, the reality is that the authorities do not know how long the fuel lasted and when it was exhausted, what altitude the aircraft was at. The gliding range from 37,000 feet is going to be huge compared to that of an airliner at 10,000 feet when the tanks run dry.

+   +   +

The human cost cannot be trivialised in any way. Seriously, there can be hardly anything more heartbreaking than waiting at an airport in joyful anticipation of being shortly reunited with loved members of your family or friends, only to find "INDEFINITE DELAY" on the arrivals board next to their flight number, shortly before being taken aside by airline officials who explain the flight has vanished and assumed to have been lost. When this loss is compounded by inadequate standards of journalism combined with apparent incompetence on behalf of the authorities, the situation is worse for all concerned. Agreed, they all picked up their game later on in the story, but the first days and weeks were atrocious.

One thing's for sure, we can expect to see several changes to the ways in which our industry 'tracks' the airliners. The financial cost of the search must have exceeded a billion US dollars already, even when you discount some of the military involvement because these resources could be said to have been already funded regardless. This is from the viewpoint that the men and materiel would have been 'on exercise' if not actively involved in the search for a missing passenger jet.

For example, the current battery life of 30 days +/- for the location devices is clearly not enough. Also, flightdeck continuous video recording is possibly being considered and this in conjunction with CVR tapes which do not self erase after so many minutes. Even if this CVR is ever found, it is quite possibly not going to be of material assistance to the investigation team if the last 'x' minutes of the 'flight' of MH370 was conducted in silence for whatever reason. Finally, the technology is currently available to ensure that every airliner is fitted with a tracking device which can be 'watched' continuously by satellites such that there is no place to hide on the surface of the earth. It goes without saying that the control of these devices would be out of reach of anyone onboard the aircraft.

+   +   +

On BBC Radio 4 in the UK last week, there was a very interesting piece of radio journalism which included an interview with one of the chief statisticians from Metron. The lady described the entire search for AF447 methodically and in an articulate way such that even those of us without an appreciation of higher Mathematics could understand the principles.

In fact it was completely fascinating to listen to an expert in the field who had the gift for facilitating the comprehension of the listener. The saddest part of the whole item however was when she was asked if she thought that the location of MH370 would ever be discovered. She paused, summarised the major factors involved and said that "No", in her opinion, the aircraft would "never be found". A sobering thought indeed.

PS. We should all say a prayer for the passengers and crew of flight 370. Until the cause is known, (and it may never be) there but for the grace of God go all of us.
**Thomas Bayes, (1701-1761). Mathematician and Clergyman, son of a Presbyterian Minister.

It is always reassuring to have a fighter escort when flying troops for HM Govt.

'Incoming choppers' – The Dog's Bed

The Dog's Bed...

(No, not the Dog House. That is something entirely different).

There is an old saying in our profession, "Never follow the airline with your house". Although the origin of this expression is not clear, the meaning is quite easy to define. It stems from the uncertainty of the future in the airline industry. What has happened many times in the past is that you start working for a company and then the employment circumstances change, such that they require you to move from your original airport where you were based to another one possibly a long way from where you call "home".

It is tempting thereafter to sell the house and move the family to the new base airport so that the commuting time (by ground transportation) is reduced. Unfortunately what often occurs within the charter airline world is that the airline goes bust, ceases operations and you are left in a city where you didn't want to live particularly and without a job to boot. The situation is made worse if your nearest and dearest has given up his/her job to be with you...

Of course we should not be surprised about the peripatetic nature of our job, after all we do work in the 'travel' industry so the clue is in the name, but we all still need somewhere to call home. In fact regardless of occupation (or even lack of it) 'home' is important to everyone. To paraphrase many clichés, there really is "no place like it*"; it's "where the heart is"; John Denver would be taken there via "Country Roads"; Capt James T. Kirk of Starship Enterprise might say "Mister Sulu lay a course for" it; ET was always trying to phone there and websites always have a page for it. In my own case, I have lost count of the number of times after arriving home from a journey halfway round the planet; I have collapsed into bed saying to my wife, "have I ever told you how much I *love* our home?"

I think it is only when you are forced to leave home that you really appreciate the value of what most people with normal jobs can take for granted. Of course they will often say they envy us 'travellers' who seem to be on a jolly for much of our lives, but there is an old saying which states that "every day you spend in a hotel... that day will never come again in your life..." and that is a really sobering thought when you consider it.

I recall a very long trip once when our crew had been away for many days, which seemed like weeks and we were all moaning about the length of time away from our loved ones. The final flight for us was a military trooping flight from somewhere very hot and dusty in the Middle East back to the UK and we were waiting for our 'passengers' to arrive. The clock ticked by and the aircraft was fully prepared. We were all fuelled up and ready to go, with all of our flight planning completed. Of course, as a commercial airline crew just having reported for duty, we all looked immaculate in our uniforms with gold stripes, bright white shirts and blouses. As the OAT was 40 degrees plus, we made the most of the air-conditioning in the cabin of the B767. Looking out from the windows of the flightdeck high above the military apron, drab sand coloured vehicles were everywhere.

Similarly dressed personnel were all sweating in the heat of a desert afternoon to load the cargo holds of military transport aircraft nearby – it was clear they were working as a closely co-ordinated team. Still there was no sign of our passengers, of which there should be over 200, all ranks. We had yet another brew of tea and chatted together with the on duty military dispatchers. Finally they perked up and said that word had been received the pax were inbound to the airbase.

Soon in a scene reminiscent of many war movies, there were several incoming helicopters, large ones with two rotors, Chinooks. As the huge thundering beasts settled onto the concrete in clouds of hot choking dust, men and women in dusty desert camouflage uniforms emerged and began to form into groups with huge amounts of baggage, body armour, weapons etc. There was more waiting for us as they were marshalled to areas to hand over weapons and ammunition then they were finally ready for boarding.

As they climbed the steps to the airliner cabin and the cool air-conditioned, civilised surroundings you could see the fatigue in their faces. Coming straight from the "Theatre of Operations" – otherwise known as a war zone, the strain of living in those conditions for weeks on end was very clear. Tired smiles from dirty faces met our impeccably dressed flight attendants with their cheerful "Welcome aboard" greetings and I noticed from my position in the forward galley that the aisle carpet was turning into a kind of beige colour with the sand from the boots of two hundred plus soldiers.

With all the able bodied passengers onboard, we now had to wait for two stretcher cases to arrive - they came in on a separate helicopter. Myself and the other pilots completed our departure briefing now and sat patiently in the cockpit while outside we could observe the medical personnel lifting the stretchers from the 'cab' into a camouflaged ambulance for the short ride across to our ship. The expertise, tenderness and care with which the medics lifted and carried the badly injured - with all their Intravenous drips and paraphernalia, was extremely moving. 'In safe hands', is a good way to describe the situation of the wounded soldiers. These were the lucky ones, we knew all too well from the TV that many more of their comrades had not been so lucky...

The DAMO (Duty Air Movements Officer) came into the flightdeck one final time to shake hands and get the final paperwork and I could see from the overhead panel that only the left forward door remained open – all cargo holds closed. Now... we were ready for the 'Home Run'. The Senior Flight Attendant came in and I confirmed to her the flight-time. She replied "two hundred and twenty one passengers onboard Captain, am I clear to close up?" I could see from her palid face she was not her usual cheery self. It was the first time she had seen them come straight from the front line and it was a shock. I tried to keep my voice steady as I said, "Yes close up please... *we're on our way Home".*

+   +   +

Over the years I suppose my kids have become accustomed to their Dad saying some pretty odd things. Like the time when they were around 7 or 8 years old and were asking me what I thought they should 'collect'? Did I think stamps or butterflies would be better? I replied *"You should try to collect pound coins like your father!"* So when it comes to talking about home and when you think about how often we have travelled and how far, it will come as no surprise that we have some in-family sayings on this subject also. Sci-fi movie aficionados may be familiar with the script of the film Blade Runner, when J.F. Sebastian arrives home and his two pet androids greet him at the door with *******"Home again, home again, Jiggity-Jig".*

I am not sure why, but I have often said this myself as I pull up outside our house in the car and apply the parking brake – it's an old family joke with the kids. A few years ago when we first moved to Athens in Greece, our children were having a difficult time adjusting to their new environment and they were still mentally thinking of the UK as their 'home' - this despite the fact that we had cut our ties there and sold the family house. Our move abroad was semi-permanent. One time when I did my Blade Runner impersonation in the car after shutting down outside our villa next to the beach, I was met with a chorus of, "NO DAD! This is NOT our HOME!"

I was taken aback by their strength of feeling on the subject and searched for a way to help them psychologically adjust to our airborne Gypsy lifestyle. I looked into their young faces and their eyes told me they really needed something to believe in, something tangible; a warm positive way of thinking about where we all lived together.

I said slowly, "Look guys. It's not places, houses or buildings which are important. People are important – the family is most important to us. You have to think of it this way... our HOME is where the dog's bed is and that's it, okay?"

They both nodded in assent, they finally understood – we were home.

* "There's no place like home" – Dorothy in Wizard of Oz..
**The origin of "Home again, home again Jiggity-Jig" is actually even older than the 1982 film. It was part of a Mother Goose nursery rhyme, "To market to market, to buy a fat pig, home again, home again, jiggety-jig.

There really is no place like Home – ask these three...

Nibbled to Death by Ducks.

(Depending on where you work, it happens a lot).

At 2pm in the afternoon, the outside air temperature was close to 40 degrees Celsius and the walkround had been an unpleasant experience; added to which there was a light breeze which brought with it plenty of hot dust from the surrounding desert, you could almost taste it in the air. Djibouti is not a great place from an aviator's perspective and if you look at a map of Africa, you can find it surrounded by Yemen, Ethiopia, Somalia and Eritrea. Come to think of it... maybe Djibouti ain't that bad a place after all? But one thing's for sure, it is not a good place to be sick...

+ + +

The Boeing 757 is a wonderful aircraft and the one which we are flying today is typical of the type. She has quite a high number of hours and cycles, but is well maintained with only a few acceptable deferred defects (ADDs) which we already know about and that are recorded in the Techlog. Our mission today is flying on behalf of another carrier from Djibouti to Paris Charles-de-Gaulle. We are predicted to have a full load of passengers and the flight time means that we are right on the limits with regard to the aircraft range. Well, we would know exactly how close to the limits if we were able to view the actual computer flight plan for the flight, but the Operations department of the airline (based in London) have been having 'Comms difficulties'. So we are working a little bit in the dark out here so very far from home. I know that it is likely there will be a headwind over most of the route to Paris and judging by our flight on the way down here two days ago, it is going to be a close run thing to get a non-stop flight out of it...

Of course it has been marketed and ticketed by the airline as a single sector even though sometimes due to adverse jet streams and strong headwinds, there is no way to do it without a fuel stop. But as I explained to my newly joined First Officer under training, "Nobody wants a fuel stop, not the airline, the charterer, the passengers, nor indeed the crew... so you see there is always mounting pressure on us, the pilots, to 'get it there in a one-er'....which would not be quite so bad, except that *we cannot even see the bloody flightplan!"*

I think he could probably tell my stress levels were somewhat raised even before we operated a flight which was at the limits of the range of the aircraft with forecast poor weather conditions on arrival. He looked at me in a diplomatic way across the cockpit, but I could tell he really wasn't feeling the same as me. He had on a new shirt, possibly brand new and a company tie without any crewfood stains and his bright shiny gold wings above his breast pocket positively gleamed. Yes he looked brand new and he was *loving this job,* you could just tell. The B757 will only hold 34,200 kgs of usable fuel with full tanks and in the absence of a flightplan, we asked the refueller to fill up to 30,000 kgs and hold. Not an uncommon thing to do when you are under pressure, but you always have to keep an eye on the fuel truck to make sure he doesn't wander off to another aircraft. Or, as we have seen in the past, he fills up to 30,000 kgs, then disconnects and drives off anyway, thinking his job is done after misunderstanding the message to hold on for the final fuel figure.

We study the weather again for Paris – it's not looking so rosy for the time of our arrival, early evening with wintry showers and low cloud forecast, combined with poor visibility. *A small duck is chewing at my ankle and I rub it absent-mindedly.* The alternate airports are all Parisian too, so the forecast is similar. Unfortunately I am aware that our particular charter airline cannot afford to unnecessarily consider alternate airports at a greater distance, with possibly much improved weather forecasts as they are so keen to get a direct flight. We are legal and it is safe enough, especially in the light of the fact that there are so many airports enroute where we could divert to in the event that Paris went below our IFR limits for landing. We need a minimum of 200 feet cloudbase above the runway plus a minimum visibility of 550 metres to complete our ILS approach – at the moment the forecast has got both of them. We are not Low Visibility Operations approved yet.

The flightplan arrives at the aircraft, "Hurrah!" I announce and then regret my enthusiasm immediately as I see that the *minimum* fuel required to complete the flight with IFR reserves... is 34,000 kgs! Ouch! Another duck nibbles at my elbow as I go down to ask the refueller to carry on fuelling till it stops. I used to joke when people asked me if we airline pilots possessed any extra special linguistic skills as we travelled so much. I often replied, "No. But we can say *'Fill Her Up'* in 23 languages!" Shortly afterwards we start the passenger boarding.

As the mass of passengers stream across the concrete towards the steps up to the cabin, it is clear they have no idea about how much overhead locker space we don't have! They seemed to be carrying everything but the kitchen sink, although there were one or two exceptionally large, heavy parcels which actually might have contained washbasins... So the boarding process is the usual chaos and also as usual I am called upon to leave the relative calm and sanity of the flightdeck to adjudicate in the inevitable argument which ensues between our Senior Stewardess and various passengers who cannot possibly allow their precious bundles of 'stuff' wrapped in brightly coloured stripy rags to be consigned to the cargo hold.

Fortunately the uniform does the trick with the Senior Stewardess quite firmly saying "If the Captain says No! Then it's NO!" While I stand next to her and try to look quietly authoritative. It is at this point when she mentions the sick Cabin Crew Member. My ankle has started itching again, as she describes the girl's symptoms and her medical history. I say to the Senior, "When did you know about this?" and she replies,

"Well she told me last night, but she won't go off sick here... She begged me to keep it quiet; she just wants to get home". We both looked around at the chaos in the cabin among the passengers with everyone talking at once, and then outside at the low-lying shanty town nearby with very little facilities and now here was the refueller who came up the steps with a semi-destroyed clipboard and a broken biro for me to sign for the fuel. I asked him how much fuel he got into the tanks and he assured me that he carried on until the valves tripped – no doubt about it we were right up to the gunwales. Or as I once heard it described by an American, *"We're up to our Ass in Gas!"* The only problem was the Specific Gravity duck, which had been nibbling away at me for the past couple of hours ever since I thought about it.

With the high OAT we would probably have such a low S.G. on the fuel that we would be lucky to get the required mass... The *litreage* would be there but not the kilogrammes. And so it proved when I re-entered the flightdeck and saw that we had only 33,100 kgs on the fuel gauges, "Nearly a tonne short – damn it!" I muttered and then explained to my young starry eyed colleague that we could not get any more *weight* of fuel in as the tanks were full due to the high ambient temperature. He nodded as if he understood, but I didn't see him offer any solution. In fact there was no solution; here we were stuck between a rock and a hard-place. We made the loadsheet and performance calculations and we were predictably at maximum takeoff weight and we would need to use full takeoff thrust to get airborne, just one more little duck...

The big plus point as I saw it, was that there was a light sea-breeze blowing now straight down Runway 09 which pointed out to sea. If we did 'lose' an engine on takeoff at least there were no obstacles in the Gulf of Tadjoura to avoid as our rate of climb would be pitifully slow. Just a few whaleshark fins sticking up above the waves. Add to that the fact that the runway was two miles long - mind you it needed to be.

Now we were getting close to time of departure and it looked like the baggage loading was nearing completion. I went out through the cabin to check and the Senior Stewardess grabbed me as I went past. "Captain, would you have look at this gentleman please, I think he is drunk...." *This is certainly a good day for ducks.* He was an old African guy with very few teeth and bad breath. I got the handling agent to translate for me as I talked to him.

It seemed that he was not entirely coherent even in French and his accent was so strong I could not follow all of what he told the representative. He strenuously denied being intoxicated however and it seemed that maybe this was his relatively normal state. His eyes were red rimmed and rheumy, they also looked a little glazed, but he did not appear aggressive in any way. I asked the Senior what she wanted to do and said that I didn't think he really was drunk, that I thought this was how he always was. Eventually she agreed and we allowed him to take his seat among the rest of the passengers, almost 230 of them.

I went to the rear galley and found Jane the Cabin Crew Member who had said she wasn't well. She was stood to one side of the melee and was letting her more able colleagues deal with all the challenges of boarding. She looked very pale and her young face looked drawn. I didn't want to pry into her condition, which had been described to me as 'women's troubles' by the Senior, but at the same time I knew I had a duty as the aircraft commander to ensure that everyone was fit to fly, and that meant passengers AND crew. Very gently I told her this and asked her if she really felt fit to fly tonight? It was going to be a long flight and even when we arrived in Paris, we were not home yet as there was another sector to London.

She told me that she had been discharged from hospital in the UK only a few days prior to the flight down to Djibouti. She had felt well enough then to operate the flight, but since arriving in the hotel 48 hours before, she had been losing blood and had abdominal pain. That being said she assured me that she would be okay for this flight and that the Senior said she could rest as much as she wanted. This little duck was a tough one, but had not *really* started nibbling yet. What to do...? I told her that if she changed her mind in the next 30 minutes before departure, we could offload her back to the hotel and a doctor, but she was not keen on that idea. There are some places in the world where you wouldn't mind being ill, but the horn of Africa is not one of them — I understood. She was lucid and appeared quite in control of herself. Also she was one of our crew, one of us; nobody wants to leave a member of the team behind. "Okay, don't worry Jane, we'll look after you. Come and rest up in the cockpit during the flight whenever you need to with the Senior's permission", were my parting words.

Back in the flightdeck and we could see the holds were closed, I checked again the fuel gauges and winced, they were now reading 32,900 as the APU had burned through a couple of hundred kilos to keep the air-conditioning packs running at full cold to cool the cabin. The last bits of paperwork were handed off and handshakes all round with the chief of the groundstaff and then the Senior came in to confirm the headcount — she looked worn out already. "Am I okay to close the doors Captain? And what did you reckon to Jane?"
I replied, "Jane says she's okay to fly, so we have to take her word for it, but she's welcome to sit in here during the night to rest if you're fine with that. Yes close up please, flight time is just under 8 hours".

I made a brief Welcome Aboard PA to the cabin and then called for "the before-start checklist". I looked at the clock, nearly an hour late according to the schedule, but we were finally on our way. Rolls Royce RB211 engines are a delight to use on the Boeing 757 and these two were no exception as they spooled up without a problem and settled down at idle. We waved away the chocks and started taxiing for Runway 09 — straight away you could tell she was heavy as the steering tiller was resistive and lots of power was needed to get her rolling forward.

The takeoff run seemed to take an age before I heard the call of "Vee-One...Rotate!" and I could start unsticking the nosegear from the runway. Nearly five seconds later and the maingear was airborne and shortly after the end of the runway shot beneath our wings as we climbed away and I called "GEAR-UP!" in a very loud voice. Those engines didn't miss a beat and they were running quite close to their maximum temperatures too. It was a blessed relief as we climbed higher and higher turning north and west as we did so. In the haze, the Red Sea stretched away ahead of us as we passed into the higher flight levels and reached our cruising altitude. Before long the sun was going down towards the horizon on our left-hand side with a beautiful crimson desert sunset for all to see.

In the cabin, the crew were hard at work with their service and I had already been informed that the passengers from Djibouti had a reputation for being as demanding as they come. In the quiet of the flightdeck we were not expecting any great attention until much later so we were surprised when another little duck called on the cabin interphone – it was the Senior's voice. "Captain, it's Jane. She's fainted in the back galley, I will let you know how she is in a few minutes I'm just going down the back..." It was certainly an anxious few minutes while we waited for another call. In the meantime we looked at all the alternatives. Do we turn back to Djibouti? Or divert to an airport in Saudi Arabia? I knew that either of these options would not be ideal and would lead to a major problem for the airline. We would not be allowed to leave Saudi again that night, then the crew would go out of hours and... *oh! Too many ducks to count here.* On the left (West) of the Red Sea, there really is nowhere to go to with any decent medical facilities and an airport that can take a 757 at short notice. Asmara had gone past the wing sometime ago and that did not appeal. There was nothing now until Cairo really.

Bong! The chime of the cabin call broke our discussion. "Captain, can I bring her in? She's here in the forward galley, she's conscious, but she needs to rest". They opened the flightdeck door and nearly carried Jane in and lowered her gently onto the lower of the two observer jumpseats behind the First Officer. Her face looked grey and her eyes were half closed with pain, she was holding her tummy and they brought blankets and pillows for her. *This duck is going to chew my flippin' leg off...* I thought to myself as I reviewed our possible options yet again – *not good, not good at all.*

I handed over control to the FO who already had the radio and left my seat and bent down near to Jane, the Senior was still there. I took her pulse, it was rapid, around 110 per minute, but you would expect that if she was in pain. "Can you please make a PA for a Doctor onboard?" I asked the Senior and she exited to the cabin, returning only a few minutes later with a negative. Jane was conscious and in pain, but she was still lucid and gave sensible answers to direct questions. I established that her gynaecological operation had not been a major one, but that she had undergone a D&C procedure. She felt that she had lost a lot of blood, but that this was now stopped while she was resting. We made her as comfortable as possible and I went back to my seat.

We called Operations in London on the long-range HF with a phonepatch via Stockholm Radio. The line was quite good and we appraised them of our situation and asked them to be sure to pass it on to the duty management pilot. At the same time we asked for an update on the Paris weather – it was not wonderful, but was no worse than the lousy forecast in the first place, this duck was being quiet for the moment. Then we contacted the airline medical advice centre and discussed it all with them. They were entirely non-committal as I described the situation and her signs and symptoms – I swore I could hear the sound of creaking fence timber in the background static of the radio. Here was a Doctor who not going to make a decision for us, "Well, it's up to you really Captain..." was all he could say – *another little hungry duck Doc, thanks.*

We went back to our Ops centre on HF. They were a lot more switched on now as they realised the gravity of our position and they had the Director Flight Operations (DFO) on the line listening to the transmissions on the wall speaker (we were high-tech in those days eh?) Between us we decided to continue while Jane was conscious and we could monitor her pain and rate of bleeding. If she slipped unconscious or if her condition made a rapid deterioration then we would immediately divert to the nearest suitable airfield in whichever country that happened to be. Fortunately the more North and West we flew, the better the options became. In the meantime Ops would inform the handling agents in Paris who would have a Paramedic Team with an ambulance ready to meet us on arrival at the parking gate. They would be advised that we had a very ill crew member who needed immediate transfer to hospital and that she would require either a stretcher or wheelchair to leave the aircraft. *If there's one city in the world where you wouldn't mind being sick, it's Paris.*

We also briefed the Senior that she should be ready to despatch one of the other Cabin Crew who spoke French to disembark with Jane at the same time so she would be well looked after all the way to hospital. Of course Jane knew nothing of these arrangements and whenever I spoke to her through the night she was keen for me to know that her Mum and Dad would come to the airport in London to pick her up and "these are their mobile numbers" etc, etc. It was a very long night as we constantly monitored our patient on the jumpseat, monitored the weather in Paris, monitored the fuel on arrival which was tight, but not disastrously low. In between playing doctors and nurses, we managed to make a bit of fuel with a better cruising level and some shortcuts across the nightskies of Europe. Egypt came and went, then Greece. Albania, Croatia, Austria all went past the window and we kept listening to the ATIS weather reports for all the airports along the way.

Jane snoozed a little which had me really worried and I woke her up a few times to check she was not really out for the count. I had to lie to her and assure her that we would get her home to London as soon as we could, but I knew that we could not take that chance. There were times when I thought we would have to commence an immediate diversion and take our chances with the medical care on arrival, but finally we were closer to top of descent into Charles-de-Gaulle than anywhere else. The latest weather? It was snowing... We had a little fuel to spare, but not much. This situation was not helped by the Paris controllers taking us round the North side of the airport for the Easterly runway at lower than desired altitudes.

Now we had engine anti-ice on and the latest weather report was giving 1000 metres in moderate snow showers – this was *one little duck that really wouldn't let go* and I felt my trouser leg being tugged this way and that. Eventually we were on finals and I could see we were going to make it *provided* we got visual at decision altitude. If we had to go around, then we would get an immediate diversion to Orly, there would be no second approach at De-Gaulle. That would be a duck too far. "One hundred above..." came the call from my right and I could still see nothing but white outside, then it cleared, "Decide...?" he called and I replied in a loud voice "VISUAL... LANDING!"

A filthy night in Paris, with less fuel than we would have liked, but still legal, we taxied in quickly and to our intense relief there was the medical crew waiting for us on the gate, blue flashing lights making pretty patterns amid the falling snowflakes. We shutdown and got the doors open in double-quick time, the Doctor came straight onboard and took care of her and the rest of the team were just as efficient. I explained to her carefully and gently what was going to happen and assured her that the other Cabin Crew Member would stay with her all the way. She had Euros, fluent French and the crewbags.

Jane started to cry as I told her and I said I was so sorry for having to lie to her, but we just couldn't take the risk of flying her on to London. I put my arms round her and now I was crying too, *this will never do.* "You'll be fine, don't worry, I'm SO sorry..."

Maybe it was the last 6 hours of intense stress and the fact that we had finally made it and now we knew she would be safe. She was one of our team and we would miss her. Or maybe one of the little ducks had finally found a way to really inflict some pain.

PS. Jane (not her real name) made a full recovery and I got a very nice thank you letter from her Mum.

Author with Captain Pat Cullen, FO Fahad Shaban and VVIP

View from the office window on a nice day. B767 at cruising altitude.

Flying with an Incompetent Captain Under Training.

(At times, it seemed like Head Office sent all of their problem pilots to fly with me)

It was a rather cold, dark Friday morning in February when I awoke and I had been rostered to fly a Geneva then a Belfast flight from East Midlands. If I had known then what the day had in store for me later, I really would have been better off staying in bed. The drive to the airport was uneventful and the forecast on the radio was for a fine day later on which was encouraging – clear skies and light winds, with plenty of sunshine in the afternoon. *'Well at least the weather won't be a problem today'*, I thought idly to myself as I locked the car and walked over to the base office.

As usual, I was not aware who the other pilot was until I actually entered the briefing room to check-in on the computer. Marian was already there and as she was the only pilot in the room and the Geneva was the only departure so early, I assumed it was her. She was a slim figure, in a Captain's uniform, with a rather elegant cravat instead of a tie which she wore with her white shirt. I estimated her age as being early 40's. She had quite a pronounced French accent which I noted as we greeted each other.

It's funny, but I quite like working with women, and I find it fascinating as to why they want to fly aeroplanes. I have flown airliners with a significant number of them in the past and I think the vast majority of them are very, very good indeed. They have got to be good to get where they are I reckon as the world of "the flightdeck" is very much a male dominated arena. In fact of course there is still much resentment from some of the more senior members of the profession and I can clearly recall one of my old Captains in years gone by commenting, *"If God had meant women to fly, he would have painted the sky PINK!"* Of course at that time, I was a very junior co-pilot, so I did not demur, but muttered encouraging words in agreement, although internally I found myself in deep disagreement.
"Erm, yes Skip, right you are then......... I'll get some weather shall I?" I said, trying to change the subject and glad that our conversation could be heard by no-one except the electronic CVR.

My own outlook on the fairer sex in the workplace is undoubtedly coloured by the experience of growing up in a family with a working mother who was also a professional in a male dominated field – Medicine. If having a working mum wasn't enough to tune me in to the idea of women in the workplace, my first job was on Saturdays in one of the big UK retail stores where I was surrounded by female employees. This early formative experience was then topped off by my entry into the Nursing Profession at the age of 18, where yet again I was surrounded by working women until I left at the age of 25, nearly 8 years later.

So when it comes to working with women, I can honestly say that I do not have a hang-up about it. Today was going to be a little different however, because I was just about to meet a woman who was out of her depth, although I didn't know it at the time. *"Good morning, you must be Marian?"* I said shaking hands with my new colleague and trainee. *"My name is James and I am your Training Captain today"*. We then went through the brief for the flight and I checked Marian's training file. I noted that she appeared to have been making some "slow progress" during her early line training sectors, but there was nothing noted to warn me that she was anything other than a normal trainee. We talked briefly about her former career prior to joining the company and I was pleased to note that she had a couple of thousand hours in command of BAe146 aircraft. It was on the strength of this experience it seemed that she had been given a Direct Entry Command to the airline by the recruitment team.

I emphasised to her that she should act as the Captain throughout the planned four sectors, with the caveat that I was the actual aircraft Commander, even though I was sat in the seat normally occupied by her co-pilot. I assured her that I would try to operate as a competent First Officer. I am always conscious of the fact that enough challenges will usually appear along the way in the course of a normal flight without having to invent problems for the trainee. Also it is vital to remember that these flights are, to all intents and purposes, ordinary line flights with passengers on board. It is therefore not possible, nor is it expected, to introduce artificial 'system failures' to assess a trainee's 'failure management skills' and I was at pains to point this out. Failure management can easily be assessed in the Simulator and that is one of the reasons we have the Sim.

We had a good scan through the weather forecast for the flights and I noted that the weather in Geneva was pretty foggy at first with low cloud. There was the possibility of a Low Visibility instrument approach being required, so I was not surprised when she mentioned casually, "But we can take a bit of fuel extra I think?" The Computer Flight Plan fuel recommendation was 6400kgs as a minimum and it would have been normal to carry perhaps another 1500kgs to allow for half an hour going round in circles while waiting our turn for the Low Vis approach, so a figure of 8 tonnes would not have been unreasonable as a ramp fuel. "How much fuel would you like to put on Captain?" I asked. She responded immediately with, "Ten tonnes for the ramp!" This pronounced in a very confident tone of voice.

I replied that maybe this would be a little excessive, even considering that a Low Vis approach may be required at Geneva and gently suggested that she could reduce the figure to prevent carrying unnecessary weight. Of course it always costs more fuel to carry extra fuel which is why accurate flight planning combined with sensible decision making are essential to an efficient operation. We did not encourage Captains to just make arbitrary decisions about fuel loading, but to give it careful consideration. It seemed to me that she picked the figure of ten tonnes out of thin air. There are times when fuel is so expensive at destination that it becomes worthwhile carrying the extra gas to come home again if you can – this is called tankering fuel. It transpired that she believed we tankered fuel to Geneva from East Midlands – I told her this was not the case.

Later on, during the return sector – Marian asked me why we tankered fuel at all and I then explained that it was due to the fact that the cost of the fuel varied at each airport. I thought it was a strange question for a Captain to ask and I was not entirely convinced that she really understood the reasons why we tankered, especially after she replied, "Oh? I just thought it was expensive everywhere!" We then completed our interactive briefing with the cabin crew and informed the Senior Cabin Crew member to refer to Marian as the Captain at all times and to ignore me sat in the First Officer's seat. Having passed all of the fuel and loading figures to the load controllers by telephone, we made our way airside to the ramp. The aircraft had been in maintenance overnight and was 15 minutes late being towed out, although this had no bearing upon events in the flightdeck that were to follow.

Prior to my doing the external checks on the aeroplane, we entered the flightdeck together and I mentioned that it was customary for the flying pilot (PF) to set up the Inertial Reference System for navigation. (The IRSs need to be programmed with Lat and Long positions and then take 10 minutes for a full align before the aircraft can be moved. Any movement before that period has elapsed means the whole alignment process must begin again.

It became apparent, that Marian didn't have the first idea about IRS alignment, which was something of a concern to me, as she had only recently completed her groundschool course as part of her training on the B737. I reassured her, "Don't worry I'll set them up for you this time", as I whizzed through the switches and then popped down the steps to do the walkround. By this time my senses were telling me that something was amiss here. I was thinking to myself, *'Alright, it's very early in the morning and we're not all bright eyed and bushy tailed first thing, but setting the IRSs up with the current Lat/Long position is not exactly rocket science – especially when the trainee has just finished the theory course......'*

I noted from speaking to the engineers on the walkround outside that there were no technical defects with the aircraft. During this time, Marian was onboard in the flightdeck, setting up the flight instruments and navigational aids ready for her departure – she would be the operating (flying) pilot on the first sector to Geneva.

After finishing the walkround outside, I re-entered the flightdeck and busied myself with the usual duties of the First Officer and prepared my half of the cockpit ready for flight. By now however, I was keeping half an eye on what 'Madame Captain' was doing and noticed that she appeared to be very slow with loading the flightplan route into the Flight Management Computer (FMC). While engrossed in this task, she seemed oblivious to all else which was going on around us. The aircraft was being refuelled at the same time as passengers were boarding and the engineers were busy trying to catch up on the paperwork to certify all the work they had done while in the hangar overnight. They still had the aircraft's Techlog which we hadn't yet seen.

There was further evidence of Marian's detachment from the scene when the Senior Cabin Crew Member popped his head through the flightdeck door and stated that all the passengers were onboard and could he close the doors? Without reference to me and before I could intervene, she imperiously gave a wave of her hand and asserted, "Yes you may close". At this time I could just see the engineer making his way towards us across the apron with the Techlog under his arm. His rush up the steps prevented the Senior from retracting the airstairs and he arrived at the flightdeck door in a bit of a huff. Of course, you could see it from his point of view. The boys had been slogging their guts out all night in the hangar doing essential maintenance on our aircraft and we then tried to repay their efforts by leaving without even a sniff of the Techlog – a legal document which the Captain must sign prior to flight. He was not a happy bunny.

As Commander of the aircraft, I reviewed the Techlog pages and showed them to Marian, at the same time I confirmed the fuel and oil state then signed the top sheet, gave the copies to the engineer with humble thanks and we were off. "Now... may I close the doors?" said the Senior with a quizzical look, having witnessed the disgruntled engineer departing the flightdeck muttering under his breath. This time I noticed he was asking me directly. "Yes indeed you may close up, thank you", I replied. I wondered to myself what sort of Captain tried to depart an airliner that has been in the hangar all night without checking the technical status with the Techlog – *'Ah well, perhaps it's just preflight nerves'* I thought.

We then proceeded through the briefing for the flight (including a full emergency brief which covered the potential rejected take-off scenario, which is always accomplished by the left-seat pilot) and went on to the before start/after start checklists. I noted that some of her responses were non-standard, but let them pass, as to interrupt the flow of the checklists at those points would have been time consuming and distracting for her. I distinctly felt that she could not cope with much in the way of distraction as she seemed to be uncomfortable enough as it was. I do recall that her response to the challenge "Speedbrake?" was "Down Detent" however. This was to become significant very shortly.

Just by chance we called for taxi clearance only seconds before a Britannia Airlines B767 and he was instructed to follow us to the holding point for runway 27. It was a little odd however, because Marian taxied the aircraft at a steady 10 knots all the way down the taxiway to the holding point for the runway – this, despite the fact that the ¾ mile of taxiway was straight and clear, (normal speed at this point would be 20 knots). As I had been thinking that maybe she didn't have much spare mental capacity, I declined to mention it, but I bet the Britannia behind us thought it most unusual and wished he'd got taxi clearance earlier.

Approaching the runway we were cleared for takeoff and completed the before takeoff checklists. At about 15 knots and with only 30% N1 on the engines after Marian had advanced the thrust levers, - normally we would see them stabilise at 40% N1 first - she pressed the TOGA button. (The TOGA button engages the autothrottle system and increases the engine power to takeoff setting – commonly around 90% N1). As the thrust levers advanced and the aircraft started to accelerate, the very loud 'Configuration Warning' horn started to sound in the cockpit. This informed us that a system was not set correctly for takeoff and as it obviously wasn't the parking brake, I immediately looked at the flap setting and stabiliser trim; not those so it must be......... *'BLOODY HELL SHE'S NOT REACTING!'* crossed my mind as I looked across and she was sat there with her hands on the controls and a puzzled look on her face, but still apparently intent upon continuing the takeoff.

"STOP!" I shouted and closed the thrust levers smartly and smoothly put the brakes on. I checked the Speedbrake lever and, yes it was just out of its' detent – there was the reason for the Config Warning. I called ATC on the radio to say that we were "Stopping" and then requested a 180 degree turn to backtrack for another attempt at takeoff. I asked Marian to turn the aircraft round as she was the only one with the steering tiller for use on the ground for tight turns. As she did so, I noticed that the autothrottle was still engaged and assisted her to close the advancing thrust levers which were trying to go up to takeoff power again, while at the same time switching off the autothrottle on the Mode Control Panel (MCP).

While in the turn on the runway, I spoke to the passengers, "Ladies and Gentlemen, this is the Captain speaking, apologies for having to stop our takeoff just back there, we had a minor technical problem. This is now resolved and we shall be taking off again in just a couple of minutes. Thank you for your patience". I noticed that my hand was shaking as my finger came off the R/T Transmit button – *this is scary stuff.*

We confirmed that the Speedbrake was now definitely gated and as the rejection had occurred at a relatively low speed (30-40 knots) there were clearly no brake cooling schedule requirements to consider, so we were ready to recommence the takeoff again from the threshold. The Britannia 767 was still sitting there patiently waiting at the holding point – those guys must have been shaking their heads in disbelief at the strange antics of our little 737 this morning. "Sorry about that Britannia, we'll try again shall we" I tried to sound cheerful on the radio, but I felt far from it.

It did occur to me then, that perhaps we could return to the gate and cancel the flight. I felt really frightened about the idea of flying with Marian by now. In reality, she was the only one who had control of the steering on the ground - just one nosewheel steering tiller on the left side of the flightdeck.

There were three factors which prevented me from taking this course of action. Firstly the passengers had all paid to go to Geneva and we were nearly on schedule. Secondly I thought, maybe she will improve, *surely she cannot be this bad for real.* And thirdly, I hadn't really seen enough evidence to cancel a training detail. Yes...... we were going to try another takeoff for Geneva.

The second attempt was fine and although she made some non-standard calls, her actual controlling of the aircraft was okay. Her knowledge of the FMC hadn't got any better when she tried to engage VNAV mode on the autopilot (Vertical Navigation profile from the FMC route) and found it wouldn't play ball. The reason was that we were now passing Flight Level 80 in the climb and there was still a 'hard altitude' in the route at 4000 feet – I showed her where it was and we cancelled it. VNAV would now engage and the climb continued. (Flight Levels in whole thousands of feet, exist above Transition Altitude, which is where all altimeters reference to a Standard Barometric Pressure setting of 1013mbs).

Part of our stock in trade as Airline Pilots is correct adherence to procedures. Standard Operating Procedures (or SOPs as they are universally known) are vitally important in maintaining a safe, *consistently safe,* standard of operation. The SOPs are written down in the operations manuals, which are approved by the regulatory authorities as the way in which public transport flights are to be carried out. The SOPs are so detailed that they even cover the actual words which should be used by pilots while flying together such that each knows what the other is doing or (going to do) at any moment in time on a flight.

These are called the "SOP Calls". They are the way in which the pilots monitor each other and the automatic flight systems while flying. At critical phases of flight (takeoff and landing for example) they are the approved method of communicating between the pilots. For example during the climb or descent with 1000 feet to go to a new altitude as cleared by ATC, the PNF (Pilot Non Flying) would call "One to go!" and the PF would respond "Check!" This is only one example, there are many others and the calls as written down in the SOPs cover every possible phase of flight – both normal and abnormal. Of course each airline is slightly different in the way they write their SOP calls and I distinctly recall that in this airline we had at least 4 complete rewrites of the SOPs in the years I was there.

During the climb out from East Mids, Marian demonstrated her lack of knowledge of company SOP calls to an alarming degree. Either the initial call was incorrect or the response was wrong. On a few occasions she did manage to get the wording right, but it was an unconvincing performance in this respect and well below the standard that we usually expect of pilots flying the line. Due allowance was made for the fact that English was not her first language (in fact she was quite fluent), but this does not account for the fact that she made calls regarding the altimeters, like *"Set QNH"* when she should have been calling *"Set Standard"* in the climb (there is a significant difference). There were many other examples of non-standard calls either because Marian did not understand the need for them or she had not learned them.

Prior to the descent phase into Geneva, I obtained the latest weather reports and airfield data from the Automated Information System on the second VHF radio (commonly known as Box Two). I told her that we should expect a LUSAR 6 Romeo arrival routing with a DINIG transition – this to enable her to properly programme the route in the Flight Management Computer (FMC). I also reminded her that Geneva Air Traffic Controllers had the habit of shortcutting the route for arriving aircraft and that it was common to be placed in the position of being "Hot and High" (too fast on the speed and too high on the descent profile). She said she understood this and gave me her approach brief for the arrival and landing on Geneva's Runway 23.

With regard to "getting the weather" on the second VHF box, it is usual for the PNF to warn the Flying Pilot that they are leaving the ATC frequency in use briefly with the words "Off Box One" or similar, ("Off the Air" Is another) while they devote their concentration to hearing the weather report on the number two VHF radio. Unfortunately during the two sectors that morning, Marian made several gross errors while I was listening on the second box. Usually I only found this out on my return to listening on the ATC frequency to find a debate going on between Air Traffic and Marian about what our flight had really been cleared to do. After a couple of these incidents, I had no confidence in her skill with the radio and always kept one ear open on the air traffic frequency even while being supposedly "Off the Air".

Marian's briefing as PF for the descent and arrival into Geneva was pretty rudimentary, however it covered the basics and I restricted my only input to being that it was likely Geneva Radar would "shortcut us onto finals down the lake". She acknowledged this, but did not take any track miles out of her proposed FMC routing which went a long way up to the Northeast prior to coming back to finals. During the descent, we started to get very high on the profile as Marian was slow to change the autopilot modes – apparently unsure of which descent mode would suit the occasion best. I monitored the distance to run to touchdown versus our altitude carefully as I expected we would get very high at some stage – sure enough Geneva ATC shortened our route.

I hinted that perhaps we were going a little high and fast on the vertical profile, (250 knots on the ASI) and asked her what we could do about it. She looked over at me and hesitated, before saying "Well, we could put the gear down…" I was taken aback at this, as although it was true we were below the limiting speed for lowering the landing gear (Max 270kts) and technically feasible, I knew from experience that the resulting loud noise of dumping the gear above 210kts is very discomfiting for the passengers. "No I don't think we will be doing that", I replied and explained the reason why.

At one stage, we had 38 track miles to the runway, passing 15,000 feet, configured clean with speedbrakes out and at this stage I intervened and asked ATC for more distance to get the height off. (Ideally we would have had more than 45 miles to play with). Marian seemed unaware of the problem and I was certain that had I not made the input, she was so far 'behind the aircraft' we would have ended up with a high, fast, unstable approach that would have ended up in a go-around from low altitude on finals. This I considered an unnecessary training experience. While we were descending at high speed, there were a number of tasks still to do, liaison with the cabin crew to see if the cabin was secure, descent and approach checklists, identifying the radio aids etc. etc. It was a busy time for me as the PNF (Pilot Not Flying) and at the same time, I had my hands full trying to monitor exactly what Marian was doing. She had the habit of deploying the speedbrakes (large drag inducing panels on the top of the wings) without announcing it and then taking her hand off the Speedbrake lever. I reminded her twice to keep her hand on the lever in accordance with SOPs. The 'brakes were still deployed through the initial flap extension, (Flap 1 and then Flap5) and when she called for "Gear Down", I had to prompt her to stow the speedbrakes to prevent airframe buffeting before it became intense.

We were established on finals, correctly configured, "in the slot" as they say at about 4 miles out. The power was still at idle, as we were still decelerating to final approach speed, however I was confident that we would be stable by 500 feet above the ground - just - so was happy for her to continue to land. The landing itself was quite good, with a nicely judged flare at 25 feet and well controlled touchdown. However, she was slow to deploy reversers until prompted and then pulled them straight through to 45% power (N1) even though she had briefed and planned for "idle reverse" on landing as per the Geneva standing orders for noise abatement. As we slowed right down and exited from the runway, I was once again busily employed in the after-landing scan as the First Officer. Marian appeared to be having difficulty deciding which taxiway to follow to our parking area and I think she had trouble visualising exactly where we were - even though we had pre-briefed this while airborne and I had obtained the parking position from the handling agent on the radio. I gave her progressive taxiing guidance from the right-hand seat.

Once we were on the stand with the engines shutdown and had completed the checklists, I took a deep breath. *'Well!....... Now what do I do?'* I thought to myself. As far as I was concerned at this point, Marian was mentally a long way behind the aeroplane and appeared to be spectacularly maxed out and requiring substantial inputs and guidance from the right-hand seat just to keep the operation safe. Once again, it came down to evidence however and the burden of proof. On the evidence I had thus far and although I felt distinctly nervous about exposing myself to her ineptitude as PF again, I simply could not put together a cast iron case to suspend her training. Add to that the fact that I had helped her all the way into Geneva, and many of her errors which would have for example resulted in a go-around were masked by the support she received from me. I couldn't help wondering what on earth the other trainers had been doing on her previous flights to let her get this far. Quite simply, I needed to see more.

There was also the slim chance that her observed performance up to now had been uncharacteristic and she was having the equivalent of 'an off day', so in some ways she deserved to be given the opportunity to redeem herself.

"Marian there are plenty of points to debrief from that sector, but we will cover them later. I would like you now to operate the next sector back to Liverpool as PF again, are you happy to do that?" She said yes she was, so I went out to do the walkround while I left her to prepare for the flight. I checked with the cabin crew to see how they were faring as by now the passengers had all disembarked and the Senior Steward commented that the seatbelt sign had been put on a little bit late in the descent for cabin secure. I apologised for that and said we were "quite busy" at that point – he raised his eyebrows and cocked his head towards the closed flightdeck door, "you've got your hands full in there today then..." I smiled and said "All in a day's work".

Outside the aircraft on the airbridge and out of earshot of anyone onboard I turned on my mobile 'phone. The first 'phonecall I made was to the Airline Crew Training Manager – there was no answer and no voicemail. I then made a second call, this time to the Flight Ops Manager. I really needed some advice and guidance here, as I expected Marian to be unable to impress me on the next flight East Midlands and if her performance was as bad as I anticipated, then she could not continue in her present role. The call went straight through to voicemail and I left a message with the FOM to the effect that Marian was frighteningly incompetent and it was quite likely she would be suspended on our return to East Midlands – I would arrange for a taxi to take her to London. The third call also went straight through to voicemail, it was to the crewing department. I asked them to organise a taxi to be waiting for Marian at East Midlands airport to take her directly to London, in addition I wanted them to ensure that a qualified Line First Officer would meet the arriving aircraft on the ramp to operate the EMA-BFS-EMA sectors with me. Later on, during the return flight while passing over London at 35,000 feet, I discreetly checked with Airline Ops on the number two VHF to confirm that this had been arranged - it had.

Once the external checks had been completed on the walkround, I now had to decide what to do. When considering that my trainee Captain was coming up to being ready for Line Check at the end of her Line Training syllabus, I should theoretically be able to passively observe while she leads the way. For the next sector, I would be supportive when she asked me to be, however I would not be seen to be 'leading the witness'.

The departure out of Geneva was planned for a full length takeoff from runway 23, the wind was calm. In the departure instructions for the airport, it specifically states that departing aircraft MUST achieve 7000 feet by the time they are 8 miles out on the climb from the runway if they wish to continue their Standard Instrument Departure (SID) routing turning to the right (North) towards high terrain. The range of hills just to the North of Lac Leman is called the Jura Mountains and the minimum safety altitude in that area is 7000 feet. The penalty for aircraft unable to get to this altitude in time is that they must turn left and climb in the holding pattern at the Passeiry VOR radio beacon (8nm from GVA) until they are above 7000 feet after which they can be cleared enroute. This then costs fuel and time while climbing round the hold and is uneconomical.

Most airliner takeoffs are accomplished at much less than full power from the engines. The engines are designed to be 'Over-Rated' if you like, so that the operating crew only needs to use a certain percentage of available thrust to get airborne safely. To do this, they must calculate the takeoff performance for every runway individually using the performance method provided by the manufacturer. In the case of the Boeing, this is done with large thick books of performance charts for each runway that we operate from. Factors which need to be taken into consideration are Weight, Altitude (of the runway above sea level), Temperature, available Runway Length, whether Dry or Wet, Wind, aircraft defects which might have performance implications etc. etc. The list seems complicated, but many times the calculations are done quite quickly as the runways are often dry, into wind and plenty long enough. When we takeoff at less than "Rated" power, this is known as a "Derated" takeoff.

In the B737 with a full load and light winds, we normally elect to do a full (Rated) power takeoff and full power climb out of Geneva on runway 23, with the speed back at 210 knots (or thereabouts) to go for the height. In this configuration, we often only just achieve the necessary altitude by Passeiry. The other option of course is to derate the takeoff and the climb and accept the fact that you have to turn Left once round the hold to get enough altitude to head North. Marian did not mention the issue, nor did she ask me what I thought, so I didn't volunteer any solution. She simply stated that "This will be a Derated takeoff, from the left-hand seat, with flaps 5", and continued with her summary of the departure.

I knew however that if we were unable to make the height, I would have to stop her turning North at 8 miles and although I was now Mr Passive the First Officer, I must keep the operation safe. *'It really has turned out to be an interesting day....'*

During her preflight departure brief she did mention the altitude restriction on the SID, but it did not seem to occur to her that it may provide us with a problem. As luck would have it there was a light passenger load on the Geneva flight to East Mids on this particular morning and therefore the Zero

Fuel Weight (weight of the aircraft disregarding weight of the fuel in the tanks) was fairly low. From experience though, I knew it was going to be very close and if she is only 500 feet short of 7000 at Passeiry I will have to tell her to go left.......

We received our clearance, Marian started the engines and taxied out for departure from runway 23 at Geneva. *'Will we? Won't we?'* I wondered as I carried out my duties as her competent Co-Pilot on the parallel taxiway.

On arrival at the holding point, the tower called, "Easy 123, the wind is light and variable, you are cleared for takeoff from runway 23", I acknowledged and completed the takeoff checklist for Marian. As she lined the 737 up on the centreline of the runway I had a last minute glance at the speedbrake lever which was securely in its detent stowage. She advanced the thrust levers and obtained 40% N1 before pushing the autothrottle 'TOGA' switch for takeoff power and the levers advanced to their predetermined setting. I called "Thrust Set" in a loud clear voice and there was no response, (the back of my neck tingled) her gaze was fixed on a point at the end of the runway, I called "Eighty Knots!" in a louder voice and that did the trick – she responded "Check". And finally I called "Vee One" and "Rotate" – she pulled back on the control column and the nose of the aircraft started to rise off the runway, accelerating all the while. "Positive Climb!" and she responded "Gear Up". I mentally breathe a sigh of relief at this point in every takeoff because I know that 'once the wheels are in the well' life is a whole lot easier in every respect – we are safe. For example in the case of an engine failure on takeoff, there is a massive amount of drag from the extended landing gear which MUST be got rid of or the machine will struggle to climb – and at that stage *climbing* is what it's all about.

She called for "LNAV" as we were passing 500 feet above the ground and that meant the autopilot would follow the magenta track of the FMC route. This assumed that we would make the altitude restriction as the route took us directly to the North at 8 miles out from the runway. We entered cloud at around 2000 feet and the Engine Anti-Ice was required as the temperature had fallen below +10° C. This and a simultaneous radio frequency change from ATC distracted me from my monitoring briefly and when I next looked at the instruments I could see that the airspeed was falling rapidly and the rate of climb had decreased! I then noted that the attitude of the aircraft was over 22 degrees nose-up and felt moved to say something about this. "The attitude's too high, you should be around 17° pitch – LOWER THE NOSE!" Fortunately she listened to me, did as I instructed and the airspeed started to increase again. I breathed another sigh of relief, at least we had not stalled.

Then after saying before departure, that she would "Maintain 210 knots to Passeiry", she engaged autopilot B and as we climbed through 3000 feet, she called "Climb Thrust" and pressed the N1 button on the autopilot MCP. Unfortunately she did not wait to observe if the N1 mode had engaged, prior to pushing the button a second time – the result was that the Autothrottle went into ARM mode. Her confusion was obvious at this point and so I tried to help by saying that she had "double pushed" the switch – so, she did it again and obtained the same result. In cartoons, this is where a large 'thinks bubble' with a question mark in it appears over the character's head, but I wasn't laughing anymore. As she had appeared to have run out of ideas now, I suggested, "Push it slowly, ONE MORE TIME!" This she did and we now had Climb Power engaged. At some stage Marian also managed to engage the Level Change mode on the Autopilot with the result that the Airspeed Command bug came back to around 165 knots. I indicated to her that this was non-standard (apart from being unsafe) and at 5900 feet she called "Bug-up" and selected 210 knots on the MCP.

At exactly 8 miles out from the runway the aircraft climbed through 7000 feet and the autopilot commenced its right turn to the North towards Dijon. There was no acknowledgement from Marian about this, it just was. Mind you, I would have been incredibly impressed if she had said to me, "You see James with a Zero Fuel Weight as low as we had today, I KNEW we didn't need a RATED power takeoff to achieve the altitude restriction!" but it was not to be.

As PNF, I had carried out the after takeoff scan including switching off the engine start switches and cycling the seatbelt signs in the cabin to release the cabin crew to start their service. In my passive role however I had not prompted Marian to call for the "After Takeoff Checklist" and it wasn't until we were passing 10,000 feet in the climb (Flight Level 100) that I asked her if she would like me to do them. The aircraft was still climbing steeply at this point with a substantial 'deck angle' of over 10° pitch above the horizon as she still had only 210 knots selected in the autopilot speed window. I imagined that this was making life a little difficult for the cabin crew as they would be trying to push their trolleys up a rather steep hill from the aft galley. Eventually I could stand it no longer and suggested that we could increase our forward speed to good effect – she engaged VNAV to follow the Vertical navigation profile for the rest of the climb.

I noticed that Marian seem to be genuinely mystified about the workings of the Flight Management Computer and the way in which information entered via the CDU was being processed and managed. On several occasions there were 'route discontinuities' that she found impossible to eliminate and twice when we had been given 'direct' to an airway waypoint after a period on Radar Heading, she had to be prompted to engage the LNAV system. There were also times when in climb or descent, the autopilot pitch mode defaulted to 'Vertical Speed' (V/S mode), just as the manufacturer intended, but she appeared unaware of the change in mode or the significance of it. At no time during the two sectors did Marian carry out any form of raw data navigation check of the LNAV system – she simply accepted the LNAV magenta track was correct and that was that. When the FMC 'MSG' annunciator lights came on – alerting the pilots to a Message on the FMC CDU screen, she made no mention of it and when the message 'Drag Required' appeared on the CDU, she did nothing to react to it while in the descents.

Several times during the two sectors we experienced light, occasionally moderate clear air turbulence (CAT). Marian as PF and nominal aircraft commander, neither reacted to these turbulent conditions, nor mentioned anything about bringing the cruise speed back to turbulent airspeed. At one point while it was particularly bumpy, I asked her what the turbulent airspeed was and she replied "280 knots", "Yes that's true", I said, "but what about the turbulent Mach Number?" She was hesitant now, "I think it is Mach 0.70....." I informed her that for the variant that we were flying it was actually Mach 0.73. I then asked her if there was any manufacturer recommended turbulent airspeed for altitudes below 15,000 feet and she responded, "Just 280 knots" - wrong again. You would have thought that given the fact that it was turbulent at this time of our discussion and as we were hacking along at M0.75, she would have taken the hint to reduce the cruising speed, especially as I had just told her what it was. Sadly it did not seem to register with her, so I asked her to fly at the lower speed while it was turbulent. She then brought the Mach number back to 0.73.

There were other areas of technical limitations on which she appeared hazy in her knowledge and overall, I found this deeply disturbing. I was just asking normal questions about B737 operations to which she did not have the answers. I kept thinking, *'Thank God the passengers don't know what's going on in here'.*

Our descent into East Mids in clear, CAVOK weather conditions was inefficiently managed. Manchester Control kept us up quite high for a long time, Flight Level 160 and then stepped us down in stages. Instead of making a definite decision regarding the airspeed to fly at for each part of the descent, she simply opted to leave the speed at 250 knots mostly with the speedbrake out. The selection of the descent speed seemed arbitrary, sometimes she would fly at 300 knots in level flight, then 250 for the next phase of the descent – whereas it would have been nice to see 210 level and 300+ with speedbrakes while actually descending (by negotiation with ATC of course). But she didn't ask and I did not suggest – I needed to see Marian operating without interference or guiding inputs from the other seat. Just as she would have to operate as a Captain on the line of course with junior Co-Pilots who were unable to offer the support which Trainers could give.

Eventually the inevitable happened. We were palmed off by the Manchester controller to East Midlands approach radar passing 6000 feet descending, at 250 knots with the speedbrakes out on a left base for runway 27 with about 10 track miles to the runway......

Due to our altitude on handover, we were put on a radar heading of 350 degrees and were 3 miles away from the extended centreline with the intention - as ATC put it - for a "Right-hand pattern, to intercept from the North". Marian could obviously see the runway clearly now through the left-hand cockpit window and said, "Are we clear to intercept the localiser?" At this time she was just about to press the button on the autopilot to engage the ILS (Instrument Landing System) Localiser, but I prevented her from doing so, explaining that ATC would be taking us through the Localiser beam and back on to it again from the North. It just didn't occur to her that we would have immediately faced a Go-Around situation had we been cleared to turn left as we were much too high and fast.

We were now doing 220 knots passing 5000 feet so she called for Flap 1, then shortly after called for Flap 5 – again she used speedbrake with Flap 5 contrary to SOPs. It was clear that ATC were going to radar vector us round for a standard ILS approach and we ended up at 2100 feet, configured with Flap 5 and (from the controller) "12 track miles to run". Marian mentioned something at this stage that perhaps she had taken flap a little too early and I agreed.

The resulting landing from the approach was not bad, except that this time, having briefed for "Standard reverse thrust after landing" she only used 52% as opposed to 70% (standard setting). She had opted for Autobrake Level 3 however and the deceleration rate after touchdown was correspondingly rapid to the point where the aircraft was nearly stationary before she deselected the brakes – halfway along the runway. She then had to use plenty of power to get the machine moving again and up to speed to vacate the runway at the end.

We taxied off the runway and I ran through the 'after landing scan' as the First Officer – calling to her when it was completed. As we turned through 90° and came onto stand nose-in to the terminal, I could see one of the East Midlands based First Officers standing in uniform with his flightbag next to the groundcrew near to where the chocks were waiting for us – *'Thank heavens somebody listens to their voicemail'.* I was conscious of the fact now that we had a very short, 25 minutes turnround on the ramp here in East Mids before we were due to depart for Belfast, so I had to be quick to keep the aircraft on schedule. Once the shutdown checklist was completed, I looked over at Marian. She had the next Computer Flight Plan in her hand and was making some comment about fuel planning for the next sector to Belfast.

She didn't look very happy, but neither was I. I asked her for her training file and said that as time was very short we would not be able to do a full debrief – I don't think she understood at that point how poor her standard of performance had been. The flightdeck door opened, it was the flight dispatcher and the engineers were just behind him. "CLOSE THE DOOR PLEASE!" I said in loud voice and they did so.

Quietly, slowly and deliberately I said, "Marian, I am very sorry to have to tell you that you are not going to Belfast with us. There is a taxi waiting to take you to London from the crewroom here in East Midlands and unfortunately your flying training is suspended with effect from now until the training department has had a chance to review your performance. Today's flights did not go well for you. There were too many mistakes and you have failed to meet the standard of performance which we would expect at your stage of training. I believe it is unsafe to continue with you flying in the left-hand seat and therefore I have made the decision to stop your training now. We don't have time for a proper debrief now, I know that you will want the feedback and you are entitled to that, so I will write a full report which you will see at a later date".

In her training file I wrote in large capital letters across the dated report page, 'SUSPENDED FROM LINE TRAINING WITH IMMEDIATE EFFECT – FULL REPORT TO FOLLOW'. Then signed and dated it.

The full report which I wrote to the Training Manager ran to 6 pages. My summary included all of the incidents as mentioned above and included all of the relevant details about the weather, ATC and technical aspects.

It concluded with the words; 'If she cannot competently carry out an RTO (Rejected Take Off) at 30 knots, then we can be certain that a high-speed rejection could well result in disaster. In short I believe this pilot is out of her depth in the seat she is occupying, i.e. Left-hand seat B737. She appears to have little spare mental capacity, insufficient experience and cannot cope with the challenge of the 737's extra inertia and greater performance over her previous type'.

In Airline Line Training, it is not unheard of for a First Officer to be suspended from training, often due to the fact that they lack experience and very occasionally because the recruitment department has got it wrong. For an allegedly experienced trainee Direct Entry Captain (DEC) to be suspended is extremely rare and almost certainly a result of flawed recruiting process.

The taxi was waiting for her right on cue and she was transported to the airline headquarters without delay. On arrival there, she went to see the Training Department Management and immediately tried to imply that she had been the victim of sex discrimination by me as her Training Captain. I shook my head sadly when I heard, but cannot say I was surprised.

I did actually meet Marian again. In those days I spent some of my time at the Airline Head Offices in London and on my visit the following week I was asked to meet with her and present her with a formal debrief and discuss the contents of my report. It was a sad event for me and I was very sorry for her, but I spent much time explaining all the reasons why each of her errors and failings were significant.

She never flew for the airline again.

Hard at work - Line Training new First Officer on B757

GLOSSARY OF TERMS AND ABBREVIATIONS.

AAIB – Air Accident Investigation Branch (of Dept for Transport UK)
ABP – Able Bodied Passenger
ADD – Acceptable Deferred Defect
ADF – Auto Direction Finder unit – often associated with NDB see below
AEW – Airborne Early Warning
AFDS – Automatic Flight Director System
ANO – Air Navigation Order
APU – Auxiliary Power Unit
AOC – Air Operators Certificate
ASR – Air Safety Report
ATA – Actual Time of Arrival
ATC – Air Traffic Control
ATD – Actual Time of Departure
ATIS – Automated Terminal Information System, gives aerodrome current weather
ATO – Approved Training Organisation
Autobrake – as it says, an automatic braking system for landing

BAe – British Aerospace
Baro – Barometric Altimeter
Basha – little house on the Prairie

The Flightdeck Survival Manual.

BER – Beyond Economic Repair
BSI – Borescope Inspection of engine

CAA – Civil Aviation Authority
CAPT – Captain or Aircraft Commander
CAVOK – Cloud And Visibility OK – very nice weather
CBT – Computer Based Training
CDL – Configuration Deviation List
CDU – Computer Display Unit
CFP – Computer Flight Plan
CFIT – Controlled Flight Into Terrain
CLB – Climb abbreviation for FMC
CONFIG – Configuration of the aircraft, flaps, gear, speedbrakes etc
Configuration Warning – warning that CONFIG incorrect for maneouvre
CPT - Captain
CRM – Crew Resource Management
CRMI – Crew Resource Management Instructor (a facilitator really)
CRS – Certificate of Release to Service (maintenance term)
CRZ – Cruise abbreviation for FMC
CRZ ALT – Cruise Altitude abbreviation for FMC
CSI – Combat Survival Instructor
CSR – Cabin Safety Report
CTBL – Contactable – referring to a crew member being available to call by crewing
CTC – Chief Training Captain (usually Postholder for Training on behalf of CAA)
CTOT – Calculated TakeOff Time
CVR – Cockpit Voice Recorder
Cyan – Colour of blue specific to Boeing EFIS displays

DDG – Dispatch Deviation Guide
DEC – Direct Entry Captain
DFDR – Digital Flight Data Recorder
DFO – Director Flight Operations
DOB – Death On Board
DODAR – Diagnose, Options, Decision, Action, Review
DV Window – Direct Vision window in flightdeck which slides open on ground

EAT – Estimated Approach Time (normally for holding aircraft in the stack)
EADI – Electronic Attitude Director Unit (part of EFIS instrumentation in Boeings)
EET – Estimated Elapsed Time (enroute on a Flight Plan)
EFIS – Electronic Flight Instrumentation System
EFOTO – Engine Failure On TakeOff
EHSI – Electronic Horizontal Situation Indicator
EMA – East Midlands Airport (IATA Code)
EMMA COUSINS – not her real name ☺
EPR – Engine Pressure Ratio – an expression of how much thrust is being produced
ETA - Estimated Time of Arrival
ETOPS – Extended Range Twin Engined Operations – often over water (eg.Atlantic)

FCTM – Flight Crew Training Manual
FCU - Fuel Control Unit
FDM – Flight Data Monitoring
FDR – Flight Data Recorder

FFS – Full Flight Simulator
Final Line Check – After Line Training is complete to release crew member to Line
Fire Handle – shuts off fuel, hydraulics and when rotated activates Fire Extinguisher
Flightdeck – the little room at the front where the pilots sit
Flight Level – or FL – an altimeter indication in 000's of feet referenced to 1013mb
FMC – Flight Management Computer
FO – First Officer also known as Co-Pilot
FOM – Flight Operations Manager – usually Postholder reporting to the CAA
FOM – Flight Operations Manual
FPL – Flightplan
FSTD – Flight Simulator Training Device
FSO – Flight Safety Officer
FTL – Flight Time Limitations

G/A – Go-Around, aborted landing. (Used to be known as Overshoot)
Glass Cockpit – refers to the introduction of computer screens in flightdecks EFIS
GPU – Ground Power Unit – provides electrics to run the aircraft without APU
GPWS – Ground Proximity Warning System (does what it says on the tin)
GRADE – Gather (info), Review, Analyse, Decide (& Do), Evaluate
Ground Lock Pins – heavy duty bolts with flags to lock landing gear down

HSI – Horizontal Situation Indicator (Orville and Wilbur called it a compass)

IFR – Instrument Flight Rules
ILS – Instrument Landing System – for precision approaches to runway in IMC
IMC – Instrument Meteorological Conditions – cloudy outside
IR – Instrument Rating – a licence to fly aircraft on instruments alone
IRS – Inertial Reference System
IRU – Inertial Reference Unit

LCA – Low Cost Airline
LCC – Low Cost Company
LCZR – Localizer (element of the ILS)
Line Check – annual event for all crew
Line Training – after basic/initial training in Simulator, training on the line
LLZ – Localizer (azimuth) element of the ILS
LNAV – Lateral Navigation system – part of the AFDS
LOFT – Line Oriented Flying Training
LPC – Licence Proficiency Check (for pilots)
LPC – Lemon Pie Club (an alternative meaning for the abbreviation)
LTN – Luton Airport (3 letter IATA code)
LVPs – Low Visibility Procedures
LVOs – Low Visibility Operations

Mach No – associated with cruise speed of airliner as percentage of Mach 1
Magenta – purple type colour specific to Boeing EFIS system
MAN – Manchester Airport (3 letter IATA code)
MEL – Minimum Equipment List
MPA – Maximum Power Assurance engine runs – Engineering Techincal
MPL – Multi Pilot Licence
MOR – Mandatory Occurrence Report – to CAA (or regulating authority)
MSA – Minimum Safe Altitude

N1 – engine gauge showing speed of front fan of large bypass engines
N2 – second stage fan
N3 – third stage fan
NDB – Non Directional Beacon – used with aircraft autodirection finder
Nipple Anti-Stretch Cream – a good substitute for facial moisturiser
NPA – Non-Precision Approach on instruments to an airfield/aerodrome

OAT – Outside Air Temperature – also known as Ambient
OPC – Operator Proficiency Check for crew

P1 – Senior Pilot onboard – another name for Captain – refers to logging the flightime
P1/S – First Pilot under Supervision/Training
P2 – Co-pilot
PA – Public Address system – aircraft loudspeaker system to cabin
PF – Pilot Flying (also known as the Handling Pilot – with hands on controls)
PIC – Pilot In Command
PAP – Passenger x 1
Paraphimosis - An emergency condition. Foreskin of penis, once retracted, cannot return to its original location.
PAX – Passengers Plural
PIREP – Pilot Report – usually of meteorological phenomena
PLI – Pitch Limit Indicators
Pusser – Generic Term for Royal Naval Supply Branch

QFI – Qualified Flying Instructor
QRH – Quick Reference Handbook – with emergency & non-normal checklists
QWI – Qualified Weapons Instructor

RA – Radio Altimeter
RADALT – Radio Altimeter
Rotate – Call by Monitoring Pilot to indicate to PF that it is speed to get airborne
RPM – Revolutions Per Minute – with reference to engine speed usually
RTO – Rejected TakeOff

SAS – Special Air Services
SBY – Standby – referring to crew usually associated with rostering/crewing dept.
SCCM – Senior Cabin Crew Member
SID – Standard Instrument Departure – defined for all flights heading that direction
SMS – Safety Management System
SOP – Standard Operating Procedure
Soup Dragon – Cabin Crew in forward galley serving flightdeck
SP – Safety Pilot – qualified observer on jumpseat in flightdeck for Line Training
Speedbird – British Airways' R/T callsign
SSA – Sector Safe Altitude – usually within 25 nm
STA – Scheduled Time of Arrival
STAR – Standard Arrival Routing – defined for all flights from that direction
STD – Scheduled Time of Departure

TCAS – Traffic Collision Avoidance System
Techlog – aircraft Technical Log a legal document – see also ATL

Thrust Reverser – on each engine deflects exhaust forward to slow down on landing
TRE – Type Rating Examiner, check airman, usually a Training Captain
TRI – Type Rating Instructor, usually a Training Captain
TRTO – Type Rating Training Organisation

UNMIN – Unaccompanied Minor – a child with a big tag round his/her neck escorted
UTC – Universal Time Coordinated (used to be known correctly as GMT)

V1 – Decision Speed on takeoff roll beyond which we must fly
VFR – Visual Flight Rules
VMC – Visual Meteorological Conditions
VNAV – Vertical Navigation System of FMC for automatic flight
VOR – VHF Omnidirectional Radio Beacon
VSI – Vertical Speed Indicator – in feet per minute for climb or descent

WTL – Worn To Limits – engineering technical